THE CAUSES OF WAR: 3000 BCE TO 1000 CE

This is the first volume of a projected four-volume series charting the causes of war from 3000 BCE to the present day, written by a leading international lawyer, and using as its principal materials the documentary history of international law largely in the form of treaties and the negotiations which led up to them. These volumes seek to show why millions of people, over thousands of years, slayed each other. In departing from the various theories put forward by historians, anthropologists and psychologists, Gillespie offers a different taxonomy of the causes of war, focusing on the broader settings of politics, religion, migrations and empire-building. These four contexts were dominant and often overlapping justifications for the first four thousand years of human civilisation for which written records exist.

The Causes of War

Volume 1

3000 BCE to 1000 CE

Alexander Gillespie

·HART·
PUBLISHING
OXFORD AND PORTLAND, OREGON
2013

Published in the United Kingdom by Hart Publishing Ltd
16C Worcester Place, Oxford, OX1 2JW
Telephone: +44 (0)1865 517530
Fax: +44 (0)1865 510710
E-mail: mail@hartpub.co.uk
Website: http://www.hartpub.co.uk

Published in North America (US and Canada) by
Hart Publishing
c/o International Specialized Book Services
920 NE 58th Avenue, Suite 300
Portland, OR 97213-3786
USA
Tel: +1 503 287 3093 or toll-free: (1) 800 944 6190
Fax: +1 503 280 8832
E-mail: orders@isbs.com
Website: http://www.isbs.com

British Library Cataloguing in Publication Data
Data Available

ISBN: 978-1-84946-500-7

Typeset by Hope Services, Abingdon
Printed and bound in Great Britain by
Lightning Source UK Ltd

This work is for Claire, for the love,
the family and the journey we have made and shared.

Table of Contents

I

Introduction

1. THE CONVERSATION ON SUNDAY AFTERNOON

THE TOPIC OF this book is the causes of war. This book is the first of four, as the timescale of this question is large. This book is accompanied by three other books which deal with the customs and laws of war with regard to the methods by which humans have fought and killed each other for the last 5,000 years. This book is different. It is about why, not how they fight.

The three original books, this book, and the two to follow, all began with a discussion I had with my mother over 13 years ago towards the end of the twentieth century, on whether the practices of humanity were better or worse than in the past. Simply put: 'Was humanity making progress or not?' Whilst I argued in the affirmative, my mother argued in the negative. As with many such lunch-time discussions on Sunday afternoons, trying to find robust benchmarks was (and is) very difficult, if not impossible. Although the conversation on this particular Sunday afternoon moved on to other topics, this question of 'progress' caught me.

My supposition is that the causes of warfare have changed, for the better – where progress has occurred – since the Enlightenment. To prove this point requires a great amount of research, to show what the causes were and how they have changed. This means that this book, which ends at 1000 CE, is a stepping stone towards my final answer.

2. UTOPIA

There are many philosophical discussions around the idea of 'progress'.[1] These discussions are often linked to various forms of Utopian thinking.[2] This is especially so for the question on which I am focusing, as the flipside of the question of the causes of war is

[1] Doren, V (1969) *The Idea of Progress* (NYC, Praeger); Hilderbrand, G (ed) (1974) *The Idea of Progress: A Collection of Readings* (Los Angeles, California University Press); Melzer, A (ed) (1995) *History and the Idea of Progress* (NYC, Cornell University Press); Marx, L (ed) (1998) *Progress: Fact or Fiction* (NYC, Michigan University Press).

[2] Manuel, F (1979) *Utopian Thought in the Western World* (NYC, Harvard University Press); Manuel, F (ed) (1969) *Utopias and Utopian Thought* (NYC, Condor); Buber, M (1949) *Paths in Utopia* (London, Routledge); Mumford, L (1962) *The Story of Utopias* (NYC, Viking); Bernini, M (1950) *Journey Through Utopia* (London, Routledge).

the search for enduring peace. I struggle to think of an appropriate figure for how many gallons of ink have been expended in debates on this question, or on suggestions of the correct path to Utopia, where the difficulties of the past are bypassed and a bright, violence-free future awaits humanity. There is no monopoly on these plans, and the libraries are full of these variations on themes which run for thousands of miles of shelving, from theology to ideology, cross-referenced with a bewildering collection of historical epochs and philosophical musings. These musings are both historical and cross-cultural.

The idea of a 'Golden Age' in which there was no warfare can be found in the scribblings of, amongst others, the scholars of ancient China and India.[3] Such views were mirrored in Greece and Rome when the Roman poet Ovid (43 BCE–17 CE) wrote of a previous time when 'men kept faith and did what was right . . . the peoples passed their lives in security and peace, without need for armies'.[4] These dreams later flowered into the eschatology and promises of times to come in religions like Christianity and Islam. Such looking back, or forward, was essential for those trying to muse their way out of contemporary conundrums of societies that were beleaguered by warfare.

These views have been supplemented by a number of scholars since the onset of the Enlightenment. Most famously, Jean Jacques Rousseau (1712–78) argued that it was demographic growth, private property, the division of class, and state coercion which forced warfare upon an otherwise peaceful species.[5] D'Holbach (1723–89) added to this thesis with his view that peace was the natural condition of mankind.[6] In modern times, Margaret Mead (1901–78) famously added in 1940 that: 'Warfare is only an invention, not a biological necessity'.[7] A similar view was later reflected by UNESCO in its constitution which was drawn up in the immediate aftermath of the Second World War. Specifically, 'since wars begin in the minds of men, it is in the minds of men that the defences of peace must be constructed'.[8] UNESCO subsequently added to this view with its 1986 Seville Statement on Violence, issued to celebrate the International Year of Peace. This suggested that it was 'scientifically incorrect to say that we have inherited a tendency to make war from our animal ancestors' or 'that war or any other violent behavior is genetically programmed in our human nature'. It affirmed that 'biology does not condemn humanity to war' and anathematised the 'alleged biological findings that have been used . . . to justify violence and war'.

I like this view, especially the idea that humanity can escape its past and what Sigmund Freud (1856–1939) saw as an underlying desire for aggression, as part of our instinctual endowment.[9] I consider this essential as I am of the belief that human-

[3] Hsiao, K (1979) *A History of Chinese Political Thought* (New Jersey, Princeton University Press) 299, 308. Bary, T (ed) (1960) *Sources of Chinese Tradition*, Vol I (New York, Columbia University Press) 99, 128–30, 237.

[4] Ovid, *Metamorphoses* trans Raeburn, D (2004) (London, Penguin) 1.89–100. Note also Hesiod, *The Works and Days* trans Most, L (2003) (Boston, Loeb) 1.146.

[5] Rousseau, JJ *The Discourses* trans Gourevitch, V (1997) (Cambridge, Cambridge University Press).

[6] D'Holbach *The System of Nature* trans Robinson, D (1995) (London, Penguin).

[7] Mead, M (1940) 'Warfare is Only an Invention' 40 *Asia* 402–405. For contemporary debates about this question, see Livingston-Smith, D (2007) *The Most Dangerous Animal: Human Nature and the Origins of War* (London, St Martins); Fry, D (2007) *Beyond War: The Human Potential For Peace* (Oxford, Oxford University Press); Brown, S (1987) *The Causes and Prevention of War* (NYC, St Martins).

[8] Preamble, Constitution of the UNESCO.

[9] Freud, S (1930) *Civilisation and its Discontents* (London, Penguin) 86.

ity has been constantly beleaguered by warfare. This is certainly the pattern of the period of this book, of the years 3000 BCE to 1000 CE. I do not think this pattern was much different to the ages that went before it although the causes for fighting were different. That is, I can find no reasonable evidence for the existence of a golden age when there was no warfare except in the imaginations of scholars who were tired of killing. I cannot even find evidence, when dealing with our evolutionary cousins, in support of the claim that peace was our original state. An alternative thesis from the 1960s suggested that our primate cousins were vegetarian, non-violent and non-territorial.[10] This was an image which resonated well with the period, but finds very little support in the science that appeared in the decades that followed. This has shown, on the contrary, that for our primate cousins violence is neither rare nor light, but often extreme and calculating.[11]

With regard to our own species, 'human' as in the genus *Homo*, and the subspecies, *sapiens* (meaning 'wise man' or 'knowing man'), it would appear that, as our species began to move out of Africa between 100,000 and 50,000 years ago, our direct ancestors gradually marginalised the 'archaic' homo varieties. It is possible that this 'wise' or 'knowing' species, in combination with natural factors including climate change, systematically drove our closest genetic relatives, such as the Neanderthals, to extinction. Once this was achieved, it is more than possible that from the Upper Palaeolithic (around 10000–5000 BCE) onwards continued warfare, of which cave art attests, was not unknown.[12]

The evidence becomes more firm as scientists have observed functioning non-literate societies within contemporary times. The evidence here suggests that 65 per cent of the societies studied were at war continuously, 77 per cent were at war once every five years, 75 per cent were war once every two years, 55 per cent were at war every year and 87 per cent were fighting more than once a year. These rates are so high that warfare may have accounted for up to 10 per cent of all male deaths. Deadly conflict, if not endemic, was ever to be expected.[13] The reasons that they killed each other include revenge, reprisal, the glory of victory (replete with rank, status, prestige and honour) and the fruits of winning, namely the women and physical resources of the opposition.[14] These reasons have a similarity to the recorded pretexts found in Homeric Greece.[15]

[10] Ardrey, R (1961) *African Genesis* (London, Delta).

[11] Robbins, M (ed) (2011) *Among African Apes* (California, California University Press); Callaway, E (2010) 'Chimpanzees Kill to Win New Territory' *New Scientist*, 26 June, 14.

[12] Gat, A (2008) *War in Human Civilisation* (Oxford, Oxford University Press) 26–30; Carman, J and Harding, A (2009) *Ancient Warfare* (Gloucestershire, The History Press) 56–58; Wong, K (2010) 'Twilight of the Neanderthals' in *Selections on Evolution* (NYC, Scientific American) 23–29; Keegan, J (1993) *A History of Warfare* (London, Hutchinson) 116–22.

[13] Gat, A (2008) *War in Human Civilisation* (Oxford, Oxford University Press) 30–35.

[14] Keeley, L (1996) *War Before Civilisation* (Oxford, Oxford University Press) 16–17, 28, 33, 108–12; Dawson, D (1996) *The Origins of Western Warfare* (Westview, Colorado) 16–17, 20–21; Davie, M (1929) *The Evolution of War* (Boston, Yale University Press) 77–87, 110–26, 147–59; Gat, A (2008) *War in Human Civilisation* (Oxford, Oxford University Press) 61–76, 87–99; Horgan, J (2009) 'The End of War' *New Scientist*, 4 July, 36–40; Holmes, B (2008) 'Born to Fight' *New Scientist*, 15 November, 8.

[15] Herodotus, *The Histories* trans de Selincourt, A (2003) (London, Penguin) 3:47 and 5:82; Hedreen, G (2004) *Capturing Troy* (Michigan, University of Michigan Press) 34, 59.

3. FACTS

The methodology of this book is somewhat complicated. The skeleton on which it is built is treaties. I place a great weight on the bilateral and international instruments of each age, as despite all of the difficulties of different languages and different ages, treaties and/or agreements reflect in the clearest way possible how different nations see a shared problem and shared solution. As such, at each point, the law, or at least the settlement by which peace has been reached, has been set out as simply as possible. In places where there were no treaties, the bones are taken from the practice of key players of the period, which often became custom. In each epoch I have attempted to read and quote the original sources. These have often been supplemented by the best monographs I can find on each epoch.

Within this methodology it is important to keep in mind when reading historical texts that there is a risk that mistakes have occurred, as the original sources may be wrong, mistaken, or may have been taken out of context. I was conscious of this risk in writing this book, as at various points there are only fragments of history. In places I think these fragments resemble dinosaur bones in the desert. A huge amount is often missing, and what remains can be assembled to make a variety of bizarre species with no relation to what actually existed. My interpretations are the way that I see the evidence. I have no doubt that others will see it differently. I particularly urge caution in the areas where the numbers of those killed have been included. Nevertheless, despite the uncertainties in this area, I have included them to provide the roughest of gauges by which the impacts of decisions for warfare can be seen.

4. *CASUS BELLI* IN PRACTICE

Casus belli is a Latin expression meaning the justification for acts of war. *Casus* means incident, 'rupture' or 'case', while *belli* refers to *bellum* and means ('of war'). The need for people to have a just cause can be the difference between an act of heroism and an act of murder. For this reason, hundreds, if not thousands, of philosophers and leaders of state listed justifications for why bloodshed was necessary, and why the loss or acquisition of property that followed was fair. This point about property is an underlying theme in all of the chapters that follow. That is, the overwhelming majority of all the wars studied in the period of this book have the control and/or ownership of resources as their result. No matter which way the causes for violence are examined, the results are nearly always the same – namely that the control and/or ownership of resources (from physical resources through to the ability to raise tax) can change hands or be defended. This is the practical result of nearly all of the conflicts documented in this book. Thus, I am broadly in agreement with the playwright Aristophanes (446–386 BCE), who noted that, despite many high-sounding justifications for conflict, warfare was really 'about seeking the silver of others'.[16] In the period of my study for this

[16] Aristophanes, *Lysistrate*, at 346. This is reprinted in Botsford, G (ed) (1929) *Hellenic Civilisation: Records of Civilisation* (NYC, Columbia University Press) 340.

volume (3000 BCE–1000 CE), I fear this is correct, as whilst countless scholars throughout the period of this work have detested the idea of warfare being based around such considerations as material (or social) wealth, the fact of the matter is that winning wars brought the ability to harness and control resources that losing did not.

Despite this base consideration, it was rare to find justifications for war being purely based on material (or social) reward. This was always implicit in any of the other four themes that I identified. The four themes that I can consistently trace – in practice – from the years 3000 BCE to 1000 CE relate to empire, migratory peoples, politics and religion.

The term empire derives from the Latin *imperium*, which means power and authority. My assumption is that the drive for empire and absolute control over a geographical and socio-political region was very strong in the period under study and this was a foremost cause of warfare. The thesis here is that the formation and expansion of empire was a constant catalyst. There are two different considerations at play in this setting. The first pertains to the formation of empire, in which a looped rhythm between formation, peak and fragmentation appears constant. The second deals with the situation where two established empires clash.

My second theme deals with the impact that migratory peoples had upon warfare in the years in the same period. I have focused on these people as, unlike more recent parts of history, the waves of migratory peoples seemed both constant and universal. The question I considered pertinent here was whether such people with no static places to defend were really covetous of the riches of others, and, if so, what were the implications of these actions, and how were they dealt with?

The third theme I identified as a catalyst for warfare was disagreement over political choices. Politics (from the Greek *politikos* 'of, for, or relating to the citizens') is a term generally applied to the art or science of running governments and/or state affairs. Within the context of this chapter, I see the issue of politics as the options of running the state, which range from monarchy or other forms of absolute rule (which occupied the vast amount of the history in question) through to democracy. The particular questions that these options raised are: what were the most common practices in this area in relation to warfare, and what were their limits and patterns?

This final theme deals with an overlapping consideration of direct applicability to all three of the above ideas, namely religion. The question that this chapter seeks to examine is: what was the influence of religion upon warfare? How constant and common was it in the years leading up to 1000 CE, and what were the nuances by which it was displayed? Most importantly, did the influence and underlying ideas change?

II

Empires

1. INTRODUCTION

THIS CHAPTER IS about the formation and clashing of empires, and the wars that both processes generated. The term empire derives from the Latin *imperium*, which means power and authority. My assumption is that the drive for empire, and absolute control over a geographical and socio-political region was very strong in the period under study from around 3000 BCE to 1000 CE, and this was a foremost cause for warfare. The thesis here is that the formation and expansion of empire was a constant catalyst. There are, however, two different considerations at play. The first pertains to the formation of empire, in which a looped rhythm between formation, peak and fragmentation appears constant. The second deals with the situation where two established empires clash.[1]

2. THE FORMATION OF EMPIRES

A. India

The Vedic Aryans came *en masse* to the Indian plains, perhaps, as early as 1800 BCE. These people, assimilated into India and the Vedic tribal social order, lasted until around 700 BCE, when it gave way to larger, more stable societies of regional scope. By around 600 BCE there were perhaps 16 separate kingdoms in northern India. This situation only changed when Bimbisara of Magadha (reigned 540–490 BCE) became the first monarch (and dynasty) of note to capture and control a sizeable part of north-east India, overriding many of the others who fought for their independence and autonomy. After his death, his dynasty struggled to maintain its coherence, and the part he had held fragmented. From this disintegration, arose Mahapadma Nanda (450–362 BCE). During the fourth and fifth centuries BCE, his dynasty occupied the same area and in addition stretched right across the top of north India. This empire of Nanda would have come face to face with Alexander the Great (356–323 BCE) had Alexander persuaded his men to advance beyond the plains of the Punjab. This

[1] Gat, A (2008) *War in Human Civilisation* (Oxford, Oxford University Press) 255–66, 274–75, 332–37, 341, 342–51.

advance beyond the plains did not happen, and the forces of Alexander did not stay. By 317, all of the outposts of Alexander in India had been abandoned.[2]

The decision of the Greeks to leave north-west India was probably assisted by the armed rebellion against their presence, led by Chandagrupta Maurya (340–298 BCE). Chandagrupta, following the advice of the remarkably pragmatic Kautilya (350–275 BCE), fought with a reputed 500,000 men to claim as much of India as he could from the fragmented kingdoms that had been created in the power-vacuum of the Greek exit and remaining autonomous areas of India. The result achieved was spectacular. The dynasty of Chandagrupta (322–185 BCE) went on to conquer and control some 5 million square kilometres, including all but the southern tip of India, as well as parts of modern-day Afghanistan, Pakistan, Bangladesh, Nepal and Iran. He achieved this by conquering both neighbours to the side of him and preventing the heirs of Alexander's empire from trying to reclaim what they had held earlier. Specifically, he stopped a reoccupation attempted by Seleucus (358–281 BCE) who crossed the Hindu Kush mountains about 305 BCE. In the subsequent peace treaty of 303 BCE, Seleucus ceded to Chandragupta not only all the disputed territories in India, but also all territories to the east of Kabul as well as Baluchistan.[3]

Chandagrupta's son Bindusara (320–272 BCE) assumed the throne on the death of his father and continued his policy of conquest. By his death, he had brought the entire subcontinent under the Mauryan Empire except for the Kalinga state on the east coast. Bindusara's son, Asoka (304–232 BCE), came to the throne in 272 BCE and immediately attacked Kalinga, bringing it within the imperial realm at the cost of 10,000 of his own men and 150,000 opposition soldiers and civilians. He was, however, riding out a dynasty that would dissolve and fragment into independent realms within a few decades of his death. The most notable to emerge out of this disintegration was Pushyamitra Sunga (r 185–151 BCE), who by killing the last Mauryan emperor, could establish the Sunga Empire (185–73 BCE). This empire, which (like many before it) seems to have followed the advice offered in the *Laws of Manu* (c 200 BCE–200 CE) to 'try hard to get what he has not got and to guard what he had got'.[4]

The Sunga Empire held the eastern portions of north India, including modern-day Pakistan and Bangladesh. This expansion coincided with the final demise of the Indo-Greek communities in Parthia and Bactria, who slowly sunk beneath waves of inter-Greek warfare and foreign invasions. The subsequent Kushan Empire under the direction of Kadphises (r 30–80), went on to occupy the footprint of Bactria, sitting upon what is now northern Afghanistan, Pakistan, Uzbekistan and north-west India. The most aggressive of this dynasty, Kanishka (r 120–160), who would boast of con-

[2] Kulke, H (1996) *A History of India* (London, Routledge) 18–22, 30–33, 59–60, 98–99; Smith, V (1962) *The Early History of India* (Oxford, Oxford University Press) 35–37, 40, 63–67, 104–106, 116–18; Raychaudhuri, H (1999) *Political History of Ancient India* (Oxford, Oxford University Press) 15–20, 25–28, 85, 163–65; Gabriel, R (2005) *Empires at War*, Vol I (London, Greenwood) 235–38.

[3] Strabo, *Geography* trans Jones, A (1943) (Loeb, Boston) 15.2.1; Smith, V (1962) *The Early History of India* (Oxford, Oxford University Press) 121–25; Raychaudhuri, H (1999) *Political History of Ancient India* (Oxford, Oxford University Press) 235–39; Kautilya, *Arthashastra* trans, Shamasastry, R (1915) (Bangalore, Government Printer) VI:2, VII:1 and VII:3.

[4] *The Laws of Manu* trans Doniger, W (1991) (London, Penguin) VII:99. Note also VII:173. For the figures, see Grant, R (2011) *1001 Battles that Changed the Course of History* (London, Penguin) 52.

tacts with both Rome and China, would style himself as 'king of kings'.[5] Following suit, having achieved a period of impressive unity and conquest, the kingdom of Kanishka broke up into fragments upon his death.[6]

Chandra Gupta (r 320–335), laid the foundations for the Gupta Empire. This was the greatest empire in India since the time of Asoka. Most of this empire was achieved by Chandra's son, Samudragupta (c 335–375), who was of the view that 'kingdom taking' was the business of kings. In southern India he subdued 13 kings, and then issued coins which proclaimed 'after conquering the earth, the Great king of kings, with the strength of an invisible hero is going to conquer the heavens'.[7] The Gupta Empire operated a system of control that was strict in the centre, but allowed for more autonomy, albeit of a type linked through a form of vassalage (broadly similar to the European system) of structuring society around relationships of fealty, homage and military assistance when required, and derived from the holding of land and exercising a measure of autonomy, as the reach expanded. Samudragupta's son, Chandragupta II (375–415), attained the greatest territorial expansion of the kingdom, knocking out the opposing Shaka-Kshatrapa dynasty and annexing their realm. At its peak, the Gupta Empire consisted of most of north and upper-central India, and also included raids resulting in the submission (but not occupation) and the requirement of tribute from of a number of kingdoms of the south.[8]

This Gupta Empire held together until the invasion of the White Huns and rebellions within the realm occurred at the same time. From here, although the initial threats were dealt with, it was a slow decline until the Empire withered in the sixth century. This decline was capitalised on by the rise of the next great Indian empire, that of Harsha (606–647), which went on to occupy a similar region as that held by the Gupta Empire, stretching from side to side over northern India, holding sway over the whole of the basin of the Ganges (including Nepal) from the Himalayas to the Narmada. Once more, size was not indicative of longevity, and upon the death of its founder, it fragmented. The fragmentation multiplied throughout north India for the following 200 years until the turn of the millennium saw a succession of kingdoms and dynasties appearing, struggling between themselves, reaching for suzerain over entire areas – or independence from such claims – and then disappearing. This pattern was in accordance with central and parts of southern Indian (the Deccan), and also the three principalities of southern India (the Cholas, Pandyas and Cheras) who appear to have spent most of the century leading up to the millennium, either fighting off invaders from the north, fighting each other and/or fighting Ceylon for the title of 'king of the south'.[9]

[5] Kulke, H (1996) *A History of India* (London, Routledge) 75–79; Smith, V (1962) *The Early History of India* (Oxford, Oxford University Press) 272–76.

[6] Raychaudhuri, H (1999) *Political History of Ancient India* (Oxford, Oxford University Press) 322–25, 329, 338–45, 376–79, 402–11, 414, 418–20; Smith, V (1962) *The Early History of India* (Oxford, Oxford University Press) 209, 254, 297–300.

[7] Smith, V (1962) *The Early History of India* (Oxford, Oxford University Press) 86–87.

[8] Smith, V (1962) *The Early History of India* (Oxford, Oxford University Press) 298–301; Raychaudhuri, H (1999) *Political History of Ancient India* (Oxford, Oxford University Press) 474–80.

[9] Smith, V (1962) *The Early History of India* (Oxford, Oxford University Press) 290, 350–52, 354, 369, 380–81, 393–94; Kulke, H (1996) *A History of India* (London, Routledge) 104, 112–16.

B. China

The formation of the Empire of China was similar to that of India. In relative isolation from the other great power-blocks, Chinese cultural memory begins with the Three Sovereigns and Five Emperors, who were a group of semi-mythological rulers who are pegged to the period 2600 to 2100 BCE. Whilst the three sovereigns were demigods who helped create humans, the five emperors were reknown as exemplary sages of great moral character. The most notable of these was the Yellow Emperor (Huang-ti, reigned c 2600 BCE), who is believed to have been the primogenitor of the centralised Chinese nation. The Yellow Emperor, having reputedly introduced, inter alia, the bow and arrow, rose to power throughout the Yellow River plain by subduing all the powerful clans around him and linking them into a type of feudal arrangement. Those in closest proximity to the Emperor (roughly within 250 kilometres) were believed to be completely submissive, whilst those at the further extremes (beyond about 500 kilometres) were considered much less reliable.[10]

The Hsia (or Xia) dynasty was established by the legendary Yu the Great (c 2300 BCE), after Shun (c 2200 BCE), the last of the Five Emperors, gave the throne to him. The Hsia dynasty lasted from around 2200 to 1600 BCE. Evidence would suggest that this dynasty occupied much of central China. This was a greater amount of territory under control than the Five Emperors achieved. It was done by expanding into new territories, crushing any potential rebellions on the periphery of existing control, and centralising control even further over thousands of semi-independent areas. Thereafter, according to Huai-nan Tzu (c 200 BCE), Yu 'destroyed the walls and levelled the moats, dispersed goods and wealth to the people, buried their armour and weapons, and overspread them with virtue'.[11]

This period of peace came to an end with the rise of the Shang dynasty (1600–1046 BCE), when King T'ang toppled the last in a line of 17 rulers of the Hsia dynasty. By the time the revolution was completed, some 10,000 feudal-type entities paid tribute to the new king. Many of these entities may have been new to the centralised system, as the Shang dynasty aggressively expanded into new areas, beyond the circumference of the realm of the Hsia. This push was achieved by a chariot-riding ruling class, who seem to have regularly assembled armies of up to 5,000 men, to enforce authority, and/or expand domains and pursue riches of those outside the kingdom. On at least one occasion a Shang army made a march of 10 days to fight in support of a so-called vassal state.[12]

As the size of the Shang dynasty expanded, the ability to control all areas in the realm weakened. When the centre weakened, many of those with local power saw greater opportunities in their autonomy than in continued loyalty to the Shang dynasty, and rebelled. What started as individual revolts ended as a unified opposition

[10] Sawyer, R (2011) *Ancient Chinese Warfare* (NYC, Basic Books) 15–17, 66, 94; Lewis, M (1990) *Sanctioned Violence in Early China* (NYC, State University of New York Press) 167–83, 207, 210–12; McNeill, W (1991) *The Rise of the West* (Chicago, Chicago University Press) 218–20, 357–58.

[11] Huai-nan Tzu, noted in Sawyer, R (2011) *Ancient Chinese Warfare* (NYC, Basic Books) 63, 71.

[12] Gascoigne, B (2003) *The Dynasties of China* (London, Robinson) 24–25.

of perhaps 800 disaffected groups under the leadership of the Chou, and the Shang fell at the battle of Mu-yeh around 1046 BCE. The Chou, who may have only intended to destroy and loot the Shang kingdom, ended up ruling the country. The *Book of Odes* which was compiled around this period would record: 'Under the wide heaven, there is no land that is not the Emperors and within the sea-boundaries of the land, there is none who is not a subject of the Emperor.'[13] In theory, this was correct, as for the following nearly 800 years until about 256 BCE the Chou held the title of Emperor.[14]

The words, 'in theory' noted above are important. From the middle of the fifth century BCE, the Chou controlled nothing but the state of Chou itself. In reality, although the Chou expanded throughout North China and began to assimilate the Yangtze River regions of the south, this was not a period of peace or propriety. The core fell apart in 771 BCE when the Chou rulers were driven from their capital in the Wei valley by an alliance of barbarian tribes and some rebel Chou dependence. The 'Spring and Autumn' period which followed, broadly from 771 to 476 BCE, was one in which some 170 lineage-based familial city-states of various sizes, either fought alone or linked themselves together via mutual defensive treaties. For example, when the state of Zheng was being attacked around 562 BCE a number of states came together and agreed, inter alia, to 'give assistance in the event of civil war or insurrection, to have the same friends and enemies, and to support the royal house'.[15] Such agreements were buttressed by the thinking of the great scholars such as Sun-Tzu (c 544–496 BCE), who authored the *Art of War*, and maintained a very cautious bottom line when thinking about going to war. Namely:

> Unless endangered do not engage in warfare. The ruler cannot mobilise the army out of personal anger. The general cannot engage in battle because of personal frustration. A vanquished state cannot be revived, the dead cannot be brought back to life.[16]

Such advice was of limited use, as over the 250 years or so which was this epoch, more than a hundred individual states were annexed or extinguished in which there were at least 450 inter-state wars and more than 130 major civil wars. The rhetoric was that many of these conflicts had more to do with prestige and honour, than outright conquest. In reality, by the end of this period, much of the original nobility – along with an estimated 1.5 million people – would be consumed by warfare. It was, as Mencius (372–289 BCE) would suggest, a period in which there were 'no righteous wars'.[17]

[13] Noted in Lee, L (1969) *China and International Agreements* (Durham, Role of Law Press) 25.

[14] Hucker, C (1994) *China's Imperial Past* (Stanford University Press, California) 28–34; Sawyer, R (2011) *Ancient Chinese Warfare* (NYC, Basic Books) 130–33, 142–43, 147; Sawyer, R (1993) *The Seven Military Classics of Ancient China* (Colorado, Westview) 3–5.

[15] Agreement at the End of the Zheng reprinted in Lewis, M (1990) *Sanctioned Violence in Early China* (NYC, State University of New York Press) 47–48; Di Cosmo, N (2002) *Ancient China and its Enemies: The Rise of Nomadic Power in East Asian History* (Cambridge, Cambridge University Press) 98–99. See also Tso Chuan, Book VII in Legge, J (1893) *Chinese Classics*, Vol I (NYC, MacMillan) 371.

[16] Sun Tzu as reprinted in Sawyer, R (1993) *The Seven Military Classics of Ancient China* (Colorado, Westview) 184; also Gascoigne, B (2003) *The Dynasties of China* (London, Robinson) 28–29.

[17] Works of Mencius in Legge, J (ed) *The Chinese Classics* (NYC, Alden) VII:II:2. For the background, see Hucker, C (1994) *China's Imperial Past* (California, Stanford University Press) 34–35; White, M (2011) *Atrocitology: Humanity's 100 Deadliest Achievements* (Melbourne, Text) 8–9; Sawyer, R (1993) *The Seven Military Classics of Ancient China* (Colorado, Westview) 9–11; Lewis, M (1990) *Sanctioned Violence in Early China* (NYC, State University of New York Press) 24–27.

By the end of the Spring and Autumn period, seven surviving states had emerged from the carnage. There was no restraining authority from the theoretical emperor above, and no guiding or controlling influence exerted by the aristocracy below. Absolute power came to be held in both name and fact by each of the leaders as what is known as the 'Warring States' era (476–221 BCE) began. This era is complex and confusing, with the only relative clarity being the cooperation when needed, but military competition when an advantage was sensed. For example, in 323 BCE two of the seven, Ch'in and Ch'u, made a peace treaty that seemed to promise the quick extermination of the nation of Ch'i. Despite this treaty, within four years Ch'u was organising an alliance against Ch'in. With such duplicity, the seven survivors (out of the original 170) of the Spring and Autumn period fought for pre-eminence and absolute control of power as each became locked into a death struggle of 'irrevocable expansionism'.[18] This quest was the exact opposite of what the philosophers such as Mencius and Mo Tzu (490–403 BCE) were advocating, when they spoke against the futility (in terms of benefits achieved and the likelihood that eventually the aggressor will be consumed by someone else) of endless wars of territorial acquisition. Specifically, when taking the territory of another State only for the purpose of acquisition, 'a benevolent man would not do it – how much less he will do so, when the end is to be sought by the slaughter of men!'.[19]

The warnings of the philosophers were not heeded. The sophistry of some such as Hsun-tzu (312–230 BCE) that warfare and conflict was natural, combined with the advocacy of others such as Lord Shang (390–338 BCE) that the expansion of territory and the rewards it gave was a good thing, carried greater weight.[20] Accordingly, Confucius (551–479 BCE), Wu Tzu (c 440–361 BCE), Ssu-ma Fa, Sun Pin Ping-fa (c 400 BCE) and Huang Shih-Kung (c 200 BCE), warned that all rulers who neglected military matters, no matter how repugnant they were, did so at their peril.[21] This was especially so as the warfare turned absolute, and as Mencius noted, the contested fields and cities became full of dead men.[22] Casualties recorded for the period suggested that 60,000 men fought to their deaths at Shih-men in 363 BCE and 100,000 at the battle of Ma-ling in 341 BCE. A further 80,000 fell in battle in 311 BCE and another 80,000 at the battle of Yi-yang in 306 BCE. Some 240,000 men are believed to have died on

[18] Lewis, M (2007) *The Early Chinese Empires: Qin and Han* (Massachusetts, Harvard University Press) 37; Lewis, M (1990) *Sanctioned Violence in Early China* (NYC, State University of New York Press) 36–37, 40–42, 83–91, 243–47; Gascoigne, B (2003) *The Dynasties of China* (London, Robinson) 38–39.

[19] For Mencius on this point, his *Works* which are reprinted in Legge, D (ed) (1885) *Chinese Classics* (NYC, Alden) VI/II/8. See also Mo Tzu's essay, 'Universal Love' at section 16:3 reprinted in De Bary, T (ed) (1960) *Sources of Chinese Tradition*, Vol I (NYC, Columbia University Press) 40–41. For the contribution of Mo Tzu, see Hsiao, K (1979) *A History of Chinese Political Thought* (New Jersey, Princeton University Press) 268.

[20] *The Book of Lord Shang* trans Duyvendak, J (1928) Vol I (San Francisco, Chinese Materials Centre) 2 and 3. See also Vol II, 6 and 7. Hsun-tzu, as noted in Sawyer, R (2011) *Ancient Chinese Warfare* (NYC, Basic Books) 3; Lewis, M (2007) *The Early Chinese Empires: Qin and Han* (Massachusetts, Harvard University Press) 30.

[21] *Analects* in Legge, J (ed) (1885) *The Chinese Classics* (NYC, Alden) Book VII:10–13. Ssu-ma Fa, is reprinted in Sawyer, R (1993) *The Seven Military Classics of Ancient China* (Colorado, Westview) 116, 126–27; Wu Tzu, also in Seven Military Classics, at 202, as is Wei Liao-tzu, at 288. Sun-Pin Ping fa, as noted in Sawyer, R (2011) *Ancient Chinese Warfare* (NYC, Basic Books) 2–3. See also page 307 of this book. Note also Hsiao, K (1979) *A History of Chinese Political Thought* (New Jersey, Princeton University Press) 271; Lewis, M (1990) *Sanctioned Violence in Early China* (NYC, State University of New York Press) 19.

[22] Mencius his *Works* are reprinted in Legge, D (ed) (1885) *Chinese Classics* (NYC, Alden) IV:I:14 and VII:II:4

the battlefield at I-ch'uech in 295 BCE and 450,000 men of the Zhao and 250,000 men of the Qin met their end at Ch'ang-p'ing in 260 BCE. It was win or lose, absorb or be absorbed, with the chaos not being resolved until one state eliminated all rivals.[23]

Eventually, the western frontier state of Qin (also known as Ch'in, from which the name *China* is derived) subdued all rivals. In 256 BCE they overran the tiny and feeble state of Chou, ending with an abrupt lack of courtesy the fiction that the kings of Chou were still the rulers of China. Then, in a sudden hectic decade, Qin annexed one by one its six rival States. By 221 BCE, Qin had expanded its circumference to an even greater size. This was achieved under a centralised, totalitarian government – as perfectly exemplified by the terracotta army left behind. This regime, which boasted about peace, was brought back to the land and achieved its victory, with philosophical guidance from the Legalists, by pure power and the pursuit of utilitarianism to the extent that it is believed to have caused the deaths of at least one million of its own citizens, including many of its own leading intellectuals. This repression, coupled with resurgent disquiet in regions lead to another civil war, between 210 and 206 BCE. This war was sparked by the revolt of a commoner, Ch'en She, against the tyrannical policies of the Qin, such as when they massacred over 100,000 of opposition prisoners. This revolt quickly spread into a coalition of 18 loosely connected states. Of this mass of 18, Liu Bang (256–195 BCE) – another commoner – rose to the top of the leadership, to found the Han dynasty, and defeat the last of the Qin at the battle of Jingxing in 205 BCE.[24]

The achievements of the Han dynasty, rivalled – if not surpassed – the achievements of Rome in the same epoch. Externally, it had relations spanning the seas directly to Malaya, Africa and India. Indirectly, it had contact with Rome. Internally, the Han created a stable, centralised, aristocratic social order within its own borders. Their foremost tool to the internal cohesion was the division (and dilution) of regional kingdoms between the siblings, upon the death of the leader. This allowed the lands to revert to the centre if there were no clear heirs, and the taking of lands if the owners were suspected of treason or rebellion. Externally, they began to expand into Vietnam, Korea and across Central Asia, to a tongue of land just above the Himalayas and Tibet. In the northern part of what became Korea, the early state of Koguryo sent tribute to the Han in 32 CE. A later state in the south of Korea copied suit, and received titles from the Chinese court as a general and deputy king, whilst other parts of the peninsular were also client states, which were occasionally occupied (if a rebellion was feared) and subject to immigration. Japan also sent tribute and sought titles from China. However, their internal controls and external pursuits were not sufficient

[23] Hucker, C (1994) *China's Imperial Past* (California, Stanford University Press) 36–41; Sawyer, R (1993) *The Seven Military Classics of Ancient China* (Colorado, Westview) 10–11; Lewis, M (2007) *The Early Chinese Empires: Qin and Han* (Massachusetts, Harvard University Press) 37–38; Grant, R (2011) *1001 Battles that Changed the Course of History* (London, Penguin) 44, 53.

[24] Lewis, M (2007) *The Early Chinese Empires: Qin and Han* (Massachusetts, Harvard University Press) 19, 51, 54, 69–71; Hsiao, K (1979) *A History of Chinese Political Thought* (New Jersey, Princeton University Press) 431–32; Hucker, C (1994) *China's Imperial Past* (California, Stanford University Press) 44; White, M (2011) *Atrocitology: Humanity's 100 Deadliest Achievements* (Melbourne, Text) 37. For the dislike of Confucian scholars by Lord Shang, see *The Book of Lord Shang*, trans Duyvendak, J (1928) (San Francisco, Chinese Materials Centre) Vol I, 3 and 4, and Vol II, 5. For the figures, see Grant, R (2011) *1001 Battles that Changed the Course of History* (London, Penguin) 63.

to prevent the disintegration of the Empire between 169 and 220 CE, as it was swept away by a combination of regions seeking autonomy and religiously inspired revolutions (the Yellow Turbans and later, the Five Pecks of Grain) which collectively reacted against the status quo.[25]

China then reverted to its traditional patterns, as a further era of violence and chaos unfolded as rising populations overlapped with a concentration of lands in fewer hands. This was supplemented by widespread misery, social breakdown, banditry and the inability of the central government to control rebellions. Externally, Korea tried to claim independence from the end of the fourth century onwards, when the former pro-China overlords were ejected. A similar situation occurred in Vietnam in the third, and later the fifth, centuries. In the north of China, wars between non-Chinese groupings and the local Chinese rose and fell with confusing rapidity, before settling into what became known as the Sixteen Kingdoms, which took turns at devouring each other and claiming their resources. In the south of China, the defeat of the Han army at the battle of the Red Cliffs in 208 CE allowed for the formation of the Three Kingdoms (Wei, Wu and Shu). Although each, originally, claimed to the be correct descendants of the Han, in time, all declared themselves independent and established their own dynasties, which took turns aligning with each other as they each tried to reconstruct a unified China. Whilst this almost occurred with the Jin dynasty, the Rebellion of the Eight Princes in the year 300 proved too severe, with too many military dynasts breeding first autonomy, and then absolute power, over all others. This ushered in another period of hundreds of years of warfare and division.[26]

It was only towards the fifth century that both the northern and southern dynasties reversed the trend and managed to reunite China at the end of the sixth century, with the rise of the Sui dynasty (581–618). This occurred when its leader, a general named Yang Jian usurped a regional throne, and then proceeded to override all of China, as he increased his forces to in excess of half a million men under arms. With these forces, the Sui dynasty brought all of China under a single ruler for the first time in almost four centuries. It lasted for less than four decades. The roots of the Sui collapse lay in their intention to bring both Vietnam and Korea under their control. Whilst this was possible to achieve with Vietnam, the two invasions (598 and 612) of Korea (which was in the stage of forging it its own unity from three contending regions) were disasters. Of the 305,000 Chinese soldiers who invaded Korea in the second invasion, only 2,700 returned. When a third invasion was attempted, a revolution was sparked, which degenerated into a situation in which China split into nine separate contenders for power. This separatism was the rule until the Tang dynasty (618–907) rose to the top.[27]

[25] Lewis, M (2007) *The Early Chinese Empires: Qin and Han* (Massachusetts, Harvard University Press) 20–21, 28, 133–37, 203; Warmington, E (1928) *The Commerce Between the Roman Empire and China* (Cambridge, Cambridge University Press) 1–35.

[26] Lewis, M (2009) *China Between Empires: The Northern and Southern Dynasties* (Massachusetts, Harvard University Press) 7–25, 31–39, 53, 55–60, 84–85; Graff, D (2002) *Medieval Chinese Warfare* (London, Routledge) 132–33.

[27] Lewis, M (2009) *China Between Empires: The Northern and Southern Dynasties* (Massachusetts, Harvard University Press) 150–54; Graff, D (2002) *Medieval Chinese Warfare* (London, Routledge) 144–47, 190–201; Gabriel, R (2005) *Empires at War*, Vol II (London, Greenwood) 618–24, 634–36.

Under the Tang dynasty, China combined prosperity, cultural grandeur, aristocratic sophistication, military power, and supremacy in foreign relations to achieve an age of greatness unapproached since the Han. Tang emperors became monarchs, acknowledged by Turkic khans in Mongolia, and their practices were copied in Vietnam, Japan and Central Asia. Tibet initially fell under Tang suzerainty after campaigns in 639–40 and 647–48, and in 648 a small Chinese force crossed the Himalayas from Tibet into north-eastern India to chastise a local ruler who had insulted a Tang ambassador. Like the Sui, they also dreamed of bringing Korea back under their control. However, their initial successes around 668 (following the battle of Baekgang, where Japan sent 800 ships – of which it lost half – to support the Koreans seeking independence) soon turned into retreats, from which they were forced out of this region and Tibet between 670 and 675. These losses appear to have forced the Tang to reject expansionist policies, and instead secure the existing frontiers with increasingly professional, but static, forces. This largely worked until some of the static forces, such as the 150,000 men under the leadership of An Lushan, rebelled in 755, due to a fear that they were about to be disbanded. The Tang forces joined with the dominant forces on the Mongolian steppe and defeated the uprising, which may have caused the deaths of tens of millions over the following half decade. The Tang then had to weather an invasion by the Tibetans in 763, who advanced against the Tang capital of Changán and overran most of the region before they were forced out. It was close to a further 50 years before peace was reached with Tibet in 822. In institutional terms, the cost of these victories was the loss of cohesion from the centre. Rebellions, mutinies and further bandit armies proliferated within China. From 780 onwards, local rulers sought absolute autonomy. The same pattern was repeated in Vietnam, where at the battle of Bach Dang in 938, a possible 100,000 Chinese soldiers were killed. Due to such defeats, the authorities of China quickly disengaged from their foreign adventures and focused on tighter border and closer neighbours. Within a century, there were around one million men under arms in China – but they were all watching each other within some 50 different provincial regimes. When the inevitable collapse and civil war occurred, it was the Song dynasty (960–1279), as seeded from one of the commanders of the Palace Corps, Zhao Kuangyin, who changed the title of the dynasty.[28]

3. THE MIDDLE EAST

A. Egypt and Nubia

Intelligible military history of Egypt begins with the conflicts between rival city-states in the southern part of the country around 3150 BCE. By 3075 BCE this had been

[28] Hucker, C (1994) *China's Imperial Past* (California, Stanford University Press) 147–48; Graff, D (2002) *Medieval Chinese Warfare* (London, Routledge) 245–47; Smith, V (1962) *The Early History of India* (Oxford, Oxford University Press) 378; Graff, D (2002) *Medieval Chinese Warfare* (London, Routledge) 173–78, 201, 218–23, 227–28; White, M (2011) *Atrocitology: Humanity's 100 Deadliest Achievements* (Melbourne, Text) 88–91; Grant, R (2011) *1001 Battles that Changed the Course of History* (London, Penguin) 123.

concentrated down to two rival kingdoms, whereupon the kings Ka (c 3075–3050 BCE) and Scorpion (c 3085–3060 BCE) battled for the right to unite Egypt and its million or so people based upon the fertility and geography of the Nile, under one religion, one culture and one man. Although Ka may have been successful, it was Narmer (c 3050–3025 BCE) who is recognised as the founder of the first dynasty. His records proclaimed 'the King has united the heavens, the King has power over the southern and northern lands'.[29] This vision of a single Egypt would endure for 30 dynasties, ending with Nectanebo II, as the last king of the thirtieth dynasty (360–343 BCE).[30]

Although Egypt had a broad geographical boundary, the Empire was continually pushed to the north, west and south. To the south (of the Nile) sat the area known as Nubia. Attempts at Egyptian control over Nubia were long standing, as were Nubian attempts to reject it. The first recorded objection was when Nubia attempted to push the Egyptians out of the area around the sixth dynasty (2345–2181 BCE). The Egyptians viewed this as a revolt of such magnitude that the response precipitated the end of the Old Kingdom. Revolt against Egyptian rule (manifested in everything from a failure to pay the correct amount of tribute through to physical eviction of Egyptian soldiers and/or citizens) was seen as a very serious act demanding an immediate and severe response. The response, 'as is done to a rebel against the king',[31] was reprisal against those challenging Egyptian authority, the re-annexation of the disputed territory and possible expansion deeper south. This was the pattern of the Pharaohs of the New Dynasty including Montuhotep (2061–2011 BCE), Sesostris I (1971–1928 BCE) and Amenemhat I (1991–1962 BCE). Sometimes these responses were believed to be so successful that the conquerors, such as Sesostris I could boast he was 'lord of mankind',[32] whilst one of his successors, Sesostris III (1887–1849 BCE), claimed he 'smited the Negro, opening the land of the Asiatic'.[33]

This was not one-way traffic. Around 1630 to 1520 BCE, following a civil war within Egypt, a great army from Nubia (the Hykos) in conjunction with forces from

[29] Narmer inscription reprinted in Hamblin, W (2006) *Warfare in the Ancient Near East to 1600 BC* (London, Routledge) 319.

[30] Wilkinson, T (2010) *The Rise and Fall of Ancient Egypt* (London, Bloomsbury) 18–19, 25–30; Edwards, I (ed) (1971) *The Cambridge Ancient History. The Early History of the Middle East* (Cambridge, Cambridge University Press) 167, 360, 422; Edwards, I (ed) (1975) *The Cambridge Ancient History: The Middle East and the Aegean Region* (Cambridge, Cambridge University Press) 478–83; Saggs, H (1989) *Civilisation Before Greece and Rome* (New Haven, Yale University Press) 41, 136–39; Kramer, S (1956) *History Begins at Sumer* (Philadelphia, Pennsylvania University Press) 20–21. Kramer, S (1963) *The Sumerians: Their History, Culture and Character* (Chicago, University of Chicago Press) 37, 54; Postgate, J (1996) *Early Mesopotamia: Society and Economy and the Dawn of History* (London, Routledge) 241–42; Hamblin, W (2006) *Warfare in the Ancient Near East to 1600 BC* (London, Routledge) 51–53, 194, 351, 378.

[31] Amenemhat, noted in Wilkinson, T (2010) *The Rise and Fall of Ancient Egypt* (London, Bloomsbury) 111, 166. See also Hamblin, W (2006) *Warfare in the Ancient Near East to 1600 BC* (London, Routledge) 382–84, 335–47, 397–98; Asante, M (2000) *The Egyptian Philosophers* (Chicago, African Images) 64, 69; Kemp, B (1989) *Ancient Egypt* (London, Routledge) 225.

[32] Inscription of Sesostris reprinted in Breasted, J (ed) (1988) *Ancient Records of Egypt*, Vol 1 (London, Histories and Mysteries) 243.

[33] Sesostris III reprinted in Breasted, J (ed) (1988 edn) *Ancient Records of Egypt*, Vol 1 (London, Histories and Mysteries) 313; also Edwards, I (ed) (1975) *The Cambridge Ancient History: The Middle East and the Aegean Region* (Cambridge, Cambridge University Press) 290–93, 313.

Kush (further south than Nubia on the Nile), pushed north, and toppled the Egyptian regime (ruling for 108 years) after both sides committed to join forces to 'divide up the towns of Egypt'.[34] This occupation only came to an end when Ahmose (r 1550–1525 BCE) pushed out the Nubians and their allies, retook the lands to the north (as far as modern-day Lebanon) and to the south, when Egyptian forces re-entered Nubia and the associated territories. These wars were justified on the assumption that the land they were retaking was rightfully theirs. Subsequent pharaohs, such as Thutmose I (r 1506–1493 BCE), Thutmose II (r 1493–1479 BCE), Thutmose III (1481–1425 BCE) and Horembeb (1319–1292 BCE) all followed suit, advancing military forces into Nubia to subdue uprisings when required and extending the imperial boundaries of Egypt. Some of these Pharaohs were particularly ambitious in this area. Thutmose I could claim that 'the entire earth is under his two feet'. He recorded that he had, 'made the boundaries of Egypt as far as that which the sun encircles . . . I made Egypt superior of every land'.[35]

B. Egypt, Mesopotamia and the Hittites

Egypt did not only battle countries to the south. It also, when needed, battled those to the north. The countries to the north (Sumer, Akkadia, Babylon and Assyria) were broadly within the area known by the Greeks as Mesopotamia – literally 'the land between the two rivers'. This was a reference to the Tigris and the Euphrates – an area which largely corresponds to modern-day Iraq, north-east Syria, south-east Turkey and south-west Iran.

These empires had to form before Egypt could do battle with them. The formation of these empires is first recorded with the Sumerian city-states some time between 3000 and 2100 BCE. These were a hotchpotch of separate and feuding independent entities which engaged in cooperative alliances and/or competition, and when appropriate, war. It is from this epoch, around 2600 BCE, that the first treaty of peace and first international arbitration occurred. The treaty of peace followed the first recorded war in which two armies, perhaps of a few hundred men each, clashed over the ownership of some fertile land that lay between the cities of the two sides. The treaty recorded the commitment of Enakale of Umma 'not [to] transgress the territory of [Lagash] . . . shift the course of its irrigation channels and canals [or] smash its [boundary] monuments'.[36]

[34] Letter of the Hykos king to the ruler of Kush reprinted in Wilkinson, T (2010) *The Rise and Fall of Ancient Egypt* (London, Bloomsbury) 206.

[35] Wilkinson, T (2010) *The Rise and Fall of Ancient Egypt* (London, Bloomsbury) 196, 208–13, 224–25, 230, 310; Spalinger, A (2005) *War in Ancient Egypt* (London, Blackwell) 46–47. *Thutmose I* is reprinted in Breasted, J (ed) (1988 edn) *Ancient Records of Egypt*, Vol II (London, Histories and Mysteries) 30 and 40. *Thutmose III* is in the same volume, at 167–70, 195.

[36] The peace imposed on Enakale reprinted in Hamblin, W (2006) *Warfare in the Ancient Near East to 1600 BC* (London, Routledge) 53. For the arbitration between Lagash and Umma with regard to a boundary dispute which was overseen by a neutral third party, see Frankfort, H (1941) *Before Philosophy* (Harmondsworth, Penguin) 231. *Cf*, Phillipson, C (1908) *Studies in International Law* (London, Harpers) 6. For the figures, see Grant, R (2011) *1001 Battles that Changed the Course of History* (London, Penguin) 20.

The ad hoc nature of such arrangements came to an end around 2350 BCE when Sargon of Agade (2334–2279 BCE), replete with the first recorded standing army of over 5,000 men, succeeded in dominating the whole land. He went on to conquer most of the region (despite a network of alliances against him), through no less than 34 wars and to create the earliest empire in history, under which Mesopotamia, Syria and the province of Elam were integrated into one political system under the rule of one man and his directly appointed governors.[37] This system was far from robust, lasting less than a century before it was toppled by Lugalzagesi (r 2296–2271 BCE), who took all of the cities and lands of Sumer – and the title of 'high king' as 'all the lands . . . from east to west [were] subject to him'.[38] A period of peace followed, in which the subsequent rulers such as Shulgi (2029–1982 BCE) could claim that they did not need to breach walls or sack cities. So deep was the belief among the Sumerians that they had reached the end of conflict, that they built a special 'gate of peace' in their holy city of Nippur. Exactly what happened next is uncertain, but it appears that an internal rebellion, fueled by outside invaders, combined to bring this period of peace to an end. The rebels made this point clear by destroying Nippur and taking apart the gate of peace with pickaxes. Thereafter, the regime and the network that held the Sumerian Empire together, disintegrated.[39]

From the destruction of one empire, arose others. The Assyrian kingdom emerged from the city of Ashur which broke free from the Sumerians around the year 2000 BCE, whilst leaders of supplementary groups such as the Akkadians, for example, Ilu-shumma (c 1900 BCE) claimed he 'established freedom' for his people.[40] Having established their own freedoms, the differing groups then attempted to expand outwards and take the autonomy of others. The problem was that the area was too fragmented to be brought together under one ruler, as a bewildering number of local and semi-regional warlords jockeyed for position. The military balance of power was described in a famous letter by Itur-Asdu to the king of Mari, in which he lamented 'there is no king who is strong by himself'. This was because '10 or 15 kings follow Hammurabi of Babylon, as many follow Rim-Sin of Larsa . . . while 20 kings follow Yarim-Lim of Aleppo'.[41] Despite these initial odds, Hammurabi of Babylon (1792–

[37] Saggs, H (1989) *Civilisation Before Greece and Rome* (New Haven, Yale University Press) 178; Postgate, J (1996) *Early Mesopotamia: Society and Economy and the Dawn of History* (London, Routledge) 46; Hamblin, W (2006) *Warfare in the Ancient Near East to 1600 BC* (London, Routledge) 54, 73; Gabriel, R (2005) *Empires at War*, Vol I (London, Greenwood) 57–60.

[38] The Lugalzagesi inscription noted in Hamblin, W (2006) *Warfare in the Ancient Near East to 1600 BC* (London, Routledge) 65–66.

[39] Kramer, S (1981) *History Begins at Sumer* (Philadelphia, University of Pennsylvania Press) 40–41, 122, 261–63; Kramer, S (1963) *The Sumerians: Their History, Culture and Character* (London, University of Chicago Press) 54, 56–57; Hamblin, W (2006) *Warfare in the Ancient Near East to 1600 BC* (London, Routledge) 45–46, 73–78.

[40] Ilu-shumma reprinted in Hamblin, W (2006) *Warfare in the Ancient Near East to 1600 BC* (London, Routledge) 167.

[41] Letter from Itur-Asdu, noted in Saggs, H (1989) *Civilisation Before Greece and Rome* (New Haven, Yale University Press) 178. For useful quotes reflecting this period, see Luckenbill, D (ed) (1989) *Ancient Records of Assyria and Babylonia* (London, Histories and Mysteries) Vol I, 49, 114, 203, 254, 275; Vol II, 3; Postgate, J (1996) *Early Mesopotamia: Society and Economy and the Dawn of History* (London, Routledge) 41; Edwards, I (ed) (1971) *The Cambridge Ancient History. Early History of the Middle East* 3rd edn, Vol I (Cambridge, Cambridge University Press) 463, 616, 650, 658, 761; Edwards, I (ed) (1975) *The Cambridge Ancient History. History of the*

1750 BCE) won this three-horse race and became the first to reunite Mesopotamia as the 'high-king' in almost 250 years since the fall or the Sumerian city of Ur around 2000 BCE. This success was short lived, as Hammurabi's achievements and dynasty fell beneath the swords of the Hittites. In between the collapse of Babylon, the rise of the Hittites and the reach of Egypt, a number of other people attempted to assert their autonomy.

It was this quest for autonomy in the Transjordan valley that made Thutmose III march out of Egypt. Claiming the right to quash a rebellion against Egyptian domination, Thutmose III advanced with 20,000 soldiers to battle a coalition under the direction of the ancient city of Kadesh (modern-day west Syria) including 330 princes and perhaps 15,000 men of the various surrounding areas, including, inter alia, Canaanites, Mitanni and forces from the region at Megiddo around 1457 BCE. After a relatively small engagement (Egyptian records report that only 83 hands were taken from the fallen enemy) the rebels retreated into Megiddo from which they were starved into submission five months later.[42] This capture of Megiddo placed control of the region firmly within the grasp of the Egyptians. The defeat of the coalition brought with it the submission of many other towns that may have been toying with idea of independence, and any further attempts at revolt were dealt with severely. Thus, when Megiddo attempted to rebel again, when recaptured, every male was executed. From such actions Thutmose III claimed that 'all lands were under his sandals' and 'all countries are my subjects'. He, as 'king of kings, ruler of rulers' claimed sovereignty 'as far as the four pillars of heaven'.[43] Subsequent pharaohs, such as Harmhab (1319–1292 BCE) would echo such grandiose claims that 'all lands are under thy feet'.[44] Seti I (1294–1279 BCE), aimed higher, trying to set 'his boundary as far as the limits of Aton illuminates'.[45]

Rhetoric aside, Egypt only possessed everything up to the borders of the Hittite Empire. Over five centuries, the Hittites had carved out an empire throughout Anatolia, north-west Syria and upper Mesopotamia, and had alliances possibly stretching out as far as Troy. Their goal was to secure their homeland by suppressing domestic revolts and increasing their power by pushing out their borders when the time was

Middle East and Aegean Region 1800–1380 BCE 3rd edn, Vol II (Cambridge, Cambridge University Press) 179–81, 420–25, 469.

[42] Hamblin, W (2006) *Warfare in the Ancient Near East to 1600 BC* (London, Routledge) 114, 159, 164, 260–63, 295, 301; Strauss, B (2006) *The Trojan War* (NYC, Schuster) 18; Edwards, I (ed) (1975) *The Cambridge Ancient History: The Middle East and the Aegean Region* (Cambridge, Cambridge University Press) 484; Wilkinson, T (2010) *The Rise and Fall of Ancient Egypt* (Bloomsbury, London) 226–29, 236–39; Spalinger, A (2005) *War in Ancient Egypt* (London, Blackwell) 49–50, 83–95; Gabriel, R (2005) *Empires at War*, Vol I (London, Greenwood) 75–77, 80–87.

[43] Thutmose III reprinted in Breasted, J (ed) (1988 edn) *Ancient Records of Egypt*, Vol II (London, Histories and Mysteries) 62, 134, 203, 254, 263, 311; Spalinger, A (2005) *War in Ancient Egypt* (London, Blackwell) 130–36; Wilkinson, T (2010) *The Rise and Fall of Ancient Egypt* (London, Bloomsbury) 258.

[44] Harmhab reprinted in Breasted, J (ed) (1988 edn) *Ancient Records of Egypt*, Vol III (London, Histories and Mysteries) 20.

[45] Seti I reprinted in Breasted, J (ed) (1988 edn) *Ancient Records of Egypt*, Vol III (London, Histories and Mysteries) 72. Edwards, I (ed) (1975) *The Cambridge Ancient History: The Middle East and the Aegean Region* (Cambridge, Cambridge University Press) 459–63, 470–71, 475–78. On the question of appeasement, and the desire to avoid conflict with Egypt, see Mercer, S (1939) *The Tell El-Amarna Tablets* (Toronto, Toronto University Press) No 6, lines 8–16.

right. The time for the Hittites was right when the city of Kadesh, rather than opt for independence as they had tried earlier, decided to opt for a change in overlords – from Egypt to the Hittites. The fact that the Hittites had been attempting to meddle in Egyptian national affairs (and almost acquired Egypt by a diplomatic marriage at a point of civil unrest) did not help matters. The act of revolt by Kadesh, which Ramses II (1303–1213 BCE) saw as particularly serious, resulted in of one the largest battles of pre-Greek Antiquity – the battle of Kadesh in 1274 BCE. In this engagement, some 20,000 Egyptian soldiers (and 2,000 chariots) clashed with 15,000 Hittites (and 3,500 chariots).[46]

The battle of Kadesh resulted in the tactical victory for Egypt – but strategic loss, as the Hittites expanded their territory southwards after the battle. Ramses had to send an army, again, into Syria to subdue an uprising, and then into southern Palestine. In both instances, it was believed that the Hittites were behind the revolt. Rather than face such ongoing problems in 1269 BCE, the world's first comprehensive peace treaty was agreed between Ramses II and Hattusili III (r 1267–1237 BCE). In terms of geography, the river and the city of Kadesh became the boundary between the two great empires. In terms of principles, the agreement promised 'peace and brotherhood . . . forever', binding their children and grandchildren alike. This utopia was to be achieved via three simple principles. First, neither shall 'pass into the land' of the other or take anything from it. Second, to lessen tensions, they also both agreed to turn over anyone from either country who attempted to flee their primary domicile and live in the other country. Finally, rather than fight the other, both sides sought to entrench the status quo via mutual assistance against both internal and external enemies.[47] In the Hittite text, this point was particularly drawn out. Thus, if the king:

> [R]ises in anger against his citizens after they have committed a crime against him and if, for this reason, [the king of Egypt was to] send his troops and his chariots and these should exterminate all those that he has risen in anger against.[48]

C. Egypt, Canaan, Assyria, Babylon and the Rise of Persia

Although both the Hittites and the Egyptians sought to defend each other and thus entrench the status quo, the reality of the times was that neither empire controlled all areas within their auspice. As such, some areas could develop independently, whilst others could regain their power. The case of the latter was obvious with the renewed rise of Assyria, while the case of the former was most obvious in the instance of Canaan.

[46] For Ramses II see Breasted, J (ed) (1988 edn) *Ancient Records of Egypt*, Vol III (London, Histories and Mysteries) 203, 259; also Spalinger, A (2005) *War in Ancient Egypt* (London, Blackwell) 225–28; Wilkinson, T (2010) *The Rise and Fall of Ancient Egypt* (London, Bloomsbury) 320–21, 324–25. The figures come from Grant, R (2005) *Battle* (London, Dorling Kindersley) 14; and Gabriel, R (2005) *Empires at War*, Vol I (London, Greenwood) 110–14.

[47] The text used for these points is the Egyptian one. The sections quoted are the preamble and articles 1, 3, 5 and 9. The treaty is reprinted in Breasted, J (ed) (1988 edn) *Ancient Records of Egypt*, Vol III (London, Histories and Mysteries) 171–72.

[48] Article 5 of the Hittite version. See also article 5 of the Egyptian text, and articles 6, 7 and 8 of both.

Canaan (broadly modern-day Israel, Palestine and Jordan) was a region which held a patchwork of ethnic groups (including, inter alia, Amalekites, Amorites, Anakim, Emim, Horites, Nephalim, Rephaim and Zuzim).[49] These peoples, who were described as ancient, warlike and fearsome were fragmented into numerous clans and city-states. Egyptian raids – to punish rebels and/or secure resources, especially copper – to the areas around Canaan, which was believed to have been under (nominal) Egyptian control, appear to have gone back, perhaps, as early as 2700 BCE. The Bible only records such Egyptian incursions at around 1500 BCE. This was roughly 300 years after Abraham and his clan left from the Mesopotamian city of Haran (because of his belief in a single God), and became swept up in the great movement of ethnic units that shook the eastern Mediterranean. Upon settling in (but not conquering) the already occupied Canaan (which God had given him), Abraham became familiar with cooperation and conflict with, and between, various local warlords. It was within one of these conflicts between multiple local warlords seeking autonomy/and or dominance from/over each other – and nominal overlord – that the Jewish people appear to have been swept up and taken to Egypt. The Egyptian regime did this 'lest they multiply, and it come to pass, that, when there falleth out any war, they join also unto our enemies, and fight against us'.[50]

It was after the exodus from Egypt that Moses began the conquest of the de facto Egyptian province of Canaan. Although much of this period is shrouded in mystery, it appears that by the time of the New Kingdom, Egypt had lost a large amount of control in the area, thus allowing local (and returning) communities to try to obtain their own autonomy from both Egypt and the other groupings in the area. Although Moses started this process, the credit for gaining a foothold in the Judean heartland west of Jordan usually goes to Joshua (c 1500 BCE), who took the city of Jericho. When the Canaanites, under the five kings of the Amorites, prepared a counter-offensive, Joshua joined forces with the Gibeonites, and then having defeated them, pushed further into Galilee, where he met another contingent of Canaanite kings who had joined 'to fight against Israel'.[51] These conflicts were without success, as subsequent leaders such as Deborah (c 1200 BCE) and her 10,000 fighters achieved military victories which look like tide marks, as disputed borders moved backwards and forwards between lesser enemies, before greater ones, such as the Philistines – a proxy of Egypt – arrived. The

[49] Eretz Israel is the Hebrew name for the Holy Land while Canaan was the name by which the area was known on the eve of the Israelite conquest. After the split of the United Monarchy in about 925 BCE, the northern kingdom retained the name of Israel, while the southern was called Judah. Eventually the term Judah was used to designate all the Jewish dominions after the Israelites return from exile in Babylon in 537 BCE. The name was later changed into Syria Palestina, hence Palestine, by the Roman emperor Hadrian, in an attempt to stamp out the Jewish uprising between 132 and 135.

[50] Exodus 1:10. The Egyptian records on the existence of Israel and Judah (who were defeated) did not appear until around 1200 BCE. For additional references from the Bible around this point, see Genesis 12:6, 12:26, 14:1–19, 21:22, 34:2; Numbers 13:32, 13:33; Deuteronomy 2:10–12; Joshua 9:7 and 9:14–15. For some of the alliances, note 1 Kings 5:12, and consult the useful Thompson, J (1963) *The Ancient Near Eastern Treaties and the Old Testament* (London, Tynedale Press). For some general commentary, see Hamblin, W (2006) *Warfare in the Ancient Near East to 1600 BC* (London, Routledge) 273–75, 283–84, 311, 320, 322, 329, 336–40, 344–45; Spalinger, A (2005) *War in Ancient Egypt* (London, Blackwell) 169, 187–95, 241–43; Herzog, C (1997) *Battles of the Bible* (London, Greenhill) 27–28.

[51] Joshua 11:5, 7–9; also Joshua 6: 2–5, 6:20 and 10:3–4; Herzog, C (1997) *Battles of the Bible* (London, Greenhill) 40–41.

Philistines, from which the name Palestine originates, were of Aegean stock and were probably related to both the Minoan and Mycenaean people of the Mediterranean islands and mainland Greece. It was due to the magnitude of the threat that the Philistines represented, that the 12 Jewish tribes decided they could only ensure their independence by acting collectively and pooling their 30,000 warriors under the leadership of one man – Saul (c 1050–1000 BCE). The continuing independence was achieved at the battle of Michmash (c 1010 BCE) and associated conflicts, at which point David (c 1040–970 BCE) fought Goliath.[52] Thereafter, Saul pushed the borders even further. Thus:

> Saul took the kingdom over Israel, and fought against all his enemies on every side, against Moab, and against the children of Ammon, and against Edom, and against the kings of Zobah . . . and withersoever he turned himself, he vexed them.[53]

The successes came to an end when Saul faced the regrouped Philistines at Mount Gilboa, and he and his son (Jonathan) were killed and his forces defeated. This allowed the Philistines to re-establish their pre-eminence in Canaan. After a civil war with Saul's heirs, David was then made king of Judah, and following the assassination of the king of the tribes of Israel (Ish-Bosheth), was made king of a united monarchy of all the Israelite tribes. Once his authority was secure, he advanced against the Negev Nomads, before going on to capture Jerusalem. This capture sparked several unsuccessful Philistine interventions before David began his trans-Jordan campaigns by conquering various kingdoms and making them satellites of Israel.[54]

With these victories David created an Israelite empire that ran from the River of Egypt (Wadi Arish) to Lebo in the Lebanon valley. This was the empire bequeathed by David to Solomon (r, c 970–930 BCE) who, as the text recorded, 'ruled over all the kingdoms from the River Euphrates to the land of the Philistines and to the border of Egypt'.[55] Such an expansion eventually came to the attention of some of the former landlords, who began to take a renewed interest in the region. The Pharaoh Shishak, launched a punitive raid (c 924 BCE) with a force of 1,200 chariots and 60,000 men, that destroyed the United Monarchy of Israel. This was followed by an invasion by the Aramean kingdom of Damascus (in association with 32 other local kings) – who decided to strike Israel before they could recover. This attack was eventually defeated after Ahab (r 869–850 BCE) forced the Syrians and their allies back out of the area. Then, to ensure that the same situation did not reoccur, Ahab secured the Golan Heights and made peace with Damascus. This peace was either good planning or good fortune, as Israel then went on to face an even greater threat – the resurgent Assyria.[56]

[52] Judges 4:6–7, 6:1–5, 8:11. Herzog, C (1997) *Battles of the Bible* (London, Greenhill) 82–87; Gabriel, R (2005) *Empires at War*, Vol I (London, Greenwood) 141–45.

[53] 1 Samuel 14:47.

[54] Thus 2 Samuel 10:19 explained: 'When all the kings who were servants of Hadadezer saw that they had been defeated by Israel they made peace with Israel and became subject to them.' See also 2 Samuel 1:17–27, 5:17–25, 8:12, 10:15–19; 1 Chronicles 19:16–19. And, Edwards, I (ed) (1975) *The Cambridge Ancient History. History of the Middle East and Aegean Region*, Vol II, 3rd edn (Cambridge, Cambridge University Press) 550–63.

[55] 1 Kings 4:21.

[56] 1 Kings 20:1; 20:19–25. Herzog, C (1997) *Battles of the Bible* (London, Greenhill) 126–28; Gabriel, R (2005) *Empires at War*, Vol I (London, Greenwood) 164–75.

By the year 1000 BCE, Assyria, despite it its long history, had been reduced to its traditional heartland around the cities of Ashur and Nineveh. By the year 700 BCE, it was the most formidable empire on the planet. It achieved this status through having up to 200,000 men under arms, which allowed it to fight through 108 recorded wars between the years 890 and 640 BCE. This persistent conflict was in accordance with their belief that their most powerful kings, would be those who, 'capture all peoples [and] enlarge boundary and frontiers'.[57] Amongst those who tried to live up to this ideal, under the reign of Shalmanezer III (858–824 BCE), the Assyrians tried to subdue the lands west of the Euphrates – namely Canaan and her neighbours. Battle was joined around 853 BCE, when the Assyrians, with a reported 100,000 men, faced off, and lost, against a united force of Israel (under the authority of Ahab) and seven others (including the Aramean kingdom of Damascus) of perhaps 60,000 men.[58]

Although the united tribes of Israel could play a vital part in keeping the Assyrians out, they faced a growing number of revolts from local communities who sought their autonomy. These attempts resulted in a series of conflicts as some of the communities, 'revolted from under the hand of Judah, and made a king over themselves'.[59] Thereafter, successive kings such as Jehoash (c 790 BCE), Amaziah (r 796–767 BCE) and Uzziah (r c 783–742 BCE) battled successfully to hold the group together.[60]

The Assyrians returned in 738 BCE under the direction of Tilgath-Pileser III (r 745–727 BCE). Tilgath-Pileser III invaded the whole of Syria under the pretext of helping a distant vassal who feared a joint attack from the forces of Damascus and Israel. This time there was no stopping the Assyrians, as they first took and occupied the Medes, neo-Hittites, and Phoenicia. In 729 BCE, they assumed total control of Babylon, and then, under the guidance of Sargon II (r 722–705 BCE), they set their sights on Israel. This campaign was one of 10 major wars of conquest or suppression within the space of 16 years that Sargon II had undertaken. Under the pretext of being invited to help friends in local squabbles and/or removing threats on the borders, Sargon established an empire that ran from the Persian Gulf to the Mediterranean Sea, from Armenia and north Persia to the Arabian desert, and farther west to include parts of the Egyptian delta. Rather than face utter destruction, Israel agreed to become a loyal vassal of Assyria.[61]

When the united tribes of Israel, despite their obligations under loyalty treaties to their Assyrian overlords, decided to join a revolt lead by Egypt against the Assyrians,

[57] In Luckenbill, D (ed) (1989) *Ancient Records of Assyria and Babylonia*, Vol 1 (London, Histories and Mysteries) 27, 29.

[58] For the Assyrian comments on the battle, see Luckenbill, D (ed) (1989) *Ancient Records of Assyria and Babylonia*, Vol 1 (London, Histories and Mysteries) 212–15; Bury, J, (ed) (1965) *The Cambridge Ancient History. The Assyrian Empire*, Vol III, 1st edn (Cambridge, Cambridge University Press) 179; Kelle, B (2007) *Ancient Israel at War* (Oxford, Osprey) 34; Grant, R (2005) *Battle* (London, Dorling Kindersley) 17; Herzog, C (1997) *Battles of the Bible* (London, Greenhill) 159–63.

[59] 2 Kings 8:20; also 1 Kings 22:34, 2 Kings 3:7–9.

[60] 2 Chronicles 26:6–8; also 2 Chronicles 25:14; 2 Kings 14:7 and 14:22.

[61] 2 Kings 16:2, 7–9; 15:29; 17:4–5. Also Herzog, C (1997) *Battles of the Bible* (London, Greenhill) 151, 246–48; Luckenbill, D (ed) (1989) *Ancient Records of Assyria and Babylonia*, Vol 1 (London, Histories and Mysteries) 143, 145, 279, 281, 284. Note also the Loyalty Treaty of Naqia-Zakutu of 670 BCE, The Covenant of Zakutu reprinted in Parpola, S (1987) 'Neo-Assyrian Treaties from the Royal Archives of Nineveh' 39(2) *Journal of Cuneiform Studies*, 161, 165.

they were confronting the largest, most aggressive military empire in the world at that point of time. The revolt was a disaster for Israel, which had to pay for the adventure in tribute and some deported populations. Undeterred, (again with the assistance of Egypt) another attempt at revolt and independence from Assyria occurred in 701 BCE, when Lachish, the second city of Judah, attempted to divorce their overlord. The Assyrians, after brutally crushing the city as a warning to others within the region who had similar thoughts, then went on to face similar uprisings in Babylonia, and a concerted attack from Egypt. With the possibilities of uprisings in different parts of their empire removed, the Assyrians, especially under the rule of Esarhaddon, and then Ashurbanipal achieved impressive victories. Babylonia was completely subdued and Egypt was invaded in 674 BCE. Just over 10 years later, Lower and Upper Egypt had been overwhelmed as far as the first cataract of the Nile, thus becoming a province of greater Assyria. Assyria's power was now supreme, and King Manasseh of Judah (709–643 BCE), reverted back to the earlier position of accepting Assyria as the overlord. This was a wise move, as Assyria was in no mood to tolerate rebellion. Elam, the former ally of Babylonia was fully destroyed between the invasions in 693 and 639 BCE, and simply vanished from history.[62]

The Egyptian pharaoh Psamtik I (r 664–610 BCE) fought back, and pushed the Assyrians out of Egypt, thus establishing the twenty-sixth dynasty. This was relatively easy to achieve as Assyria became distracted by a resurgent Babylon, and sought an alliance with Egypt. Babylon then fought battles independently against both Assyria and Egypt in 616, 614 and 612 BCE before Assyria and Egypt joined forces to fight the greater enemy. The last fight (and loss) as a united force against the Babylonians occurred in 605 BCE. Thereafter, Egypt was fighting alone as Assyria had ceased to exist. The Babylonian-led forces which sacked the Assyrian capital of Nineveh were so comprehensive that two centuries later when Xenophon (430–354 BCE) and his army passed the ruins of the former centre of Assyria, they were unaware of what they were passing. Not a single vestige of Assyrian power remained. A people who had lived on the Tigris for more than 2,000 years had now been erased from history. At the same time, those – such as Israel – who had been under 'the heavy yoke' of Assyria broke free. Israel was sucked into this very high-stakes game. This occurred when Pharaoh Necho in 609 BCE tried to convince King Josiah (r 628–609 BCE) not to interfere with his progress through Judah territory, to fight the Babylonians. Joshua refused the offer of neutrality and within a short time, the Egyptian armies were crushing the Jewish ones. This was, however, a time of declining Egyptian influence, for despite this victory, as the book of Kings explained, 'the king of Babylon had taken all his territory, from the Wadi of Egypt to the Euphrates River'.[63] Unimpressed by this remarkable new power, the people of Jerusalem continued to seek their independence and autonomy, staging revolts against their new Babylonian overlords in 598 and 591 BCE.

[62] Wilkinson, T (2010) *The Rise and Fall of Ancient Egypt* (London, Bloomsbury) 416–17, 424–27. Hamblin, W (2006) *Warfare in the Ancient Near East to 1600 BC* (London, Routledge) 404–405; Herzog, C (1997) *Battles of the Bible* (London, Greenhill) 195–98, 254. For the inscriptions of Esarhadon, see Luckenbill, D (ed) (1989) *Ancient Records of Assyria and Babylonia*, Vol II (London, Histories and Mysteries) 127 and 207.

[63] 2 Kings 24:7.

Both were failures, and ended up in tens of thousands of people being killed during the sieges and/or subsequently carried off into slavery in Mesopotamia.[64]

The celebrations of the neo-Babylonian empire were cut short because of the rise of Persia. Credit is usually given for this rise to the Medean king, Cyaxares (625–583 BCE) for forging the first army out of rival groups operating in the Zagros mountains in Iran. This was to become the heart of the Persian Empire once Cyrus the Great of Persia (600–529 BCE) successfully established himself and then toppled his Babylonian overlords at the battle of Hyrba in 552 BCE and Opis in 539 BCE. Cyrus then orchestrated his troops and territory to grow at rapid speed. At its peak, it is possible that the king of the Persian Empire had up to 300,000 men at his disposal. Xenophon in his *Education of Cyrus*, an enormous, quasi-historical work, had Cyrus justify his new empire on three grounds. First, it was a law of nature that all possessions of the conquered becomes the property of the conquerors; second, it was a just war because his enemies had plotted against him and finally; the Persians had proved themselves better than their enemies, and therefore deserved to rule them. Cyrus then went on to conquer much of the rest of the known world, sometimes after using arbitration as a stepping stone towards his final goal of conquest. Allowing any people who had, 'done us such wanton injury, to escape our vengeance'[65] was unacceptable. Such drive to possess the territories of others meant that when Cyrus was finally killed at the age of 70, still trying to expand his empire, the queen of the tribe which had killed him was said to have decapitated his corpse. She then dropped his head into a blood-filled wineskin, so the old man's thirst might be filled.

Although the mortal Cyrus could be stopped, the empire he bequeathed could not. His son and successor, Cambyses (559–530 BCE) continued the work. This was most notable in Egypt; on hearing of the death of Ahmose II – who had held the Persian forces at bay for four decades – Cambyses quickly invaded, and toppled the untested Pharaoh, Psamtek III (r 526–525 BCE). He then incorporated a united Egypt under the Persian realm, where it would remain, despite rebellions in 486, 465, 404 BCE until Alexander the Great would take it. This achievement was only part of the pattern which Herodotus (484–425 BCE), saw as the Persians making their empire 'border only on the sky that belongs to Zeus himself' as they 'make all lands into one land'.[66] At its height, Persia covered all of western Asia, from modern-day Pakistan to north-east Africa, encompassing four great cultural/linguistic zones. Over 20 provinces provided tribute, which amounted to over 14,500 talents of silver. By comparison, the Athenians, at the height of their power could only get close to 400 talents of silver in the mid fifth century.[67]

[64] Jeremiah 39:9. See also 2 Kings 25:2–4. Note also Roux, G (1964) *Ancient Iraq* (NYC, Pelican) 342. Gabriel, R (2005) *Empires at War*, Vol I (London, Greenwood) 200.

[65] Herodotus. *The Histories* trans De Selincourt, A (London, Penguin) 7:9. The point about arbitration is at 6:4. The sections in the *Education of Cyrus* are found at 1:5.13, 7:5.72–86 and 8.6.20–23. The background figures are from Grant, R (2005) *Battle* (London, Dorling Kindersley) 19; and Gabriel, R (2005) *Empires at War* (London, Greenwood) 153–67.

[66] Herodotus, *The Histories* trans De Selincourt, A (Penguin, London) 8:2.

[67] Billows, R (2010) *Marathon: How One Battle Changed Western Civilisation* (NYC, Scribe) 105–107, 129–30; Bury, J (ed) (1969) *The Cambridge Ancient History: The Persian Empire and the West*, Vol IV (Cambridge, Cambridge University Press) 348–52. Holland, T (2005) *Persian Fire* (London, Abacus) 19–20; Wilkinson, T (2010) *The Rise and Fall of Ancient Egypt* (London, Bloomsbury) 446–70.

4. GREECE

The theory is that some time around 2000 BCE, warriors of Indo-European stock came down upon the Aegean world from lands of the north. The last wave from the north, invaders called 'Dorians', reached down into central and western Greece. Over this time, the invaders absorbed the advanced civilizations of Crete that had perhaps begun 1,000 years earlier. The new people fused their culture with that of the older inhabitants and became the Greeks of antiquity. Their expansion also covered Rhodes, the lower shores of Asia Minor – including Ionia, an ancient region of central coastal Anatolia, in present day Turkey. These people developed in relative isolation from the sound of empires clashing in the Middle East, until the rise of Persia. At this point, the communities of Greek ancestry managed to run directly into the two largest empires on the planet at that stage, the Persians to the Carthaginians.

A. Greece and Carthage

Carthage was the most dominant colony of the civilisation of Phoenicia. This civilisation appears to have grown out of the turmoil that wrought havoc in the Middle East between 1800 and 1200 BCE, as communities of the ancient Canaanite civilisation sailed from the area and established thriving, trading cities down the west coast of the Mediterranean and along the top of north Africa. These included, inter alia, Beirut, Tripoli, Tyre and Carthage (beneath modern-day Tunis). Carthage, which developed its own Punic culture that was distinct to that of its forebears, went on to become the most dominant of all of the Phoenician family, seeking to colonise far and wide. It was this goal that took their settlers to Sicily some time around 730 BCE, if not earlier.

The settlers from Carthage were not alone. Greek communities of both Ionian and Dorian roots arrived on the east coast of Sicily around the same time. The Greek and Punic Wars, or as they were more commonly known, the Sicilian wars, were a series of conflicts between the Carthaginians and a collection of Greek communities, led by the city of Syracuse. The importance of this point is that although Greek communities outside of Sicily took an interest in these matters, with Athens, Sparta and Corinth all sending sizable forces to help (or intervene) at various points, there was never a collective 'Greek' front as such. Rather, the efforts against Carthage were primarily lead by the city (and province) of Syracuse, which was mostly of Dorian (Sparta and Corinth) ancestry. This was unlike the Phoenician communities, which first sought and then became fully intertwined with Carthage as a unified front. With this context, the longest lasting series of related wars of classical antiquity, lasting in total over 300 years from 600 to 265 BCE, were undertaken.

The Greek and Phoenician communities, in addition to the original indigenous inhabitants, existed in a relative cooperative existence until the beginning of the sixth century BCE, when the Phoenicians, feeling resentment at the growing economic strength and population size of the Greeks, called for assistance from their mother-source, Carthage. This call suited Carthage, which may have been seeking reasons to expand its hegemony over the Western Mediterranean. It is also possible that this quest was in agreement with the other great power-broker of the age, Persia. This possible alliance between Persia and Carthage for a joint invasion of the Greek communities from both ends at the same time would have been consistent with the other Carthaginian treaties of the period where they divided spheres of influence. This was first seen with the Punic treaty with the Etruscans (in 535 BCE) and then the Romans (508 BCE). It is possible that Carthage had a similar agreement with Persia, aimed at preventing the expansion of the Greeks, if not extinguishing them. Although there is no copy of such an arrangement, the fact that the Greek mainland was attacked by Persia and the Greek communities in Sicily were attacked by Carthage – in exactly the same year – 480 BCE – has given some weight to this theory, as has the remarkable coincidence that the Persian defeat at Salamis occurred on the same day that the Carthaginian attack was also defeated in Sicily.[68]

The Greek and Phoenician communities began clashing swords around the first half the sixth century. When Carthage responded to the Phoenician request for assistance, they interpreted their mandate somewhat widely, deciding to try to conquer all of Sicily, and not just defend the autonomy of the existing Phoenician communities. This decision was assisted by the fact that some of the Greeks (the Ionians) were initially welcoming the Carthaginian intervention in 481 BCE, as it would give weight against the Dorian Greeks, as lead by the city of Himera, who they also saw as threatening their independence. Thus, three blocks of power existed. The Ionian Greeks dominated the north, the Dorian Greeks the east and south and the Phoenician colonies held the west. The indigenous peoples were sandwiched in the middle. The total number of men Carthage sent to take Sicily may have been around 100,000, but this was not sufficient to defeat the plague and storms or the Greek opposition under the direction of the tyrant of Syracuse, Gelon (540–478 BCE). Gelon trumped the opposition at the battle of Himera in the year 480 BCE. Despite the comprehensive victory, the peace treaty was surprisingly light. Specifically, Carthage was only obliged to pay an indemnity of 2,000 talents, enough to pay for the costs of the war. Other than that, the Phoenician colonies were allowed to remain and did not lose territory, nor were they forced off the island as some feared would happen.[69]

Although peace between the Greeks on Sicily and Carthage reigned for some 70 years, in the intervening years, Carthage grew in strength (consolidating much of North Africa), whilst the Greeks bickered and fought their way through political systems which fragmented upon the death of one tyrant, and then reformed into 11 feuding commonwealths representing mixtures of oligarchies and democracies, that appear to have been somehow tied to the leadership of the city of Syracuse. This grip tightened after the Athenian invasion of Sicily was defeated. Undeterred by this failure, one of the cities (Segesta) which had invited Athens to help defend its autonomy from

[68] Herodotus, *The Histories* trans De Selincourt, A (London, Penguin) 7:166; also, Bury J (ed) (1969) *The Cambridge Ancient History: The Persian Empire and the West*, Vol IV (Cambridge, Cambridge University Press) 358, 375–82.

[69] Champion, J (2010) *The Tyrants of Syracuse: War in Ancient Sicily* (London, Pen and Sword) 38, 44–45.

Syracuse then made a similar request to Carthage. Carthage responded favourably in 410 BCE sending a new force most probably in excess of 50,000 men. Although largely victorious, the Carthaginian forces were again decimated by plague and agreed to another peace treaty in 405 BCE, with the commander of the anti-Carthage forces, the tyrant Dionysius (432–367 BCE).

The new peace treaty effectively split the island into the areas subject to Carthage, the area subject to Dionysius (Syracuse) and the areas to be unfortified and subject to 'laws of their own making'.[70] Dionysius had no intention of honouring this treaty and when the time was right, he struck out, making a conquest of eastern Sicily. Again, when the Carthaginians responded, their forces were wrecked by plague, and they could force no more than a stalemate, that resulted in a treaty similar to that of 405 BCE. The difference was that now, Dionysius was granted Tauromenium to compliment Syracuse. Dionysius opened hostilities again in 383 BCE, with a view to forcing all of the Carthaginian communities out of Sicily. Although he won some victories, faced with rebellions at home and the destruction of one of his armies, Carthage and Dionysius settled another peace treaty. Again, both parties agreed to keep what they largely held already, with the exception that the Carthaginians would receive the territory they had recently won, thus leaving Carthage again in charge of all of western Sicily, and Dionysius had to part with 1,000 talents.[71]

The same pattern of Dionysius striking out when the time was opportune was repeated in 368 BCE and in 341 BCE following a confused invitation to Carthage to enter Syracuse followed by another military fight. In both cases, the peace treaties of 367 and 341 BCE saw Carthage with reduced sizes of the territory, west of the Halcyas and Himeras rivers. When the tyrant of Syracuse, Agathocles (361–289 BCE), tried to claim the last Carthaginian holdings on Sicily, he provoked a massive response in which over an eight-year period of 315 to 307 BCE, the Carthaginians conquered the entire island, except Syracuse. This position was ratified in the following peace treaty, after Agathocles had taken the initiative and gone so far as leading a strike against the city of Carthage itself. This was the situation in which three Greek cities in Sicily requested Pyrrhus (319–272) to come and 'drive out the Carthaginians and rid the island of tyrants'.[72] These three communities were trying to counter a similar invitation from some Sicilian tyrants to Carthage, for a similar purpose. In both cases, the respective sides were acting beyond the earlier peace treaties which allowed, in essence, the two communities to co-exist, with a river being used to divide the two peoples. Although Pyrrhus would go on to capture the whole island, except for one stronghold of Carthage, his terms of peace for Carthage – that they completely abandon Sicily – were unacceptable. Negotiations with Carthage then collapsed. So too did the will of the Sicilian communities to keep supporting Pyrrhus as the military requirements that Pyrrhus placed upon the people of Sicily to obtain the goal, had ended up with him being a military dictator over Sicily (as well as the Greek cities of Italy). The people of

[70] Diodorus (1963) *Library of History* trans Wells, B (Boston, Loeb) 13.114.
[71] Diodorus (1963) *Library of History* trans Wells, B (Boston, Loeb) 15.17.
[72] Plutarch, *Greek Lives* trans Waterfield, R (2009) (Oxford, Oxford University Press) 'Life of Pyrrhus' at 22, 23.

Sicily were nearly impossible to subdue and govern, and rather than face continuing waves of revolt, Pyrrhus chose to abandon Sicily and return to Italy. This was the end point of the substantive Greek involvement in the affairs of Sicily, and thus Carthage. It was the starting point of Roman involvement in the affairs of Sicily, and thus Carthage.[73]

B. Greece and Persia

The wars between Greece and Persia can be divided into three parts. The first part had to deal with the Persian invasions, against Greek communities on the defensive. Whilst on the defensive, they came together in moments of urgency. When these moments passed, they went back to battling each other. The second part dealt with the end of the inter-Greek warfare, with the rise of Macedon. The final part was when all of Greece was united to point against a common enemy, and carry out a war of conquest and invasion against them.

(i) Defensive War against Persia

The first part of the wars between Greece and Persia began when Cyrus, whilst at war with the Lydian Empire in 546 BCE, came to discover a number of important city-states whose inhabitants were not Lydian, but Greek. These Greeks were part of a flourishing civilisation that, between the years of 800 and 500 BCE, had spread throughout the Propontis and the Black Sea, the north-west Aegean and the western Mediterranean. The part of Greek culture that the Persians came into contact with, and conquered with relatively little bloodshed, was Ionia. The Ionians resented this foreign imposition. They preferred their own autonomy – and choice of political institution in particular – to a mild Persian rule. They expelled the pro-Persian tyrants in an act of revolt under the banner of autonomy and democracy, around 514 BCE.

This situation was compounded by the fact that the Athenians had earlier agreed an alliance with Persia (around 544 BCE) against the Spartans, who were supporting tyrants in Athens. The price of help was nominal submission to Persia. The Athenians ended up dealing with the problem of the Spartans without Persian help, and subsequently declared their treaty with Persia to be null and void. Persia was outraged. In the mind of Darius I (550–486 BCE), the Greeks had reneged on their word and deprived him of a territory which he now considered his. The Athenians then went to the defence of the Ionian Greeks under the banner of 'freedom for the Greeks'. The assistance was futile, with the Ionians being crushed with the fall of Miletus in 494 BCE. When the walls fell, the city was plundered and the people were carried off to the Persian capital as slaves. Herodotus (485–425 BCE) could confidently state that the act of the Athenian assistance, was 'the beginnings of the evils for Greeks and barbarians'.[74] These evils,

[73] Champion,J (2009) *Pyrrhus of Epirus* (London, Pen and Sword) 103–105; Champion,J (2010) *The Tyrants of Syracuse: War in Ancient Sicily* (London, Pen and Sword) 202, 206–29.

[74] *Histories*, 5.97.48. For the fall of Miletus, see section 5.116.

between the years 549 and 448 BCE would consume, perhaps, 57,000 Greek soldiers and a quarter of a million Persians.[75]

The Greek assistance to Ionia triggered the invasion of Greece in 491 BCE, in reply for their meddling in what Persia considered to be their affairs and as a chance to settle some old scores against Athens. The fact that both Athens and Sparta had joined forces as a united Hellenic force and would not, even now, submit – even symbolically – to Persian authority made conflict inevitable. The first conflict in Greek territory with the Persians occurred at the battle of Marathon in 490 BCE, when some 11,000 Hoplites (of which 10,000 were from Athens) met and defied the Persian army of, perhaps, 25,000 combatants. The two sides then met 10 years later at Thermopylae (where an estimated 7,000 Greeks fought off a Persian force perhaps 10 times that number) and Salamis (where perhaps 350 Greek ships fought off some 475 ships sailing under the Persian flag). The following year in 479 BCE, some 80,000 Greeks essentially broke the army of 100,000 Persians at the battle of Plataea. The independence of ancient Greece was the result of these battles.[76]

The formal inter-Greek response to the Persian invasion was agreed at the joint Hellenic Proceedings Conference of 481 BCE.[77] The proceedings occurred before the battles of Salamis and Thermopylae. The military cooperation agreement that followed was the Confederacy of Delos of 478 BCE – the year after the Persians had been ejected from Greece. Such collective defensive agreements between the Greeks (typically against other Greeks) were long standing, with the 300 plus years before the Confederacy of Delos being well marked by a collection of military alliances, based upon 'friendship faithful and without guild forever'.[78] In the instance of Delos, the Greek cities were obliged to either supply ships or money in the war against 'the Barbarians.'[79] This allowed Greeks to move towards an offensive alliance, to complete 'the liberation of their enslaved brothers' whilst also pursuing the Persians in their other contested domains such as Turkey and Egypt. In the case of the former, the victory of the Confederacy at the Battle of the Eurymedon River (Aspendos in southern Turkey) in 469 BCE destroyed Persian power in the region. The same result was not replicated in Egypt where Greek forces served until peace was reached with Persia in 449 BCE, at which point they withdrew. This was in accordance with the Peace Treaty

[75] Hansen, V (2002) *Culture and Carnage: Landmark Battles in the Rise to Western Power* (NYC, Anchor) 27–59; Holland, T (2005) *Persian Fire* (London, Abacus) 155; Billows, R (2010) *Marathon: How One Battle Changed Western Civilisation* (NYC, Scribe) 176–85.

[76] Billows, R (2010) *Marathon: How One Battle Changed Western Civilisation* (NYC, Scribe) 92–93, 102, 196; Holland, T (2005) *Persian Fire* (London, Abacus) 178–79; Bury, J (ed) (1969) *The Cambridge Ancient History. The Persian Empire and the West*, 1st edn (Cambridge, Cambridge University Press) 215–24; Regan, G (2006) *Battles That Changed History* (London, Carlton) 9–12.

[77] See, for example, the later union of 481 found in the Proceedings of the Hellenic Congress reprinted in Botsford, G (1915) *Hellenic Civilisation Records* (NYC, Columbia University Press) 166–73.

[78] This language is from the treaty from approximately 550 BCE between Sybaris and Serdaioi. This is reprinted in Meiggs, R (ed) *A Selection of Greek Historical Inscriptions to the End of the Fifth Century BC* (Oxford, Oxford University Press) 19. For very early Greek examples, see the *Iliad* 18.207–13. For the seventh century BCE, see Meiggs, at 32.

[79] Thucydides, *History of the Peloponnesian War* trans Finley, M (1984) (London, Penguin) I:95–96. Note also the Alliance Between Boetia and Athens reprinted in Ferguson, J (ed) (1978) *Political and Social Life in the Great Age of Athens: A Sourcebook* (London, Open University Press) 74.

negotiated by Callias between Persia and the Confederacy of Delos, whereby the autonomy of Greece and a line of demarcation was agreed. Specifically:

> All the Greek cities of Asia are to be autonomous; no Persian satrap is to come closer than a three day's journey from the sea; no Persian warship is to sail in the waters between Phaselis and the Cyanean rocks; if the King and his generals respect these terms, the Athenians are not to send any expedition against the country over which the King rules.[80]

This peace with the Persians allowed the Athenians and their allies to focus on the threat of the Spartans and their allies, in the Peloponnesian War of 431 to 404 BCE. During this conflict, as discussed in chapter four,[81] the activities of Persia were largely in the background, and did not come back into focus until the beginning of the fourth century BCE, at which point the political landscape of Greece was very different. This was so much so that when the Corinthian war exploded between 395 and 387 BCE, the new alliance was a resurgent Athens (and Argos, Corinth and Thebes) – as well as Persia – against an expansionist Sparta. When the time was right, Persia swapped sides, and gave assistance to the Spartans. Reflecting this complicated situation, the 'King's Peace' that concluded this war in 387 BCE, recorded a three-way split. It stated:

> King Artaxerxes [the Persian king] thinks it just that the cities in Asia should belong to him, as well as Clazomenae and Cyprus among the islands, and that the other Greek cities, both small and great, should be left independent, except Lemnos, Imbros, and Scyros; and these should belong, as of old, to the Athenians. But whichever of the two parties [of Athens and Sparta] does not accept this peace, upon them I will make war, in company with those who desire this arrangement, both by land and by sea, with ships and with money.[82]

Thus, it came to pass that Persia would again control all of Ionia, and that a dividing line was reached with Greece, and within the non-Greek territories, another dividing line was settled, whereby the independence of most was a foremost objective. To further this, the Boetian League (under the leadership of Thebes), which had earlier fought for Persia in the original conflict, and then later, against Sparta and Persia, was disbanded. Again, following earlier patterns, the Greeks then diverted their attention from Persia, to each other.

(ii) The Unification of Greece

The second stage of the Greek wars against Persia occurred when the Greeks were forced to be united under a common plan. This was only achieved when the inter-Greek wars ended when Macedon managed to rise to mastery over all Greece. This was not an easy position to achieve, for the Greeks had perfected the art of inter-Greek warfare over several centuries. Even at the end of the Peloponnesian wars and

[80] The Peace of Callias reprinted in Diodorus *Library of History* trans Wells, B (1963) (Boston, Loeb) 12.4.5–6. Note, some scholars are of the opinion that the Peace of Callias was a fabrication. See also Zimmern, A (1962) *The Greek Commonwealth* (Oxford, Oxford University Press) 186, 190–91; Kagan, D (1989) *Pericles of Athens and the Birth of Democracy* (NYC, Secker) 96–97.

[81] See ch 4 s 3 The Greeks and the Wars for Freedom.

[82] Xenophon *Hellenica* trans Brownson, E (1918) (Boston, Loeb) 5.1.31.

the ascendency of Sparta, the dominance was short lived. As such, the fourth century BCE had seen a reversion to the traditional patterns of inter-locked Greek alliances, such as the Second Athenian Confederacy of 377 BCE.[83] However, many of the Greeks soon came to realise that the threat was not their traditional Greek foes, but new ones, as Isocrates (436–338 BCE) correctly foresaw, such as the monarchy of Macedonia.[84]

Whether the monarchies of Macedon were any more 'rooted in greed and violence'[85] than other Greek communities, as Demosthenes (384–322 BCE) asserted, is a matter of debate. What is not a matter of debate was the military genius of both Philip II (382–336 BCE) and his son Alexander. Philip's empire expanded rapidly, through a combination of diplomacy, bluff and the build up of a highly professional, and rewarded, military. Philip came to blows with Athens over the Athenian refusal to hand over Philip's half-brother (to whom they had given asylum, as a possible alternative to the Macedonian crown); and Philip's failure to honour his promise to lease to Athens the gold mine regions within a disputed region. To make matters harder, Philip II persuaded a number of the allies of Athens to rebel against their Athenian overlords whilst also supporting a number of the anti-Athenian forces in Sacred War of 355 to 346 BCE. When Philip finally declared war on Athens in 341 BCE, the conflict was short lived, as he strangled the food supply of the isolated Athenians. When the opposing forces of some 50,000 Athenians and Thebans were defeated by some 32,000 Macedonians at Chaeronea in 338 BCE, the domination of Greece by Philip II was reached, and the ideal of each region exercising autonomy was destroyed.[86]

Undisputed leadership of the Hellenic world now passed to Macedon. This transfer was codified in the Common Peace/League of Corinth of 338 BCE. Under this peace, the signatories agreed, 'nor shall I overthrow the kingdom of Philip or his descendants, nor the constitutions existing in each State when they swore the oaths concerning the peace'.[87] In practical terms, although some Greek areas (such as Thebes) were occupied and lost local autonomy, others, like Athens, were treated leniently and allowed to retain their democratic institutions – provided they accepted the hegemony of Philip. When some of the cities were tempted to challenge this hegemony, such as the attempt

[83] The Founding of the Second Athenian Confederacy, 377 BC reprinted in Botsford, G (ed) (1915) *Hellenic Civilisation Records* (NYC, Columbia University Press) 391. See also the Oaths of the Allies (377 BC); also in Botsford, at 396. For similar arrangements, see the Alliance between Athens and the Thessalians of 361 BCE reprinted in Rhodes, P (ed) (2003) *Greek Historical Inscriptions 404–323 BC* (Oxford, Oxford University Press) 221.

[84] Isocrates, 'Panegyric'. This is reprinted in Saunders, A (ed) (1970) *Greek Political Oratory* (London, Penguin). The sections within the Panegyric are 24, 72, 80, 91, 104–106.

[85] Demosthenes. The key works of Demosthenes are reprinted in Saunders, A (ed) (1970) *Greek Political Oratory* (London, Penguin). See his *Olynthiac II, Philippic I and III.* The pages in Saunders are at 188–89, 190, 206–207, 221. The point about democracies and peace can be found in *On the Chersonese* at 40–43.

[86] Worthington, I (2008) *Philip II of Macedonia* (New Haven, Yale University Press) 29–34, 40–43, 130–35. Also Philip's War Upon Olythus reprinted in Botsford, G (ed) (1915) *Hellenic Civilisation Records* (NYC, Columbia University Press) 401. Note also Philip's alliances with the Chalchidians and Rhodes reprinted in Rhodes, P (ed) (2003) *Greek Historical Inscriptions 404–323 BC* (Oxford, Oxford University Press) 221, 244; Grant, R (2005) *Battle* (London, Dorling Kindersley) 26.

[87] Reprinted in Rhodes, P (ed) (2003) *Greek Historical Inscriptions 404–323 BC* (Oxford, Oxford University Press) 375–76; also reprinted in Barker, E (1959) *From Alexander to Constantine: Passages and Documents Illustrating the History of Social and Political Ideas* (Oxford, Oxford University Press) 68.

by Thebes to break free after the assassination of Philip in 334 BCE, they found their city violently sacked by Alexander to such a degree 'that the Greeks would be so struck by the magnitude of the disaster that they would be frightened into submission'.[88]

(iii) Aggressive War against Persia

The Common Peace did two things. First, it forced the Greeks to stop fighting each other. Second, it allowed Philip II to channel this energy into an outward expansion of his empire towards the traditional enemy – Persia. This idea, to channel Hellenistic energy towards a common enemy, as opposed to each other can be traced to the Greek scholars such as Isocrates (436–388 BCE) who had recognised earlier that 'it is impossible to reach a secure peace [within Greece] without sharing in war against Persia'.[89] Philip may have accepted this advice, for shortly after the meeting which established the Common Peace, around 337 BCE, Philip was also making known throughout Greece that his desire to attack Persia was 'to punish them for the profanation of the temples'[90] in the earlier Greek and Persian wars. Philip may also have desired to attack Persia for reasons of personal glory and economic reward.[91]

Philip did not see the fruition of the plan to attack Persia, as he was assassinated the following year in 336. The invasion of Persia – and more – by the combined forces of Greece fell to his son, Alexander. The conquests of Alexander were so *great* that he even found mention in the Bible as the man who, 'fought many battles, and won many strongholds, and slew the kings of the Earth, and took spoils of a multitude of nations. And the earth was quiet before him'.[92] The geographic scope of his achievements was breathtaking. A soldier with him from the time he crossed the border in 335 BCE to the time Alexander died in 323 BCE would have covered 20,870 miles (33,587 kilometres). He also would have seen a remarkable amount of death. Estimates suggest that in the space of just eight years Alexander had slain well over 200,000 men in pitched battle. His battle at Granicus in 334 BCE had 40,000 Macedonians facing 35,000 Persians. Thirty-five thousand Macedonians opposed 110,000 Persians at Issus. At Gaugamela in 331 BCE, an estimated 47,000 Macedonians fought

[88] The quote is from Plutarch, 'Life of Alexander' in *Greek Lives* trans Waterfield, R (2009) (Oxford, Oxford University Press) 10:6–11; also Rhodes, P (ed) (2003) *Greek Historical Inscriptions 404–323 BC* (Oxford, Oxford University Press) 375–76; Barker, E (1959) *From Alexander to Constantine: Passages and Documents Illustrating the History of Social and Political Ideas* (Oxford, Oxford University Press) 65–68, 420; Sheppard, R (2008) *Alexander the Great At War* (London, Osprey) 72–77; Austin, M (ed) (1992) *The Hellenistic World from Alexander to the Roman Conquest: A Collection of Readings* (Cambridge, Cambridge University Press) 35–36; Waterfield, R (2011) *Dividing the Spoils: The War for Alexander the Great's Empire* (Oxford, Oxford University Press) 28. Bozeman, A (1994) *Politics and Culture in International History* (London, Transaction) 90–95, 103–104.

[89] Isocrates, *Panegyricus* reprinted in Saunders, A (ed) (1970) *Greek Political Oratory* (London, Penguin). The section in the *Panegyricus* is found at 171–76. Note also Atticus on this point, 'On the Constitution' (400 BC) reprinted in Botsford, G (ed) (1915) *Hellenic Civilisation Records* (NYC, Columbia University Press) 375, 379.

[90] Diodorus, *Library of History* trans Wells, B (1963) (Boston, Loeb) 16.89.2.

[91] The important speeches are in Barker, E (1959) *From Alexander to Constantine: Passages and Documents Illustrating the History of Social and Political Ideas* (Oxford, Oxford University Press) 65–68; Worthington, I (2008) *Philip II of Macedonia* (New Haven, Yale University Press) 29–34, 40–43, 130–35, 168–70.

[92] 1 Maccabees 1:1–3.

200,000 Persians, whilst at Hydaspes, when Alexander battled for a corner of India against King Porus (died 317 BCE), Alexander commanded 41,000 men against 50,000 for his opponent.[93]

Aside from inheriting the goals of his father, the commonly believed purpose for the invasion of Persia were revenge (as he believed the assassination of his father was orchestrated by Persia) and a cosmopolitan view of humanity which could lead to the benefit of all under his rule, as well as personal glory and economic rewards for both him and his men.[94] For all of these things, Alexander was prepared to fight, for as he told the Persian king, Darius III (380–330 BCE) 'if you wish to lay claim to the title of king, then stand your ground and fight for it', for he was clear that 'it is war that will determine the boundaries of our respective empires'.[95] Alexander then set out the grounds for the invasion, in a letter he sent to Darius:

> Your ancestors invaded Macedonia and the rest of Greece and did us harm although we had not done you any previous injury. I have been appointed commander-in-chief of the Greeks and it is with the aim of punishing the Persians that I have crossed into Asia, since you are the aggressors. You gave support to the people of Perinthus, who had done my father harm, and Ochus sent a force to Thrace, which was under our rule. My father died at the hand of conspirators instigated by you, as you yourself . . . gained your throne through unjust means, in defiance of Persian custom and doing wrong to the Persians. You sent unfriendly letters to the Greeks about me, to push them to war against me, and sent money to the Spartans and some other Greeks, which none of the other cities would accept apart from the Spartans. Your envoys corrupted my friends and sought to destroy the peace which I established among the Greeks. I therefore led an expedition against you, and you started the quarrel. But now I have defeated in battle first your generals and satraps, and now you in person and your army, and by the grace of the gods I control the country.[96]

Alexander aimed for the boundaries of the Earth. After defeating Persia, he invaded India. To spur on his troops he rallied:

> All Asia shall belong to us, and the boundaries of our empire in that direction will coincide with those which the deity has made the boundaries of the earth . . . glory crowns the deeds of those who expose themselves to toils and dangers.[97]

[93] Sheppard, R (2008) *Alexander the Great At War* (London, Osprey) 199–200, 215–17; White, M (2011) *Atrocitology* (NYC, Norton) 6–7; Grant, R (2005) *Battle* (London, Dorling Kindersley) 26–28; Grant, R (2011) *1001 Battles that Changed the Course of History* (London, Penguin) 49.

[94] Arrian, *Anabasis of Alexander* trans Brunt, P (1956) (Boston, Loeb) Books VII:4, VII:9–10 and VII:20. Diodorus, *Library of History* trans Wells, B (1963) (Boston, Loeb) 18.22; also Plutarch, 'Life of Alexander' in *Greek Lives* trans Waterfield, R (2009) (Oxford, Oxford University Press) 15; Polybious 3.6 and Justin *Epitome of the Philippic History* trans Heckel, W (1994) (Oxford, Oxford University Press) XI:5; Waterfield, R (2011) *Dividing the Spoils: The War for Alexander the Great's Empire* (Oxford, Oxford University Press) 28; Bozeman, A (1994) *Politics and Culture in International History* (London, Transaction) 90–95, 103–104; Sharples, R (1996) *Stoics, Epicureans and Sceptics* (London, Routledge) 123–28.

[95] The first part of this quote is Arrian, *Anabasis of Alexander* trans Brunt, P (1956) (Boston, Loeb) Book II.14. The second part is from Quintus Curtius Rufus, *The History of Alexander* trans Yardley, J (1984) (London, Penguin) IV.II.21.

[96] Arrian, *Anabasis of Alexander* trans Brunt, P (1956) (Boston, Loeb) Book II:14.

[97] Arrian, *Anabasis of Alexander* trans Brunt, P (1956) (Boston, Loeb) Book V:26.

In crossing the Indus, Alexander was pitching his ambitions even beyond the confines of the defeated Persian Empire. Alexander would have been aware of this region when he conquered the last corner of the Achaemenid Empire. Here three provinces remained: Parapamisadae, which lay beyond the passes of the Hindu Kush east of the city of Bactra; Gandhara (now part of northern Pakistan) and Hindush, the valley of the Indus. In 327 BCE Alexander crossed the Hindu Kush mountains in eastern Afghanistan with some 50,000 to 60,000 soldiers. A year later in 326 BCE he would cross the Indus River. His pretext for crossing into the land of India was to support a local ruler (Taxiles c 320 BCE), who at the time was hard pressed by his enemies to the north and west. In exchange for support, Taxiles accepted a Macedonian garrison and an overseer – although Taxiles remained the nominal head of the territory. From this act, Alexander then pushed as far as the River Hyphasis (Beas), east of the present city of Lahore, before his soldiers refused to go any further. This was despite Alexander's attempt to urge his men on, in which he recited the glories of their wondrous conquests from the Hellespont to Hyphasis, and promised them the dominion and riches of all Asia. To these entreaties Koinos (d 326 BCE), his cavalry general, replied on behalf of his men, 'moderation in the midst of success, O king, is the noblest of virtues'.[98]

Whether Alexander would have kept going forward if his armies agreed to follow him (before he died at the age of 33) is a matter of debate. The Roman historian Arrian (86–150), suggested that Alexander was limitless in his desire to acquire new lands, with only his untimely death at a young age preventing him from going forwards. Had it been otherwise 'he would not have been able to remain satisfied with his conquests so far, not even if he had added Europe and Asia and the British Isles to Europe. He would always have been seen seeking out some unknown land, attempting to rival himself if not anybody else'.[99] Certainly, his last plans involved the building of 1,000 warships, larger than *triremes*, to prepare for a conflict with Carthage. In addition, his testament called for, inter alia, conquest of Arabia and the entire Mediterranean Basin. Such views and records, lead many commentators from Antiquity to suggest that his passion for glory and associated warfare was insatiable.[100]

5. ROME

A. The Formation of Rome

The Roman classicist Virgil (70–19 BCE) had the god Jupiter promise the Romans unlimited power – *imperium*, from which the word 'empire' is derived. The god asserted:

[98] Speech of Koinos reprinted in Smith, V (1962) *The Early History of India* (Oxford, Oxford University Press) 52–53, 79–80.

[99] Arrian, *Anabasis of Alexander* trans Brunt, P (1956) (Boston, Loeb) VII.I:1–4.

[100] Quintus Curtius, *The History of Alexander* trans Yardley, D (1974) (London, Penguin) 4.7.5; 7.1–2, 7.8, 12–30; also Diodorus, *Library of History* trans Wells, B (1963) (Boston, Loeb) XVIII:4.1–6.

'I place no limits on them of time or space; I have given them power without boundaries.'[101] Although Rome received this gift, it took centuries of warfare to achieve. It began around 3000 BCE, when settlers, some from North Africa, others from Spain, Gaul and the Danube Valley, and perhaps from across the Adriatic, entered the lands of Italy. Indo-Europeans came in several waves in the second millennium BCE. Around the ninth century BCE, a people from the eastern Mediterranean conquered much of central Italy and established the first city-states. Called the Etruscans, these people reached the height of their power in the sixth century BCE. Within Italy, recorded alliances for collective defence and coordinated expansion can be traced to the Etruscans around 650 BCE. These were necessary as from their early period, the Romans (people of the city of Rome, founded some time around 1000 BCE), had sought an independent polity from the Etruscans. The Romans were part of a larger group of people, the *Latium*, who occupied central-west Italy, on the hills and plains south of the River Tiber. The Etruscans could not hold the people of *Latium*, under the leadership of Rome, in their grasp.[102]

Rome rose to dominance through a combination of military force and diplomatic promises, by which their security could be achieved. Their ability to win over friends and make enemies swap sides was reknowned. They did this with commitments that enemies could face either physical destruction if they lost in war, or all of the benefits of Roman civilisation and its associated commonwealth if they joined them. These benefits, in time, came to be known as the *Pax Romana* (Roman Peace) and *Concordia*. *Concordia* often came to be linked with social orders domestically within Italy, and *pax* with foreign concerns. *Pax* came to represent the unity of the Roman people and, at the same time, was the commitment to the *humanitas* created by the Roman power – which came to be shared with the conquered peoples who entered the Roman system. Uniting these two strands was the association of *pax* and imperium as virtual synonyms in which security, peace, economic growth and urbanisation (replete with medicine, education and science and of the goods that flowed with these, from aqueducts to sanitation) coincided to form the perfect society. This society was built as a community designed for the general good which ranged from a shared language (Latin), and a shared law based upon principles of equality of citizens and inter-state arbitration (if under the Roman umbrella) through to the prohibition of repugnant practices such as human sacrifice.[103] It also came to encompass basic considerations of safety within the realm, as problems such as piracy the 'the common enemy of all' were dealt with by

[101] Virgil, *Aeneid* trans Fitzgerald, H (1978) (London, Vintage) I:278–79.

[102] Livy, *The Early History of Rome* trans, De Selincourt, A (1960) (London, Penguin) 1:32. Bury, J (ed) (1969) *The Cambridge Ancient History. The Persian Empire and the West* 1st edn (Cambridge, Cambridge University Press) 411, 412, 439–40; Cook, S (ed) (1964) *The Cambridge Ancient History. The Hellenistic Monarchies and the Rise of Rome*, Vol VII (Cambridge, Cambridge University Press) 378–87, 404–405.

[103] Livy, *The Early History of Rome* trans, De Selincourt, A (1960) (London, Penguin) 1:28; also sections 1:33 and 1:39; Bozeman, A (1994) *Politics and Culture in International History* (Boston, Transaction) 166–84; McLynn, F (2010) *Marcus Aurelius* (London, Vintage) 113. For some of the arbitrations at work, see Lewis, N (ed) (1955) *Roman Civilisation: Selected Readings*, Vol 1 (NYC, Columbia University Press) 333–37; Phillipson C (1911) *The International Law of Greece and Rome*, Vol 1 (London, Macmillan) 152–57; Ralston, JH (1929) *International Arbitration From Athens to Locarno* (California, Stanford University Press) 168–69. For a critical view of the general philosophy of the Roman rule, see Morley, N (2010) *The Roman Empire: Roots of Imperialism* (London, Pluto) 39–41, 103–20.

ever greater means of efficiency (and ruthlessness) as the Republic gained absolute control over all people and areas, within its grasp unlike the ad hoc control of other areas, such as with the Greeks.[104]

Whilst the Roman kings had been familiar with 'treaties of friendship'[105] it was with the formation of the Latin League in the Treaty of Cassius in 493 BCE, that a coordinated approach between the 30 or so settlements in the region of *Latium* – and Rome – joined forces for collective offensive and defensive purposes. In addition to the promise of perpetual peace ('as long as the heavens and the earth shall remain where they are') both parties agreed 'to assist one another with all their might when warred upon'.[106] Rome came to dominate this League and defeat a combined force of their foremost enemy – the Etruscans – at the battle of Cumae in 474 BCE. In the following decades, security was far from secured as both internal and external forces jockeyed for the control of resources. Internally, Rome continued its expansion, dividing and conquering her opponents with combinations of carefully planned truces, aggression or the choice of peace and the benefits of joining Roman civilization. Even when the enemies were defeated, they were brought within the Roman juggernaut. For example, after defeating the Aequians, the subsequent peace treaty of 467 BCE stipulated:

> The Aequians should be subject to the Romans without being dispossessed either from their cities or from their territories; and that they should not be obliged to send anything to the Romans except troops, when ordered, to be maintained at their own expense.[107]

Around the early decades of the fourth century BCE, Rome began to abandon her natural boundaries, crossed the Tiber and advanced on the long-standing and notably powerful (and independent) Etruscan city of Veii. This city was besieged and then destroyed by the Romans in 396 BCE. Rome then discovered that she could get involved in other conflicts by being invited into them by one of the belligerents. This process, which began with invitations from other independent Etruscan cities requesting help, ended up with entire countries requesting assistance. From this simple

[104] The quote is from Cicero, *Offices*, 3:29.107. See also sections 2.26 and 3.107. For the legal focus, see for example, 'The Measure Against Pirates' reprinted in Lewis, N (ed) (1955) *Roman Civilisation: Selected Readings*, Vol 1 (NYC, Columbia University Press) 325–26. For some general history of this area, such as the involvement of Caesar, Pompey and Augustus in tackling the problem, see Plutarch, 'Life of Cato' and 'Life of Caesar' and 'Life of Pompey' in *Roman Lives* trans Waterfield, R (2009) (Oxford, Oxford University Press) xxv.i–xxvi.i; ii and X:xiv.1–6; *The Res Gestae Divi Augustus: Accomplishment of Augustus* trans Brunt, P (1967) (Oxford, Oxford University Press) 25. For the Greek practices on piracy, see the 200 BCE Treaty Between Rhodes and Hierapytna in Crete reprinted in Austin, M (ed) (1992) *The Hellenistic World from Alexander to the Roman Conquest: A Collection of Readings* (Cambridge, Cambridge University Press) 165–67; Diodorus, *Library of History* trans, Wells, B (Boston, Loeb) 20.83; Strabo, *Geography* trans Jones, A (1943) (Boston, Loeb) 14:5.2; Mayor, A (2010) *The Poison King: The Life and Legend of Mithradates* (New Jersey, Princeton University Press) 119, 276.

[105] Dionysius of Halicarnassus, *Roman Antiquities* trans Cary, E (1937) Vol IV (Boston, Boston) xlix.

[106] Treaty of Alliance with the Latin League, Dionysius of Halicarnassus. *Roman Antiquities* trans Cary, E (1937) Vol VI (Boston, Loeb) 95.2. The treaty is also reprinted in Lewis, N (ed)(1955) *Roman Civilisation: Selected Readings*, Vol 1 (NYC, Columbia University Press) 85.

[107] Dionysius of Halicarnassus, *Roman Antiquities* trans Cary, E (1937) Vol IX (Boston, Loeb) lix; also Bury, J (ed) (1964) *The Cambridge Ancient History. The Hellenistic Monarchies and the Rise of Rome*, Vol VII (Cambridge, Cambridge University Press) 502–509.

pattern, as Cicero (106–43 BCE) recognised, 'by defending their allies' the Romans, 'gained dominion over the whole world'.[108]

Before absolute dominance in the Western world could be achieved, Rome had to balance the needs of security from both near and far enemies. Rome ensured that all the dissident Italian cities within *Latium* (such as Aequi and Volsci) were brought within the Latin League with Rome at the forefront. This consolidation of power was balanced by peace treaties with greater enemies such as Samnium (a collection of peoples' within central and southern Italy) – in 354 BCE – before they were ready to face them. This facing, as occurred in First Samnite War (343–341 BCE) overlapped with the Latin War (343–338 BCE), in which a number of the allies in the League vented their anger at both Roman dominance and their own lack of autonomy.[109]

The Roman involvement in the First Samnite War, despite a peace treaty which was a little over a decade older, occurred because Rome answered the call of the people of Campania (with whom they were not in an existing alliance) to protect them against the marauding Samnites who coveted their lands. Before this point, the Romans and Samnites were 'friends and allies . . . [however] . . . simply because they were stronger, they made an unprovoked attack upon [the people of Campania, who] were compelled to ask for help from Rome'.[110] When Roman envoys came to investigate the dispute, the Samnites accused Rome of aggression, denied that they were stoking turmoil in the area and suggested it was Rome who was in the wrong for placing colonies in their territory. The war which followed saw Rome retain much of the territory of Campania in addition to a number of new Latin cities to her hegemony. The peace terms were traditional, with the defeated retaining varying degrees of autonomy (depending on how much they had challenged Rome), reaping the benefits of Roman civilization but charged to provide soldiers when required.[111]

The Roman actions against the Samnites were short lived as the Romans had to remove their military forces to put down a revolt by their allies of the Latin League who, already resenting the dominance of Rome, believed they had been forced into the Samnite War without their consultation or agreement. The conclusion of the Latin War was the dissolution of the Latin League in 338 BCE. If the allies were dissatisfied with the arrangement before the conflict, after the conflict they were even more annoyed, as Rome renamed all of the cites now under its auspice *municipiae* and established *coloniae* inside them via the export and planting of thousands of Roman citizens. Meanwhile, those who instigated rebellions were deported, if not enslaved. In practice, this now meant that they were all directly ruled by Rome and that each was considered a Roman colony.[112]

[108] Cicero, *The Republic* trans Powell, J (1977) (Oxford, Oxford University Press) Book II 34. Note also *Offices* trans Warrington, J (1954) (London, Penguin) Book II, xxvi; also Frank, T (1914) *Roman Imperialism* (NYC, Columbia University Press) 73–125; Errington, R (1971) *The Dawn of Empire: Rome's Rise to World Power* (New York, Ithaca) 43–56.

[109] Cook, S (ed) (1964) *The Cambridge Ancient History. The Hellenistic Monarchies and the Rise of Rome*, Vol VII (Cambridge, Cambridge University Press). 574–75, 578–79.

[110] Livy, *The Early History of Rome* trans De Selincourt, A (1960) (London, Penguin) 7:29.

[111] Livy, *The Early History of Rome* trans De Selincourt, A (1960) (London, Penguin) 8:14.1–11 and 8:23.1–7

[112] Livy, *The Early History of Rome* trans De Selincourt, A (1960) (London, Penguin) 8:9.1; 7:5 and 13:8–10; Cook, S (ed) (1964) *The Cambridge Ancient History. The Hellenistic Monarchies and the Rise of Rome*, Vol VII (Cambridge, Cambridge University Press) 541–43.

The Second Samnite War broke out in 327 BCE, again between the Samnites and those on the plain of Campania. According to Dionysus of Halicarnassus (60–7 BCE) this was a war that was driven by the increasing population numbers of the Samnites who were forced to form colonies elsewhere as, 'their lands no longer sufficed for them all'.[113] Against the incursions of the Samnites, the city of Capua in southern Italy (just north of Naples) appealed to Rome for help. Rome responded favourably to this request, and after initially being held to a truce (following the large-scale capture of their men who had to pass 'under the yoke') they returned to a series of battles and evenly-balanced victories. This balance swung when the Etruscan cities, seeing a chance to settle some old scores and gain the dominance of Italy, joined the Samnites in 311 BCE in opposition to Rome. This was not to be. The forces of Rome were too strong. Rome emerged victorious against the Etruscans in 308 BCE, (with harsh terms due to be former allies) and the Samnites in 304 BCE, (with harsh, but not crushing terms). Undeterred, the Third Samnite War (298–290 BCE) broke out for very similar reasons as for the Second, when another independent people (the people of Lucania, a district of southern Italy) appealed to Rome for assistance in defeating what they feared to be an imminent attack by the Samnites. At this point, the Samnites rejoined with the Etruscans and the peoples from Umbria (the landlocked section of central Italy) to confront Rome. Some 38,000 Romans then faced off against 60,000 opponents, of which 8,500 Romans and 25,000 of the opposition, lay dead on the battlefield of Sentinum in 295 BCE. Once more the Roman forces were victorious through a combination of further peace treaties and military colonies over all of the defeated areas. This was especially so when, seeing the fate that awaited them if they acted otherwise, the few unallied cities opted to become Rome's friend. By this point Rome had gained absolute control over most of the Italian peninsula, with the exception of the Greek areas in Italy's extreme south and the Po valley.[114]

The peace which Rome offered was shallow, and warfare broke out again. The difference was that now the conflict was about the insistence that all citizens within the Roman empire should have the same – and equal – benefits. To those with no direct lineage to Rome, the argument was a simple one – if they were expected to fight and die for wars at the direction of Rome, they should share equally in all the political benefits of the citizenship. This problem became so difficult that war broke out between the Latins and Rome in 91/90 BCE, and over the next three years some 300,000 people would be killed in what Mithridates (r 120–63 BCE), one of the great enemies of Rome described as a conflict whereby 'peoples are demanding not just independence, but also a share in the government and the rights of citizenship'.[115]

[113] Dionysius of Halicarnassus, *Roman Antiquities* trans Cary, E (1937) Vol I (Boston, Loeb) xvi; also Lewis, N and Reinhold M (eds) (1955) *Roman Civilisation: Records*, Vol 1 (Columbia, Columbia University Press) 76–77.

[114] Cook, S (ed) (1964) *The Cambridge Ancient History. The Hellenistic Monarchies and the Rise of Rome*, Vol VII (Cambridge, Cambridge University Press) 594–600; Grant, R (2005) *Battle* (London, Dorling Kindersley) 37.

[115] Justin, *Epitome of the Philippic History* trans Heckel, W (1994) (Oxford, Oxford University Press) 38:3–7; Appian, *The Civil Wars* trans Carter, J (1982) Vol I (London, Penguin) 6.49; Velleius Paterculus, *Compendium of Roman History* trans Shipley, J (1924) Vol II (Boston, Loeb) xv; White, M (2011) *Atrocitology* (NYC, Norton) 32–33.

Although Rome won this war they clearly recognised the justice of the cause both during and after the conflict, as they granted the Latins exactly what they wanted. This began in 90 BCE, when the Romans passed the *Lex Julia*, granting full citizenship en masse to all communities in Italy that had not revolted (and thus check the spreading of the rebellion). The following year in 89 BCE, the *Plautian–Papirian* Law offered citizenship to individuals even in rebellious Italian communities. The result was that even though the war was lost, there emerged for all Italy south of the Po valley a uniform citizenship which, in the next two generations was to weld the peninsula into a common culture. The collective result of these acts was that by 70 BCE, there were 450,000 citizens on the civil role. When the Republic fell, successive emperors continued to expand the franchise of citizenship. By the end of the time of Augustus, the number of full Roman citizens had increased to just under 5 million. This process reached its culmination in 212 CE, when all free inhabitants of the Empire were admitted to Roman citizenship en masse, by a sweeping edict of the Emperor Caracalla (188–211). This act, whereby citizenship and prima facie equality of opportunity were made available to all within the boundaries of Roman-protected territory, was revolutionary.[116]

B. Rome and Carthage

The year 509 BCE was the point that Rome branched out into the wider world, striking its first treaty with Carthage. This treaty, which may have been similar to an earlier one between the Etruscans and Carthage, was based on the principle that there 'shall be friendship between the Romans and their allies, and the Carthaginians and their allies'.[117] Aside from some allowance of commercial considerations, the core of this treaty was that the Romans would not intentionally sail past Cape Bello (that is, into the Gulf of Carthage). Conversely, the Carthaginians were not to attack certain settlements named in the treaty that were 'subject to the Romans'. They were also not to attempt military actions in *Latium*, even if the townships were not subject to Rome. This quid pro quo allowed both Carthage and Rome free hands to pursue their military interests elsewhere. Very similar treaties were reiterated in 348 BCE and again in 306 BCE, by which clear boundaries were reiterated, with Carthage promising not to take any cities within *Latium*, and Rome promising, 'not to maraud, traffic or found a city east of 'the Fair Promontory, Mastia, Tarseium'.[118] The relationship between Carthage and Rome was enhanced in 279 BCE, when the two came together to form

[116] Scullard, H (1982) *From the Gracchi to Nero* (London, Methuen) 65–68; also Lewis, N (ed) (1955) *Roman Civilisation: Selected Readings*, Vol II (NYC, Columbia University Press) 427–30.

[117] The 509 BC Treaty between Rome and Carthage, Polybius, *The Histories* trans Waterfield, R (2010) Vol III (Oxford, Oxford University Press) 22. Also Lewis, N and Reinhold M (eds) (1955) *Roman Civilisation: Records*, Vol 1 (NYC, Columbia University Press) 73; Bury, J (ed) (1969) *The Cambridge Ancient History. The Persian Empire and the West*, 1st edn (Cambridge, Cambridge University Press) 411, 412, 439–40. Cook, S (ed) (1964) *The Cambridge Ancient History. The Hellenistic Monarchies and the Rise of Rome*, Vol VII (Cambridge, Cambridge University Press) 378–87, 404–405.

[118] As noted in Cook, S (ed) (1964) *The Cambridge Ancient History. The Hellenistic Monarchies and the Rise of Rome*, Vol VII (Cambridge, Cambridge University Press) 586–87.

a defensive pact and military aid against the common enemy – Pyrrhus – who was busy battling both the Romans in Italy and the Carthaginians in Sicily.[119]

In both cases, the military assistance never eventuated as Pyrrhus sailed back to Greece, leaving the Greek communities in both Sicily and Italy to their fates. In the instance of Italy, the result was easy enough to conclude. That is, the Romans eventually swallowed the offending communities. Before Tarentum fell to the Romans in 272 BCE, rumour had it that Carthaginian forces had turned up, with the intention of either assisting the Romans, or taking the city.[120]

The situation was more nuanced in the case of Sicily. The difficulty was that tradition, supplemented by the earlier treaties and the practice of over 300 years of intervention, had it that this was an area of Carthaginian influence. However, as centuries of warring against the Greek communities present showed, the entire area had not been subdued and strong independent Greek sectors remained. Some of these sectors played both ways when it came to calls for powerful friends. For example, Messana, which sits strategically between Italy and Sicily, controlling the straits between the two areas, had not been part of the recent conflict with Pyrrhus. It had been caught in the ebb and flow of earlier conflicts, swinging between the authority of the Carthaginians and later the Greek Dionysisus I of Syracuse. When an internal revolt (conducted by mercenaries of Italian descent, known as Mamertines) occurred within Messana in 288 BCE, they came into conflict with the much stronger Hiero II (308–215 BCE), a latter tyrant of Syracuse. To survive their conflict, Messana (and its mercenaries) called upon the assistance of Carthage to defeat Hiero II. Carthage was happy to provide troops for this purpose, and with their help, the mercenaries survived the initial conflict. When Hiero II attacked a second time in 264 BCE, the mercenaries attempted to swap protectors and petitioned the Roman Republic for an alliance. In doing so, the mercenaries, who feared that the authorities of Carthage were already talking to Hiero II and were about to be betrayed, hoped for enhanced protection. As such, the Mamertines were ultimately asking for support against Hiero and Carthage – with the latter being asked to remove their own troops.

The debate in the Roman Senate was multi-layered. The legal question was whether there was a treaty restricting spheres of influence, whereby Sicily was off-limits to Rome. As a question of fact, this is difficult to answer, as although there were treaties suggesting a division of realms of influence in 509, 348 and 306 BCE, and a treaty of military assistance of 279 BCE when Pyrrhus was battling in Sicily, none of the treaties, allegedly, explicitly identified Sicily as an area of Carthaginian influence. Some commentators, such as Philinus (c third century BCE) who wrote a now lost history of the First Punic War from the Carthaginian perspective – argued that an additional treaty stating that Sicily was in the realm of Carthage did exist. Polybius (200–118 BCE) denied the existence of such a treaty. The Senate followed the position of Polybius, that there was no treaty – and therefore – there were no restraints in this area. In addition, whilst accepting the duplicitous nature of the mercenaries who were requesting help, the

[119] Polybius, *The Histories* trans Waterfield, R (2010) Vol III (Oxford, Oxford University Press) 25.

[120] Cook, S (ed) (1964) *The Cambridge Ancient History. The Hellenistic Monarchies and the Rise of Rome*, Vol VII (Cambridge, Cambridge University Press) 655–56.

Senate opted to take a somewhat larger view. This larger view was that Carthage was expanding at a rapid rate and was intending to invade Italy in the longer term. Specifically, the Senate, was in 'great apprehension lest, they [Carthage] became masters of Sicily, they would be most troublesome and dangerous neighbours, hemming them in on all sides and threatening every part of Italy'.[121] When the assertion was added that great plunder could be taken from the expedition, the scales were tipped in favour of intervention. Thereafter, for the first time ever, Roman troops acted outside the Italian peninsula, beginning a war which would burn between the two empires for the next 24 years at both land and sea. The human cost of this conflict, for the Romans alone, was around 400,000 lives. For this price, Rome, via the 241 BCE with the Treaty of Lutatius, (named after the Roman he negotiated it) forced Carthage to evacuate 'the whole of Sicily'. They were also obliged not to pursue conflict against the allies of Rome, pay tribute, return prisoners of war, and agree to be 'friends'.[122]

The first act of the new 'friends' was the Roman occupation of Sardinia. Like Sicily, this island, also garrisoned by mercenaries in the pay of Carthage who were in a situation of revolt against their overlords. Rome attacked the mercenary rebels, due to the risk that these independent forces apparently represented to Rome. An additional justification was that the taking of Sardinia was 'by way of penalty' for the killing of Roman merchants at sea.[123] Although the taking of Sardinia was condemned by subsequent historians as being wrongful due to lack of reasonable cause, the result for Carthage was clear. The final treaty of peace (the Lutatius treaty had been rejected by the Roman senate due to the insufficient size of the economic penalty, which was increased from 2,200 talents to 3,200 talents) added Sardinia to the booty. Although, in theory, both parties were not to fortify, enrol soldiers or form alliances with the peoples of either Sicily or Sardinia, the treaty clearly stipulated that the Carthaginians had lost these territories as they were 'to evacuate Sardinia . . . the whole of Sicily and all the islands lying between Italy and Sicily'.[124]

In addition, a dividing line between the two empires in the area of Spain was also set down. Specifically, 'the Carthaginians are not to cross the Ebro in arms'.[125] This point about the River Ebro was added to in 226 BCE, when an additional treaty was signed between Rome and Carthage. This addition, following a Roman request that the forces and allies of Carthage, not cross the river in question, clarified that the River Ebro in Iberia was meant to be the boundary between the two powers. In practical terms this meant that Carthage would not expand north of the Ebro, as long as Rome did not expand south of the river.[126]

[121] Polybius, *The Histories* trans Waterfield, R (2010) Vols I and III (Oxford, Oxford University Press) I: 10–11 and III:26. Cook, S (ed) (1964) *The Cambridge Ancient History. The Hellenistic Monarchies and the Rise of Rome*, Vol VII (Cambridge, Cambridge University Press) 655–56.

[122] Polybius, *The Histories* trans Waterfield, R (2010) Vol I (Oxford, Oxford University Press) 12. The figures are from White, M (2011) *Atrocitology* (NYC, Norton) 13–14; Grant, R (2005) *Battle* (London, Dorling Kindersley) 38.

[123] Appian, *The Civil Wars* trans Carter, J (1982) (London, Penguin). The particular section is the Punic Wars, at 86.

[124] See Polybius, *The Histories* (trans Waterfield, R (2010) (Oxford, Oxford University Press) III:27; Livy, *The War with Hannibal* trans De Selincourt, A (1972) (London, Penguin) 21:1.4–5.

[125] Polybius, *The Histories* trans Waterfield, R (2010) (Oxford, Oxford University Press) III:27.

[126] Polybius, *The Histories* trans Waterfield, R (2010) (Oxford, Oxford University Press) II:13.

Despite the clarity of the Ebro treaty, Rome still had friends on the south side of the river, from times prior to the 226 BCE treaty. Specifically, Rome had a connection with the 'free and autonomous' town of Saguntum. Moreover, Rome saw no difficulty in her supporting 'pro-Roman' factions within this city when a dispute arose. These forces, despite being on the south side of the river, therefore, looked to Roman support when a dispute developed with Carthage. Those within Saguntum who had lost power, appealed for assistance to Carthage, of which the Carthaginians, under the leadership of Hannibal (247–182 BCE) responded. However, when the forces of Hannibal approached the walls of Saguntum in 218, they were told, by Roman legates, that although there were no Roman military forces in the city, Saguntum 'was under their protection'.[127] Hannibal, perhaps looking for a reason for revenge for the earlier Carthaginian losses of Sicily and Sardinia, replied that the forces of Carthage were responding to a political dispute within Saguntum, of which some of the leading men (sympathetic to Carthage) had been 'unjustly put to death'. Moreover, and most obviously, Saguntum was on the south side of the river, and therefore within the Carthaginian sphere of influence. The Carthaginian weapons of war were then released against the city, which was eventually subdued in 218 BCE.[128]

Although Saguntum was on the south side of the river and within the auspice of interest for Carthage, as agreed by the treaty of 226 BCE, the Romans saw the acts of Hannibal as an unacceptable attack on a Roman friend. Accordingly, the Romans sent a delegation to Carthage demanding the surrender of Hannibal for this offence. The Carthaginian Senate refused to hand over Hannibal. They refused because they denied that they were under any formal obligation not to attack Saguntum. They interpreted the Roman request as simply a very weak pretext for war – of which the Carthaginians were happy to oblige, as they quickly aligned with some other potential Roman enemies such as Macedon and Syracuse.[129]

The human cost of the 16-year conflict known as the Second Punic War was close to 770,000 people. This figure includes people lost both on the battlefields that entombed tens of thousands of soldiers (Cannae took 48,200 Romans in one day, whilst Zama took 20,000 Carthaginians) and in the cities that became ensnared between the opponents and were sacked without mercy. When Carthage surrendered, in addition to standard requirements of handing over prisoners, paying tribute, and handing over the leader (Hannibal), the geographical loss for Carthage was all of her possessions outside of North Africa. This meant that Spain was now added to the earlier losses of Sardinia and Corsica, thus making the western Mediterranean a Roman sea. Sicily, despite its theoretical independence agreed at the end of the First Punic War, was brought squarely under the power of Rome following an attempt by Syracuse to become a republic and a distance itself from pro-Roman policies. Carthage also lost the ability to have its own independent foreign policy. These were the costs for the city

[127] Polybius, *The Histories* trans Waterfield, R (2010) (Oxford, Oxford University Press) III:15.

[128] Appian, *The Roman Histories* trans White, H (1912) (Boston, Loeb) section 11; Livy, *The War with Hannibal* trans De Selincourt, A (1972) (London, Penguin) 21:11 and 30.

[129] The 215 Treaty Between Carthage and Macedon. Polybius, *The Histories* trans Waterfield, R (2010) (Oxford, Oxford University Press) VII:9; also Lewis, N (ed) (1955) *Roman Civilisation: Selected Readings*, Vol 1 (NYC, Columbia University Press) 169.

of Carthage not being occupied and its people killed or enslaved.[130] The Treaty with Carthage of 201 BCE which concluded the Second Punic War explained:

> Carthage was to retain all the cities she formally possessed in Africa before entering on the last war with Rome, all her former territory, all flocks and herds, slaves and other property. From that day onward the Carthaginians were to suffer no injury, they were to be governed by their own laws and customs and to receive no garrison . . . they were not to make war at all on any nation outside Africa, nor on any nation in Africa without consulting Rome . . . they were to restore [to the King of Numidia] all lands and cities and other property which had belonged to him or his ancestors.[131]

Although Carthage survived, intact (albeit, stripped), the Second Punic War, she would not survive the Third. Unlike the second war, there was no question about the cause of the third war or who breached the treaty. In the third instance Carthage clearly violated the treaty of 201 BCE, as when they felt that Rome was not protecting them as expected, and after 50 years of tribute (which they believed ended their obligations under the 201 BCE treaty) they were forced to declare war against the King of Numidia (a friend of Rome) without Rome's approval in 151 BCE. This was done to repel a Numidian invasion of their territory. This invasion was the last in a sequence of provocations from Numidia, of which Rome invariably decided against Carthage whenever they complained to Rome. When Carthage took matters into their own hands, Rome declared war against Carthage. The Carthaginians made a series of attempts to appease Rome, ranging from the provision of hostages through to the disarmament of their city. After this had been achieved, the Romans demanded that they abandon and burn their city, whilst moving their population at least 10 miles inland. When the Carthaginians learned of this demand (whereby they were, in essence, ordered to live or die without trade and without protection), they abandoned negotiations and the city was immediately fortified in preparation for their final conflict with Rome. The declaration of war was the subject of intense debate in the Roman Senate. A minority argued that to destroy Carthage was an act more akin to 'a lust of domination'. This was especially apparent in this case as 'the Carthaginians had been guilty of no immediate offence to Rome, but the Romans had treated them with irremediable severity, although they had accepted all their conditions and consented to obey all their orders'. Opposing, Cato the Elder (234–149 BCE), argued to the satisfaction of the Senate that the Romans were facing a strong and irreconcilable enemy. He suggested that this enemy was again, 'preparing themselves for a contest against the Romans [and as such] the peace and treaty were but names to disguise their postpone-

[130] Livy, *The War with Hannibal* trans De Selincourt, A (1972) (London, Penguin) 2:18, 21:30, 26:16 and 29:11. Appian, *The Roman Histories* trans White, H (1912) (Boston, Loeb) section 13; Goldsworthy, A (2003) *The Fall of Carthage* (Cassel, London) 304–10. Cook, S (ed) (1970) *The Cambridge Ancient History. Rome and Mediterranean*, Vol VIII (Cambridge, Cambridge University Press) 28–29, 64–69. The supplementary treaties on the handing over of Hannibal can be found in the Treaty of Apamea in 188 BCE under which Antiochus III agreed to, inter alia, 'surrender, if it is in his power to do so, Hannibal'. Polybius, *The Histories* trans Waterfield, R (2010) (Oxford, Oxford University Press) XXI:43; also Lewis, N (ed) (1955) *Roman Civilisation: Selected Readings*, Vol 1 (NYC, Columbia University Press) 184. The figures are from Regan, G (2006) *Battles That Changed History* (London, Carlton) 24–26. White, M (2011) *Atrocitology* (NYC, Norton) 18–19.

[131] Polybius, *The Histories* trans Waterfield, R (2010) (Oxford, Oxford University Press) XV:17.

ment of war until a proper occasion presented itself'. Therefore, 'Carthage must be destroyed'.[132] The Senate broadly concurred with this view, 'since they felt sure that its inhabitants would never remain entirely at peace'.[133] The majority therefore agreed that war was necessary:

> For to destroy this source of perpetual menace, this city which had constantly disputed the supremacy with them and was still able to dispute it if it had the opportunity and thus to secure the dominion of the own country, was the act of intelligent and far-seeing men.[134]

The war which followed these views ended after three years in 146 BCE, when the city of Carthage – and with it, the entire Punic civilisation – was completely destroyed. Within this loss were perhaps 65,000 killed and 50,000 enslaved. There was no peace treaty to conclude the destruction of this civilisation.[135]

Although the war with Carthage finally ended in 146 BCE, the Roman military adventures did not end in North Africa for a few more decades. The last conflict related to Numidia (modern-day Algeria and western Tunisia), which had become an economic powerhouse. Whilst this held together when King Micipsa (148–118 BCE) was alive, upon his death a dispute arose between his two sons and his nephew, Jugurtha (160–104 BCE), whom he had adopted as a son. Jugurtha turned on the other two and a civil war quickly broke out. When Rome became involved, the Senate divided the country between the one remaining brother and Jugurtha. The latter was unhappy with his half, and attacked the forces of the remaining brother. Jugurtha argued he had the right to do this because the others had tried to kill him first. As such, he argued, 'it would not be right or just for Rome to deny him the rights to which the law of nations entitles him'.[136] Irrespective of what Rome may have thought of the merits of Jugurtha's justification to expand his area, what was completely unacceptable to them was the killing of Italian merchants in the newly occupied territory – even if it was not Roman land. The Senate demanded action and soon after war was declared on Jugurtha. Jugurtha replied that the real reason the Romans were seeking war against him was because the Romans were men 'of insatiable greed . . . [their] motive is . . . lust for empire'.[137] This assertion was not strictly correct, as although Jugurtha was finally defeated, brought to Rome and publically defrocked before being thrown into a prison to starve to death, the territories in question were not annexed and the Roman province of Africa was not enlarged. This was unlike the destruction of the Punic Empire, of which the Romans acquired everything.

[132] Plutarch, 'Life of Cato' in *Roman Lives* trans Waterfield, R (2009) (Oxford, Oxford University Press) XXV.1 and XXVII.1.

[133] Zonaras, *Epitome* trans Dindofius, L (1912) (London, Macmillan) IX.xxx.

[134] Polybius, *The Histories* trans Waterfield, R (Oxford, Oxford University Press) XXXVI:9.

[135] For the figures, see Grant, R (2011) *1001 Battles that Changed the Course of History* (London, Penguin) 67.

[136] Sallust, (1970) *The Jugurthine War* trans Handford, S (London, Penguin) IV:23.

[137] Sallust, (1970) *The Jugurthine War* trans Handford, S (London, Penguin) VI:81.

C. Rome and Europe

This section on Rome against Europe is divided into two parts. Roman advances to the west, against the Greek populations; and Roman advances to the north, against the broader European populations. The similarity in both instances is that in this context, the Romans never fought a unified opposition as they did with Carthage. Rather, they fought a successive series of wars against relatively divided oppositions. This division meant that the conquests were not so much the result of a clash of empires (as there was no unified opposition such as a conflict with Alexander the Great would have been), but more the expansion of Roman power over individual enemies.

(i) Greece

The Romans never fought a collective force of the Greeks under the leadership of one man, such as with Alexander. However, many of the fragmented Greek kingdoms of note that followed in the wake of the collapse of Alexander's empire did fight Rome. These were all battles between the singular Greek leaders of Pyrrhus (319–272 BCE), Philip V of Macedon (238–179 BCE), Antiochus III (241–187 BCE) and Mithridates VI (134–63 BCE).

Of the Greek kings to fight Rome, Pyrrhus was the only one to fight the Romans in Italy (and the Carthaginians in Sicily). Whilst the Romans portrayed him as being driven by an unquenchable desire to conquest, linked by 'bloodshed and toil and danger', the fact remains that in the case of both Italy and Sicily, he was asked in by local communities to help.[138]

The request for Pyrrhus to come to Italy came in 281 BCE, when Tarentine, on behalf of the Greek cities asked for his military assistance to help them fight the Romans. This request came after an existing treaty had been breached by both sides, and the Romans were unhappy with the Tarentines for their support of the Samnites in the wars (as noted above) which had just ended. The earlier treaty related to Tarentine hegemony over Greek cities around the bay of Tarentine, in exchange for the Tarentines' recognising the Roman conquests in Apulia and Samnia. The Romans also agreed not to send ships east of the Cape of Lacinum and into the Bay of Tarentum.[139] This clause was violated around 303 BCE. Roman ships, by chance, ill-fortune or bad weather, entered the Bay and attempted to seek shelter in the harbour of Tarentum. The people of Tarentum took this act as an invasion, attacked the five ships whilst at anchor, captured and looted the vessels, killed the commander and imprisoned the crews. They then followed up their action with an attack on a Roman ally. The Romans demanded that the fleet and prisoners be returned, compensation paid, and the Tarentine commanders handed over to Rome for punishment. The

[138] Plutarch, 'Life of Pyrrhus' in *Greek Lives* trans Waterfield, R (2009) (Oxford, Oxford University Press) at 14; also Austin, M (ed) (1992) *The Hellenistic World from Alexander to the Roman Conquest: A Collection of Readings* (Cambridge, Cambridge University Press) 91–92.

[139] Appian, 'The Samnite Wars' in *The Roman Histories* trans White, H (1912) (Boston, Loeb) section 15.

Tarentine assembly debated this request and came to the conclusion that the Roman terms were not acceptable, because they were tantamount to surrender, subordination and finally annexation by Rome.[140]

Aware that they could not fight Rome alone, the Greek communities living on the coast of Italy, under the leadership of Tarentine, requested the help of the Pyrrhus to help, 'defend their liberty'. Pyrrhus accepted the offer, and duly informed the Romans of his intention to defend 'his allies' who were 'free men'.[141] He added that he would 'not permit [the Romans] to make desolate the country of men who are my allies, to plunder Greek cities . . . and treating all men arrogantly as if they were slaves'.[142] Pyrrhus then fought the Romans to a standstill at the battle of Heraclea in the same year he arrived in Italy, before advancing to within six kilometres of Rome. The victory that he achieved was very expensive (in terms of manpower) to both his enemies and himself. That is, of the 35,000 Romans who fought him at the battle of Heraclea, up to 15,000 were casualties by the end of the day. Similarly, of the 30,000 Greeks under his command at the beginning of the battle, up to 11,000 were no longer alive when the conflict ended. His frank acknowledgement of what his victory had cost him passed into a proverbial phrase – a 'pyrrhic victory' – which is still current. Thereafter, he then tried to make an agreement with the Romans, offering a military alliance, in exchange for the principle that, 'the Greeks dwelling in Italy should remain free under their own laws'.[143] Rome refused the offer, suggesting, 'you dare to call this peace instead of servitude'.[144]

The fact that the Romans would not make peace with Pyrrhus resulted in the Greek communities in Italy questioning his methods. Pyrrhus responded by placing military garrisons in the Greek cities and removing all of their democratic liberties to ensure his wars could go as he wished. A very similar situation occurred with his next involvement in Sicily, where he was also invited in, ended up being a military dictator, but then discovered he could not be in two places at once. This became apparent when the conflict with Rome flared up again, and he had to return to Italy. Once on the mainland, he had to fight the regenerated Roman forces; he found their army of 18,000 men, ground his force of 23,000 soldiers (of which only 9,000 survived) to a halt, at the Battle of Beneventum in 275 BCE. At this point, Pyrrus embarked with the remnant of his forces, some 8,000 foot and 500 horse, less than one third the force with whom he had arrived in Italy six years earlier, and left the region. In 272 BCE, Tarentum finally surrendered – on terms – to Roman forces. Although this allowed Tarentum to retain some autonomy, it also became a city which was garrisoned by Roman troops. This

[140] Matyszak, P (2009) *Roman Conquests: Macedonia and Greece* (London, Pen and Sword) 17–18.

[141] Appian, *The Civil Wars* trans Carter, J (London, Penguin). The particular section is the 'The Samnite Wars' at 17 and 22. See also Dionysius of Halicarnassus *Roman Antiquities* trans Cary, E (1937) (Boston, Loeb) XIX:9.

[142] Dionysius of Halicarnassus, *Roman Antiquities* trans Cary, E (1937) (Boston, Loeb) XIX:ix; Appian, 'The Samnite Wars' in *The Roman Histories* trans White, H (1912) (Boston, Loeb) section 17.

[143] Appian, 'The Samnite Wars' in *The Roman Histories* trans White, H (1912) (Boston, Loeb) 22; Grant, R (2005) *Battle* (London, Dorling Kindersely) 37.

[144] Appian, 'The Samnite Wars' in *The Roman Histories* trans White, H (1912) (Boston, Loeb) section 22; also Fragment 10 as reprinted in Lewis, N and Reinhold M (eds) (1955) *Roman Civilisation: Records*, Vol 1 (NYC, Columbia University Press). 76–77; Champion, J (2009) *Pyrrhus of Epirus* (London, Pen and Sword) 98–99; Grant, R (2005) *Battle* (London, Dorling Kindersley) 37.

loss was much greater than one city. It was, in essence, the end of independent Greek influence in Italy, and supremacy in the eastern Mediterranean. This left the way open for Rome to complete her domination of Italy.[145]

The second set of Greek monarchy that the Romans fell into conflict with was Philip V, Antiochus III (241–187 BCE) and the son of Philip, Perseus (212–166 BCE). As discussed in chapter four,[146] Philip V, through some astute maneuvering between the Aetolian and Achaean Leagues, had come to control most of Greece – but not Athens, Rhodes or Pergamon. He attempted to cement this control through the Peace of Naupactus in 217 BCE, which brought conflict between Macedon and the Greek leagues to an end. The parties agreed: 'Above all the Greeks should never go to war against each other.'[147] After this peace, Philip began to mirror his famous forebears, and find an external enemy which he could focus (most) of the Greek attention on. With this goal, he settled his intentions upon the eastern shores of the Adriatic where he went forward and captured Illyria (the Western part of the Balkan peninsular). This was a tipping point, as Illyria had been associated with Rome since 229 BCE, as despite being Greek, it felt its security was more enhanced with Roman friendship.[148]

Philip did this as he saw the opportunity of replacing Roman influence, due to their attention being diverted by the Second Punic War. To ensure solid footing in this adventure, an agreement between Macedon and Carthage was struck in 215 BCE, which promised mutual assistance and a prima facie division of territories (as that point, as held by the Romans). The treaty stipulated:

> King Philip and the Macedonians and those Greeks who are allied to him shall protect the Carthaginians as a sovereign people, and Hannibal their general . . . The Carthaginians . . . shall guard and protect King Philip and the Macedonians . . . If the Romans make war on either of us, we will help each other in that war as either side requires.[149]

The Roman response to the agreement between Macedon and Carthage was a mutual defensive agreement with Macedon's old enemy, the Aetolian League – and its associated Greek allies in 211 BCE. Under this treaty of military assistance, it was agreed that 'the Aetolians should immediately wage war against Philip by land and the Romans should assist them' and a tentative division of the geographical spoils of the enemies' cities and areas was set down.[150]

[145] Appian, Fragment 10 as reprinted in Lewis, N and Reinhold M (eds) (1955) *Roman Civilisation: Records*, Vol 1 (NYC, Columbia University Press) 76–77; Regan, G (2006) *Battles that Changed History* (London, Carlton) 21–23.

[146] See ch 4 s 3C Autonomy, Monarchy and the Rise of Rome.

[147] Polybius, *The Histories* trans Waterfield, R (2010) (Oxford, Oxford University Press) V:103; also II:37; IV:25 and XII:10–12.

[148] Matyszak, P (2009) *Roman Conquests: Macedonia and Greece* (London, Pen and Sword) 20–32.

[149] The 215 Treaty Between Carthage and Macedon. Polybius, *The Histories* trans Waterfield, R (2010) (Oxford, Oxford University Press) VII:9.

[150] The quote is from the Roman Alliance with the Aetolian League reprinted in Lewis, N (ed) (1955) *Roman Civilisation: Selected Readings*, Vol 1 (NYC, Columbia University Press) 170. Note the breakdown of the terms, see Livy, *The War with Hannibal* trans De Selincourt, A (1972) (London, Penguin) 26:24.7–15 and a historical inscription. They are collectively reprinted in Austin, M (ed) (1992) *The Hellenistic World from Alexander to the Roman Conquest: A Collection of Readings* (Cambridge, Cambridge University Press) 121–22; Matyszak, P (2009) *Roman Conquests: Macedonia and Greece* (London, Pen and Sword) 32–40.

As it was, Rome was too exhausted from fighting Hannibal to give substantive assistance to the Aetolians, who received a beating from Philip and then retreated behind their walls, waiting for the Romans to help. The Romans were unable to help as, after clearing Hannibal out of Italy, they had committed all of its reserves to the subjugation of Spain (now that Carthage had lost this region). Realising this, the Aetolians made a separate peace with Philip, in which they surrendered many of the territorial gains they had initially made. In this context, the Romans also agreed to end hostilities with Philip. The peace was concluded in the Treaty of Phoenice. The political importance of this treaty was that Philip effectively repudiated his alliance with Hannibal. The geographical importance was that although Philip had to return most of their recently acquired territories, he was allowed to keep Illyria, which had previously been the tipping point for Rome.[151]

Philip then turned his attention elsewhere. This time the opportunity arose when he and Antiochus III, around 205 BCE, made an agreement to capture and partition the entire Ptolemy kingdom. Philip thus proceeded to battle his way to the acquisition of some Egyptian territory, which caused great alarm to a number of neighbouring states including Pergamum and Rhodes. In the latter case, although he left 9,000 of his own men in the ocean after his 53 heavy warships came off second best to the 65 heavy warships of Pergamum and Rhodes, his real loss was that Rhodes was an ally of Rome. Rhodes, joined by Pergamum and Athens, then appealed to Rome for help against the expansionism of Philip V. To the great surprise of Philip, the Roman Senate informed him in 200 BCE that he must 'make war henceforth upon no Greek State'.[152] Philip, who saw such threats as a violation of his peace treaty with Rome, had no intention of changing direction. He discovered the magnitude of this mistake when Rome, with assistance from the Aetolian League, went to war against him. In doing so, the Romans carefully pointed out that they did not want to conquer Greece, but to defeat Macedon, as Macedon was a threat to Rome when Philip commanded all of the resources of Greece. This threat was removed at the battle of Cynoscephalae in 197 BCE, when a force of 26,000 Romans decimated the opposing Macadonian army of an equal size, leaving at least 8,000 dead and a taking a further 5,000 men away in chains. The consequence of this loss was that Philip was obliged to accept the Treaty of Tempe the following year. Through this, although he was allowed to survive and remain in Macedon, he had to pay a penalty of 1,000 talents and had to give up the bulk of his navy. In geographical terms, all of the non-Macedonian regions he had occupied were to be returned and 'free, exempt from tribute, and subject to their own laws'.[153]

The same pattern was followed after the Romans subdued Sparta, which had continued to battle on alone. Afterwards, in addition to the reiteration that each area was to be free and autonomous, all of the military forces were removed from the area

[151] Livy, *The Early History of Rome* trans De Selincourt, A (1960) (London, Penguin) 29:12.11–16.

[152] Polybius, *The Histories* trans Waterfield, R (2010) (Oxford, Oxford University Press) XV:20, XVI:27; Cook, S (ed) (1970) *The Cambridge Ancient History: Rome and the Mediterranean*, Vol VIII (Cambridge, Cambridge University Press) 156–63; Grant, R (2005) *Battle* (London, Dorling Kindersley) 31.

[153] Livy, *The Early History of Rome* trans De Selincourt, A (1960) (London, Penguin) 33:32.4–10; Polybius, *The Histories* trans Waterfield, R (2010) (Oxford, Oxford University Press) XVI:34 and XVIII:44; Matyszak, P (2009) *Roman Conquests: Macedonia and Greece* (London, Pen and Sword) 60–64, 95–99; Grant, R (2005) *Battle* (London, Dorling Kindersley) 31.

– Macedonians *and* Romans. All of the property occupied and/or possessed by the Romans, was returned. Titus Quinctius Flamininus (c 229–174 BCE) could then proclaim that Rome sought, 'absolutely no financial profit, esteeming good will and reputation above all others'.[154]

When the Romans marched out of Greece, the forces of Antiochus III marched into it. This act, in conjunction with some of the members of the Aetolian League (which had swapped from supporting Rome due to a belief it had been more deserving of booty after the battle of Cynoscephalae) occurred in the year of 192 BCE. Antiochus, who had earlier been warned by Rome not to expand his empire and stay away from autonomous cities, did not heed the advice and advanced into Greece with 10,000 soldiers. This force was defeated the following year by a Roman force at Thermopylae. The Romans followed up their success by attacking Antiochus in Anatolia. The battle of Magnesia (on the plains of Lydia, in modern-day Turkey) in 190 BCE was a further disaster for Antiochus, in which well over half of his army, some 53,000 men, died on the battlefield, destroyed by the smaller Roman force of 40,000 men.[155]

Rome then dealt with the joint enemies separately. The Aetolians were required to become a subject ally of the Roman Republic. In doing so, they agreed to respect 'the empire and majesty of the Roman people'. In addition, they lost their 'territories, cities or populations which were formally under their jurisdiction but were conquered by, or voluntarily submitted to, the Romans'.[156] The settlement for Antiochus III was concluded in the Treaty of Apamea in 188 BCE. Under this treaty, Antiochus III agreed, in addition to the provisions of hostages and tribute and becoming 'a friend of Rome'. He also agreed to 'stay out of Europe and withdraw from all of Asia on this side of the Taurus mountains'. His son, Antiochus IV was also held to these commitments, and was clearly warned by Rome not to cross 'the line in the sand' and attack Egypt, as to do so would bring a fatal reaction for him delivered from Rome.[157]

Although the peace and associated autonomy for most of Greece held together during the lifetime of Philip V, following the accession by his son Perseus (212–166 BCE), the situation unravelled. Perseus was quick to make alliances with a large number of Greek regions in his attempt to restore Macedonian hegemony and force the Romans out of Greece. He also attempted to secure the support of the lower classes and dispossessed Greek citizens in these regions, by championing revolutionary measures for the relief of economic and social distress. The fact that he defended the silver mines within Macedonia against outsiders who tried to take them, was the final proof for Rome that this was a popular king who was planning a full-scale war against Rome. The resulting Third Macedonian War of 171 BCE was concluded at the battle of Pydna in 168

[154] Letter of Flamininus reprinted in Lewis, N (ed) (1955) *Roman Civilisation: Selected Readings*, Vol 1 (NYC, Columbia University Press) 309. See also Livy, *The Early History of Rome* trans De Selincourt, A (1960) (London, Penguin) 33:32.4–10; Polybius, *The Histories* trans Waterfield, R (2010) (Oxford, Oxford University Press) XVIII:44.

[155] Matyszak, P (2009) *Roman Conquests: Macedonia and Greece* (London, Pen and Sword) 106–113; Grant, R (2005) *Battle* (London, Dorling Kindersley) 31.

[156] Polybius, *The Histories* trans Waterfield, R (2010) (Oxford, Oxford University Press) XXI:32.

[157] Polybius, *The Histories* trans Waterfield, R (2010) (Oxford, Oxford University Press) XVIII:51, XVIII:49, XXIX:27; also Lewis, N (ed) (1955) *Roman Civilisation: Selected Readings*, Vol 1 (NYC, Columbia University Press) 309.

BCE, at which an army of 37,000 Romans left some 25,000 Macedonian soldiers dead on the battlefield and a further 11,000 captured. Macedon was totally and unconditionally crushed. This war ensured that the balance of power in Greece was turned conclusively towards Rome, with Macedon and her allies, although still free, being deprived of their associated territories, and both these and the original centres divided at the end of the conflict (Macedon was split into four parts) and settled upon by Roman veterans and bolstered by the property classes which had generally been opposed to the views of Perseus. The monarchy was also dissolved. These acts marked the effective end of the Macedonian line of the Antigonid dynasty.[158]

The Fourth, and final, Macedonian War began in 150 BCE and ended two years later, when a pretender (Andriscus d 149 BCE, the alleged son of Perseus) sought to claim the throne of Macedon and bring back the kingdom to its former glory. To assist this goal, he sought the assistance of Carthage. By this stage, the Romans had reached the end of their tether with any form of toleration of Greek rebellions or transgressions against the peace imposed upon the region. The Romans dealt with the pretender quickly, before moving onto the Achaean War in 146 BCE, when the Achaean League erupted in open revolt. The soldiers of the League were comprehensively crushed in a series of direct and pre-emptive acts which culminated in the utter destruction of Corinth, which came to symbolise the Roman wrath with the Achaean League as a whole. From this point, not only were the Greek cities of the defeated destroyed that had the potential to cause problems in the future, so too were their political institutions. Thereafter, institutions which were favourable to Rome were cemented into place. This allowed the Greeks to be free – within the Roman understanding of the word: namely it was a freedom in which they were subordinate to Rome, and bound with a series of duties and obligations towards their master.[159]

The final Greek-derived king to clash with Rome was Mithridates VI (134–63 BCE). Mitridates ruled Pontus and Armenia Minor in northern Anatolia (now Turkey). Mitridates, with a rich Persian and Macedonian ancestry, had a taste for acquiring the territory of others. He began this by providing protection for the small kingdoms around the Black Sea, creating independent allies, and taking tribute – but of a smaller amount than that taken by the Romans. With such policies, he absorbed the Crimea and the Taman Peninsular into the kingdom of the Bosphorus. He added satraps from Anatolia, Persia and what became Germany into his realm. He also made good use of palace intrigues to advance into the territories of others, such as Paphlagonia and Cappadocia. These actions brought him into conflict with Rome, who told him to restore certain kings who had been toppled. Mithridates would either feign innocence, claim that they were originally his territories, and/or accuse Rome of looking for a

[158] See the 171 BCE Letter of the Romans to the Delphic Amphictyony Concerning Perseus reprinted in Austin, M (ed) (1992) *The Hellenistic World from Alexander to the Roman Conquest: A Collection of Readings* (Cambridge, Cambridge University Press) 140–41; also Livy, *The Early History of Rome* trans De Selincourt, A (1960) (London, Penguin) XLII:30; XLV:26–33; Matyszak, P (2009) *Roman Conquests: Macedonia and Greece* (London, Pen and Sword) 128–32, 149–56; Grant, R (2005) *Battle* (London, Dorling Kindersley) 31.

[159] Pausanias, *Description of Greece* trans Jones, W (1933) (Boston, Loeb) VII:xvi.7–10; Barker, E (1959) *From Alexander to Constantine: Passages and Documents Illustrating the History of Social and Political Ideas* (Oxford, Oxford University Press) 80–82; Botsford, G (1915) *Hellenic Civilisation Records* (NYC, Columbia University) 579–84; Matyszak, P (2009) *Roman Conquests: Macedonia and Greece* (London, Pen and Sword) 175–80.

fight due to its uncontrollable imperialism. Then, to ensure the declaration of war would truly catch fire, he had the Roman envoy executed, along with some 80,000 to 150,000 Roman and Italian residents he had within his countries. The three conflicts which made up the Mithridatic wars followed, resulting in the deaths of at least 400,000 people.[160]

The First Mithridatic War (89–85 BCE), was the only one of the three conflicts to be fought in Greece, under which Mithridates disastrously enticed many Greek communities to join his struggle to regain their autonomy from their Roman overlords. Mithridates escaped oblivion by being offered a good deal by the Roman general Sulla (138–78 BCE), who was keen to leave Greece in a hurry to return to the pressing issues in Italy. The good deal Mithridates was offered was the Treaty of Dardanos in 85 BCE. This was built around a return to the status quo, as it existed before the war. This meant that Greece belonged to Rome, whilst Mithridates was allowed to keep the possessions he held in 89 BCE, but had to withdraw from his recent acquisitions (Paphlagonia, Bithynia and Cappadocia). Sulla also promised that Mithridates would be declared a friend and ally of Rome, upon Mithridates' payment of a fine equal to the cost of the war. The difficulty was that the Treaty of Dardanos was never ratified by the Roman Senate and, therefore, the peace was tenuous, reliant on the strength of Sulla.[161]

The Second Mithradatic War of 83 to 81 BCE, began when a pre-emptive strike into Pontus was made due to concerns that Mithridates was again getting too powerful and rearming. This was not a success and after failing to do much damage, Mithridates pushed the Roman forces back out of the regions they had entered. Sulla, recognising a stalemate, ordered the peace to be restored, but when Sulla died in 78 BCE, conflict broke out again. The last war occurred when Mithridates persuaded an old ally (Tigranes of Armenia, 140–55 BCE) to invade Cappadocia, whilst also linking forces with Sertorius (126–73 BCE) a former Roman General who had revolted in Spain. Sertorius could not defeat Rome and Tigranes sued for peace when the Romans crossed his borders (in exchange for being able to keep his kingdom). The end for Mithridates followed soon after as he could not hold them back when they invaded Pontus. He chose to end his life by suicide, whilst the Romans snuffed out the Pontic kingdom.[162]

[160] Appian, *The Roman Histories* trans White, H (1912) (Boston, Loeb) XII:9 and 21; Justin *Epitome of the Philippic History* trans Heckel, W (1994) (Oxford, Oxford University Press) 38.3–7; Plutarch, *Roman Lives* trans Waterfield, R (2009) (Oxford, Oxford University Press) 'Life of Marius' at 31.2–2; Mayor, A (2010) *The Poison King: The Life and Legend of Mithradates* (New Jersey, Princeton University Press) 116–17, 119, 128–29, 131–32, 139–46, 153–54, 226; Cook, S (ed) (1966) *The Cambridge Ancient History: The Roman Republic*, Vol IX (Cambridge, Cambridge University Press) 254–56; White, M (2011) *Atrocitology* (NYC, Norton) 34–35.

[161] Mayor, A (2010) *The Poison King: The Life and Legend of Mithradates* (New Jersey, Princeton University Press) 208–13, 218–22.

[162] Mayor, A (2010) *The Poison King: The Life and Legend of Mithradates* (New Jersey, Princeton University Press) 220–23, 256, 293–94, 300, 330, 341; Cook, S (ed) (1966) *The Cambridge Ancient History: The Roman Republic*, Vol IX (Cambridge, Cambridge University Press) 365.

(ii) Continental Europe

Rome opposed a conglomerate of opposing, non-unified, forces on the continent of Europe. These forces were not an empire like Carthage or Persia, as much as an ocean of peoples who existed beyond the Roman borders in Europe. This 'discord among our foes' was, as Tacitus (57–117 CE) noted, fundamental for the defence of the empire.[163] This division allowed Rome the ability to practice a divide and rule approach. This was particularly useful in the types of conflict Rome was engaged in within this sector, which tended to be dealing with revolts against occupation and what Cicero called 'Roman greed and Roman injustice' – covering everything from political inequality, to heavy taxes and corruption.[164]

Within the period of the Republic, such problems first came to light when Rome acquired the territories of the former Carthaginian Empire and had to learn how to deal with local communities who desired independence of both overlords. This problem became obvious in Spain, where the Roman rule until the end of the Republic was brutal. This brutality was evident in all three of the wars which were needed to subdue rebellions in Spain with the Celtiberian War of 181 to 179 BCE, the Nurantine War between 151 and 143 BCE and finally the Sertorian War, over half a century later. It was only by the time of Augustus when the country had become organised and Romanised that the bloodshed ended.[165]

The pacification process over the Pyrenees was different, as Rome did not inherit this land from a defeated foe. Rather, through the actions of Julius Caesar (100–44 BCE), they entered the province. Whilst Suetonius (69–122) suggested that 'he lost no opportunity picking quarrels – however unfair and dangerous',[166] the official pretext was that he entered the region to protect tribes which were the 'friends' of Rome who were threatened by some of the particularly large tribes coming into their territory. Caesar helped the friends of Rome by demanding the large tribes turn back and not migrate through the region (territory near modern-day Geneva). When they persisted in their attempt, he attacked, 'the Germans [who] formed a habit of crossing the Rhine an entering into Gaul in large numbers'.[167] He defeated these people and ordered them back to their homeland. Caesar then went one step further and invaded Britain (with its rumoured – but exaggerated – reputation of wealth), of which he said he received a nominal submission, under the pretext of cutting off British assistance to Gaul. In human terms, the death toll of the war in Gaul between 58 and 51 BCE was about 700,000 people. In geographical terms he reduced the whole of Gaul to the form of a province, enclosed by the Pyrenees, the Alps, the Cevennes, the Rhine and the Rhone. This taking of some 640,000 square miles was supplemented by an exacted annual tribute of 400,000 gold pieces. In political terms, Caesar has achieved a remarkable

[163] Tacitus, *The Agricola and Germania* trans Mattingly, W (1974) (London, Penguin) X:xxiii.

[164] Cicero 'Second Speech Against Verres'. This is in Cicero, *Ten Speeches* trans James, Z (2009) (NYC, Hackett) III:lxxxix; also Morley, N (2010) *The Roman Empire: Roots of Imperialism* (London, Pluto) 60–67.

[165] Appian, 'The Spanish Wars' in *The Roman Histories* trans White, H (1912) (Boston, Loeb) section 60.

[166] Suetonius, *The Twelve Caesars* trans Graves, R (1989) (London, Penguin) 23.

[167] Ceasar, *The Conquest of Gaul* trans Handford, S (1982) (London, Penguin) 130; Caesar, *Gallic War* trans Edwards, H (1942) Vol I (Boston, Loeb) i–vii; also Gelzer, M (1968) *Caesar* (Oxford, Blackwell) 102–16.

victory. Accordingly, the Senate passed an unprecedented 15-day public thanksgiving to celebrate 'binding Gaul with eternal chains'.[168]

Augustus (63 BCE – 14 CE) was granted powers, to, inter alia, 'extend and advance the boundaries of the pomerium [the lands which Rome possesses] whenever they deem it to be the interest of the State'.[169] He recognised such interests to the extent that he annexed more territory to the Roman Empire than did any of the famous generals of the Republic. At the end of this period he would record that he:

> [E]xtended the [western] frontiers of all the provinces of the Roman people on whose boundaries were people not subject to our empire. I restored peace to the Gallic and Spanish provinces and likewise to Germany . . . I caused peace to be restored in the Alps, from the region nearest to the Adriatic Sea as far as the Tuscan Sea, without undeservedly making war against any people. My fleet sailed the ocean from the mouth of the Rhine eastward . . . to which no Roman had previously penetrated by land or sea . . . At my command, two armies were lead into Ethiopia and Arabia . . . I added Egypt to the realm of the Roman people . . . I conquered and subjected the Pannonian tribes [present day western Hungary, eastern Austria and northern Croatia], to which before my principate no army of the Roman people had ever penetrated; and I extended the frontier of Illyricum [present day Balkans] to the bank of the Danube river . . . The following kings fled to me as suppliants . . .[170]

On the last point, the kings who expressed subservience to Augustus were part of the continuing policy of cushioning the empire at various points by vassal states, ruled by client princes who were invested with their power by the emperor. He made the client kings swear allegiance to Rome, in which they personally requested, 'utter destruction' if they violated their oath.[171] If the clients failed to live up to expectations they were commonly absorbed into the provincial system during the first century of the Principate. This was unlike the client-kings on the Rhine Danube frontiers and along the Euphrates, who were such essential buffer states that their indiscretions and mistakes were overlooked. This was, as Tacitus suggested, 'the old, long established policy of the Roman people of employing kings too as their instruments of enslavement'.[172]

In addition to the zones of client princes outside direct Roman rule, Augustus divided the parts of the Empire that were under direct rule into imperial and senatorial provinces, with the former being under his direct control (rather than as occurred formally with individual commanders holding areas) and the repository of the vast majority of the military resources. Before these lines were finally settled, Augustus had undertaken a series of 'inroads' into territory which had not previously been under

[168] Cicero, *On the Consular Provinces* XII:30, XIII:32; Caesar *Gallic War* IV:xx-xxiii Suetonius *The Twelve Caesars* trans Graves, R (1989) (London, Penguin) 23–24. The figures are from Suetonius, *The Twelve Caesars* trans Graves, R (1989) (London, Penguin) 24–25; also Collingwood, R (1958) *Roman Britain and the English Settlements* (Oxford, Oxford University Press) 32–33, 52; White, R (2011) *Atrocitology* (NYC, Norton) 37.

[169] This fragment from Egypt is reprinted in Lewis, N (ed) (1955) *Roman Civilisation: Selected Readings*, Vol II (NYC, Columbia University Press) 89.

[170] *The Res Gestae Divi Augustus: Accomplishment of Augustus* trans Brunt, P (1967) (Oxford, Oxford University Press) 25–28.

[171] Oath of Allegiance to Augustus reprinted in Lewis, N (ed) (1955) *Roman Civilisation: Selected Readings*, Vol II (NYC, Columbia University Press) 35 and 89; also Suetonius, 'Life of Augustus' in *The Twelve Caesars* trans Graves, R (1989) (London, Penguin) X:xi.

[172] Tacitus, *The Agricola and Germania* trans Mattingly, W (1974) (London, Penguin) X:iv.

direct Roman rule. Suetonius suggested that such actions were always 'just' and with 'due cause' and 'he was far from the desire of increasing his dominion or military glory at any cost'. The end result was that 'other peoples . . . that were not entirely peaceful he reduced to submission'.[173]

Augustus also desired to strengthen the position of Rome by having enhanced defences that were identified as strong, easily defendable, natural barriers. These were to be shortened wherever possible, and reinforced by advanced communication and transport systems which supported permanent – not mobile – garrisons, supplemented by colonies of veterans, auxiliaries and general colonialism. In the north, the frontier was the Danube and in 5 CE Roman armies stood on the Elbe. Having established the boundaries, on his deathbed, Augustus told his heir, to keep the empire within its existing borders.[174]

The political exhortations of Augustus were matched by the philosophical recommendations of Seneca (4 BCE–65 CE). Seneca, although aware of the inconsistency between the private murder of one which is a crime and the public murder of thousands which is celebrated, did not suggest that all warfare was wrong. He did, however, strongly advocate policies of restraint of any further expansion of the Roman Empire, especially based only on goals of glory.[175] This philosophy, combined with the pragmatic request from Augustus meant that in the two centuries that followed the death of Augustus, most of the emperors took little interest in further territorial expansion. The exceptions of no-expansion in this period were of the invasions of Britain, Germany and Dacia. In all three instances, the invasions and/or occupations were steadfastly blocked by campaigns based on national autonomy in opposition to Roman hegemony. This resistance combined with high economic costs meant that many, such as Appian (95–165 CE) questioned the value of ruling over 'poverty-stricken and profitless tribes of barbarians'.[176]

With regard to Britain, Augustus had originally declined to push for a second invasion, seeing that the people of Britain could not harm Rome, nor provide her any good. Claudius (10 BCE–54 CE), came to a different conclusion and crossed the channel under two pretexts. The first was that he was helping a British chieftain who had been driven out of the island as the result of an uprising. The second was that he had been invited in to help the British as they feared the *Picts* – who at this point, may have been groups of separate tribes. Certainty in this area is difficult as little is known of this period, in which various local groups may have been mingling together, with the Romans also identifying Hiberian (north-eastern Irish) pirates in this region, whom they called *Scotti*. The possibility that Britain represented a beacon of Celtic nationalism was added weight for invasion. Whatever the actual pretext, the result was that southern Britain was rapidly overrun after a two-day battle at Medway (near Rochester

[173] Suetonius 'Life of Augustus' in *The Twelve Caesars* trans Graves, R (1989) (London, Penguin1989) X:xi.

[174] Tacitus, *The Annals of Imperial Rome* trans Grant, M (1965) (London, Penguin) 1:11.

[175] Epistle 113, as reprinted in Cooper, J (ed) (1995) *Seneca: Moral and Political Essays* (Cambridge, Cambridge University Press). Note also Epistle 95, see 27–29, 45–47, 76–79, 119–20.

[176] Appian, *The Roman Histories* trans White, H (1912) (Boston, Loeb) at 7. Tacitus, *The Annals of Imperial Rome* trans Grant, M (1965) (London, Penguin) 4:32; also Tacitus *The Agricola and Germania* trans Mattingly, W (1974) (London, Penguin) 39–40.

in Kent) in 43 CE and was organised into a province through prolonged military operations, lasting about a century.[177]

The Roman occupation of the British Isles was not extensive. The Romans declined an invitation to enter into Ireland (after an Irish prince sought refuge with Agricola (40–93) and they could not subdue Scotland, where despite constructing the Antonine wall, they had to fall back to the more robust line made famous by Hadrian (76–138). The Roman occupations were also not peaceful. The first uprising occurred following the will of Prasutagus, king of the Icenian people, who held sway over Norfolk and Suffolk, before dying in 61 CE. As a client king of Rome, he made Nero (37–68) his heir jointly with his own two daughters, hoping to save both his kingdom and his fortune. The Romans did not honour this. Upon his death, they took his land, desecrated his house, raped his daughters and denied any political power to his wife, Boudicca (d 61 CE). With such concerns she sparked a rebellion (that ended in disaster for a reputed 80,000 Britons at the battle of Watling Street in 61 CE) alleging that Roman occupation was akin to slavery, in which those who had not been robbed of their possessions were being over-taxed 'and trampled underfoot by men who know nothing else than how to secure gain'.[178] A little over two decades later in 83 CE, Calgacus, a Caledonian chieftain argued (before he and his army of at least 10,000 were destroyed at the battle of Mons Graupius in 84 CE), that the Romans were without limit in their desire for domination and riches. He famously added 'they rob, butcher, plunder, and call it "empire", and where they make a desolation, they call it "peace"'.[179]

In the case of the northern/German frontier, although the region had been relatively quiet for 40 years after the time of Caesar, Augustus decided on a policy of expansion. He advanced and held the Alpine range, east Switzerland, the Tyrol and Austria, to advance the frontier to the Danube from Lake Constance to Vienna. He further judged that the southern Balkans would never be secure unless the Romans advanced northwards, also to the Danube. He also advanced north-east, over the Rhine and through west Germany, towards the Elbe. The exact reasons for these acquisitions of new territory are somewhat obscure, although individual instances were often linked to broken truces and/or attacks on Roman clients, and/or raids into Roman territory.[180]

[177] Dio Cassius, *Roman History* trans Cary E (1967) (Boston, Loeb) LX:19; Bede, *The Ecclesiastical History of the English Nation* trans Jane, L (1910) (London, Dent) I.12. Collingwood, R (1958) *Roman Britain and the English Settlements* (Oxford, Oxford University Press) 72–78; Davies, N (2011) *Vanished Kingdoms: The History of Half Forgotten Europe* (London, Penguin) 35–39.

[178] Dio Cassius, *Roman History* trans Cary, E (1967) (Boston, Loeb) LXII:iii, I-IV:2. Also Franzero, C (1954) *The Life and Times of Nero* (London, Redman) 134–38; Collingwood, R (1958) *Roman Britain and the English Settlements* (Oxford, Oxford University Press) 95–101; Everitt, A (2009) *Hadrian and the Triumph of Rome* (NYC, Random House) 212–25; Cook, S (ed) (1968) *The Cambridge Ancient History: The Augustan Empire*, Vol X (Cambridge, Cambridge University Press) 797–800; Cook, S (ed) (1965) *The Cambridge Ancient History: The Imperial Peace*, Vol XI (Cambridge, Cambridge University Press) 154–56; Collingwood, R (1958) *Roman Britain and the English Settlements* (Oxford, Oxford University Press) 115, 118, 121, 123, 140, 153.

[179] *Tacitus on Britain and Germany* trans Mattingly, H (1951) (London, Penguin) 80; Collingwood, R (1958) *Roman Britain and the English Settlements* (Oxford, Oxford University Press) 115–16.

[180] Jordanes, *The Origins and Deeds of the Goths* trans Miero, C 1910 edn, 2009 reprint, Vols II, III and XIII (London, Theophania); Polybius, *The Histories* trans Waterfield, R (2010) (Oxford, Oxford University Press) XXXVI:13.6–7; Cassius Dio 76[77].11.1. See also Champion, C (2004) *Roman Imperialism* (London, Blackwell) 190; Cook, S (ed) (1965) *The Cambridge Ancient History: The Imperial Peace*, Vol XI (Cambridge, Cambridge University Press) 160–66.

The new territories were not peaceful. The first great rebellion, due to the overt nature of the requisitions placed on the locals by the occupying armies, occurred in Pannonia (the area bounded north and east by the Danube, roughly the western half of modern-day Hungary, with parts of Austria, Croatia, Serbia, Slovenia, Slovakia and Bosnia in the mix) between years 6 to 9 CE. As this uprising was drawing to a close, Augustus suffered his greatest loss in 9 CE when three of his legions – some 35,000 men – were completely wiped out in the Teutoburg Forest of Germany. Although this region was eventually subdued, it took decades to achieve, and was only held by the weight of some 200,000 Roman men or allies, sitting upon the region. Before this point, many of the German tribes went on to repeatedly rebel against the excessive demands of the Romans and 'disgraceful servitude' and rallied under the cry of their ancient traditions as opposed to 'foreign domination'.[181]

The final example of the Roman dealing with Europe pertains to Dacia and the rise of Emperor Trajan (53–117). Trajan, the 13th Emperor of Rome, despite explicit warnings from the philosopher Dio Chrysostom (40–120) that most causes for war were unjust and based upon a type of madness, was the first emperor since Augustus who knew how to harness the traditional Roman ideals to his own ends and make his ambitions seem like the natural ones of Rome. This was unlike the policy of Domitian (51–96), the 11th Emperor, who preferred a more diplomatic approach. Specifically, following an invasion of the neighbouring Roman province from Dacia in the year 86, the Romans regrouped and counter-attacked into Dacia. Rather than enter into a war of attrition, Dominitian agreed to pay the Dacian king, Decebalus (r 86–107) 8 million sesterces each year in exchange for becoming a Roman client. For Trajan, this approach was intolerable. The invasion of Dacia in 101 by 180,000 Roman soldiers was justified because Trajan 'took into account the [Dacian] past deeds and was grieved at the money they were receiving annually, and he also observed that the [Dacian] power and arrogance was increasing'.[182]

Although Decebalus came to terms with Trajan, swearing obedience, surrendering territories and much of his military hardware, and (again) accepting the status of a loyal client king, he appears to have disregarded the peace treaty, fermented revolt against Rome, and then launched a preemptive strike and attacked Roman forces which were occupying south-west Dacia. The second time Trajan fought in Dacia in 105 and 106, there was no formal surrender document. The forces of the king were completely destroyed, whilst the country was fully digested before emerging as a new Roman province. The Dacian treasure turned out to be of almost unbelievable value – some 165 tons of gold and 330 tons of silver. In addition, the mines of Dacia continued to produce vast amounts of wealth. Even the conservative Hadrian, who sought to abandon the unproductive and difficult to defend areas of the Empire, elected to keep

[181] Tacitus, *The Annals of Imperial Rome* trans Grant, M (1965) (London, Penguin) I:lvii; Dio Cassius, *Roman History* trans Cary E (1967) (Boston, Loeb) LVI:xviii; Wells, S (2003) *The Battle That Stopped Rome: Augustus, Armenius and the Slaughter of the Legions* (NYC, Norton) 17–35, 89–113; also Scullard, H (1982) *From the Gracchi to Nero* (London, Methuen) 253–55. For the figures, see Grant, R (2011) *1001 Battles that Changed the Course of History* (London, Penguin) 83.

[182] Dio Cassius, *Roman History* trans Cary, E (1967) (Boston, Loeb) LXVIII:vi; Dio Chrysostom, *Discourses* trans Cohoon, J (1932) (Boston, Loeb) XII:16–20, XV:28 and XXXVIII:29.

Dacia within the realm. Here it remained until Aurelian abandoned it due to it being too difficult and too expensive to defend at a time of repeated uprisings by Germanic tribes.[183]

(iii) Parthia and Sassanid Persia

The kingdom of Parthia, in the north-east of modern-day Iran, was originally part of the Seleucid Empire – the realm founded in Persia by Alexander's successors. In the second century BCE, the Arsacid kingdom of Parthia overthrew the Seleucids and became the dominant power in Persia and the Middle East. Until its point of collapse in the third century CE, this empire came to cover 648,000 square miles, from modern-day Pakistan to Saudi Arabia. Such power and expanse drew it into centuries of 'constant wars and great expense' with Rome, without any real success for either, until they fought themselves to exhaustion, at which point a third power – Islam – arose and eclipsed Persia before going onto consume Byzantium 800 years later.[184]

The feud between Parthia and Rome owed its origin to the arrangements of Pompey (106–48 BCE) which spilled over into disputed territories of Parthian interest. Later events suggest the real problem appears to have been the aggression of the proconsul Marcus Crassus (115–53 BCE). Crassus was widely viewed as the weak partner in the famous triumvirate that he formed with Julius Caesar and Pompey to rule Rome. To compensate, Crassus decided to invade Parthia to win a martial glory that would equal that of Caesar in Gaul. With the acquiescence of both Pompey and Caesar, Crassus crossed the Euphrates from the Roman province of Syria. There was no justification for this war, beyond a general feeling that the potential triumph for Crassus would be good for the man, whilst the riches of the East would be good for Rome. Neither was the case. At least 20,000 Roman men were lost in battle. A further 10,000 were taken prisoner and never seen again. Crassus was then executed, allegedly by having molten gold poured down his throat, in mockery for his insatiable desire for material rewards. When the Parthians eventually decided to strike back, taking Syria and Judea from Rome during the time of their civil war, they provoked a reaction whereby Mark Antony (83–30 BCE) recovered the lost territories and entered into the country on the promise of a disgruntled royal, who had promised him the Parthian crown. This folly cost the lives of a further 32,000 Roman soldiers.[185]

Before Antony had a chance to re-engage with Parthia, he was consumed in his own war with Octavian/Augustus. Upon the success of Augustus, the decision was made to reach for a truce. Augustus judged that the two empires could live at peace, with the Euphrates as a limit of their spheres of interest. The sticking point was the country of Armenia – the territory that buttressed the Euphrates. Rather than fight over the issue, the Parthian king Phraates IV (r 37–2 BCE), agreed to recognise Roman suzerainty

[183] Dio Cassius, *Roman History* trans Cary, E (1967) (Boston, Loeb) LXVIII:9; Cook, S (ed) (1965) *The Cambridge Ancient History: The Imperial Peace*, Vol XI (Cambridge, Cambridge University Press) 168–70, 224–32.

[184] Dio Cassius, *Roman History* trans Cary, E (1967) (Boston, Loeb) LXXV:3.

[185] Dio Cassius, *Roman History* trans Cary, E (1967) Vol LX (Boston, Loeb) 26; Cook, S (ed) *The Ancient Roman History. The Roman Republic*, Vol IX (Cambridge, Cambridge University Press) 605, 611. For the figures, see Grant, R (2011) *1001 Battles that Changed the Course of History* (London, Penguin) 73.

over Armenia. This was not a permanent arrangement, as when swords were drawn over the country a few decades later, the new settlement (of Nero) in the treaty of Rhandeia of 63 CE, had the Parthians nominate the king, but the Armenians had to acknowledge Roman over-lordship. This was not satisfactory to future emperors, who, being distrustful of the Parthians due to their possible fermenting of rebellion elsewhere, demanded greater control over the client king.[186]

When the Parthian monarch disposed of the pro-Roman puppet ruler, Asidares (unknown date) without consulting Trajan (r 98–117), war was the result. Trajan advanced deep into Parthia with 80,000 armed men, advancing as far as the Tigris and sacking the Parthian capital (Ctesiphon) en route. When he withdrew his forces, he decided to claim Armenia and most of southern Mesopotamia as new Roman provinces. Trajan explained that was done because it had been no part of the Nero's treaty that the Parthian king should depose Armenian rulers, once lawfully invested, at pleasure and without consulting Rome. The victory of Trajan was crowned with another Roman puppet king placed on the Armenian throne, and remarkably, also on the throne of Parthia. With the latter, Trajan had to satisfy himself with approving the king, and not attempting to make Parthia another Roman province.[187]

Hadrian adopted a different policy to Trajan. Upon his accession, Hadrian issued orders to immediately abandon the newly acquired provinces, including, among others, those of Armenia and Mesopotamia and to regroup behind Rome's traditional border, the Euphrates. Furthering this approach, and a belief that he could achieve more by negotiation than warfare, in 123 CE, in direct negotiations with the Parthian king Chrosroes (r 109–129), the two agreed to balance the kingship of Armenia between the two empires. This balance only lasted for as long as the two leaders existed. Thus, when Vologases IV (r 147–191) came to power, having reunited Parthia after a civil war, he invaded Syria and Armenia, and installed a new client king in these territories. Marcus Aurelius (121–180) responded with a war which raged between 161 and 166. It ended with Aurelius recapturing the disputed territories, vanquishing the Parthian forces and advancing deep into the Parthian Empire, sacking Ctesiphon as Trajan had before him, before retrenching on the borders of the disputed territories that were now solidly, once again, in Roman hands.[188]

Severus (145–211) followed a similar pattern to Trajan, again crossing the Euphrates and ensuring the loyalty of the king of Armenia, by taking his children hostage. In 198 he declared war on Parthia, in retaliation for the support that they had given to one of the contenders for the title of Emperor or Rome. The Parthian capital, Ctesiphon, was again sacked by Roman legions and the northern half of Mesopotamia was annexed to the Empire. Although the Romans, once more, withdrew from the central territories of Parthia, any hope of a reconciliation was smashed when the Emperor Caracella

[186] Dio Cassius, *Roman History* trans Cary, E (1967) (Boston, Loeb) LXIII:i.2–4; also Franzero, C (1954) *The Life and Times of Nero* (London, Redman) 130–34; Cook, S (ed) (1968) *The Cambridge Ancient History: The Augustan Empire*, Vol X (Cambridge, Cambridge University Press) 263, 272–76; Cook, S (ed) *The Cambridge Ancient History: The Imperial Peace*, Vol XI (Cambridge, Cambridge University Press) 142–44.

[187] Everitt, A (2009) *Hadrian and the Triumph of Rome* (NYC, Random House) 162; Dio Cassius, *Roman History* trans Cary, E (1967) (Boston, Loeb) LXVIII:17, 1–3.

[188] McLynn, F (2010) *Marcus Aurelius* (London, Vintage) 194–203; Cook, S (ed) (1965) *The Cambridge Ancient History: The Imperial Peace*, Vol XI (Cambridge, Cambridge University Press) 238–47.

(180–217) tricked the Parthians into believing that he accepted a marriage to the daughter of the Parthian king, Artabanus (r 216–224), and just before the ceremony had his men attack the unarmed and completely deceived bride and wedding party. The Parthian king was lucky to escape alive. Caracalla then destroyed many of the surrounding towns and villages, before returning to Mesopotamia. From there he sent word to the Senate and the Roman people 'that the East was subdued and that all the kingdoms in the regions had submitted to him'.[189]

In fact, what Caracalla had created was the perfect conditions for the Parthian Empire to dissolve in through a series of dynastic struggles, civil war and ambitious local warlords. The result was the creation of the Sassanid Persian Empire which existed from 226 to 651 CE, at which point it was extinguished by the forces of Islam. During its existence, the Sassanid Empire encompassed all of the territories found in modern-day Iran, Iraq, Afghanistan and parts of west Pakistan. It repeated contested territory with Rome in the form of eastern Syria, the Caucasus and parts of modern-day Turkey.

The founder of the new Sassanid Empire, Ardashir I (d 242), did not contain himself to the Parthian territories of those he overthrew. His forces invaded the recently acquired Roman territory of Mesopotamia and threatened Syria. The watchword of the campaign was the restoration of the ancient frontiers of the Persian Empire. The Roman forces of Gordian III (225–244) met those of Ardashir, with the latter being forced to retreat from the Euphrates to the Tigris. Although the borders stayed intact, no peace was concluded until Philip the Arab (204–249) was emperor. There was no talk of a cession of Mesopotamia or Armenia in this agreement, and it was only a matter of time until the Persians advanced again. This occurred around 252, when both Antioch and Armenia were taken by Shapur I (240–272). Emperor Valerian (193–264) attempted to blunt these advances by the force of both arms and diplomacy. His diplomatic efforts resulted in the Persians treacherously capturing the emperor himself, who died in Persian captivity. Successive Roman emperors battled with Persia, including Carus (224–283) who took advantage of a succession debate following the death of Shapur to invade the disjointed territory. Carus battled to, and then sacked Ctesiphon in 283, before returning to the Roman side of the Euphrates.

In the following decade Diocletian (244–305) brokered a peace that inched its way forward in the last decade of the third century. Before this could be concluded, the son of Shapur I, Narseh (293–302), declared war on Rome and invaded the provinces of Armenia and Mesopotamia. The Roman forces of Diocletian (244–311) and Galerius (260–311) met and defeated the Persian armies. The resultant Treaty of Nisbis of 299, oiled by the fact that Galerius had also captured the family of Narseh, reflected the Roman victory. Rome was acknowledged its suzerain rights over Armenia and Caucasian Iberia (the eastern and southern parts of modern-day Georgia). Rome also received a part of the Upper Mesopotamia that extended beyond the Tigris, encompassing five satrapies between the Tigris and Armenia. According to the Chronicle of

[189] Herodian, *History of the Roman Empire* trans Whitaker, C (1969) (Massachusetts, Loeb) section 4.11; Cook, S (ed) (1965) *The Cambridge Ancient History: The Imperial Crisis and Recovery*, Vol XII (Cambridge, Cambridge University Press) 5–9.

Joshua the Stylite (early sixth century), this treaty not only agreed the above considerations, it was also a military alliance by which both sides committed to help the other (via the provision of 300 cavalry, or a provision of financial assistance) if at war 'with any nation'.[190]

This peace held until the resurgence of Shapur II (309–379) in the 330s. This was the beginning of two long drawn-out wars (with nine major battles recorded between 337 and 350, and 358 and 363). Shapur, who had been expanding his empire in all directions, eventually came into conflict with (now Christian) Rome, when he crushed a rebellion within his borders. The crushing brought him to the borders of Armenia and Mesopotamia which he crossed with his forces. Although religion may have been a consideration in these conflicts, the desired provinces were now largely Christian. Shapur felt justified in these actions as the areas of Armenia and Mesopotamia had been 'fraudulently taken from my grandfather'.[191] Unconvinced, the Romans bided their time, until following Shapur's deep penetration into Roman Mesopotamia in 359, the (non-Christian) emperor, Julian, struck back, as it was his belief that 'peace was not consistent with the public welfare' of Rome. He advanced at the head of an army of 83,000 men – which fought its way to the base of Ctesiphon, before being trapped (and killed, along with 60,000 of his men) with his army deep in enemy territory. Julian's successor, Jovian (331–364) was forced to make a new treaty, in exchange for safe passage back to Roman territories. The cost of the treaty was the return of the five satrapies between the Tigris and Armenia conquered by Galerius in 298 (east of the Tigris) that Diocletian had annexed. This was in addition to the two strongholds of Nisbis and Singara. In addition, both Rome and Persia promised not to intervene in the affairs of Armenia.[192]

Both Rome and Persia found it too difficult to disengage from the affairs of Armenia. This was brought back into conflict in 374. Realising that this was a situation in which they both, inevitably, would be drawn into conflict again, a more permanent solution was suggested by Shapur III (r 383–388) through which Armenia should be partitioned and annexed between the two superpowers, with each having a different vassal king. The broad division which was agreed in 387 was four fifths going to Persia and one fifth going to Rome. Emperor Theodosius (347–392) accepted these terms, as he needed peace to march against his rivals in the west. The peace between Rome and Persia survived for 36 years. A further treaty between Constantinople/Byzantium (as western Rome was in its dying stages) and Persia was agreed in 441, with one term of

[190] *Chronicle of Pseudo-Joshua the Stylite* trans Wright, W (2001 edn) (Liverpool, Liverpool University Press) VIII; Rawlson, G (1972) *The Seven Great Monarchies of the Ancient World* (London, Georgias Press) 305.

[191] Letter from Shapur, noted in Norwich, J (1988) *Byzantium: The Early Centuries* (London, Guild) 86. Stephenson, P (2009) *Constantine* (London, Quercus) 248; Cook, S (ed) (1965) *The Cambridge Ancient History: The Imperial Crisis and Recovery*, Vol XII (Cambridge, Cambridge University Press) 126–37; Gibbon, E (1926 edn) *The Decline and Fall of the Roman Empire*, Vol 1 (London, Methuen) 404–405; Millar, F (1981) *The Roman Empire and Its Neighbours* (London, Duckworth) 250–67.

[192] Ammianus Marcellinus, *The Histories* trans Rolfe, J (1940) (Cambridge, Harvard University Press) 17:5, 22:12, 25:7; Gwatkin, H (ed) (1957) *The Cambridge Medieval History. The Christian Roman Empire*, Vol 1 (Cambridge, Cambridge University Press) 57–59, 71–74. Last testament of Julian reprinted in Gibbon, E (1929 edn) *The Decline and Fall of the Roman Empire*, Vol II Bury, J (ed) (London, Methuen) 535–45; Grant, R (2005) *Battle* (London, Dorling Kindersley) 50.

particular importance. Specifically, 'neither party should construct any new fortification in his own territory in the neighbourhood of the boundary line between the two countries'.[193] Moreover, the two sides even learnt how to cooperate in accordance with their treaty of 299 in terms of military assistance. This was done when the Persians requested, of which the Romans obliged, to pay a financial contribution (which was used to free Persian hostages) from their common enemy – the Huns.[194]

The division of Armenia, demilitarisation of the flash points and cooperation against a common enemy could not hold the peace between the two empires in the sixth century. The point of conflict was twofold. First, the new Byzantine emperor – Anastasius (430–518) gained the throne after the death of Zeno, via the favouritism of Zeno's widow (who soon married Anastasius). This was the cause of severe discontent within the family of Zeno, who believed better candidates for the Byzantine throne existed. These 'better candidates' were supported by Persia. As such, Anastasius began on the wrong foot with Persia. Second, after the initial contribution was paid to the Persians towards fighting the Huns, the expectation developed that the payments would become annual. In time, this meant that Kavadh I (449–531) instructed his ambassador to go Constantinople and explain: 'If you wish to make peace, give us 10,000 pounds of gold, and make an agreement with us that we shall receive every year the customary sum of money.'[195] Anastasius could not agree to this and war broke out when the forces of Kavadh crossed the border. The two sides traded sieges and exchanged fortresses along the shared borders from 502 to 504, before agreeing to a seven-year truce and a return to the geographical status quo as it was before the conflict started.[196]

Although the peace lasted longer than seven years, it could not hold back war indefinitely. The process of disintegration was fourfold. First, a proposed diplomatic marriage in 518 between the leading families of Persia and Constantinople ('to bind them together in kinship and goodwill') failed to eventuate. Second, revolts against Persian rule in Caucasian Iberia and upper Mesopotamia were believed to be linked to the meddling of Constantinople. Third, Persia continued to harbour the belief that it was bearing the brunt of the Hun attacks for which the Romans obtained peace, and that if the Romans were sincere in their military alliance with the Persians, they would have a joint force – rather than what the Persians saw as a build-up of Roman troops on the Persian border.

Finally, an emerging concern was that in 505 Anastasius had purchased a small estate named Dara (now Oguz in south-east Turkey), located just two miles from the border and10 miles from the great Persian border stronghold of Nisibis. Within a year, this small estate began to grow into one of the largest forts of the period. The Persians saw this as something forbidden by the treaty of 441, and something against which

[193] Procopius, *History of the Wars* trans Dewing, H (1914 edn) (Massachusetts, Harvard University Press) I:2; Gwatkin, H (ed) (1957) *The Cambridge Medieval History. The Christian Roman Empire*, Vol 1 (Cambridge, Cambridge University Press) 240; Hussey, J (ed) (1966) *The Cambridge Medieval History: The Byzantine Empire*, Vol IV(1) (Cambridge, Cambridge University Press) 594–98.

[194] *Chronicle of Pseudo-Joshua the Stylite* trans Wright, W (2001 edn) (Liverpool, Liverpool University Press) VI, IX, X.

[195] *Chronicle of Pseudo-Joshua the Stylite* trans Wright, W (2001 edn) (Liverpool, Liverpool University Press) LIX, XIX, XXI, XXIV and LIV.

[196] Procopius, *History of the Wars* trans Dewing, H (1914 edn) (Massachusetts, Harvard University Press) I:9.

they needed to create a counter-weight. The counter-weight was a new (larger) fortification of their own, and a supporting field army. With such concerns just before the Persian invasion of 530, they warned the Romans they could either 'choose peace or elect war . . . either help them in guarding the [Caspian] gates [against the Huns], as is just and right, or dismantle the city of Daras'.[197] The Romans did neither and the Persian forces flooded over the border of Mesopotamia in 530 and the Caucasus in 531. The culmination of these invasions was at the battle of Daras, when the fresh new and inspirational, Emperor Justinian (482–565) who had come to power a few years earlier, defeated an army of 50,000 Persians (leaving 8,000 of them dead on the battlefield), with a Byzantine force of only half the size.[198] Justinian was surprisingly lenient in the 'Eternal Peace' which was agreed the following year in 532. The terms specified:

> [T]hat both sides should give back all the places which each nation had wrested from the other in that war, and that there should no longer be any military post in Daras; as for the Iberians, it was agreed that [although Iberia was to remain in Persian hands] the decision rested with them whether they should remain there in Byzantium or return to their own fatherland. And the Romans gave the Persians Pharangium and the fortress of Bolum together with the money [110,000 pounds of gold as a one-off payment], and the Persians [retained the province but] gave the Romans the strongholds of Lazica [effectively north-west Iberia, modern-day west-Georgia, beneath the Caucasus mountains].[199]

The treaty of 'Eternal Peace' lasted for a total of eight years. In 540 the new ruler of Persia, Khosrau I/Chosroes (r 531–579) decided to invade Syria and Mesopotamia. Persian forces were repulsed and then defeated (again) at the strongpoint of Dara. A further peace agreement was reached in 545 whereby the Persians promised to no longer feel 'resentment' about Daras, and the Romans agreed to pay the Persians 20 centenaria as a cost for the Persians guarding Caspian Gates (and thus preventing the Huns from advancing).[200] The Persians saw this as a payment akin to the 'annual payment of gold to some of the Huns . . . not as tributary subjects to them, but in order that they may guard your land unplundered for all time'.[201]

The arrangement of 545 only kept the peace for three years until 548. The next breach occurred when the kingdom of Lazica found Persian protection oppressive and asked Justinian to establish a Roman protectorate. Justinian accepted, and when his forces entered the territory, warfare raged for 13 years, before in 561 another peace agreement was concluded. After a large amount of correspondence over whether the peace would involve a financial tribute for Persia (this was not to be the case), the

[197] Procopius, *History of the Wars* trans Dewing, H, (1914 edn) (Massachusetts, Harvard University Press) I:16.

[198] Procopius, *History of the Wars* trans Dewing, H (1914 edn) (Massachusetts, Harvard University Press) I:10 and 11; Gwatkin, H (ed) (1967) *The Cambridge Medieval History: The Rise of the Saracens and the Foundation of the Western Empire*, Vol II (Cambridge, Cambridge University Press) 7; Grant, R (2005) *Battle* (London, Dorling Kindersley) 64.

[199] Procopius *History of the Wars* trans Dewing, H (1914 edn) (Massachusetts, Harvard University Press) I:21; also Gwatkin, H (ed) (1967) *The Cambridge Medieval History: The Rise of the Saracens and the Foundation of the Western Empire*, Vol II (Cambridge, Cambridge University Press) 29.

[200] Procopius, *History of the Wars* trans Dewing, H (1914 edn) (Massachusetts, Harvard University Press) II:10 and 28.

[201] Procopius, *History of the Wars* trans Dewing, H (1914 edn) (Massachusetts, Harvard University Press) II:28.

treaty was concluded and the Persians agreed to evacuate Lazica whilst the Romans gave up, in exchange, Suania (modern-day north Georgia). In addition to terms agreeing to the facilitation of the work of ambassadors and expansion of trade, the important terms of this treaty were four-fold. First, the Saracens (from whom Islam would blossom) were mentioned (for the first time), as allies of both sides who had to be tied into, and comply with, the peace. Second, although refugees from the conflict could return home, in the future, neither side was to accept people fleeing from one side to the other. Third, the Persians promised (again) not to complain about the fortification of Daras – in exchange for the town only having an 'adequate' force within it, and that in the 'future neither state shall fortify or protect with a wall any place along the frontier, so that no occasion for dispute shall arise from such an act and the treaty be broken'. Finally, it was agreed again that 'the Persians shall not allow the Huns or Alans or other barbarians access to the Roman Empire, nor shall the Romans either in that area or any other part of the Persian frontier send an army against the Persians'.[202]

This peace treaty lasted for little more than a decade. Further war broke out in 572 and lasted for nearly two decades. Whilst the early chroniclers recorded that the Persians broke the peace treaties, and attacked and took Daras, later scholarship showed that this attack coincided with Byzantine advances into Persian territory, to assist Armenia and Iberia which were both rebelling against Sassanid rule. Late payment of Byzantine tribute to Persia was also causing disquiet to the Persians.[203]

Both sides fought themselves to a stalemate, punctuated by some truces, paid for in gold and failed attempts at further peace treaties, before a remarkable event occurred in 589. This event was the attempted coup on the Persian throne by a disgruntled general which led to the rise of Khosrau II (r 590–628). Khosrau II, who was no stranger to fighting for the throne, had earlier led a successful civil war against his own father to gain the Persian throne. When he could not hold this against his own usurper he fled to Byzantine territories – with whom he was also fighting. The Byzantine emperor Maurice (539–602), recognising the opportunity that this presented, overruled his advisers and succeeded in helping Khosrau II to regain his Persian throne with an army of 35,000 Roman soldiers. The cost of this military assistance to the Persian crown was the Treaty of Peace of 591 by which half of Armenia and half of Iberia, including the two great cities of Daras and Martyropolis (which had been lost in recent fighting), were to be restored to Byzantium. To cement the deal, Khosrau II married Maurice's eldest daughter. Khosrau II was probably also adopted by Maurice.[204]

It was this personal relationship between the Persian king and the Byzantine emperor which lead to the final war which destroyed the Persian Empire. The catalyst was the revolt by the Byzantine army against Maurice, which saw the death of him

[202] This treaty is recorded in *The History of Menander the Guardsman* trans Blockley, R (2006) (Liverpool, Cairns) 73–75.

[203] John of Biclaro, *Chronicle* reprinted in trans Wolf, K (1999) *Conquerors and Chroniclers of Early Medieval Spain* (Liverpool, Liverpool University Press) 63; Gwatkin, H (ed) (1967) *The Cambridge Medieval History: The Rise of the Saracens and the Foundation of the Western Empire*, Vol II (Cambridge, Cambridge University Press) 271–72.

[204] See Menander the Guardsman, in *The History of Menander the Guardsman* trans Blockley, R (2006) (Liverpool, Cairns) 159, 161, 185; also Hussey, J (ed) (1966) *The Cambridge Medieval History: The Byzantine Empire*, Vol IV(1) (Cambridge, Cambridge University Press) 600–603.

(and his six sons) in 602. Khosrau II used the coup by Phocas (r 602–610) and the murder of the man who helped him retain his crown (and the father to his wife, and possibly his adoptive father) as the reason for a renewed war against the Byzantine Empire. For the following 20 years, despite the fact that Heraclius (575–641) had toppled Phocas, the Persian forces continued to advance through the Roman territories as Khosrau II refused to recognise Heraclius as the rightful imperial successor. In so doing, for the first time ever, the Persians experienced unprecedented victories as the Byzantine armies virtually collapsed between 609 and 615. In this situation, what started out as victories in the territories of Armenia and Mesopotamia, advanced to the high-tide marks of the Persian forces as they submerged the Caucasus, Syria, Palestine and Egypt. Whilst some regions and cities barely fought the Persians, others, like Jerusalem, were the subject of intense fighting and subsequent sack, resulting in the deaths of tens of thousands.[205]

From the then lowest point in the history of the Byzantine Empire, Heraclius, drawing inspiration from religious faith, fought back. The results were staggering. Heraclius reclaimed many of the lost territories, before advancing deep into Persian territories, destroying a number of Persian palaces and threatening to attack the capital Ctesiphon, as the Roman Emperors had done centuries earlier. At this point, Khosrau II was overthrown in a coup led by his own son, Kavadh II (59—-628). Upon success, Kavadh II at once sued for peace. The memorandum sent from him to Heraclius expressed his desire to reach an agreement to 'live in peace and love with you, the emperor of the Romans and our brother, and the Roman State and the remaining nations and other princes who surround our states'.[206] Following through, the subsequent peace treaty was agreed on the basis of the return of all prisoners of war, the withdrawal – of both sides – from all occupied territories and a restoration to the borders agreed in the treaty of 591.[207]

This was a poisoned victory. Protracted Byzantine–Persian warfare had reduced both empires 'to a wretched and miserable condition'.[208] Kavadh II only survived a few more months, as Persia descended into several years of further dynastic disputes, civil wars, economic decline, religious unrest and lack of control of its own provinces. In this situation, the conditions were perfect for the germination of the new religion which would quickly kill the Persian Empire. Nine hundred years later it would consume Byzantium.

[205] Kaegi, W (2007) *Heraclius: Emperor of Byzantine* (Cambridge, Cambridge University Press) 65–70, 74–75, 77–79, 85.

[206] The Persian Memorandum reprinted in Kaegi, W (2007) *Heraclius: Emperor of Byzantine* (Cambridge, Cambridge University Press) 178; Kaegi, W (2007) *Heraclius: Emperor of Byzantine* (Cambridge, Cambridge University Press) 168–69, 175.

[207] *The Chronicles of Theophanes Confessor* trans Mango, C (2006) (Oxford, Clarendon Press) 453, 455. See also Maas, M (ed) (2010) *Readings in Late Antiquity: A Sourcebook* (London, Routledge) 342–43.

[208] Persian envoy, noted in Kaegi, W (2000) *Byzantium and the Early Islamic Conquests* (Cambridge, Cambridge University Press) 32.

6. THE FORMATION OF MODERN EUROPE

The formation of modern Europe was preceded by the collapse of the Roman Empire in the west. It is my contention that western Rome did not collapse because it was crushed by another empire. The collapse of the west was due to the migratory waves of fighters that overran the defences, combined with the fatal preoccupation of the western emperors who spent as much time fighting internal contenders within the empire, as their external enemies. The conclusion was hammered home when the last Roman emperor in the west, Romulus Augustus (c 460–476) was deposed in 476 by the German chieftain Odoacer (433–493) – the first 'barbarian' king of Rome. This was the end point of ancient Rome, and the beginning of the Middle Ages in Western Europe.[209]

Anglo-Saxon England refers to the period between the end of the Roman occupation and the evolution of the Anglo-Saxon kingdoms around the beginning of the fifth century CE, until the Norman Conquest in 1066. The pattern in this country was very similar to that in Spain, which Isodore (560–636) explained as being one whereby kings would set about 'enlarging their kingdoms through warfare to increase their riches . . . illegitimately taking the kingdoms of others . . . [as they] lived by the sword, died by the sword'.[210]

Until the ninth century, Anglo-Saxon England was the Heptarchy, a region dominated by seven kingdoms (Northumbria, Mercia, East Anglia and Wessex as the dominant kingdoms, and Essex, Kent and Sussex as the minor kingdoms). These kingdoms developed following the departure of the Romans in 410 CE, leaving the people to fend for themselves, and defend their communities against foreign invaders who swarmed into their country during the fifth and sixth centuries. Although the legendary (but perhaps mythical) Arthur tried to re-establish the older Roman frontiers and reassert both unity and authority, this proved impossible when the armed forces he had assembled, disbanded after the war and went on to fight each other, dissolving into five, six or seven native kingdoms. It was a time, according to Bede (672–735), when 'all the bonds of sincerity and justice were so entirely broken, that there was . . . no trace of them remaining'.[211]

The disorder and discord that was created in the wake of Arthur's victories meant that when the English, who were contained within substantial defined reservations, rebelled for a second time at the end of the sixth century, they could not be stopped and the English triumphed because the Britons could not unite. Thereafter, local kings fought each other, seeking the dominance of their dynasty and the reward of the resources of the defeated which could then be redistributed. Such actions became part

[209] Gibbon, E (1926 edn) *The Decline and Fall of the Roman Empire*, Vol IV (London, Methuen) 47–53.

[210] Isidore of Seville, *History of the Kings of the Goths* reprinted in trans Wolf, K (1999) *Conquerors and Chroniclers of Early Medieval Spain* (Liverpool, Liverpool University Press) 101–104; John of Biclaro, *Chronicle*; also in Wolf, 68, 70–71, 74–75.

[211] Bede, *The Ecclesiastical History of the English Nation*, trans Jane, L (1910) (London, Dent) I:22; Morris, J (2004) *The Age of Arthur: A History of the British Isles* (London, Phoenix) 200–203; Stenton, F (1985) *Anglo Saxon England* (Oxford, Clarendon Press) 2–5; Davies, N (2011) *Vanished Kingdoms: The History of Half Forgotten Europe* (London, Penguin) 46–57.

of larger set of patterns where constant warfare became the norm. In seventh-century England 12 battles were recorded involving the death of at least one king or major royal figure, besides 10 other battles and 11 other instances of warfare. Pretexts ranged from glory to feud, through to religion to revenge. In other instances, wars are recorded, but the causes are not clear other than oblique references that they were caused by people of 'royal race' who had been 'banished from the country'. Sons also fought against their royal fathers or brothers against their enthroned siblings within a mix of conflicts caused by 'kings of doubtful title, or foreigners'.[212]

Once a local throne was secure, then outward adventure would often follow, such as when King Egfrid around 684, pushed outwards, invading – allegedly without cause – both Ireland and the land of the Picts, who by the seventh century, were seen as the dominant group in the North. Such attacks were consistent with the period. Between 600 and 850, 14 wars are recorded between the dominant Anglo-Saxon kingdoms of Mercia and Wessex. In the same period Mercia waged 11 wars against the Welsh and fought other opponents on 18 recorded occasions. The kings all took turns either losing their lives, being chased from their domains, creating alliances (either via marriages or agreement) 'to give them peace and protection against the terror' of other kingdoms, or accepting 'terms of obedience and subjection' in exchange for retaining their kingdoms.[213] From this turmoil, arose increasingly powerful regional leaders, such as Offa of Mercia (r 757–797) coming to hold most of southern England, before even greater leaders such as Egbert (769–839) emerged, conquering the opposing Mercian kingdom and thus becoming 'sovereign of all the British dominions'.[214]

Exactly how much control over the dominions outside of England was achieved is questionable. In the case of what is now known as Scotland, the first king of the country, worthy of the title, was Kenneth (d 858), son of Alpin, who in the year 843, murdered the earls of Dalriada, and absorbed the lands of the Picts. By this point of history, the Picts were parts of local communities seeking to assert their independence, situated between the dangerous tides of groups challenging for dominance to both their north and south, before the tsunami of the Vikings arrived. When Egbert ventured into Wales to subdue the locals, he discovered not only angry Welsh, but also previously unforeseen invaders – Danes. It was all of these enemies that the grandson of Egbert – Alfred the Great (848–899), would attempt to bring under his control. This was finally achieved under the leadership of Athelstan (893–939). In 927, this leader of the kingdom of Mercia and Wessex launched a lightening northern campaign, destroying the Viking kingdom of York, overrunning Northumbria as far as the Forth, and

[212] Bede, *The Ecclesiastical History of the English Nation*, trans Jane, L (1910) (London, Dent) III:2. For the other important parts of Bede, see I:12, II:6, 14, 15, III:4, 7, 21, 22; IV:13–15, IV:21; Collingwood, R (1958) *Roman Britain and the English Settlements* (Oxford, Oxford University Press) 291–301, 423. Morris, J (2004) *The Age of Arthur: A History of the British Isles* (London, Phoenix) viii, 17, 71–86, 110–15, 140–41, 245–48, 488–91; Stenton, F (1985) *Anglo Saxon England* (Oxford, Clarendon Press) 30–73, 78–84.

[213] The quotes are from *The Anglo Saxon Chronicle* trans Swanton, M (1998) (London, Routledge). See years 813, 827 and 823. See also Bede, *The Ecclesiastical History of the English Nation*, trans Jane, L (1910) (London, Dent) IV:26; Halsall, G (2003) *Warfare and Society in the Barbarian West 450–900* (London, Routledge) 2–3; Gwatkin, H (ed) (1967) *The Cambridge Medieval History: The Rise of the Saracens and the Foundation of the Western Empire*, Vol II (Cambridge, Cambridge University Press) 548, 552, 559.

[214] *The Anglo Saxon Chronicle* trans Swanton, M (1998) (London, Routledge) 827; also Stenton, F (1985) *Anglo Saxon England* (Oxford, Clarendon Press) 38–41, 46–47, 206–15, 220, 232–34, 236.

obliging the Scottish king Constantine II (r 900–943) to sue for peace. A meeting of five kings at Eamont Bridge in Cumbria acknowledged Athelstan's overlordship. This peace was solidified after the battle of Brunanburh around 937 which finally confirmed Athelstan's control of a united English kingdom. The defeated coalition of Scots, Irish and Northumbrian Danes lost five 'kings' and two Viking chieftains and an unknown number of men.[215]

The unification of the tribes of the Franks (a confederation of Germanic tribes) under one monarch within the geographical areas that are broadly recognised today as Germany and France, was achieved with the conquests and organisation of Clovis (466–511). After uniting the Franks in 481, Clovis went on to defeat the Gallo-Roman ruler in Gaul, Syagrius (430–487) in 486. This victory extended Frankish dominion and greatly increased his prestige as Syagrius was the last Roman official in Gaul. This was 10 years after the point that the Western Roman Empire had, in essence, ceased to exist. In this power-vacuum, Clovis began the building of the foundations of the Merovingian dynasty, which would rule Gaul and neighbouring Burgundia for the next 250 years. To achieve this expansion, spurning offers of arbitration, he adopted many reasons for warfare. Before – and after – he was Christian, he attacked the neighbouring kingdoms for a multitude of reasons. These ranged from assertions to the territories previously belonging to his family, through to, inter alia, them harbouring his enemies, not paying tribute and/or punishing those who did not give him military support. He encouraged disgruntled sons to depose their ailing father kings, and even intentionally provoking wars by sending gifts of bronze disguised as gold.[216]

Upon the death of Clovis, his realm was divided amongst his four sons. This partitioning, from which the Merovingian dynasty grew, created four separate kingdoms – and civil strife. His four sons, (Clothar, Childebert, Chloromder and Theuderic) and their successors – (which grew to a total of 32) could maintain a type of concord when the circle was not too large. This peace was supported by treaties, such as that of Andelot of 587, whereby stability was reinforced by the clear delineation of property, promises of military assistance, the cross-adoption of children, and agreement (in advance) on succession. The ability of kings to honour such agreements or respect peaceful neighbours, was always limited by the nobles and men beneath them who, eager for the material benefits of conflict (in terms of both land and titles), could drive their leaders into battle, or attempt to usurp them in rebellion, as eventually occurred with the rise of Charles Martel (686–741) and the beginning Carolingian dynasty which followed him.[217]

[215] Davies, N (2011) *Vanished Kingdoms: The History of Half Forgotten Europe* (London, Penguin) 58–73. For the figures, see Grant, R (2011) *1001 Battles that Changed the Course of History* (London, Penguin) 123.

[216] Gregory of Tours, *History of the Franks* trans Thorpe, L (1974) (Baltimore, Penguin) II 27, 37–42; Jordanes, *The Origins and Deeds of the Goths* trans Miero, C (1910 edn, 2009 reprint) (London, Theophania) lvii; Davies, N (2011) *Vanished Kingdoms: The History of Half Forgotten Europe* (London, Penguin) 95–100; Ralston, JH (1929) *International Arbitration From Athens to Locarno* (California, Stanford University Press) 174.

[217] The treaty of Andelot is in Gregory of Tours, *History of the Franks* trans Thorpe, L (1974) (Baltimore, Penguin) III:15, IV:14, VI:31, VII:2, IX:20. See also Halsall, G (2003) *Warfare and Society in the Barbarian West, 450–900* (London, Routledge) 14–15, 17, 22, 71, 74, 76, 85, 87, 89, 136; Gwatkin, H (ed) (1967) *The Cambridge Medieval History: The Rise of the Saracens and the Foundation of the Western Empire*, Vol II (Cambridge, Cambridge University Press) 122–23.

The Carolingian king who reached the apex of power was Charlemagne (742–814). Charlemagne was known as 'the Great' due to being king of the Franks, the (Italian) Lombards, and, via the endowment of the Papacy, Emperor of the Romans. He was responsible for pushing the Carolingian empire to its furthest limits, adding, inter alia, Saxony, Bavaria, half of Italy and Aquitaine (modern-day Spain, Andorra and France) into his realm. At its peak, he held nearly 400,000 square miles within his grasp. Where he did not conquer, he made treaties of friendship or division. He developed relations with Islamic Baghdad, as well as friendship treaties with Britain and the Christian communities at the top of Spain.[218]

With Byzantium, after the failure of a proposed marriage alliance involving Empress Irene (752–804), war broke out in 788, as Byzantine forces were shipped to help the Lombards in Italy. This was a disasterous failure which finally ended in 798 in the cession of Byzantine Istria and Benevento to Charlemagne. The following year Charlemagne was crowned *Imperator Romanorum* (Emperor of the Romans) by Leo III. Irene was in no position to dispute Charlemagne's new dignity by force of arms. Charlemagne, in turn, seems to have had no intention of asserting a claim to Constantinople. He sought nothing more than Byzantine recognition of his right to imperial title. This recognition arrived in 811 via treaty. In exchange for a number of territories held by the Franks, including Venice and Liburnia (Croatia), the Byzantine Emperor Michael I Rangabe (r 811–813) recognised Charlemagne as emperor of the western half of the Roman Empire, except for the Iberian peninsula and the few Byzantine outposts in Italy.[219]

Cognisant of the difficulties that competition between his children could cause upon his death, Charlemagne had, on paper, divided his kingdom into three parts, so that his children could be 'co-rulers' and not fight each other. Although this held for one generation, it could not hold for two, and the Carolingian Empire ended up being split with the 843 Treaty of Verdun. This treaty ended the dream of a united Europe dividing the empire amongst the three Carolingian brothers. The treaty gave Charles (823–877) the western portions of the empire, most of what eventually became France: East Francia) as far as Spain. Louis (804–876) took and went on to solidify, the eastern portion of the empire, consisting of the land to the east of the Rhine and to the north and east of Italy (which became Germany: West Francia). Lothair (795–855) received the central portion of the empire, known as Middle Francia (consisting of the Low Countries, Lorraine, Alsace, Burgundy, Provence and the Frankish Kingdom of Italy).[220]

[218] See the Letter of Charles to Offa reprinted in Loyn, H (ed) (1975) *The Reign of Charlemagne: Documents on Carolingian Government and Administration* (London, Edward Arnold) 113. For the earlier treaty, see the 790 Treaty Between Charlemagne and Offa reprinted in Roy C (ed) *A Source Book for Medieval Economic History* (1965) (NYC, Tannen) 96–97; Costambey, M (2012) *The Carolingian World* (Cambridge, Cambridge University Press) 171–73.

[219] The 811 Treaty Between Charlemagne and Michael I Rangabe reprinted in Axelrod, A (ed) (2001) *Encyclopedia of Historical Treaties and Alliances*, Vol I (NYC, Facts on File) 14; Hussey, J (ed) (1966) *The Cambridge Medieval History: The Byzantine Empire*, Vol IV(1) (Cambridge, Cambridge University Press) 88–89, 96.

[220] The 843 Treaty of Verdun is reprinted in Laffan, R (ed) (1929) *Select Historical Documents: 800–1492* (New York, Holt) 8–9; Wallace-Hadrill, J (1962) *The Barbarian West: The Early Middle Ages AD 400–1000* (NYC, Harper) 7, 124–28; Gwatkin, H (ed) (1968) *The Cambridge Medieval History: Germany and the Western Empire*, Vol III (Cambridge, Cambridge University Press) 25.

In the decade that followed, the three kings, equal in dignity and power, ruled cooperatively, whilst battling to retain the integrity of their own realms, such as when the Bretons fought and succeeded in carving out an independent Brittany from Charles. After the death of Lothair in 855, the situation rapidly deteriorated. This coincided with Louis coveting the throne of West Francia possessed by Charles. His subsequent invasion, justified by an alleged invitation into the region by the people of the county because of the cruelty and poor governing of Charles, was only denied by the loyalty of the Aquitanian bishops, who refused to crown Louis as the German king. Being unable to hold the region, Louis withdrew, and in cooperation with Charles, focused upon dividing the lands of Lothair, and manipulating Lothair's goals of leaving his portion of Charlemagne's empire to his three children. The result of this process was the 870 Treaty of Mersen. This treaty set the shape of eastern and central Europe until the eighteenth century. It was roughly divided along the Meuse and Ourthe Rivers, allocating the west of these to Charles, whilst the Rhineland and former Duchy of Alsace went to Louis.[221]

This is not to suggest that the Franks of East and West lived peacefully thereafter. An attempted invasion in 920 by the West Frankish king, Charles the Simple (879–929) came to nothing, and the following year in 921, the two concluded a 'pact of friendship' which was recorded as the Treaty of Bonn. This treaty between Charles – the king of the East Franks – and Henry I (876–936) – king of the West Franks – recognised the existing border of the two realms and the authority of the respective kings. This was a short-lived peace. Upon hearing of the civil war in France in 921, Henry tried to wrest the Duchy of Lorraine from the Western Kingdom. By 924, the eastern part of Lorraine was in Henry's possession, but it would swing back again as nobles in the region would later wish to switch overlords, and rebel in 938, 940, 942 and again in 946. Otto I (912–973), who was the first to entice English forces to help against his enemy in France, was followed by his successor, Otto II (955–93) who continued the war against France, going so far as besieging Paris, before retreating. Peace was only reached in this area in 980, when his French counterpart Lothair (in fact, the nephew of Otto I), renounced his claims on the Lorrain, in exchange for Otto II recognising the rights of his son, Louis.[222] In addition to fighting in the West, the Ottos also fought in the East. Most notably, Otto I achieved a monumental victory over the Magyars in 955, thus extending his influence further into the East. Most notably, allowing the independence of new regimes, which accepted both Christianity and his overlordship. From such foundations, Poland (perhaps traceable to the names of one of the many original Slavonic tribes – *Polanie* – although also linked to the Slavonic word – *pole* – as in field) emerged towards the end of the tenth century.[223]

In other parts of the empire, where the centralisation of power was not as concentrated, such as in Italy, local magnates arose to take control when the opportunities

[221] Carlyle, A (1936) *A History of Medieval Political Theory in the West: The Second Century to the Ninth*, Vol 1 (London, Blackwood) 249–50; Gwatkin, H (ed) (1968) *The Cambridge Medieval History: Germany and the Western Empire*, Vol III (Cambridge, Cambridge University Press) 42–46.

[222] Gwatkin, H (ed) (1968) *The Cambridge Medieval History: Germany and the Western Empire*, Vol III (Cambridge, Cambridge University Press) 80, 179–84.

[223] Davies, N (2005) *God's Playground: A History of Poland*, Vol I (Oxford, Clarendon Press) 39–41, 43, 52–57; Stenton, F (1985) *Anglo Saxon England* (Oxford, Clarendon Press) 346–48.

presented themselves. Guy of Spoleto (d 894) went from being a local margrave, to Duke, to being crowned king of Italy in 883 (he had earlier tried to claim the West Frankish throne) and the Holy Roman Emperor in 894. His primary protagonist, Berengar I (845–924, the son of a daughter of Louis the Pious) who began as a layman, followed the same pattern, carving a small niche, becoming an established margrave, king of Italy and then Holy Roman Emperor (the last until Otto the Great was crowned in 962). Berenger I had to contend with no less than seven other contenders for the Italian throne. Such contenders were willing to make deals with whoever was required. Some, like Louis the Blind (880–928) a maternal relative of the Carolingians, lost both his armies and his eyes – after failing in his objectives in 900 and again in 905.

The death of Berengar I in 924 created a power vacuum in Italy. The kings of Upper and Lower Burgundy (which at this point was existing in oscillating degrees of independence slipping between the grips of France and Germany) held competing claims, as did Berengar II (900–966), with all being manipulated by various Italian nobles into the country to defend their interests. The mix of arrangements with power sharing, divisions and marriage alliances produced the result which was an arranged marriage for the throne of Italy. The only problem was that the groom was soon murdered and his widowed bride, Adelaide, quickly became the object of desire for a number of men who wished to marry her (by force, not love) for the throne of Italy. This situation lead to her requesting a German intervention by Otto I. Otto invaded in 951, appeased some Italian nobles, beat off the offended ones (especially Berengar II) and married Adelaide himself in 952. Otto the Great was also asked for assistance by Pope John XII (937–964), due to the political turmoil in Italy and the need to bring some stability to the region. In return, he was crowned as Emperor in 962. Thus, Otto, as Duke of Saxony and King of Germany, also became King of Italy. He was the first German to be called 'Emperor of Italy', and later crowned head of what became the 'Holy Roman Empire'. At this point, he became the most powerful man in Europe, gaining control over much of Europe and the Church (as he was, in essence, granted a veto over any papal candidates).[224]

7. CONCLUSION

This chapter was about the formation and clashing of empires, and the wars that both processes generated. My reading of history from around 2400 BCE to 1000 CE suggests that as states formed, where geographical boundaries, internal peace, economic and social growth, and religious syncretism came together on one hand; on the other hand, cooperation, coercion and conquest matched the process. Quite simply, war made the State, and the State made war. A push to expand the boundaries of the State, including into areas contested by equal heavyweights appears unavoidable, even

[224] Norwich, J (2011) *Absolute Monarchs: A History of the Papacy* (London, Random House) 81.

if punctuated by a number of peace treaties, as the power from the centre continued to push outwards – until only one heavyweight remained. At the same time, the desire for autonomy appeared as a powerful catalyst for many of those under the yolk of others.

India was a good example of the last point. India did not really fight other empires. The warfare India experienced in this bracket had more to do with establishing itself. It dealt with successive waves of migratory peoples, some of who settled, and some who were pushed back. Some foreign empires, like the Greek, took bits out of the top of the country, before regurgitating what they ate after a relatively short period of time. Others, like Islam, fought their way into north India and digested what they held. For most of the time, dynasties within India spent the majority of the 3,500 years fighting themselves as multiple leaders sought the ultimate goal of uniting the realm (and accompanying territories north of India, such as modern-day Afghanistan, Pakistan and Uzbekistan) under one ruler. This goal saw seven successive dynasties rise and fall, with all failing in terms of either completely subduing all of the areas, and/or holding what was held for a prolonged period of time. Each dynasty expanded and then collapsed as areas eventually broke free under the flag of autonomy, before snowballing to a weight heavier than the ruling dynasty. Accordingly, the geo-political landscape and the goals of the Indian kings of 1000 CE was not radically different to what it had been 2,500 years earlier.

China replicated the pattern of India, progressing through centuries of warfare as successive dynasties, with each attempt at centralisation expanding the empire until eventually the glue at the centre would weaken and the empire would fragment into separate parts seeking autonomy. Sometimes these fragments were in hundreds of parts, from which the competition to absolute control would again take off. The Han dynasty was the first to really push the circumference of their empire into what may be viewed as non-Chinese areas, such as Korea and Vietnam, whilst taking tribute from Japan. It, too, became unstuck when fired from internal revolt and then the attraction to many of the provinces, for autonomy. This overlapped with the ejection of Chinese influence in Korea and Vietnam, the mass disintegration of North China, and the splintering of the South into large sections following the Lulin rebellion in 23 BCE. This fragmentation pattern held until the Sui dynasty reunited the country under one rule. When the Sui attempted to retake Vietnam, and especially Korea, the conflicts involved were of such magnitude that revolt broke out against their reign, and the regime which solidified China after 400 years of separatism fell after 40 years of rule. This time, the process of fragmentation and the rise to power of a single overlord, the Tang, was much quicker. This regime suffered the same fate, after adventures in Korea and Tibet had turned the attackers into defenders. Although the Tang could survive the invasions, their reorganisation of military forces to defend the existing borders turned poisonous; when some of its own forces turned on the State, the State weakened, and once again fragmented. From this fragmentation, the Sung dynasty first rose to the surface, and then to dominance over all others.

The 2,500 years of history of the Middle East, as made up of Egypt, Mesopotamia, Canaan, Assyria and Persia repeated the same pattern. The pattern begins with the rise of one king seeking to expand their territory at the expense of other locals. This momentum of expansion spread into the wider region. In the case of Egypt, after a relatively quick and clear consolidation, the regimes pushed west, south and north. The push to the north was problematic as the north was much more solidified than the other neighbours. It was also much more familiar with the rise and fall of different dynasties, in which minor kings rose to prominence, as Sumer, Babylon and the Hittites took turns evolving, then crushing each other, whilst smaller players, such as Israel, moved between the carnage. In the trumping process, as the boundaries and influence expanded, they inevitably came into conflict with the more established power of Egypt. When neither side could reach military victory, they opted for a peace which set a boundary, non-meddling and protection of the status quo for each other. This type of peace was unusual, as the pattern before it, and the pattern after it, was peace was only achieved by victory – or submission as a type of vassal. The alternative was destruction. The civilizations of Elam, Assyria, Babylon and even Egypt fell in this sequence before Persia was left holding the trump card.

Once Persia became dominant, it continued to push its boundaries until eventually this pushing lead them to independent Greek communities. When these communities called for help from other Greeks, the response led Persia (and possibly the other great power-bloc of the day, Carthage) into a full scale invasion of Greece. At this point, the autonomous communities of the Greeks stopped their tradition of fighting each other, and joined together in defence of their collective territories. When the threat of invasion passed, they went back to their traditional antagonisms against each other. It was only when the Macedonians managed to defeat, and then unite, all of the Greek communities into the same direction, that aggressive war against Persia was possible. This was an absolute war of conquest, in which an emergent empire completely consumed the original antagonist. This success of Alexander against Persia was unlike the Greek practices in Sicily against Carthage. Here, five treaties punctuated the end of each conflict, with the majority of these always reflecting the status quo where the two sides agreed to redivide the island into respective spheres of influence. Whilst a divided island was the military reality, the dream for all sides, especially as the centuries wore on, appears to have been more comprehensive with the complete control of the island, and all of the treaties were broken for this purpose. To avoid being swallowed, the threatened communities would invite in whoever they felt was best to guarantee their survival. Whilst this approach allowed for a divided island for four centuries when it was only the Greeks and Carthaginians in the game, when the emergent Rome was invited in for the same purpose, the dynamic quickly changed, ending up with the two superpowers clashing.

By the time that Rome was ready to fight Carthage, it had already achieved most of its own formation. This process which had begun with joint and equally-held defensive alliances such as the Etruscans, had eventually ended up with Rome at the forefront, continually pushing the boundaries within the Italian peninsular until, through processes of provocation and invitations to help, they had brought the entire area under their authority. Uniquely, even once under Roman direction, the warfare continued as all within the realm fought, and ultimately succeeded, in obtaining equal rights. This demand for equal rights increased as the conquests of Rome and the benefits thereof, began to be become even more dominant. This dominance increased as the boundaries of Rome increased in both northern and western directions, as Rome continued to advance over small, decentralised, regions. The wars against the peoples north of Italy, be they in Gaul or Germany, both began – and ended – Roman history. From the outset, Rome was aware of the raw power of Gaul, and their covetous intentions on the assets of Italy. The original success of the Gauls in 390 BCE, was not repeated (despite several attempts) until the middle of the third century. Between that point, Rome entered into a series of wars under Caesar and Augustus, to pacify large parts of the north, and advance further to build strong defensive lines to protect future incursions. Before the eventual collapse of the western side of the Roman Empire, there was a constant stream of uprisings by communities under the Roman yolk seeking their autonomy. Whilst Rome could bring all of these under control, they became increasingly aware that it could not control all of the forces beyond the borders and developed elaborate systems of support for those in the buffer zones, who were meant to keep the troubles from getting too close.

This approach was different to what the Romans originally envisaged in Greece, where, having first secured the formerly autonomous Greek parts of Italy, the goal was to keep Greece divided and prevent the resurgence of another, united, Alexander-type of scenario. To do this, the Greeks fought two regimes, under Philip V and Antiochus III. Although the Roman rhetoric was about ensuring the autonomy of the Greeks, the overlap of ensuring that the Greeks were not united under a single monarch, was implicit. The limits of Roman patience with allowance of autonomy for the Greeks was tested to the limits when subsequent Greek monarchs, such as Perseus and Mithridates, attempted to revive the absolute autonomy of all Greek communities and reunite all of Greece. When Rome had dealt with these threats, the Greek communities were controlled with pro-Roman factions, being cemented in place.

The only two – unified – empires that Rome fought were Carthage, and then Sassanid Persia. The war with Carthage happened after 200 years of peaceful co-existence and collective defence agreement against common enemies. As noted above, the first instance occurred because the Romans were invited into a conflict which they had traditionally ignored, as it did not buttress their territory. However, after taking all of Italy, their boundaries and interests changed. They feared the Carthaginians were taking territory, much like they were, despite the fact that after 400 years of conflict, the Carthaginians had never completely consumed Sicily. Nevertheless, the Roman fear was real, and since their treaties with Carthage did not explicitly say they could not get involved in Sicily, they did. Given that this war which was largely permitted because the treaties over what areas were of influence to which superpower, were not clear, the peace treaties which concluded the Punic War, attempted to draw much sharper lines. The problem was, that the sharp lines were not sufficient to stop the Roman intentions to defend their friends (and/or the Carthaginian attempts to provoke them), even though they were on the wrong side of the line. The peace treaty which followed the Second Punic War allowed the survival and limited autonomy of Carthage, but stripped her of all of her possessions and foreign policy options. Eventually, when Carthage acted without Roman approval defending herself against a provocative Roman ally, Rome categorically crushed (and consumed) the rump of the once great empire of Carthage.

Rome also fought Sassanid Persia for over 600 years. These wars, which ranged from the end of the Republic to the middle years of the Byzantine Empire, were punctuated by four treaties that continually tried to resolve the sticking points. The original attacks flying out of the Republic appear more concerned with glory than any substantive considerations. This was not the case in subsequent centuries. Then, the sticking point for both was originally the control over disputed areas, particularly Armenia (and later Mesopotamia). The mechanisms to deal with this were first promises of autonomy for Armenia, and when neither side could stop meddling in the supposedly autonomous regions, a division of Armenia was agreed. Supplementing the split were promises of regional demilitarisation (to reduce tensions in the area) and cooperation against new enemies (the Huns). When the sincerity of demilitarisation promises were tested (via the building of new super-forts just outside the agreed zone) and the commitments to provide financial assistance against common enemies were not solidified, warfare broke out again. This warfare which raged over large areas throughout the sixth century, despite a number of truces and attempts to return to the status quo, could not be stopped when both sides became involved in the dynastic politics of each. Specifically, the Byzantium emperor Maurice became the saviour of Khosrau II, who attempted to return the compliment when Maurice was toppled. At this point, the warfare between the two sides appears to have reached new levels of intensity, fuelled by a much stronger religious background than in the past, and absolute. That is, the war between the two sides was not over disputed provinces, but was for absolute mastery, in which there could be no negotiated outcome.

When the western side of the Roman Empire eventually collapsed, the process of the tension between groups seeking autonomy and those seeking to re-establish the authority over all areas repeated itself. In this instance, the fragmentation of the empire of the west was spectacular. Whilst some areas battled for absolute dominance over relatively small spaces such as in Britain for hundreds of years, in the case of continental Europe, the size was larger, and the conquest was quicker. This was found in the efforts of the Merovigian and Carolingian dynasties. However, this grasp on the collective area only lasted until the grandchildren fought and split the core of western Europe into three parts, which effectively became France, Germany and Italy.

III

Migratory Peoples

1. INTRODUCTION

THE THIRD CHAPTER of this book seeks to examine the impact that migratory people had on warfare in the years 3000 BCE to 1000 CE. I have focused on these people as unlike more recent history, the waves of migratory peoples seemed both constant and universal. The question that this raised for me was whether such peoples with no settled home were covetous of the riches of others, and if so, what were the implications of these actions, and how were they dealt with?

2. EGYPT

The Bible, reaching back thousands of years, recorded the problems of nomads and other landless people invading and threatening the territories of the Israelites. These nomadic people had the rhythm of their existence set by their flocks of animals which they moved in search of water and pasture. Sometimes the water and pasture was occupied by other peoples. The Bible recorded one of these invasions in the following terms: 'they came up with their cattle and their tents, and they came as grasshoppers for multitude; for both they and their camels were without number: and they entered the land to destroy it'.[1]

By the time this problem was recorded in the Bible, the process was at least 1,500 years old. The sixth dynasty of Egypt (2345–2181 BCE) was the first civilization to record landless people, or nomads, who were starting to view the fertility and wealth of the Nile Valley with covetous eyes. These 'sand-dwellers' as the Egyptians disparagingly called them, were difficult to control, and even when the Egyptians offered them land to settle on, preferred the alternative of self-selecting and occupying more desirable areas. The Egyptian Akhtoy III (2090–2070 BCE) suggested these peoples were always lurking, like 'a crocodile on the riverbank'.[2] What he did not know, was that the same (or very similar) crocodile had been devouring large sections of the ancient Near East in what is commonly seen as the end of the Bronze Age. In the latter case, peoples known as *Gurians* quickly migrated between regions as lawless and fierce mass migrations. Amorite (ancient Semitic peoples) and other Zagros highlanders (from the

[1] Judges 6:1–5.
[2] Hamblin, W (2006) *Warfare in the Ancient Near East to 1600 BC* (London, Routledge) 379.

mountains of Iran and Iraq) responded in a similar way. The target was the agricultural land along the middle of the Euphrates, and later Syria, Mesopotamia and Canaan. Whilst some areas could hold back the tide (or more likely allowed them access and the resources they wanted until they were depleted), many others such as Ur could not and after decades of warfare ended up as rubble.[3]

Although Egypt was not subsumed beneath such invasions, by the twelfth dynasty (1991–1778 BCE) many Egyptians were concerned at the continual flow of 'Asiatics' attempting to flow over their borders. This became a particular problem when the *Hykos* (broadly, 'foreign shepherd kings') arrived. For over a century (1630–1520), these Semitic-speaking peoples – possibly from coastal Lebanon – ruled most of north and south Egypt, which was easily acquired after the civil war. The *Hykos* were only defeated when the Pharaoh Taa (reigned 1560–1558 BCE), striking out of the safe-haven of Thebes, began the fight back. Although Taa had the misfortune to be killed in battle (leaving his mummified head for posterity, replete with the fatal axe wound in its forehead), he began the process which would, after the eviction of the Hykos was complete, give rise to the New Kingdom (1541–1322 BCE).[4]

No sooner was this reclamation achieved, than Egypt had to battle with other migratory peoples' who originated from around the coastal areas of modern-day Libya. Again, whole communities of peoples on the move in search of better sustenance formed the backdrop for at least eight wars down to the thirteenth century BCE. By the time of Ramses II (1303–1213 BCE), these peoples had morphed into, or with, 'the Sea Peoples'. This grouping, which may have included such Aegean and Aetolian populations, who may have previously been in the employment of the Egyptian military, saw a series of large-scale battles (especially that of Perirer of 1208 BCE) at which the Egyptians defended their space and the invaders were forced to turn their attention to the eastern seaboard of the Mediterranean.[5]

This turn of attention saw cities being sacked and torched, harbours burned and looted, and entire nations laid low. Whilst coastal communities had been harried by pirates for decades, this new onslaught was of an entirely different order of magnitude as massive hordes of migratory warriors, followed by their families and all of their possessions, attacked a series of cities without warning. The first great maritime city to fall was Ugarit. The king of Ugarit wrote an urgent letter to his counterpart in Cyprus: 'The enemy ships are already here, they have set fire to my towns and have done very great damage to the countryside.'[6] This letter was never sent. It was later found in the kiln where it was being fired, amid the rubble of a devastated city. Next to be attacked was Egypt's ally, the Hittite kingdom. In a desperate flurry of diplomatic correspondence, the last Hittite ruler spoke of fighting a seaborne enemy. This enemy was so

[3] Hamblin, W (2006) *Warfare in the Ancient Near East to 1600 BC* (London, Routledge) 103–104, 107, 115–18, 154–57, 250–51, 288–89.

[4] Wilkinson, T (2010) *The Rise and Fall of Ancient Egypt* (London, Bloomsbury) 108, 182–83, 190–98; Gabriel, R (2005) *Empires at War*, Vol I (London, Greenwood) 67.

[5] Spalinger, A (2005) *War in Ancient Egypt* (London, Blackwell) 178–82, 197–203, 235–38; Hamblin, W (2006) *Warfare in the Ancient Near East to 1600 BC* (London, Routledge) 345; Herzog, C (1997) *Battles of the Bible* (London, Greenhill) 80–81.

[6] Letter from Ugarit reprinted in Wilkinson, T (2010) *The Rise and Fall of Ancient Egypt* (London, Bloomsbury) 351.

strong that it overpowered the entire kingdom, and a people who had occupied the Anatolian peninsula from approximately 1900 to 1000 BCE, vanished from history. The same result was recorded in Asia Minor, in cities like Miletus and Troy and elsewhere in the eastern Mediterranean, ranging from north Cyprus to Palestine. Achaean Greece was subject to a number of invasions who completely destroyed their civilization. So complete was the destruction that even writing disappeared. For 400 years until the eighth century BCE, Greece was plunged into a dark age of which almost nothing is known. Only Assyria, on the far bank of the Euphrates, survived unscathed, whilst Egypt was given breathing space. This changed in the period of Ramses III, when he had to battle the invaders in 1182 and 1176 BCE, on both land and sea. Whilst he stemmed the invasion, it is possible that part of the peace package involved the resettling of many of these communities both within Egypt, and/or in some of the vassal states of Egypt, such as Canaan.[7]

This was a short-term measure as it was only a matter of time before Ramses VI (1145–1137 BCE) was facing the familiar problem of mobile tribespeople trying to invade the fertile Nile Valley. In this period, it was recorded that these peoples who are believed to have originated from around modern-day Libya, 'spend all day marauding the land, fighting daily to fill their bellies, they came to the land of Egypt to seek sustenance for their mouths'.[8] Ramses VI saw off two attacks, before a third rampaged right through the region of Thebes, before settling. Within 100 years, these Libyan people had become fully integrated in Thebes with many, in time, becoming integrated with Egyptian society.[9]

3. INDIA

The established states of the ancient Near East were not alone in having to fight against swarms of migratory peoples. The same problem was also recorded in ancient India. As long ago as 2500 BCE, the inhabitants had developed a thriving culture that included their own written language in the Indus River valley. This language was captured in the early Vedic texts, as recorded by the new migrants to the area – the Vedic Aryans. The Vedic Aryans were probably Indo-Europeans who also invaded Anatolia (and became the Hittites), and imposed themselves on the native Hurrians (and became the Mitanni). Over several centuries they moved further south-east, invading what is modern-day Iran, and eventually India.

The Vedic Aryans came en masse to the Indian plains, perhaps around 1500 to 1200 BCE. These were not the first peoples to sweep into north India. Earlier, possibly Aryan groups crashed the Indus civilisation around 1800 and 1700 BCE destroying cities and settlements with what appears remarkable speed. The Vedic Aryans, who shared traces of an Indo-European language, made their first recorded appearance in

[7] Spalinger, A (2005) *War in Ancient Egypt* (London, Blackwell) 248–52, 258–60.

[8] Inscription from the time of Ramses VI reprinted in Wilkinson, T (2010) *The Rise and Fall of Ancient Egypt* (London, Bloomsbury) 371.

[9] Wilkinson, T (2010) *The Rise and Fall of Ancient Egypt* (London, Bloomsbury) 386–90, 398–99, 406–10.

history in 1350 BCE. At this point, a peace treaty from Boghazkoi in Western Asia had a king of the Hittites conclude an agreement with the ruler of the Mitanni kingdom. With this, the Aryan gods were invoked as witnesses. As these gods thereafter reappeared in the sacred literature of the Vedic Aryans in India, it may be that at least the ruling elite of the Mitanni kingdom were either the ancestors of the later Indo-Aryans or that this elite was a branch of the much larger Indo-Aryan community. It is also possible that Mitanni, Iranian and Indo-Aryans were branches of one Indo-European family of languages who migrated in waves in various directions from central Europe, perhaps through Iran and/or Afghanistan at the beginning of the second millennium. Whilst the ancestry of these peoples who pushed into north India may be in dispute, the causes for their invasion into the ecologically fertile areas appears relatively clear, as many hymns mention 'the great struggle for water and sun' and record prayers that the gods may grant 'undivided fallow land'.[10] The Vedic tribal social order lasted until around 700 BCE, when it gave way to larger, more stable societies of regional scope.

4. CHINA

The 'Inner-Asian frontiers of China' is a general term for the eastern part of the continental mass of Eurasia. It included three geographical regions: in the east, Manchuria; in the centre, Mongolia; and in the west, the Minusink Basin and the northern parts of the Altai Mountains. From these areas, at least since around 1000 BCE, multiple Chinese administrations had difficulties with (despised) nomadic cultures who attempted to spill over their borders. This problem first became evident with the advent of the Chou (1046–221 BCE), who, although they may have enjoyed the support of non-Chinese-speaking tribes to topple the Shang, were very clear over the following centuries that these nomadic people were quite different to the Chinese, in lacking in education and 'virtue and righteousness'. This lack allowed a lesser standard in terms of justifications for warfare, with attacks on the non-Chinese deemed acceptable, when judged in the national interest such as for an expansion of territory, despite treaties of peace. This problem was reversed (with the non-Chinese being the ones attacking) towards the end of the Chou period, with the centralisation of the *Hsiung-nu* Empire, under the leadership of one man. This empire, broadly a 'Tartar' grouping, comprised Turks, Huns and Mongols as a type of *Pax Nomadica*.[11]

Hsiung-nu armies of up to 300,000 men streamed into north China. This resulted in the Han dynasty (206 BCE–220 CE) launching a series of raids into the territories of the nomads (north and west), at the same time as building a series of defensive walls (the predecessors to the 'Great Wall') down parts of their poorly defended borders.

[10] The *Rig Veda* section VI:25, VI:28 and VI:46; Kulke, H (1996) *A History of India* (London, Routledge) 18–22, 30–33, 98–99; Raychaudhuri, H (1999) *Political History of Ancient India* (Oxford, Oxford University Press) 15–20, 25–28.

[11] Hsu, I (1960) *China's Entry into the Family of Nations* (Boston, Harvard University Press) 7–10. Di Cosmo, N (2002) *Ancient China and its Enemies: The Rise of Nomadic Power in East Asian History* (Cambridge, Cambridge University Press) 13, 45, 57–60, 98–100, 102, 104–108, 110–15, 119–21, 194–95; Grousset, R (2010) *The Empire of the Steppes: A History of Central Asia* (New Jersey, Rutgers) 19–20.

The walls and the reprisals could not stop the *Hsiung-nu* and a treaty had to be struck with them in 198 BCE. The essence of this treaty was that the Han had to provide tribute (annual payments of silk, wine and grain) to the *Hsing-nu* and a marriage alliance was accepted with the emperor's daughter being advanced as the prize. A further treaty in 162 BCE divided their shared world into two great cultural zones – the realm of the nomads and that of the Chinese – each forming its own empire. It also entailed recognition of each other's dominion of lesser states within their respective spheres. Underlying this treaty was the obligation of continued (and expanded) tribute to the *Hsing-nu*, along with their right to establish frontier markets and further high-level marriage alliances.[12]

The *Hsing-nu* also expanded westward towards India around 170 BCE. This push seems to have acted in the same way as dominoes, with the *Hsing-nu* advance forcing other non-aligned nomadic tribes in front of them to push westward. In the first instance, the *Hsing-nu* fought then pushed the *Yue-chi* out of their way, before they hit upon a second nomadic tribe, the *Sai-Wang* or *Shakas* (a Chinese word, which has the same meaning as king, master or lord) who in turn, bounced to the west into India in a mass migration of perhaps one million people, with a couple of hundred thousand warriors at the forefront. Together with the Scythians (a catch-all phrase for inhabitants of eastern parts of the Northern European Plain, an Indo-European family, who probably originated from north Iran), the *Shakas* became a major threat to the Indo-Greek provinces of Bactria (now part of modern Afghanistan) and Parthia (roughly north-east of modern Iran) around 140 to 120 BCE. Two Parthian rulers Phraates II (171–128 BCE), and Artebanus II, (r 128–124 BCE) lost their lives fighting against these people. Whilst Bactria was consumed, the *Shakas*, whilst appearing to have recognised Parthian suzerainty after Mithridates II (r 123–88 BCE), defeated them and settled down in what is now southern Afghanistan, before they too dissolved around the beginning of the Common Era, before reforming into another nomadic conglomeration.[13]

The relationship between the *Hsing-nu* and the Han dynasty held until the Emperor Wu (156–87 BCE) had enough forces to end the policy of appeasement and stop paying tribute and then quickly advanced into the *Hsing-nu* territories, pushing them deep into upper Mongolia in 133 BCE. He then split the *Hsing-nu* into two parts, placing military colonies between them and then focused on eradicating one part of the nomadic regime which was distracted by dynastic disputes. The nomadic survivors of this war were then relegated to a subservient position of being an outer vassal that had to provide tribute to the Han. Any further attempts at revolt were quickly crushed, with Chinese armies of up to 60,000 strong being sent directly into the territories of the nomads, to both punish (destroying a capital) and take tribute (3,000 horses) when the offence (killing of an ambassador) occurred. At other times of revolt, the imperial

[12] Di Cosmo, N (2002) *Ancient China and its Enemies: The Rise of Nomadic Power in East Asian History* (Cambridge, Cambridge University Press) 161–63, 194–95, 200–201; Graff, D (2002) *Medieval Chinese Warfare* (London, Routledge) 28; Hucker, C (1994) *China's Imperial Past* (California, Stanford University Press) 44–45; Lewis, M (2007) *The Early Chinese Empires: Qin and Han* (Massachusetts, Harvard University Press) 58–59; Grousset, R (2010) *The Empire of the Steppes: A History of Central Asia*. (New Jersey, Rutgers) 27–28.

[13] Smith, V (1962) *The Early History of India* (Oxford, Oxford University Press) 239–41, 263–64; Raychaudhuri, H (1999) *Political History of Ancient India* (Oxford, Oxford University Press) 381–86.

Chinese authorities utilised their preferred method of control outside the borders, using (and rewarding) one nomadic group to attack another.[14]

The subservient position of the nomadic tribes changed when the Han state collapsed and the non-Chinese (by this time, the *Hsiung-nu* had been supplanted around 150 CE by the *Hsien-pi*, a group who appear to have originated on the Mongol–Manchurian borders) suddenly found themselves in the majority of the armed forces within the borders of China. The North of China was consumed in wars between the 16 Chinese successor regions, and non-Chinese migrants (a combination of the *Hsiung-nu* and the *Hsien-pi*) moved between them all, making alliances and enemies as required. In this climate, Liu Tsúng (r 310–318), China's equivalent of Attila, arose raiding into central China, capturing the imperial palace at Loyang, burning it to the ground and taking the emperor prisoner. Soon after, the Chin imperial family fled south (effectively abandoning the North, as happened with Rome in the West), sheltered by the line of the Yangtze River, with the new basis of power being in Nanking (similar to Constantinople with the Roman Empire).[15]

In the South, rather than attempt to conquer new territory in the chaos that unfolded, the *Hsiung-nu* sought out new patrons among the warlords, including the Cao-Wei, one of the States in the Three Kingdoms period (220–265 CE), and then the Jin dynasties (265–420 CE). This worked in two ways. First, many of the *Hsiung-nu* were allowed to settle within the borders of China in exchange for giving military service. Second, money and/or trading rights were given to those outside the border in exchange for their military service. This situation continued until the Jin dynasty was destroyed, and with it, any centralised authority. This lead to a series of quick-moving, non-Chinese, nomadic rooted, uncoordinated governments in a period of civil war and political chaos. This chaos only ended when the Northern and Southern parts of China, (420–589) and then the Sui Dynasty (589–618) solidified and the loosely united confederation of northern nomads could again be split, and much of the country reclaimed. These splits were often timed to coincide with dynastic disputes within the groupings. This pattern was also repeated with the Turkic groups which had come to dominate half of Asia from Manchuria to Khurasan. When they were split and turned on each other, new alliances with China were quickly renegotiated and tribute either continued or stopped, and offers of peace were accepted or declined. More often than not, the giving of Chinese tribute was linked to the beneficiary attacking another nomadic group, or the Chinese doing the work themselves, without scruple. Thus, as one Chinese court responded to a request for a peace treaty: 'Amity, what do they know of amity? The barbarous savages! Give them war as the portion due to our natural enemies.'[16]

[14] Di Cosmo, N (2002) *Ancient China and its Enemies: The Rise of Nomadic Power in East Asian History* (Cambridge, Cambridge University Press) 210–15, 220–29, 252; Lewis, M (2007) *The Early Chinese Empires: Qin and Han* (Massachusetts, Harvard University Press) 144–50; Grousset, R (2010) *The Empire of the Steppes: A History of Central Asia* (New Jersey, Rutgers) 31–32, 36, 44, 48. For the idealised theories, see Hsu, I (1960) *China's Entry into the Family of Nations* (Boston, Harvard University Press) 9.

[15] Grousset, R (2010) *The Empire of the Steppes: A History of Central Asia* (New Jersey, Rutgers) 38–39, 55, 57, 58.

[16] This is noted in Bandyopadhyay, P (1982) *International Law and Custom in Ancient India* (Delhi, Goyal Printers) 31; Lewis, M (2009) *China Between Empires: The Northern and Southern Dynasties* (Massachusetts, Harvard University Press) 31–34, 146–49; Graff, D (2002) *Medieval Chinese Warfare* (London, Routledge) 40–41, 58–60, 65–68, 73, 120, 143; Grousset, R (2010) *The Empire of the Steppes: A History of Central Asia* (New Jersey, Rutgers) 86–93.

The Northern Nomads (by the seventh century, the Eastern Turks/Toba, a half-Sinicised Turko–Mongol horde) played the same game, supporting various regimes in North and South, in order to keep China weak and divided. When it became apparent that one side was gaining the upper hand, such as with the ascendency of the Tang, they would swap support to give aid to their opponents. When the tables turned, such as when the Turkic Empire was in a state of palace revolutions, family rifts and civil war in the sixth and seventh centuries, the Tang forces advanced en masse, using a combination of brute force and treaties which placed the various nomadic groups into subservient positions. This process made them masters over the Mongolian steppe, thus becoming Lords of Central Asia. Many of the defeated were subsequently incorporated into the Chinese forces and developed loyalties to their various commanders. This became a problem with the rebellion of An Lushan (703–757) which erupted in 755, where some 150,000 men (who were by now a mixture of Chinese and East Turks) rebelled. The Tang forces joined with the dominant forces on the Mongolian steppe during the period (now the Turkic *Uigur* peoples) and defeated the uprising over the following half decade. As a reward, the emperor bestowed upon them acknowledgements, titles and the promise of 20,000 pieces of silk per year. A series of diplomatic marriages between the Chinese and non-Chinese sealed the bargain. This mutually supportive relationship worked until the Tang dynasty collapsed in 907, at which point, whilst the Chinese were trying to reorganise themselves, the over-Sinicised *Uigurs* were overthrown by another Mongolian group, the *Khitan*, who quickly went on to create their own Liao Dynasty (916–1125), which dominated a vast area of north China and treated the Chinese as a separate and inferior class. The Sung dynasty responded with an equally defiant attitude of elitism and snobbery towards the migrant peoples who tried to get close.[17]

5. ROME

Whilst the pre-Archaic period (pre 900 BCE) of ancient Greece most probably had a lot to do with the impacts and settlements of migratory peoples, the world of classical Greece did not. These Greeks did not leave a history of having to deal with the invasions of migratory peoples. This may have been because of geographical distance and the fact that the Persians, under the leadership of Darius, had launched expeditions around the years 514 to 512 BCE, against the only such peoples known at that time around Europe, the *Scythians*. These actions, against peoples who Herodotus (484–425) portrayed as vicious nomadic head-hunters, may have pushed the *Scythians* deeper into the Ukraine. Or, the *Scythians* may have been displaying the skills that made such migratory peoples so dangerous – their ability to avoid confrontation and move, leaving nothing to defend, whilst drawing their pursuers into dangerous and unknown

[17] Hsu, I (1960) *China's Entry into the Family of Nations* (Boston, Harvard University Press) 9–12; Graff, D (2002) *Medieval Chinese Warfare* (London, Routledge) 173–78, 187–95, 218–23; Grousset, R (2010) *The Empire of the Steppes: A History of Central Asia* (New Jersey, Rutgers) 60–62, 65, 109–12, 120–21, 127–33; Legge, J (1893) *Chinese Classics*, Vol III (NYC, MacMillan) 165.

locations. The *Scythians* then developed in isolation of the West, but in contact with similar peoples such as the *Sarmatians* (people who originated from north of the Danube, probably around modern-day Iran), who together occupied the western part of the Eurasian steppe. The eastern part seems to have been under the sway of Turko-Mongol peoples. Of these, the dominant nation in antiquity was the Chinese who were battling as the *Hsiung-nu* and who western nations came to battle as the Huns.[18]

The *Hsiung-nu*/Huns were not the migratory peoples that first came into contact with the civilisations of the West. The people in question were the Celts, and in particular, a sub-group known as the Gauls – a people living in the region that roughly corresponds with what is now France, Belgium, Switzerland and Northern Italy, as well as parts of the Netherlands and Germany on the left bank of the Rhine. Their first recorded interaction with Rome occurred in the beginning of the fourth century BCE. In the words of Polybius (200–118 BCE) these peoples possessed 'covetous eyes on the beautiful country'[19] of Italy. The covetous intentions became clear in the early parts of the fourth century BCE when an alleged 30,000 Gallic warriors sprung forth and succeeded in defeating the 15,000 Etruscans who tried to defend the area, subduing large amounts of Northern Italy. The testament of the ancient Etruscan city laid bare at Marzabotto is notable in this regard. Here, a thick layer of ashes covers the foundations of public buildings and private houses, whilst skeletons are scattered over the soil and piled up in the wells, and the ground is thick with a medley of Gallic and Etruscan weapons. Whilst the Etruscans of the Po were destroyed (and this civilization slowly disappeared) the Romans were luckier. Thus, although Rome was sacked in 390 BCE, they were able to buy off the Gauls, despite the weight of the cry *vae victis* ('woe to the vanquished').[20]

Although Rome survived the ordeal, and went on to renew the Latin League for the purpose of defence against the nomadic peoples of the North, the threat did not materialise. Despite this failure of further conflict to eventuate, the Romans were haunted by the fear of aggressive barbarian neighbours who wanted their land and resources. Three hundred years later, the manifestation of this concern was most obvious with the *Cimbri* and *Teutones*, two German tribes that had started a mass movement from their homes, somewhere in the Jutland area, and advanced southward, bringing with them their entire households and possessions. Before advancing into Roman territory, the tribes requested of the Senate in 109 BCE that they be allowed to settle on the Roman frontiers. The Senate declined this request, deeming it too dangerous to accept. Unwilling to accept this decision, warfare broke out. The first clash with the Roman forces in 105 BCE saw the defeat of a Roman army of 80,000 men – in one day. Some experts have suggested that the death rate from this battle made it the fourth largest casualty rate in history, before the twentieth century. Plutarch (46–120 CE) suggested that this invasion occurred because 'they were seeking land to support their vast hordes and cities in which to settle and live, just as they had heard the Gauls

[18] Herodotus, *The Histories* trans de Selincourt, A (London, Penguin) IV:64–65; Grousset, R (2010) *The Empire of the Steppes: A History of Central Asia* (New Jersey, Rutgers) 9, 18, 22.

[19] Polybius, *The Histories* trans Waterfield, R (2010) (Oxford, Oxford University Press) II:xvii.

[20] Grant, R (2005) *Battle* (London, Dorling Kindersley) 36.

did, when they seized the best lands from the Eruscans'.[21] The second clash occurred in 102 BCE, in which some 35,000 Romans fought up to 150,000 *Teutones* and *Ambrones* at Aquae Sextae. Of this conflict, a casualty rate of over 100,000 was recorded – as the German women killed themselves and their children after the defeat of their men, so as to avoid slavery.[22]

In the early centuries following the collapse of the Republic, the threat of Rome being invaded by 'barbarians' was small. Rather, the opposite was the case, with both Caesar and Augustus pushing the Roman boundaries in Europe. These boundaries were reinforced by a policy of the settlement of 'friendly' or 'loyal' barbarian tribes on the Roman side of the frontier in exchange for border military service to Rome. This giving of land and the economic and social benefits of friendship in exchange for military service was an age-old Roman approach. Now, it was being given to military forces that were not Roman, yet wanted the same benefits. The giving of the right to settle within the borders to some peoples, was often supplemented by reprisals into territory (and possible occupation) against other groups which troubled Rome outside of the borders. At the same time, tribute could also be paid to loyal tribes outside of the border.

This situation turned into a problem at the end of the first century CE, when a number of tribes outside the northern borders, including the Germanic *Quadi*, pressed for their economic admission (but not loss of political sovereignty) into the Roman Empire. This would have provided them with economic opportunities consistent with what the Romans possessed. Alternatively, they wanted a large subsidy. The simple solution for Rome would have been to annex the region and grant Roman citizenship to everyone. However, these peoples wished to remain independent, and did not want to be annexed. Marcus Aurelius (121–180) did not want to annex any more territory, or permit the entry of tribes who only wanted the economic benefits, without the political compromises required. He also objected to the idea of paying tribute as a price of peace. The precedent value in both cases was too expensive. The tribes responded by attacking the Roman forces in the area in 170, specifically citing the Roman refusal to grant them a subsidy. Aurelius defeated these peoples, and enforced a treaty upon them. This required them to hand over hostages and precious booty, to trade under the auspices of Roman control, and to stay away from a five-mile zone along the River Danube.[23]

The peace which ended the First Germanic War in 175 was submerged beneath the Second Germanic War, which raged from 177 to 180. This conflict occurred as tribes in Pannonia, the Lower Danube and Upper Rhine, also demanded the payment of gold as the price of peace. Although Aurelius defeated these tribes, it was a near run victory. He had to face down rebellions along almost the entire length of Rome's European frontiers, from which he had some very lucky escapes and the actual invasion of north

[21] Plutarch, 'Life of Marius' in *Roman Lives* trans Waterfield, R (2009) (Oxford, Oxford University Press) 11.2–6.

[22] McLynn, F (2010) *Marcus Aurelius* (London, Vintage) 308–309; Gabriel, R (2005) *Empires at War*, Vol II (London, Greenwood) 500–514.

[23] Ferris, I (2009) *Hate and War: The Column of Marcus Aurelius* (Gloustershire, Mill) 22–26.

Italy was not fully repelled until the end of 179. Following through, hostile kings were replaced with pliant ones, enemy territories were occupied, trading rights were given (or removed) and some groups were allowed to move to new territories.[24]

The son of Aurelius, Commodus (161–192) was later presented with the same demands from the same tribes. Namely:

> It would be best for you to make peace and obtain the advantages accruing from harmony, and to come to a settlement with us . . . gifts of . . . gold and silver guarantee friendship. If we are denied this, we will . . . fight with all our might.[25]

Unlike his father, Commodus accepted the requests of payment of tribute in exchange for peace. Yet within two decades the tribes pressing against the northern borders were again threatening Rome. Alexander Severus (208–235) had to war in Gaul against an invasion of tribes from the area now recognised as Germany, before his successor, Gordian (159–238), induced the invaders to withdraw in exchange for the grant of an annual payment. When the military was strong, this policy of offering money in exchange for peace stopped, and warfare followed as Philip the Arab (204–249) discovered in the year 245, when a number of German tribes including the Goths (an east Germanic tribe of Scandinavian origin, from whom the *Visigoths* and *Ostrogoths* – as the two main branches of the Goths – would emerge) moved through Dacia. Perhaps pushed by other migratory groups, and/or driven by the promise of better living conditions and/or economic benefits, they crossed the Danube and threatened the Balkans. Peace was only brought back when Decius (201–251) brought them to heel, in a battle that included his own death, but brought about a treaty which promised tribute if the Goths stayed on their side of the border. Two years later in 253, due to non-payment of tribute, the Goths reinvaded, attacking Cappadocia, Pessinus and Ephesus before completely overrunning Greece. These forces did not leave the territories until Gallus (206–253) made peace with them. The cost of their departure was an annual subsidy, and in addition they were permitted to take all the movable property (including slaves) they had captured with them.[26]

No sooner had the Goths been dealt with than other Germanic tribes including the *Alamanni* (a loosely connected group of tribes originating from around the upper Rhine) and *Juthungi* (originating roughly from modern-day Bavia) crossed the Rhine in 258. These tribes rampaged through Gaul and Spain and even crossed the borders into north Italy, before being defeated by the forces of Gallienus (218–268). However, Gallienus lost control over the provinces of Germania, Britain, Spain and a large part of Gaul as civil disturbances coincided with a lack of clear authority, with some regions, like Gaul (including Britain and the Iberian Peninsula), remaining independent until 274. Britain went from revolts to substantial invasions from Scotland around 280 CE,

[24] McLynn, F (2010) *Marcus Aurelius* (London, Vantage) 324–35; Heather, P (2009) *Empires and Barbarians: Migration, Development and the Birth of Europe* (London, Pan) 96–100.

[25] Negotiations with the Juthungians as reprinted in Lewis, N (ed) *Roman Civilisation: Selected Readings*, Vol II (NYC, Columbia University Press) 435–36.

[26] Jordanes, *The Origins and Deeds of the Goths* trans Miero, C (1910 edn, 2009 reprint) (London, Theophania) XVII and XIX; Dio Cassius, *Roman History* trans Cary, E (Boston, Loeb) LXXI:iii and LXXVII:xiv; Cook, S (ed) (1965) *The Cambridge Ancient History: The Imperial Crisis and Recovery*, Vol XII (Cambridge, Cambridge University Press) 84–86, 141–50; Cook, S (ed) (1964) *The Cambridge Ancient History: The Hellenistic Monarchies and the Rise of Rome*, Vol VII (Cambridge, Cambridge University Press) 66–71, 101.

leading to periods of retreat, rebuilding and pushing back against the people of the North for the following century.[27]

Claudius Gothicus (213–270) went back to the battlefield, defeating a large Gothic army, before driving their people back across the Danube River. He also drove back the *Alamanni*, and reconquered the parts of Gaul that had claimed independence. Aurelian (214–275) followed through expelling the Vandals (a tribe originally from the area identified as modern-day east Germany), *Juthungi* and *Sarmatians* from Roman territory, before advancing into the Balkans, beyond the Danube. He decided to abandon the province of Dacia due to it being too difficult and too expensive to defend. For his work, Aurelian was given the title by the Senate of *Restitutor Orbis* ('restorer of the world'). Probus (232–282) would follow through, strengthening the frontiers in some areas, before withdrawing to the lines of the Rhine and Danube rivers as the outermost points of the Roman Empire. This withdrawal was buttressed with the provision of 16,000 recruits made up of the bravest and most robust of the German youth to serve Rome. As part of the peace-deal with the Germanic tribes, these men were dispersed throughout the empire.[28]

After a peace lasting five decades, the Goths, *Alamanni* and Franks (a confederation of Germanic tribes first attested in the third century as populating a broad strip of land on the right bank of the Lower and Middle parts of the Rhine River) crossed the Danube in 322. The Emperor Constantine I (250–306) fought back and 'reduced them all to obedience, and brought them from their savage state to one of gentleness'. This involved pushing back those he felt 'incapable of the settled order of civilized life'.[29] He battled many, such as the *Scythians* after he refused to pay any tribute as he believed the annual giving of such money made the Romans 'servants to barbarians . . . this was an unbearable indignity'.[30] He also made peace with, and incorporated groups who were capable of settling within the empire, making them liable to serve as auxiliaries, and promoting economic benefits for those who settled. The same policy was followed in Britain, where groups of Picts and Scots were allowed to settle on the Roman side of Hadrian's Wall. This was not an outright rejection of the principle of tribute – but rather one which had to be strictly controlled by Rome, where it would be used as a strategic tool when in the interests of Rome.[31]

Peace was short lived. Invasions by the *Sarmatians*, *Alani*, *Quadi*, Franks and Picts occurred throughout the empire. In 355 the Franks took Cologne and 45 other towns as the valley of the Rhine was lost to the Romans. In Britain, a full-scale invasion appears to have taken place, in which the Picts, Scots, Saxons and Franks acted in

[27] Collingwood, R (1958) *Roman Britain and the English Settlements* (Oxford, Oxford University Press) 155–59, 274–75.

[28] Cook, S (ed) (1965) *The Cambridge Ancient History: The Imperial Crisis and Recovery*, Vol XII (Cambridge, Cambridge University Press) 150–60, 311–15. Elton, H (1997) *Warfare in Roman Europe* (Oxford, Oxford University Press) 48–56.

[29] Eusebius, *The Life of the Blessed Emperor Constantine*, Vol 8 trans anon (2009 reprint of 1854 edn) (London, Bagster, Christian Roman Empire Series) I:25.

[30] Eusebius, *The Life of the Blessed Emperor Constantine* trans anon (2009 reprint of 1854 edn) (London, Bagster, Christian Roman Empire Series) III:5, 6; Stephenson, P (2009) *Constantine* (London, Quercus) 225–28.

[31] Collingwood, R (1958) *Roman Britain and the English Settlements* (Oxford, Oxford University Press) 282–83.

conjunction, attacking Britain on three sides at exactly the same time and swamping much of the entire country. This overall situation was only reversed when the future emperor Julian (d 363) met the primary barbarian army in 357 at the battle of Strasbourg. Julian, at the head of 13,000 men evicted the *Alamnni* forces of 35,000 men, leaving 6,000 dead on the battlefield. Afterwards, he imposed a number of treaties on the different groups. All the treaties differed in detail, but they had in common demands for foodstuffs, for raw materials such as wood for construction purposes, for wagons, and for physical labour to carry out rebuilding projects such as the restoration of the Roman defensive line of fortifications along the Rhine. Within this line, he allowed some groups to settle if they provided military service and acquiesced to Roman demands. Outside of the border, tribute was used to prop up the preferred loyal groupings where necessary. This meant that the loyal barbarians on the outside of the line had a direct interest, with their deliveries of Roman gold and commodities, in keeping the peace.[32]

Within 10 years, the Rhine and the Danube were crossed by the hostile forces of, inter alia, the *Alamanni*, *Quadi* and *Sarmatians*, and there was another general barbarian uprising in Britain. The reason recorded for this invasion was a reduction in the quantity and quality of tribute given by the Romans to these peoples, contrary to expectations of either custom or treaty. Valentinian (321–375) fought back, with combinations of set-piece battles, reprisals into enemy territory (and possible occupation) and the re-instigation of tribute to friendly barbarian groups. In addition, some groups were invited to live within the Roman borders, as long as they provide fresh recruits for the Roman army. Despite stability being reached in this instance, the overall situation was becoming considerably unstable. The average diplomatic settlement was only lasting about 20 to 25 years and uprisings were occurring in multiple locations. Established groups wanted more and new groups began to appear outside the line, requesting the same benefits and/or taking war to the Roman clients with the hope of replacing them and taking their rewards.[33]

Valens attempted a similar move to Valentinian in 376, allowing hundreds of thousands of Goths (who were being displaced by the Huns) to enter into the Roman borders within Illyria. This was to be in exchange for them submitting to Roman laws, providing some 10,000 auxiliaries per year to the Roman forces, and paying some form of tribute. However, before the people could be settled and the deal delivered, disaster struck. The exact cause of the revolt of 377 is unclear, but may have had to with over-crowded conditions due to much greater numbers and types (the Goths were

[32] Heather, P (2009) *Empires and Barbarians: Migration, Development and the Birth of Europe* (London, Pan) 40–41, 73–76, 84–85; Gibbon, E *The Decline and Fall of the Roman Empire* ed Bury, J (1929 edn) Vol II (London, Methuen) 230–33, 278–80, 298–99; Gwatkin, H (ed) (1957) *The Cambridge Medieval History. The Christian Roman Empire*, Vol 1 (Cambridge, Cambridge University Press) 68–72, 209; Collingwood, R (1958) *Roman Britain and the English Settlements* (Oxford, Oxford University Press) 283–86; Grant, R (2005) *Battle* (London, Dorling Kindersley) 50.

[33] Gwatkin, H (ed) (1957) *The Cambridge Medieval History. The Christian Roman Empire*, Vol 1 (Cambridge, Cambridge University Press) 229–30; Collingwood, R (1958) *Roman Britain and the English Settlements* (Oxford, Oxford University Press) 287–89; Gibbon, E *The Decline and Fall of the Roman Empire* ed Bury, J (1929 edn) Vol III (London, Methuen) 33–34; Heather, P (2009) *Empires and Barbarians: Migration, Development and the Birth of Europe* (London, Pan) 86–87.

accompanied by Huns and *Alani* (Alans) – a group of Sarmatian tribes who spoke an eastern Iranian language) and a reaction against their loss of political and national autonomy within the borders of Rome. When Valens attempted to bring this matter under control in 378 with 60,000 men at the Battle of Adrianople, he failed. He paid for his failure with his life along with two thirds of the army of the eastern half of the Roman Empire (at least 20,000 men) which was cut to pieces by a Gothic army which was estimated to be between 100,000 and 200,000 men in size.[34]

This was only the thin end of the wedge. For the next 80 years, the western side of the Roman Empire would disintegrate, with an estimated 7 million people losing their lives, as population, culture and ecological resources all suffered with the weight of the barbarian takeover. The root problem was that the Goths no longer considered themselves subservient to the Romans. Moreover, they were already within the Roman borders, and the Roman army which should have defeated them was destroyed. As such, offers of the right to settle within the borders and subservice to the laws of Rome, in exchange for the provision of auxiliaries were dismissed out of hand. This was not to suggest that the Goths sought to destroy Roman civilisation, but rather, to control it to ensure that their people could reap its benefits.[35]

Peace could only now be achieved, as by Theodosious (347–395) in 382, by the granting of generous terms. Thus, in exchange for the new occupiers serving the armies of Rome, Theodosius agreed to grant them tax-free land (the Visigoths could settle along the southern Danube frontier in the province of Thrace, whilst the Ostrogoths were settled in Phrygia and Lydia), an annual sum of money, and the right for the Goths to fight as a national unit under their own leaders.[36]

Outside of the borders, the situation changed again. The change now was that the Goths became unified under one leader – not multiple leaders, as in the past. This leader was Alaric (370–410), who had earlier seen combat – fighting for Rome. When the new emperor, Honorius (384–423) adopted a different approach to Theodosius and opted for non-payment of tribute to the favoured allies, coupled with a diminished military status for the Goths, the response was war. The Goths, Vandals and associated tribes rampaged through Greece before invading Italy in 402. Although initially defeated by Roman forces, Alaric regrouped his forces and added in *Ostrogoths*, *Alani* and *Quadi* to a total of hundreds of thousands of men, before reinvading Italy in 406

[34] Ammianus Marcellinus, *History* trans Rolfe, J Vol III (Cambridge, Harvard University Press) 401 (section 31.4); Jordanes, *The Origins and Deeds of the Goths* trans Miero, C (1910 edn, 2009 reprint) (London, Theophania) xxv; Isidore of Seville, *History of the Kings of the Goths* reprinted in trans Wolf, K *Conquerors and Chroniclers of Early Medieval Spain* (1999) (Liverpool, Liverpool University Press) 85; Gwatkin, H (ed) (1957) *The Cambridge Medieval History. The Christian Roman Empire*, Vol 1 (Cambridge, Cambridge University Press) 213; Barbero, A (2005) *The Day of the Barbarians* (London, Atlantic) 68–69, 99.

[35] Orosius, *History Against the Pagans* trans Fear, A (1992) (Liverpool, Liverpool University Press) VII:43; Isidore of Seville, *History of the Kings of the Goths* reprinted in Wolf, K trans *Conquerors and Chroniclers of Early Medieval Spain* (1999) (Liverpool, Liverpool University Press) 86; Wallace-Hadrill, J (1962) *The Barbarian West: The Early Middle Ages AD 400–1000* (NYC, Harper) 24, 34; Barbero, A (2005) *The Day of the Barbarians* (London, Atlantic) 17–35; Grant, R (2005) *Battle* (London, Dorling Kindersley) 51; White, R (2011) *Atrocitology* (NYC, Norton) 72–73.

[36] Zosimus, *New History* trans Ridley, R (1982) (Canberra, Australian Association for Byzantine Studies) section 4.56; Jordanes, *The Origins and Deeds of the Goths* trans Miero, C (1910 edn, 2009 reprint) (London, Theophania) XXVII.

and being temporarily forced out of Italy. They then regrouped, snowballed, and with a population of perhaps one million people, rolled into Gaul.[37]

Determined rebellion against Roman rule in Britain found Emperor Honorius (384–423) telling those requesting help to fend for themselves, as he had no help to give. This the government of Roman Britain attempted to do, when facing repeated waves of Picts, Scots and Irish devastating the lands and resources. Their solution, which may have been supported by the Franks who were seeking a way to funnel warlike and migratory peoples away from Gaul, was found in calling in outside assistance by inviting former Roman auxiliaries to help in the defence of the country. The Saxons, Angles and Jutes (the last being Scandinavian, not Germanic, in origin) responded to this call. Whilst initially successful, this approach became disastrous when the visitors refused to leave due to their recognition of, inter alia, 'the fertility of the country'.[38] It fell to Ambrosius (fifth century) and later the legendary Arthur (late fifth century), to lead the British on the one side (when they were not fighting each other), against Anglo-Saxons on the other, in battles such as that at Mount Badon and Deorham (in 577). At the latter, in the Cotswold Hills outside the city of Bath, three kings died fighting in the defence for Romano–British culture against the encroachment of Germanic Saxon invaders. Although the British could hold back the water for a while, they could not turn the tide and within centuries, the new migrants and the established local populations had blended.[39]

Honorius was correct that Rome could not help Britain as the Romans had their own problems to deal with. When Alaric returned to Italy in 408, Rome found the price of peace to be 4,000 pounds of gold, and the promise of Alaric being master-general of all the Roman armies throughout Illyricum. In exchange, it was expected that the Huns would fight at the direction of Rome. When Alaric returned the following year, demanding to be made commander of all the Roman armies in the west, and to be granted an allowance for his people to settle within the territory of Italy, negotiations collapsed. The price of this failure was the sack of Rome. Although Alaric's men did occupy Rome, Alaric died soon after, thus allowing its reconquest by Roman forces. The reconquest was also made possible by the repatriation of some of the property taken in the sack, including the sister of Honorius, and by subsequent treaty. The treaty of 418 which Honorius oversaw was fundamentally different to all the earlier precedents. The debate was now about how much territory they were going to get and on what terms. It was no longer about whether or not their existence was going to be tolerated. The conclusion was that both the Visigoths and Vandals were given land within the Empire, in exchange for continued military service. The Visigoths were

[37] Jordanes, *The Origins and Deeds of the Goths* trans Miero, C (1910 edn, 2009 reprint) (London, Theophania) XXIX; Gat, A (2008) *War in Human Civilisation* (Oxford, Oxford University Press) 365–67.

[38] Bede, *The Ecclesiastical History of the English Nation*, trans Jane, L (1910 edn) (London, Dent) I.15 Also sections I;12, I.14, I.16 Gildas, *On the Ruin of Britain* trans Winterbottom, M (1978) (London, Phillimore) 19.1–4; Collingwood, R (1958) *Roman Britain and the English Settlements* (Oxford, Oxford University Press) 314–17; Morris, J (2004) *The Age of Arthur: A History of the British Isles* (London, Phoenix) 64–67, 158–59; Stenton, F (1985) *Anglo-Saxon England* (Oxford, Clarendon Press) 12–14.

[39] Bede, *The Ecclesiastical History of the English Nation* trans Jane, L (1910 edn) (London, Dent) I:12, I:16 and I:20; Zosimus, *New History* trans Ridley, R (1982) (Canberra, Australian Association for Byzantine Studies) section 6.10; Heather, P (2009) *Empires and Barbarians: Migration, Development and the Birth of Europe* (London, Pan) 270–80, 290–92; Stenton, F (1985) *Anglo-Saxon England* (Oxford, Clarendon Press) 27–31.

granted two thirds of Gaul (the Franks held north-east Gaul already), and the Vandals were awarded Spain. They were not, however, given payments of gold or appointments to high office within the political structure of the Roman state, as Alaric had earlier demanded.[40]

Attila (d 453) and his Huns were originally a coalition of different groups of nomadic pastoralists from the Great Eurasian Steppe. This vast landscape runs for thousands of miles from the fringes of Europe to the western borders of China. Attila united the clans of the Huns under his undisputed command by a combination of dynastic legitimacy, or at least, a respected lineage, insofar as the Huns were not especially wedded to dynastic principle; the equitable sharing out of the revenues of loot and tribute; and charismatic leadership. The Huns were joined by the Iranian-speaking *Alani* and Germanic-speaking *Sciri*, and at least three clusters of Germanic-speaking Goths. With these hordes behind him, Attila began to negotiate with Rome. His initial relationship was built around a treaty of peace in 435 which cost Rome 350 pounds of gold per year and open access for all Hun traders to Roman markets. In return, it was expected that the Huns would respond to the orders of Rome, as they duly did, progressing into Burgundia, and reputedly killing 20,000 difficult-to-govern Burgundians, under the orders of Valentinian III (419–455).[41]

In 440 Attila declared war on his paymaster and crossed the Danube. He did this under a belief that Rome was harbouring Hun fugitives and the need to find a priest who Attila suspected had fled to the west with his secrets and some of his favourite treasures. In between destroying two opposing field armies, he took Naissus, plundered Philippopolis and ravaged Thrace as far as Acadiopolis, which he sacked. At the peace of 448, the western side of the empire had to cede to Attila a belt south of the Danube, extending in length from modern Belgrade to modern Svishtov. This was supplemented with the handing over of 6,000 pounds of gold as a one-off payment, and increasing the yearly tribute to 2,100 pounds of gold per year. The Romans also agreed that in the future no Hun fugitives would be given refuge in their empire.[42]

Attila could not settle, and in 447 he attacked the eastern side of the empire. He attempted to besiege Constantinople after the Emperor of the East, Marcian (392–457) repudiated payments of tribute. In the year 450, when Attila's attacks in the east failed, Attila turned his forces to the west. The primary reason this time was over Honoria, the sister of Emperor Valentinian III, who asked to be rescued by Attila (from her marriage which her brother had organised to keep her from trying to claim the throne) and promised she would marry him (Attilla) as a reward. Attila wanted this and half of the Roman Empire as the accompanying dowry. When Valentinian

[40] Jordanes, *The Origins and Deeds of the Goths* trans Miero, C (1910 edn, 2009 reprint) (London, Theophania) XXX and XXXII; Isidore of Seville, *History of the Kings of the Goths* reprinted in Wolf, K trans (1999) *Conquerors and Chroniclers of Early Medieval Spain* (Liverpool, Liverpool University Press) 87; Gibbon, E *The Decline and Fall of the Roman Empire* ed Bury, J (1929 edn) Vol III (London, Methuen) 290–303, 340–50, 352.

[41] Davies, N (2011) *Vanished Kingdoms: The History of Half Forgotten Europe* (London, Penguin) 93–94.

[42] Grousset, R (2010) *The Empire of the Steppes: A History of Central Asia* (New Jersey, Rutgers) 74–76; Jordanes, *The Origins and Deeds of the Goths* trans, Miero, C (1910 edn, 2009 reprint) (London, Theophania) XXXV and XXXIX; Luttwak, E (2009) *The Grand Strategy of the Byzantine Empire* (London, Harvard University Press) 44–45, 53–56; Gwatkin, H (ed) (1957) *The Cambridge Medieval History. The Christian Roman Empire*, Vol I (Cambridge, Cambridge University Press) 362–63, 412–14; Gibbon, E *The Decline and Fall of the Roman Empire* ed Bury, J (1929 edn) Vol III (London, Methuen) 440–58.

attempted to deny the legitimacy of the marriage proposal, Attila argued that the proposal was valid and that he would come to claim what was rightfully his. In the war that followed, Attila's forces were checked at the Battle of Chalons. Had the Huns not been held to a draw at Chalons, it is likely that the remaining part of Roman civilisation in the west would have been destroyed. However, Attila was not destroyed either. Undefeated, he returned in 452 to claim his marriage to Honoria anew, invading and ravaging Italy, sacking Aquilea en route to Rome. He got no further than the River Po before disease broke out in his army and his progress south halted. This piece of luck, coupled with the fact that Attila died of natural causes the following year, saved the city of Rome from being sacked. Even better for Rome, the Empire of Attila quickly dissolved into a civil war over questions about succession. The former allies, the *Ostrogoths* and *Gepidae* (an east German Gothic group, possibly originally from south Sweden) and many others rose up and crushed the Huns in a great battle in Pannonia in 454. Within 17 years of the death of Attila, the Huns simply ceased to exist as an independent force in the trans-Danubian world.[43]

Although Rome was saved, thousands of miles away, the so-called 'White Huns', *Epthalites*, having morphed from the earlier conglomerations that had occupied Bactria and become amalgamated into Parthia, attempted a failed invasion of India in 460. As palace quarrels broke out in the Sassanid dynasty, the *Epthalites* turned and invaded Persia in 483. The following year they defeated a large Persian army. Realising that they could not conquer all of Persia, the *Epthalites* volunteered to leave Persia, if they were paid for their exit in gold. In 501 when the Romans were approached to contribute to this cost (as the *Epthalites* were a common enemy) but declined, the Persians made an alliance with the *Epthalites* and together they attacked Byzantium, making inroads in Armenia and along the Tigris. It was only in 505 that the Romans relented and paid subsidies to the Persians for the maintenance of the Persian fortifications on the Caucasus. In theory, these fortifications were meant to keep the *Epthalites* in check, although some of this money probably went directly to the *Epthalites*. Against such a formation, the *Epthalites* once more changed direction and launched another invasion of India, crossing over from Afghanistan around the year 510. These peoples, who were recorded as 'having no cities, but roam freely and live in tents'[44] were forced out of India around 530 CE by a coalition of Hindu princes. In addition, following a loss by the *Epthalites* to the Turks in Central Asia around 550, the flow of immigrants stopped, and those remaining either left (being forced back to the Kashmir) or became assimilated. Either way, by the seventh century, the Huns of India had vanished from history.[45]

[43] Man, J (2006) *Attila the Hun* (NYC, Bantam) 138–42, 147–56, 168–70, 191–93, 221, 236–37, 247–57; Grousset, R (2010) *The Empire of the Steppes: A History of Central Asia* (New Jersey, Rutgers) 73–79; Norwich, J (1988) *Byzantium: The Early Centuries* (London, Guild) 152–55; Jordanes, *The Origins and Deeds of the Goths* trans Miero, C (1910 edn, 2009 reprint) (London, Theophania) XXXVI and XLII.

[44] This quote is from Raychaudhuri, H (1999) *Political History of Ancient India* (Oxford, Oxford University Press) 522.

[45] Kulke, H (1996) *A History of India* (London, Routledge) 94–96; Smith, V (1962) *The Early History of India* (Oxford, Oxford University Press) 328, 336–41; Holland, T (2012) *In the Shadow of the Sword* (NYC, Brown) 97–101; Grousset, R (2010) *The Empire of the Steppes: A History of Central Asia* (New Jersey, Rutgers) 65–72; Grant, R (2005) *Battle* (London) 57.

In the West, although the threat of the Huns had passed, the situation was in freefall. Between the years 395 and 410, 80 regiments (close to 50 per cent of the field armies) were ground to dust. Although some of this occurred in the civil wars that flared up, more appears to have been lost with the continual heavy fighting with different invaders. This loss of manpower, coupled with a loss of control over many of the provinces, was the beginning of the end of Roman rule in the West.

Whilst Roman influence declined, the competition amongst the invaders increased. Under the leadership of Geiseric (389–477) 80,000 Vandals departed from the province of Hispania they had been granted and settled in. They left because they began to suffer strong attacks by their previous allies, the more numerous Franks and Visigoths, who had earlier been granted two thirds of Gaul, but decided they also wanted the Spanish lands held by their Christian – but Arian – neighbours. One particular bruising encounter between the Franks and the Vandals in 406 was said to have left 20,000 dead Vandals on the field. Just over 100 years later in 507 the Franks would deliver a body-blow to the Visigothic kingdom at the battle of Vouille.[46]

Before the Franks and the Visigoths came to fight, the Visigoths had made their progress into Spain, by pushing others – the Vandals – out. The Vandals took advantage of the civil disputes surrounding Rome and with the initial support of the local regional leader Bonifacius (d 432) who invited the Vandals to support him in his military adventures in North Africa, Geiseric and his people set sail in 429. When Bonifacius told Geiseric his services were not required, Geiseric rebelled and refused to return to Spain. In doing so, he quickly acquired what is modern-day Morocco and northern Algeria. He besieged, and took, the city of Hippo Regius (in which the scholar Augustine died during the siege). In 439, Carthage fell and during the next 20 years, Sicily, Sardinia, Corsica and the Balearic Islands were added to his domain. All of the property in these regions passed to the victors. The former landowners who had not been killed or exiled, were given the option of making their home elsewhere, or remaining as servants of the new rulers.[47]

In the year 442, the Emperor of the West, Valentinian III, recognised Genseric as king of the lands he had acquired, and that his kingdom was independent – rather than subservient to Roman rule. Although this should have brought stability, when Valentinian III was murdered and a power vacuum developed, Genseric and his men landed in Italy and marched on Rome. Although a primary concern was likely to have been that 'much money would come to him',[48] he preferred to base his justification on the assertion that the treaty of 442 had never been finalised, as it was promised, with the marriage of one of Valentinian's daughters (Eudocia) to one of his sons (Huneric). Like Attila before him, he believed that such a royal marriage would entitle him (or at least, his son) to a just proportion of the patrimony of the empire. With Valentian III

[46] Davies, N (2011) *Vanished Kingdoms: The History of Half Forgotten Europe* (London, Penguin) 20–24.

[47] Gwatkin, H (ed) (1957) *The Cambridge Medieval History. The Christian Roman Empire*, Vol I (Cambridge, Cambridge University Press) 307; Heather, P (2009) *Empires and Barbarians: Migration, Development and the Birth of Europe* (London, Pan) 175–79, 186.

[48] Procopius, *History of the Wars* trans Dewing, H (1914 edn) (Massachusetts, Harvard University Press) III:iii–vii.

dead and the treaty never concluded, he duly sailed to Italy, marched to Rome, and sacked the city in the year of 455, before going back to Africa.[49]

From this wreckage a succession of emperors in the West attempted to reassert authority. The deal-making of some such as Avitus (385–457), or the limited military reconquests by others, such as Majorian (420–461) who brought the Goths to heel for a short period, could not disguise the fact that the Franks, Vandals and Visigoths were the major stakeholders in what was once the Western half of the Roman Empire. The further conquests by the Visigoths in Spain and Gaul between 462 and 472 only accelerated the decline. The succession of leaders of the West, namely Olybrius (d 472), Gycerius (420–480), Nepos (430–480) and finally Romulus Augustulus (c 460–488) was punctuated by continuing threats by the Visigoths and Ostrogoths to consume Italy, demanding one third of it as the price of their peace. Before this demand could be resolved, the German chieftain Odoacer (433–493), who had gained prominence in what remained of the western Roman army, with the strong support by the Eastern Emperor Zeno, deposed Augustulus. This taking of the title by a non-Roman 'barbarian' in the year 476 is commonly seen as the end of the Western Roman Empire. This was the fall of ancient Rome, and the beginning of the Middle Ages in Western Europe. Although a momentous point in history, for Odacer, it was a tenuous one, as he too, was deposed (and killed), with the conniving support of the Byzantine Emperor Zeno. This time, the agent of change was Theodoric the Great (454–526) who was the king of the Ostrogoths. Theodoric agreed to act as Zeno requested, as Zeno was fearful that Odacer was assessing the eastern Empire. For the killing, Zeno promised Theodoric all of the Italian lands. Theodoric then destroyed the armies of his opponent, and strangled Odacer with his own hands. He then went on to rule Italy from 493 to 526.[50]

6. FURTHER MIGRATORY PEOPLES IN THE WEST TO 1000

The last substantive attempt to reclaim all of the Roman Empire from the Barbarians, in both East and West came from Justinian I (482–565). His first target was the African lands under the control of the Vandals. Within Byzantium, the third emperor before Justinian – Zeno, had agreed a peace treaty with the Vandals in 477 after his forces had failed to take back north Africa. The core of this treaty was the mutual promise, 'never in all time [to] perform any hostile act' against the other.[51] Justinian did not believe this treaty applied to him and quickly sought to reclaim the occupied lands in which he lead some 35,000 men against 50,000 Vandal warriors, in what is known as the Vandalic War of 533 to 534. The pretext for his invasion was the dynastic dispute between Hilderic (a relatively pro-Byzantine Vandal king) and his usurper, Gelimer

[49] Gibbon, E *The Decline and Fall of the Roman Empire* ed Bury, J (1929 edn) Vols III and IV (London, Methuen) Vol III, 430–33 and Vol IV, 30–31; Laing, J (2000) *Warriors of the Dark Ages* (London, Sutton) 65–66.

[50] Jordanes, *The Origins and Deeds of the Goths* trans Miero, C (1910 edn, 2009 reprint) (London, Theophania) LV, LVI, LVII. Also Maas, M (ed) (2010) *Readings in Late Antiquity: A Sourcebook* (London, Routledge) 355–56; Norwich, J (1988) *Byzantium: The Early Centuries* (London, Guild) 172–73, 178–79.

[51] Procopius, *History of the Wars,* 7 vols trans Dewing, HB (1914; reprint edn 1953–54) Vol II (Cambridge, Mass and London, Harvard University Press and Wm Heinemann) 23–73.

(r 530–534). Justinian supported Hilderic and declared war on the Vandals, ostensibly to restore Hilderic. Justinian justified this pretext by alleging the right of a free people to remove or punish a chief magistrate who had failed in the execution of his kingly duties. For Justinian, the usurpation of the Vandal throne was treason and the antithesis of suitable behaviour for a king. As discussed in chapter five[52] this was supplemented by a strong religious background and a desire for conquest which would result in restoration of the Empire to its former glory. Once the war was won, the Roman – not the Vandal – administration was reinstated. Thereafter, aside from some small rebellions, the province entered into an era of relative stability. In the meantime, having lost North Africa, rather than continue to fight it out, Gelimer surrendered to Justinian for the price of his freedom and estates in Galatia, where he lived to be an old man. Similarly, the Vandal forces were incorporated and dispersed through the Byzantine armed forces. Finally, to accompany the return, the properties, lands and customs of the original east Roman inhabitants were reset. This setting back of the clock in combination with the victory parades which he was forced to watch led Gelimer on his abdication to achieve a degree of anecdotal fame by crying out the verse from Ecclesiastes: 'Vanity of vanities; all is vanity'.[53]

Justinian also reclaimed Italy on behalf of the Eastern side of the Roman Empire. The war between the Roman forces from the Eastern part of the empire against the Goths who occupied Italy lasted for just under 20 years, from 535 to 554. The war, like the war which reclaimed North Africa from the Vandals, also lay in the ambition of Justinian to recover the provinces of the former Western Roman Empire. 'Recovery' is an interesting word in this context, as the Goths, as noted above, had been invited to take Rome by the Emperor Zeno. The Goths were quite aware of this history, and thus considered their acquisition of Italy, due to being authorised by an earlier Byzantine emperor, as 'legitimate', and the Byzantine actions against them as both an 'injustice' and 'wrongful'.[54] Conversely, whilst Justinian conceded that Zeno had sent him to Italy to make war on Odoacer, this authorisation was 'not in order to hold the dominion of Italy for himself . . . he sent him in order that Italy might be free and obedient to the emperor'.[55] The Goths, he contended, having seised Italy, should have returned it to its rightful position within the Empire.[56]

After buying the neutrality of the Franks with large gifts of gold, timing his intervention to coincide with a dynastic dispute, and mixing in a little religious fervour, Justinian invaded Italy. The forces of Justinian met with relatively easy success in the early years of the war, invading Sicily and then advancing into Italy, taking both

[52] See ch 5 s 5 Christianity.

[53] Ecclesiastes 1:2. Gwatkin, H (ed) (1967) *The Cambridge Medieval History: The Rise of the Saracens and the Foundation of the Western Empire*, Vol II (Cambridge, Cambridge University Press) 12–14; Gibbon, E *The Decline and Fall of the Roman Empire* ed Bury, J (1929 edn) Vol IV (London, Methuen) 289–91; Grant, R (2005) *Battle* (London, Dorling Kindersley) 64.

[54] Procopius, *History of the Wars* trans Dewing, H (1919) Books VI:V (Massachusetts, Harvard University Press); also Jordanes *The Origins and Deeds of the Goths* trans Miero, C (1910 edn, 2009 reprint) (London, Theophania) LX.

[55] Procopius, *History of the Wars* trans Dewing, H (1919) (Massachusetts, Harvard University Press) Books VI:V.

[56] Procopius, *History of the Wars* trans Dewing, H (1919) (Massachusetts, Harvard University Press) Books V:V.

Naples and Rome in 536. This progress was not sustained, with attempts being made to retake Rome (which 50,000 Goths failed to achieve after one year), and Milan being won, then lost, by the Byzantine forces. Around this point, the death of the Gothic king Theodahad occurred and the Goths devolved into a series of self-destructive dynastic struggles. After three blood-stained preceeding reigns Totila (d 552) came to power. Totila brought back military victories for the Goths, including retaking much of Italy, with key centres like Rome being caught in the tide of war, being reclaimed by the Goths in 546, taken back by the Byzantines in 547, and then lost again to the Goths in 550. Totila achieved his successes as a result of a combination of weak Byzantine leadership and a new Byzantine–Persian war which served to drain troops and attention from the conflict in the west. However, when a truce was negotiated with Persia, 20,000 Byzantine troops were transferred to Italy, thus allowing the Byzantines to finally defeat and kill Totila (and 6,000 of his men) on the battlefield of Mons in 552. By the terms of the consequent treaty, the Goths undertook to leave Italy and engage in no further warfare against the Empire, receiving in return the guarantee that they would be permitted to take all their movable property with them and that they would never again be forcibly conscripted into the imperial army.[57]

After defeating the Vandals and the Goths, Justinian flattered himself on having restored 'perfect peace'.[58] The perfect peace lasted 14 years. Three years after the death of Justinian, the mainland Italian territories fell into the hands of another Germanic tribe, the Lombards, in 568. These peoples, who had earlier suffered under the policies of Odocacar, rebuilt their forces over the following decades before marching over the Italian frontier in a largely uncontested process, forcing out another group, the *Heruli* (a tribe, perhaps from around east Germany) who had also sought to establish settlements in the rich lands of Italy. The Lombard success was also found in destroying the independent cities, before turning on the Byzantine enclaves. When the Lombards attempted to dominate the lands of the Papacy (contrary to their earlier promises), the Papacy turned to the Franks to defend their lands. As discussed in chapter five[59] this request would lead to the end of the Lombards as an independent political and military force in Italy.[60]

A new threat of migratory invaders to the people now resident in Italy and east Europe arose in the ninth century in the form of the *Magyars*. The history of these people appears to begin some time in the fourth millennium BCE when the Uralic-speaking people, who were living in the central and southern regions of the Urals, split up. Over the succeeding centuries a number of groups appeared, one of which, the *Mayars*, seem to have solidified by ninth century CE, between the Ural mountains and

[57] Procopius, *History of the Wars* trans Dewing, H (1919) (Massachusetts, Harvard University Press) Books V:VI and VI:V; Regan, G (2006) *Battles that Changed History* (London, Carlton) 39–40; White, M (2011) *Atrocitology* (NYC, Norton) 74–77; Grant, R (2005) *Battle* (London, Dorling Kindersley) 64.

[58] Norwich, J (1988) *Byzantium: The Early Centuries* (London, Guild) 253; Gwatkin, H (ed) (1967) *The Cambridge Medieval History: The Rise of the Saracens and the Foundation of the Western Empire*, Vol II (Cambridge, Cambridge University Press) 18.

[59] See ch 5 s 7, The Rise of the Papacy and the East–West Tension.

[60] Gwatkin, H (ed) (1967) *The Cambridge Medieval History: The Rise of the Saracens and the Foundation of the Western Empire*, Vol II (Cambridge, Cambridge University Press) 195–97; John of Biclaro, *Chronicle* reprinted in Wolf, K trans *Conquerors and Chroniclers of Early Medieval Spain* (1999) (Liverpool, Liverpool University Press) 69; Norwich, J (1988) *Byzantium: The Early Centuries* (London, Guild) 269.

the Volga, and later Don Rivers, before migrating into the Carpathian basin, and then the Ukraine. Tradition has it that the Magyars were organised into a confederacy of tribes called *hetmagyar* which translates to 'seven hungarians'. These groups may have been supplemented by others who were fleeing various civil wars and/or other disturbances on the Steppes. Collectively, by the middle of the ninth century, they began raiding both the Eastern Frankish Empire (Germany) and, amongst others, the *Bulgars* (a semi-nomadic people who flourished in the Pontic Steppe and the Volga basin from around the seventh century CE, being directed to fight them via an alliance with Byzantium in 895) and the territory of Greater Moravia (which was made up of parts of modern-day Slovakia, Czech Republic, Poland, Austria, Serbia, Ukraine, Germany, Poland and Hungary). Their entry into Greater Moravia may well have been at the instigation of others, such as the minor regional lord, Arnulf (850–899) who splintered Moravia through successful attacks at the end of the ninth century, to obtain valuable slices such as Baviaria.[61]

Feeling confident in their growing powers, the Magyars decided to become masters of their own destiny, rather than the handmaidens of other superpowers. The first instance occurred in the year 900 when they tried to take Italy. Magyar raids continued through the reign of Louis the Child (893–911) as they raided far and wide across northern Italy and southern France, defeating no fewer than three major east Frankish armies between 907 and 910. This situation only changed when Henry the Fowler (876–919) successfully fought the Magyars in 921 when they again invaded the area of Germany and Italy. For the first time the Magyars agreed to a nine-year truce in 926, for the cost of tribute and the promise not to harm one of the Magyar princes that Henry had captured. Henry then refused payment in 932 – after he unified all of the German groups – and lead them to victory at the Battle of Riade in 933, thus stopping the attempted Magyar advance. Undeterred, the Magyars returned, and made a further five attempts to invade Saxony and/or Bavaria in the following 10 years, before they staged their mass invasion in 955. At this point, an army of perhaps 30,000 Magyars poured into Bavaria, advancing as far as Augsburg. Otto I (912–973) responded, and defeated the Magyars with 8,000 heavy cavalry, leaving at least 5,000 of the enemy dead on the battlefield. Otto's success at the battle of Recknitz two months later in October 955 was followed by peace for over three decades with opposing forces. Aside from some further failed attacks in 991, fundamentally, the victories of 955 brought an end to a period of great uncertainty and ended the centuries-long cycle of nomadic raids from steppe nomads in Central Europe. Conversely, this failure to penetrate any further into the west meant that the Magyar armies began a series of raids into Byzantine territories in 934, 943, 959 and 969, before appearing to becoming integrated with the marauding armies of the Rus.[62]

[61] Hussey, J (ed) (1966) *The Cambridge Medieval History: The Byzantine Empire*, Vol IV(1) (Cambridge, Cambridge University Press) 500–504, 568–70.

[62] Gwatkin, H (ed) (1957) *The Cambridge Medieval History: Germany and the Western Empire*, Vol III (Cambridge, Cambridge University Press) 182–86, 199, 207–209; Hussey, J (ed) (1966) *The Cambridge Medieval History: The Byzantine Empire*, Vol IV(1) (Cambridge, Cambridge University Press) 570–74; Regan, G (2006) *Battles that Changed History* (London, Carlton) 47–48; Heather, P (2009) *Empires and Barbarians: Migration, Development and the Birth of Europe* (London, Pan) 366–70.

7. BYZANTIUM

The Slavs (a self-identifying term often linked to 'word' meaning people who speak the same language) were the migratory threat that challenged Byzantium. In the twenty-first century, although Baltic seeds are suspected, the origins of the Slavic peoples are hotly debated. Wherever they came from, from relative obscurity in the sixth century, Slavic speakers spread across vast tracts of central and eastern Europe over the next 200 years. This mass migration was largely facilitated by the depopulation of the region of the previous Germanic speakers, many of whom had moved west with the collapse of this side of the Roman Empire.[63]

The first notable group which was loosely tied into the Slavic groupings was the *Avars*. The *Avars* were a highly organised confederacy of nomadic horse warriors of mixed tribal origins. They descended from the Great Eurasian Steppe and built an empire in central Europe. They dominated the Huns, Turks and Bulgars and took possession of the Russian steppes. Their first noted formal recognition as an independent political and geographical entity occurred in 557 when they made an offer to Constantinople whereby, in exchange for gold, they would subdue the unruly populations within the eastern empire, on behalf of Byzantium. Justinian was sympathetic to this request and directed them into Germania. However, as this area was contested by the Franks, they returned, and against the wishes of Justinian, established a control over considerable areas of Central and Eastern Europe, before expanding into Thrace (modern-day south-east Bulgaria and north Turkey). They then told the Emperor that they could 'not be a good friend of . . . the Roman state, unless . . . they receive [their] customary gifts'. Justinian replied he would not, 'purchase peace with gold, but win it at the sword's point'. He added, that whilst he did not object to the giving of gold to such peoples 'as a free gift for your service' it could not be demanded as 'a tax upon us'.[64]

Irrespective of the label under which the gold changed hands, the *Avars* served at the paid direction of Byzantium to attack and destroy other problematic barbarian groups (such as the *Gepids* in North Italy in 567). They were, however, prone to change direction when it suited them and attack Byzantine forces, as they did in 568 in Dalmatia (part of modern-day Croatia). Eighty thousand pieces of Byzantine gold were then offered for them by treaty in 574 to change direction and attack another Barbarian tribe (the *Sclavenes*). When the money stopped in 580, and the Byzantines made treaties with other migratory peoples who were the enemies of the *Avars*, the *Avars* turned on their paymasters. Through a series of short and violent conflicts, Byzantium relented, and in 584 handed over 100,000 pieces of gold as the price of peace. When Emperor

[63] Heather, P (2009) *Empires and Barbarians: Migration, Development and the Birth of Europe* (London, Pan) 9, 375–77, 386–88, 390.

[64] This is actually two quotes. The first and third part is from *The History of Menander the Guardsman* trans Blockley, R (1985) (Liverpool, Cairns) 93 and 95. The second part from Justin is noted in Gwatkin, H (ed) (1967) *The Cambridge Medieval History: The Rise of the Saracens and the Foundation of the Western Empire*, Vol II (Cambridge, Cambridge University Press) 265.

Maurice (539–602) refused their incessant demands for tribute, the *Avars* aligned themselves with the traditional enemy of Byzantium, the Persians. Peace was reached in the year 600 when a treaty fixed the empire's frontier with the *Avars* on the Danube, and an increase in tribute was added. However, this was a weak peace, and when Byzantium was rocked by internal struggles and external threats from Persia, the *Avars* and their Slav allies, went on to invade the Balkans, north Italy, and even attempt a siege of Constantinople in 617.[65]

When Emperor Heraclius (575–641) came to power in a point of crisis, realising he could not fight his greater enemy (Persia) at the same time, broadly kept the peace with the *Avars*, and in 619 he agreed to keep away from conflict with them, for the annual cost of 200,000 pieces of gold. Despite such success, the *Avars* could only stay peaceful against Byzantium for a short time, reforming in a combination with Bulgars, Slavs and *Gepids* and again attacked Constantinople in 629. Their failure to take Constantinople was soon overtaken by greater problems. First, Turkic groups pushed out of Central Asia in the East and battled them. Then the *Wends* (west Slavs) attacked. Byzantium seems to have also orchestrated the Serbs and Croats, who had by this time been converted to Christianity, to attack the *Avars*. Finally, Charlemagne's Franks attacked the *Avars*, after repeatedly warning them to stop crossing the frontiers and attacking the allies of the Franks. The war with the Franks was fatal for the *Avars*. The result was that 'all the [*Avar*] nobility died in this war, all their glory departed. All their wealth and their treasures assembled over so many years were dispersed'.[66]

Whilst the *Avars* dissolved from history, the Bulgars and other Slav populations such as the Croats and Serbs (who may have had Iranian origins) rose to take their place. Ethnically mixed, the Bulgars – perhaps, with Turkic, *Sarmatian* and *Alani* influence – were fighting Byzantium by the middle of the seventh century. Successive emperors attempted to deal with them in different ways. Whilst some allowed them to settle and forge independent areas, others, such as Justinian II in 689, brought them to heel and resettled them where he wanted them (in Antatolia). However, the Bulgars were difficult to control even though they resettled, swapping paymasters (to serve Muslim forces) when it suited them, and/or taking advantage of civil strife in the empire and carving out and/or plundering areas for themselves. Peace between the two sides was only achieved when Byzantium was forced to make a deal to contend with other threats and required either the neutrality or the assistance of the Bulgars. For example, in 716, the borders of the Bulgars, including their recently grabbed areas, were acknowledged, along with market access to Byzantium and an annual tribute – in exchange for their military assistance against the Muslims. This was particularly good

[65] Luttwak, E (2009) *The Grand Strategy of the Byzantine Empire* (London, Harvard University Press) 60–64; Hussey, J (ed) (1966) *The Cambridge Medieval History: The Byzantine Empire*, Vol IV(1) (Cambridge, Cambridge University Press) 476–85.

[66] The quote is from Thorpe, L (ed) *Einhard and Notker the Stammerer: Two Lives of Charlemagne* (1969) (London, Penguin) 67. Also *The History of Menander the Guardsman* (1985) trans Blockley, R (Liverpool, Cairns) 59–61, 129, 141–43; Gwatkin, H (ed) (1967) *The Cambridge Medieval History: The Rise of the Saracens and the Foundation of the Western Empire*, Vol II (Cambridge, Cambridge University Press) 34, 268–70; Costambey, M (2012) *The Carolingian World* (Cambridge, Cambridge University Press) 70–72; Kaegi, W (2007) *Heraclius: Emperor of Byzantine* (Cambridge, Cambridge University Press) 95–96, 118–20.

timing, as the Bulgars were responsible for the killing of perhaps 20,000 of the Muslim soldiers as they tried to take Constantinople in 717 to 718.[67]

War broke out again between the Bulgars and Byzantium in 756. The causes were Bulgar demands for an increase in tribute and the attempts by Constantine V (718–775) to fortify their shared border. Seven decades of local warfare, coupled with intermittent truces, followed, before the legendary Bulgar leader – Krum (d 814) – arose. Krum fought the Byzantine emperors Nikephoros I (r 802–811), Michael I (770–813) and Leo V (775–820). These engagements began in 809 when Krum, already sovereign of a realm that stretched from northern Thrace to the northern Carpathians, attempted to annex further territory around Anatolia. Soon after, he captured Sardica (the modern Sofia). Nikephoros took these acts as justifications to enter into Bulgaria in 811 with an army of 60,000 men, laying waste to the land and the Bulgarian capital, Pliska – of which Nikephoros ordered his army to kill the entire population. When the progress of the Byzantine forces ground to a halt, and they attempted to withdraw, Krum fell upon the enemy force with devastating impact. Nikephoros was the first Roman Emperor to die in battle for nearly 500 years. The emperor was decapitated and his skull used by Krum as a drinking cup. Seising the initiative, Krum then invaded Byzantine Thrace the following year.[68]

It fell to Leo to deal with Krum – or at least Krum's son Omurtag (r 814–831), after his father died. By this stage the Bulgars had advanced to Constantinople and blockaded the city. A peace treaty was reached in 815 and then renewed in 821. The treaty between the two parties defined the Bulgaro–Byzantine border, which the Bulgarians were empowered to fortify. In exchange, the Bulgarians were required to provide military assistance when required. Although the arrangement worked, when the Byzantines agreed to grant the Serbs independence, the Bulgars were outraged and attacked the newly independent State. A decade later, under the leadership of Boris I (d 907), the Bulgars launched a new campaign against Byzantium in 852, taking a number of cities in Thrace and the Black Sea. These were not held for long, as Boris, recognising he was about to be crushed between the Byzantines and the Franks, decided to opt for an alliance with Byzantium. Accordingly, he renounced any possibility of an alliance with the Franks, and adopted Orthodox Christianity for both himself and his people in 864. Despite some settling in required by the introduction of the new orthodoxy, this resulted in Bulgaria being allowed to keep some disputed regions (such as Zagora) whilst Byzantium reaped a huge political and cultural influence.[69]

A shared religion did not stop war breaking out again at the end of the ninth century. The background was Leo VI (866–912) restricting the entry of Bulgar goods into

[67] *The Chronicles of Theophanes Confessor* trans Mango, C (2006) (Clarendon Press, Oxford) 507–508, 552–54; Heather, P (2009) *Empires and Barbarians: Migration, Development and the Birth of Europe* (London, Pan) 405–406; Luttwak, E (2009) *The Grand Strategy of the Byzantine Empire* (London, Harvard University Press) 174–77.

[68] Norwich, J (1992) *Byzantium: The Apogee* (NYC, Knopf) 7–13; Luttwak, E (2009) *The Grand Strategy of the Byzantine Empire* (London, Harvard University Press) 180–85.

[69] For the conversion of Boris, see Geanakoplos, D (ed) (1986) *Byzantium: A Sourcebook on Church, Society and Civilisation Seen Through Contemporary Eyes* (Chicago, Chicago University Press) 349–50. Also 'Letter to the Bulgar Khan' reprinted in Rosenwein, B (ed) *Reading the Middle Ages: Sources from Europe, Byzantium and the Islamic World* (Ontario, Broadview) 143–47; Hussey, J (ed) (1966) *The Cambridge Medieval History: The Byzantine Empire*, Vol IV(1) (Cambridge, Cambridge University Press) 97–98; Grant, R (2005) *Battle* (London, Dorling Kindersley) 65.

the marketplaces of Byzantium. The spark was the failure of Emperor Alexander III (870–930) to send the traditional tribute at the time of the accession of the new Bulgar king, Simeon (r 893–927). After the resultant conflict, Byzantium agreed to pay annual tribute and allow Bulgar goods into the Byzantine markets without restriction. When the tribute was late in arriving, and further civil disturbance was bubbling in Byzantium, Simeon struck. Peace was achieved by a promise to pay all of the arrears quickly, recognition of Simeon as Emperor of the Bulgars, and more importantly, an agreement that the new emperor, Constantine VII (905–959), would marry one of Simeon's daughters. When a reshuffled regency (the mother of Constantine VII) came to power, Byzantium disowned the idea of the marriage and obscured recognition of Simeon's imperial title. Simeon immediately went to war. The conflicts that followed, including the Battle of Achelous in 917 (one of the largest battles of the period, in which over 100,000 men stood on the battlefield) resulted in Bulgarian victory, allowing them to again rampage up to the walls of Constantinople. To find success in his siege with Constantinople, Simeon attempted to strike a deal with the Fatimids, but the Byzantines got there first and also struck a deal with the Croats to stay neutral. A truce agreed between Simeon and Byzantium in 924 (which became a treaty in 927), saw the agreement of an annual tax to be paid Bulgaria in exchange for the return of a number of the cities taken on the Black Sea coast. This peace also allowed Byzantines to regain control of a number of associated regions, such as around coastal Dalmatia, and the increasingly independent Serb and Croat populations.[70]

Upon taking the Bulgar throne, Peter I (d 970), the son of Simeon, threatened continued war with Byzantium unless a new treaty could be agreed. Peter wanted a Byzantine bride (the granddaughter of Romanus I), an annual tribute and the imperial recognition of his title. Peter also wanted the Bulgars' control over inland Macedonia recognised. This was granted in exchange for all of the Bulgarian conquests of Thrace being fully returned. This peace lasted until 966, when Peter's empress died and the Byzantine Emperor Nikephoros II refused to pay the annual tribute, complaining of a Bulgarian alliance with the Magyars. Then, in alliance with Kiev (cemented by the marriage of Basil's younger sister Anna (993–1011), which in turn created the link to Russia) a combined attack was launched against Bulgaria. These attacks, built around the principles of recovering stolen imperial provinces and removing a threat to Constantinople, quickly subdued much of Bulgaria. The follow-through was bringing the Bulgarian king back to Constantinople, having him ritually divested of his imperial insignia (and given a lesser title as compensation), whilst the Bulgarian lands in Thrace and lower Moesia were brought once more into the Byzantine Empire.[71]

The discerning reader will have noted in the above paragraphs that a new actor entered the stage sometime in the ninth century. The name of the Russians was first divulged in the early part of ninth century in some diplomatic correspondence within Christendom. Exactly where this character, *Rus*, came from is the subject of debate.

[70] Hussey, J (ed) (1966) *The Cambridge Medieval History: The Byzantine Empire*, Vol IV(1) (Cambridge, Cambridge University Press) 128–32, 135–39, 506–509.

[71] Luttwak, E (2009) *The Grand Strategy of the Byzantine Empire* (London, Harvard University Press) 190–95; Norwich, J (1992) *Byzantium: The Apogee* (NYC, Knopf) 222–26; Runciman, S (1954) *A History of the Crusades*, Vol 1 (Cambridge, Cambridge University Press) 83.

Long before there was any recorded history in the area known as *Rus*, a succession of nomadic warriors dominated the steppes of modern-day Russia and Ukraine. Cimmerians, Scythinas, Huns, Avars, Turks, Bulgars, Khazars and those in possession of the Slavic language have all explored parts of this region, before a new wave of people arrived. Of this new wave, although Scandinavian scholars have argued that the word *Rus* is derived from the Finnish name for Swedes, the debate is far from settled. Scandinavian infiltration along the River Volga can be traced in archaeology to the eighth century CE. In the following century around 860, the Scandinavian rulers of Kiev and their new Slav subjects tried to attack Constantinople. This attack came from somewhere in what is modern-day Russia as 200 ships sailed across the Black Sea. These Vikings, known as *Varangians*, appear to have laid the foundations for a unified state. However, by about the year 900 it was the Slavic-speaking groups which had come to dominate, and occupy a truly vast area of eastern Europe. The only source of this period, the *Primacy Chronicle*, records that the Slavic and Finnish tribes refused to pay further tribute to the Varangians and drove them 'back beyond the sea'.[72] Although the Varangians may have been driven back, some of their leaders (notably Rurik, c 830–879) may have been invited to return, to help solidify the foundations of a new country. These foundations can be seen in the change of representation of identity, as by the time further attacks were launched against Byzantium in 904 and 907, they were recognised as Russians, *not* Vikings.[73]

The fruits of the 911 attack was a treaty with Byzantium. The essence of this treaty was the ability of *Rus* merchants to come in peace and trade in Constantinople.[74] This deal held the peace for around three decades, when armed *Rus* reappeared before the walls of Constantinople in 944. Their demands (three pounds of gold for each man) were too high for the Byzantines. The *Rus* ended up accepting a lesser amount, following debate within their own ranks after reflecting that their bargaining position was not that strong. Peace was duly reached in 945 and the relationship between the *Rus* and Byzantium began to prosper. The Russian Princess Olga of Kiev was probably the first *Rus* of noble status to be converted to the Orthodox Christian faith, about 955. However, this was not an entrenched peace, and war broke out in 971, when Olga's pagan son Sviatoslav (c 942–972) decided to try his luck, pushing deep into the Balkans, attacking the Volga Bulgars and associated Byzantine forces. He demanded an enormous ransom for the prisoners he held and inordinate compensation in exchange for the territories he had conquered. He ended with these words, 'if the Romans do not want to pay, the only course open to them is to withdraw from Europe, where they have no right to be, and to retire to Asia. There can be no other way of establishing peace between the Romans and the Russians.'[75] Sviatoslav was mistaken in this, as the Byzantines had persuaded one of Sviatoslav's migratory allies, the *Pechenegs*, to swap

[72] *The Primary Chronicle* as reprinted in Kaiser, D (1994) *Reinterpreting Russian History: Readings, 860–1860* (Oxford, Oxford University Press) 9–10.

[73] Moss, W (2005) *A History of Russia* (London, Anthem) 9–10, 15–18. Heather, P (2009) *Empires and Barbarians: Migration, Development and the Birth of Europe* (London, Pan) 414–18, 441, 444–51, 469–80.

[74] The Rus-Byzantine Treaty of 911. This is reprinted in Geanakoplos, D (ed) *Byzantium: A Sourcebook on Church, Society and Civilisation Seen Through Contemporary Eyes* (1986) (Chicago, Chicago University Press) 284.

[75] As quoted in Hussey, J (ed) (1966) *The Cambridge Medieval History: The Byzantine Empire*, Vol IV(1) (Cambridge, Cambridge University Press) 159.

sides – via promises of friendship, recognition and tribute. At the same time, the Byzantines pushed back hard against the *Rus*, trapping and overwhelming their forces in a corner of Bulgaria. At this point in 971, Sviatoslav agreed a treaty with Byzantium in which he pledged himself never again to attack the empire or Bulgaria. In exchange, he was promised an alliance and the restoration of their traditional trading privileges. Following through with the withdrawal required with this treaty, the *Rus* forces (including Sviatoslav) were set upon by the *Pechenegs* near the Dnieper rapids, and utterly destroyed.

The *Rus* successor, Vladimir (958–1015), initially carried on the fight in the Balkans, before making peace with the Bulgars in 985, at which point, according to the *Primary Chronicle*, a peace agreement was concluded which recorded: 'May peace prevail between us till stone floats and straw sinks.' Following through, Vladimir then made peace with Byzantium. This was secured by his marriage to the sister of the Emperor, and his conversion to Christianity.[76]

8. NORTHERN EUROPE

The word *Viking* encompasses people who are commonly recognised as Norwegians, Danes and even Swedes. For these people, the years between 500 and 1000 were ones of expansion and warfare. This was a time when folk-chiefs rose against each other, battled each other incessantly for power, making, and collapsing, kingdoms. Then, sometime around the eighth century, they started to expand outwards at a remarkable rate. Their outward push was due to a mixture of limited opportunities in North Europe (in ecological and social terms), the possibilities of glory, plunder and/or colonisation in the lands of other peoples and the civil disturbances in North Europe.

The Viking advances were not chaotic. Where the potential enemy was strong, such as with Charlemagne, peace treaties were made (in 811 and renewed in 839) which divided the two kingdoms and set the boundary at the Eider River.[77] Where the enemy was weak, the Vikings would combine favourable sailing conditions, political opportunity and military guile. Records survive of their adventures into, inter alia, Byzantium, what became Russia, the Netherlands, Germany, Greenland, Iceland and possibly North America. They attacked numerous Christian countries, parts of Muslim Spain, and even sent 200 ships to try to sack Rome (but mistakenly sacked Luna instead in 859) before trying to attack Constantinople in 860.[78]

[76] Mango, C (1994) *Byzantium: The Empire of the New Rome* (London, Paladin) 55; Moss, W (2005) *A History of Russia* (London, Anthem) 28–30; Hussey, J (ed) (1966) *The Cambridge Medieval History: The Byzantine Empire*, Vol IV(1) (Cambridge, Cambridge University Press) 510–11.

[77] Thorpe, L (ed) *Einhard and Notker the Stammerer: Two Lives of Charlemagne* (1969) (London, Penguin) 157–60.

[78] Richards, J (2001) *Blood of the Vikings* (London, Hodder) 18–20; Brink, S (2012) *The Viking World* (London, Routledge) 193–95; Griffith, P (1995) *The Viking Art of War* (London, Greenhill) 47; Gwatkin, H (ed) (1957) *The Cambridge Medieval History. Germany and the Western Empire*, Vol III (Cambridge, Cambridge University Press) 311; Heather, P (2009) *Empires and Barbarians: Migration, Development and the Birth of Europe.* (London, Pan) 455–59; Grant, R (2005) *Battle* (London, Dorling Kindersley) 68–69.

The Vikings also made inroads into Wales, Scotland and Ireland. In the case of Scotland, they may have run so roughly over the territory that they helped, inadvertently, to form a united kingdom of Alba (later Scotland, from which Kenneth I (d 858) the legendary king of the Picts and the Scots arose). In Ireland they went from raiding at the end of the eighth century, settling in the middle of the ninth, to being evicted at the beginning of the tenth – after forging an independent kingdom (which linked Dublin and York), before ending fighting as mercenaries on both sides of a civil war between contesting Irish kings.[79]

The first recorded attacks of 'Northmen from the land of the robbers' against the Anglo-Saxons in Britain took place in the year of 787. Lindisfarne was attacked 'by rapine and slaughter' in the year 793.[80] As the English kings battled each other and their non-English neighbours and advanced into Wales, they discovered that the Welsh had requested military assistance from the Danes. These military adventurers soon became independent of their original paymasters, and by 835, Danish raiders were heading directly for England. During the next 30 years, at least a dozen large-scale expeditions were launched to attack England, with hundreds of boatloads of Northmen arriving and expanding throughout the country, learning how to exploit the divisions between the English who were fighting each other and to offer protection services to threatened communities (by both other English and Vikings) via 'the promise of money'.[81]

From this turmoil arose Alfred the Great (848–899). Alfred watched the 'Great Heathen Army' (perhaps 5,000 men) invade in 865. This army took advantage of a succession struggle that had divided the military capacities of the kingdom and set them behind two contenders (Osbert and Aelle). The two kings eventually united, but by then it was too late. The Vikings broke into the city of York and killed them both. In 868, the Great Army turned its attention on East Anglia and then Mercia. This left only Wessex under King Alfred, as the last English king left – of which he (or at least, with 5,000 warriors) stemmed the tide of conquest (of an equal number of Vikings made up of perhaps 11 contingents fighting under different leaders). This successful defence left the province of Wessex as the last of the Anglo-Saxon kingdoms, but intact, and ruled by descendants of their ancient kings. Alfred then continued his fight, defeating a Viking army at Edington in 878 and forcing the Viking leader, Gunthrum, to accept an independent Wessex via treaty. The treaty, between Alfred (and 'all of the English nation') and Guthrum (and 'all the people that are in east Anglia'), divided the land boundaries 'up on the Thames, and then up on the Lea, and along the Lea unto its source, then straight to Bedford, then up on the Ouse unto Watling Street' [perhaps London]. Gunthrum promised to be baptised (the requirement for baptism of Viking

[79] Brink, S (2012) *The Viking World* (London, Routledge) 14, 82–92, 195–96, 198–99, 388–89, 403, 411, 422, 432, 458–59, 535, 543; Wallace-Hadrill, J (1962) *The Barbarian West: The Early Middle Ages A.D 400–1000* (NYC, Harper) 132–35; Griffith, P (1995) *The Viking Art of War* (London, Greenhill) 110; Grant, R (2005) *Battle* (London, Dorling Kindersley) 70.

[80] Years 787 and 793 from *The Anglo-Saxon Chronicle* trans Swanton, M (1998) (London, Routledge) 'The Sack of Lindisfarne' is also recorded in Loyn, H (ed) (1975) *The Reign of Charlemagne: Documents on Carolingian Government and Administration* (London, Edward Arnold) 110.

[81] The quote is from Year 865. See also Years 827, 832, 833, 840, 845, 851 and 854; Stenton, F (1985) *Anglo-Saxon England* (Oxford, Clarendon Press) 242–50.

leaders being notable in a number of similar engagements of this period). Subsequent articles set down rules for dealing with financial rates for murder or manslaughter, rules on the acquisition of property and provision of hostages. Although this peace was not long-standing, it gave Alfred time to reorganise Wessex (in social, cultural and military terms) and when further waves of Danish invasions occurred in 891, he successfully resisted them.[82]

Alfred's descendants progressively reclaimed Mercian lands, and other parts of England under Danish control. This was not an easy struggle, as their enemies formed into large, inter-locked alliances. One instance in the 930s, saw the English fighting a Viking lead alliance, with allies drawn from Scotland and Ireland brought into the conflict. This battle at Brunanburh in 937, left five Viking leaders, seven earls from Ireland, and the son of the king of the Scots, dead on the field. From such victories, further Anglo-Saxon lands were retaken. This reconquest reached an apex when King Edgar (959–975), 'the strongest of all kings over the English nation',[83] established England as a relatively complete land (replete with varying degrees of autonomy for some Viking communities via their own *Danelaw* (by which mixed communities were brought together with different – but not discriminatory – laws).[84]

English solidarity became unstuck, when his son, Aethelred (978–1016), came head-to-head with new migratory swarms of Vikings, with further large-scale raids recorded in 980, 981 and 982. Many of these men entered Britain, where they offered 'peace in exchange for gold' – but were rebuffed. Historical records suggest the British replied 'not so easily shall you win tribute; peace must be made with point and edge, with grim battle play before we give tribute'.[85] With this attitude at the battle of Maldon in 991 some 3,000 Vikings were seen off by an equal number of Anglo-Saxons. In other areas, such as when the Vikings appeared at Ipswich, Aethelred decided that rather than fight the Vikings he would close their safe havens and buy them off. The safe havens were ended with a treaty by which (the Viking descendant) Richard of Normandy promised, inter alia, not to harbour the enemies of Aethelred any longer. Second, as the *Anglo-Saxon Chronicle* explained, 'it was resolved that tribute should be given, for the first time, to the Danes, for the great terror they occasioned by the sea-coast. That was first 10,000 pounds [of silver].'[86]

The fact that the treaty for 10,000 pounds of silver was made with a Viking resident in Normandy reflected the fact that the Northmen were working on both sides of the English Channel. These efforts began about three decades into the ninth century, after

[82] The 878 Treaty Between Alfred and Guntrum reprinted in Whitelock, D (ed) (1955) *English Historical Documents: 500–1042* (London, Eyre) 73; Abels, R (1998) *Alfred the Great: War, Kingship and Culture in Anglo-Saxon England* (London, Longman) 29, 112–15, 136, 164–65, 170–76, 194–98; Stenton, F (1985) *Anglo-Saxon England* (Oxford, Clarendon Press) 250–69; Grant, R (2005) *Battle* (London, Dorling Kindersley) 69. See also the years 867–872 in the *Chronicle*.

[83] This quote is from Aelfric, an 11th century source reprinted in Baker, D (ed) (1966) *The Early Middle Ages* (London, Hutchinson) 49.

[84] Stenton, F (1985) *Anglo-Saxon England* (Oxford, Clarendon Press) 339–48.

[85] See the Anglo-Saxon poem, the Battle of Maldon as reprinted in Herlihy, D (ed) *The History of Feudalism* (NYC, Harper) 88, 89.

[86] Year 991. Also Stenton, F (1985) *Anglo-Saxon England* (Oxford, Clarendon Press) 320–25, 327–30, 375–77; Crouch, D (2002) *The Normans: The History of a Dynasty* (London, Hambledon) 33–35. Also Brink, S (2012) *The Viking World* (London, Routledge) 376–77; Grant, R (2005) *Battle* (London, Dorling Kindersley) 70.

the empire of Charlemagne had ceased to be a collective to be feared, and had been broken up and divided amongst his disgruntled grandchildren. With this opportunity the Vikings began to seek weaknesses they could exploit. The rich monastery of Saint Wandrille was sacked in 841, the port of Quentovic in 842, and the city of Nantes in 843. Two years later they raided up the Seine to reach Paris, where they attempted to loot probably the richest monastic foundation of western Europe at the time: Saint Germain. The price of them leaving was over 6,000 pounds in weight of gold and silver, as a mixture of loot, ransom and protection money.[87]

By 850 the Vikings had stopped being visitors in the region and decided to overwinter in western Europe. Their application for residency was often supported by local rulers who saw their value as auxiliaries in their regional political struggles. Soon after, some of these groups attempted to raise the stakes and threaten the king directly. Rather than take this threat on, in 866, Charles the Fat (839–888) bought peace with the Vikings at the cost of 12,000 pounds of silver. This was short lived, as the Vikings made a further attack on Paris in 885. This attack was also bought off by Charles, for the price of 700 pounds of silver. For that price, the 30,000 Vikings were directed to go and ravage elsewhere. With this incentive, a composite group of Vikings went on to pillage Cambrai, Utrecht and Charlemagne's great palace at Aachen, as well as burn Cologne and Bonn. When they returned, Charles allowed them to stay in his realm, in exchange for them accepting Christian baptism and becoming his subjects.[88]

Later Viking leaders, such as Rollo (846–931), having learnt the patterns of 885, invaded the northern coasts of France and established independent kingdoms. The price of peace with Rollo, as agreed in the treaty of St Clair-Sur-Epte (with Charles the Simple, 879–929) in 911, was Rollo's conversion to Christianity and his agreement to defend his lands against other Vikings.[89] For this price, Rollo was made a duke and given a large piece of land (which still bears their name: *Normandy*, the land of the Northmen) in north France. This grant was renewed and expanded in 924 and 933 to Rollo's son (William Longsword, c 900–942) and his son, (Richard of Normandy, 933–996). This treaty turned Rollo and his descendants into vassals, with which the Franks and Scandinavians, who created the Norman people, mixed well. The collective result was that by the 960s the area was known as 'the land of the Normans'.[90]

[87] Heather, P (2009) *Empires and Barbarians: Migration, Development and the Birth of Europe* (London, Pan) 455–57.

[88] Heather, P (2009) *Empires and Barbarians: Migration, Development and the Birth of Europe* (London, Pan) 460–62.

[89] See the 911 Treaty of St Clair-Sur-Epte reprinted in Laffan, R (ed) (1929) *Select Historical Documents: 800–1492*. (NYC, Holt) 13.

[90] Brink, S (2012) *The Viking World* (London, Routledge) 453–54; Griffith, P (1995) *The Viking Art of War* (London, Greenhill) 16–17; Gwatkin, H (ed) (1957) *The Cambridge Medieval History: Germany and the Western Empire*, Vol III (Cambridge, Cambridge University Press) 59–62, 85–86; Crouch, D (2002) *The Normans: The History of a Dynasty* (London, Hambledon) 1–7, 19–21; Abels, R (1998) *Alfred the Great: War, Kingship and Culture in Anglo-Saxon England* (London, Longman) 114–15; Grant, R (2005) *Battle* (London, Dorling Kindersley) 69.

9. CONCLUSION

A large amount of warfare between the years 3,000 BCE and 1000 CE was due to the covetous nature of migratory peoples. These people constantly sought the riches of others. The riches would begin as plunder, before advancing to tribute, and then territory within an empire, if not the empire itself. These people who had no formal home and no ideology beyond seeking the riches of others had a strong military advantage due to their mobility. For thousands of years they learnt how to advance where they wanted, and easily disappear when challenged as they possessed no territory that they were attached to.

The threat that these people represented was both universal and constant. It was also potentially cataclysmic, resulting in the downfall of a number of empires – to which they were attracted like parasites. The waves that swept through the ancient Near East toppled everything from the Empire of the Hittites to the communities of Achaean Greece. Only Egypt survived the onslaught. The same pattern was not repeated in India and China, where the regions were too large to be consumed by the nomadic hordes – not for lack of appetite. In the case of the western side of the Roman Empire, when the breach finally occurred, the dam burst with such ferocity that what is euphemistically known as 'the dark ages' accurately described the splintering, chaos and warfare that would take Europe five centuries to gestate through. Byzantium survived similar threats, although a number of the threatening peoples' combined into independent countries/entities within what was once Byzantine territory. In all instances, the attacks by the migratory peoples were most likely to succeed when the empires they targeted were distracted by internal difficulties.

All of the regions that had to deal with migratory peoples who were drawn to the riches of established communities worked out the same solutions in dealing with them. These were divide and rule strategies, in which the best defence was keeping the migratory hordes divided. To do this multiple treaties were utilised in all regions, whereby favoured groups were given benefits. The benefits ranged from tribute to trading rights, through to the ability to settle in certain areas. In exchange, they were expected to either provide troops for the empire, or battle others – normally other migratory peoples – at the direction of the empire. Those who were not given benefits were battled. The necessity to battle migratory peoples who were divided or demanding too much was recognised by all empires, who saw the omnipresent need to keep those preying on the fringes of empire subdued. In many instances, it was only when the migratory peoples were denied their requests for benefits, and were battled to a standstill, that peace could be achieved.

However, keeping the migratory peoples subdued was an issue of management and adaptation, rather than a complete and final victory. This was a constant problem due to the nearly endless supply of migratory groups who possessed a clear ability to form, mutate and turn on either a different empire or their fellow migratory allies. That is, their threat to each other was often just as great as it was to the settled populations they targeted. Awareness of the benefits that one group had, could force other groups to seek the same rewards, either by threat or demand to the paymaster, or extinction of the original recipient. Only as a last resort would an empire give territory and/or legitimisation of the rulers (often via royal marriages and/or religious recognition). Even when this occurred and the migratory people settled in the lands of others, their position was never secure as the former owners always possessed long memories, and when the time was right, would often attempt to squash them either by themselves, or in conjunction with other allies, before their roots got too deep, thus either destroying them, or reverting them back to a subservient and servile status.

IV

Politics

1. INTRODUCTION

THE QUESTION WHICH this chapter seeks to examine is the extent to which wars occur over political choices. Politics (from the Greek *politikos*, 'of, for, or relating to the citizens') is a term generally applied to the art or science of running governments and/or state affairs. Within the context of this chapter, I see the issue of politics as concerning the options of running the state, which range from monarchy through to democracy. The particular question to examine is what were the more common practices, limits and patterns which became linked to warfare?

2. THE NEAR EAST, EGYPT, CHINA AND INDIA

A. Monarchy

Monarchy is a form of government in which sovereignty, as in the supreme, independent authority over a geographic area, is embodied in a single individual. Monarchy is the oldest type of political order known to humanity. Monarchy was the overwhelming pattern of the Near East. This pattern was traceable in all regions. The omnipotent and absolute power of the king, replete with the quintessential emblems of a crown and a throne, was perfectly manifested in ancient Egypt under the title of *Pharaoh*. This title originates in the term '*pr-aa*' which meant 'great house' and was used to describe the royal palace. In time, it came to signify one man, whose absolute authority and mystery was portrayed in everything from the pyramids to hieroglyphics. Although these kings took advice from some of their helpers within the bureaucracy, priestly or otherwise, there were no constitutional checks on the power of the pharaoh. Freedoms were permitted as a matter of custom and convenience, not political principle. Commoners, although able to progress through the levels of society, had no political rights and no voice in government. They existed to serve the pharaoh, not the other way around. This was clearly ordained in the elaborate cosmology within which they existed. The Egyptian pharoahs' power of life and death over their subjects was so great that they could take their servants with them when they died; a number had their throats cut before being left in the royal tombs.[1]

Dynasties emphasised a single unbroken succession of kings, stretching back to the 'time of the gods' and the deity of Atum – the creator and father of the first king. Atum was usually represented as wearing the double crown of kingship, identifying himself as the creator not just of the universe, but also of the political system. The created cosmological and political order was independent, inextricable and absolute. The pharaohs claimed to be directly linked to (or to be) gods, and demanded all the power that went with such embodiments of divinity. The Loyalist Inscription of c 1790 BCE reflected some of these claims, when it stated that all citizens must venerate the king, for 'he is the sun god under whose governance one lives . . . It is [the god's divine] power that fights for him [the king].'[2] Similar rhetoric was common throughout the region.

Although, in ancient Mesopotamia, there may have been some communal influence over the king via councils (which had a heightened say on questions of war), actual restraints on the monarchy were few and far between. It was religion, rather than popular ascent that was seen as the dominant legitimate factor of authority. Thus, for rulers such as Hammurabi (d 1750 BCE), it was the gods that guaranteed the 'eternal seed of royalty'.[3] This link between monarchy and religion was always strong in the ancient Near East. Originally, the men who led the early Sumerian societies were known as *en* and, later, as *ensi* – literally, 'priest who laid the foundation of a temple'. The title changed to *lugal* – literally, 'big man' at some time around 2500 BCE.[4]

For Israel, it appears that independent communities initially governed themselves by a type of primitive democracy under a council of elders for, as the Book of Judges recorded, 'there was no king in Israel'.[5] However, the Jewish people wanted to change from the existing theocratic–democratic model. This was felt necessary to deal with the growing military threats in the region, which they believed required a unified approach under one man. Thus, 'we will have a king over us, that we also may be alike all the [neighbouring] nations and that our king may judge us, and go out before us, and fight our battles'.[6] Samuel, speaking on behalf of God, warned directly of the consequences of instituting a monarchy. He explained:

[1] Wilkinson, T (2010) *The Rise and Fall of Ancient Egypt* (London, Bloomsbury) 30, 32, 38–39, 43–44, 46, 94, 280–81; Muller, H (1961) *Freedom in the Ancient World* (NYC, Harper) 45–51, 56–58. See also the records of Thutmose III reprinted in Breasted, J (ed) (1988) *Ancient Records of Egypt*, Vol II (London, Histories and Mysteries) 180–81, and Ramses II, Vol III, 145–46; Hamblin, W (2006) *Warfare in the Ancient Near East to 1600 BC* (London, Routledge) 313–15, 319, 353–54, 412–13; Saggs, H (1989) *Civilisation Before Greece and Rome* (New Haven, Yale University Press) 32; Kemp, B (2001) *Ancient Egypt: Anatomy of a Civilisation* (London, Routledge) 197–200.

[2] The Loyalist Inscription reprinted in Hamblin, W (2006) *Warfare in the Ancient Near East to 1600 BC* (London, Routledge) 412–13.

[3] The quotation is from Hamblin, W (2006) *Warfare in the Ancient Near East to 1600 BC* (London, Routledge) 178. See also Kramer, S (1963) *The Sumerians. Their History, Culture and Character* (Chicago, University of Chicago Press) 37; Kramer, S (1981) *History Begins at Sumer* (Philadelphia, University of Pennsylvania Press) 30–35, 229; Saggs, H (1989) *Civilisation Before Greece and Rome* (New Haven, Yale University Press) 35–40; Jacobsen, T (1970) 'Primitive Democracy in Ancient Mesopotamia' in Moran, W (ed) *Towards the Image of Tammuz* (Boston, Harvard University Press) 157–70.

[4] Gat, A (2008) *War in Human Civilisation* (Oxford, Oxford University Press) 270.

[5] Judges 21:25.

[6] 1 Samuel 8:20.

> This is what the king who will reign over you will claim as his rights: He will take your sons and make them serve with his chariots and horses, and they will run in front of his chariots. Some he will assign to be commanders of thousands . . . and others to plough his ground and reap his harvest, and still others to make weapons of war and equipment for his chariots. He will take your daughters to be perfumers and cooks and bakers. He will take the best of your fields and vineyards and olive groves and give them to his attendants. He will take a tenth of your grain and of your vintage and give it to his officials and attendants. Your male and female servants and the best of your cattle and donkeys he will take for his own use. He will take a tenth of your flocks, and you yourselves will become his slaves.[7]

The Jewish people were undeterred by this warning, and they duly chose Saul (1079–1007 BCE) to be their king. After Saul fell in battle, the kingship was passed on to David (1040–970 BCE), of whom God agreed with the tribes of Israel that he 'will shepherd my people Israel, and [he] will become their ruler'.[8]

Within the realm of India, the institution of monarchy can be traced in the early Vedic texts. The earliest of dynasties (Parikshit and Kuru) were battling in the Mahabharata War (in a struggle between rival cousins) some time between 3000 and 1300 BCE. The following centuries saw a bewildering array of tribal groupings battling for position before the Mauryan Empire managed to secure itself above the others. Within this empire, the practice of monarchy held sway. Prior to this point, and sometimes on the edge of this empire (and subsequent empires) within India, it is possible that some groupings (especially to the south of the country) were democratic and did not have kings. Such democratic systems were noted by both Diodorus (c 50 BCE)[9] and Arrian (86–160).[10] It is also possible that, at some points when the great dynasties and associated empires dissolved and local regions became independent, some tribal republics reappeared for short periods.[11]

By the later Vedic period most of the tribal republics had been eclipsed and a 'strong-man' was either elected or seised power of the group. This control of power, coupled with the ability to preserve and correctly administer laws whilst promoting the common weal, were the original attributes of kingship in both the political and religious worlds. In the case of the Hindu system, the appointment of a king, who was 'made from particles of these lords of the gods',[12] was agreed to so as to bring back the order and stability to society that had been lost in chaos. For, as the *Book of Manu* explained, 'when this world was without a king, people ran about in all directions . . . the Lord emitted a king in order to guard this entire realm . . . [as] a protector of the classes and the stages of life'. [13] Tribes without kings were viewed with disdain.

[7] 1 Samuel 8:11–17.

[8] 2 Samuel 5. See also 1 Samuel 10:17–24 and 1 Samuel 12:1.

[9] Diodorus *Library of History* trans Wells, B (1963) (Boston, Loeb) II 35–36.

[10] Arrian *Anabasis of Alexander* trans Brunt, P (1983) (Boston, Loeb) Books 5–7, 'Indicia' IX.

[11] Raychaudhuri, H (1999) *Political History of Ancient India* (Oxford, Oxford University Press) 15–20, 25–28, 141–45, 169, 455. Sharma, J (1968) *Republics in Ancient India* (Leiden, Brill) 15–30; Thepar, R (1961) *Asoka and the Decline of the Mauryas* (Oxford, Oxford University Press) 94–95.

[12] *The Laws of Manu* trans Doniger, W (1991) (Penguin, London) VII:5; Raychaudhuri, H (1999) *Political History of Ancient India* (Oxford, Oxford University Press) 43, 140, 153.

[13] *The Laws of Manu* trans Doniger, W (1991) (Penguin, London) VII:3 and VII:35. See also The Origin of Kingship reprinted in de Barry, R (ed) (1958) *Sources of Indian Tradition*, Vol 1 (NYC, Columbia University Press) 236–38. Morgan, P (ed) (2007) *Ethical Issues in Six Religious Traditions*. (Edinburgh, Edinburgh University Press) 6–7.

Although the kings were sometimes given advice by aristocratic councils, they had a greater reliance upon the Brahmins, who held a mutually reinforcing position between the sacred status of monarchy, the hierarchical caste system, and those who interpreted and held the keys to the divine sanction of this institution.[14]

The Jain attitude to political systems varied widely. Like Hindus, they recognised that social order was conducive to well-being, leading to spiritual liberation. They were not, however, leaders in the sense of theories of preferred types of political governance. In this they were unlike the Buddhists, who appear to have originally possessed an ideal which valued decentralised, democratic decision-making. Although people in authority were usually treated with respect, Buddhists were commonly wary of hierarchical forms of government even though they accepted in principle that such forms may have been necessary to maintain social order. The early Buddhist belief was that the king was appointed to meet social needs – and was not mandated by the gods. Monarchy was a social, not a divine, creation. Later – *Mahayana* – Buddhism changed regarding the above concerns and suggested that, although the king was not himself divine, the kings held their power by the authority of the gods. This link with the gods became greater for many of the emperors of the various Buddhist dynasties as time progressed, with a succession of them leaving epithets recording just how important they were, stipulating that they were not merely beloved by the gods, but were actually their children – that is, the king himself was to be regarded as a divinity. Either way, the result was the same: Buddhist kings, such as Asoka, although being counselled by any number of advisers and allowing variations of autonomy in some areas, retained the final and absolute voice in all decision-making.[15]

A similar pattern of absolute power wrapped up in one man, the emperor, was reflected in China. In a manner akin to ancient India, chaos was thwarted and disorder quelled to the benefit of the populace by the force of a single man, both wise and strong. Huai-nan Tzu (c 200 BCE) suggested that in an earlier age, such a man brought peace to the land, preserved those about to perish, pacified the chaos under heaven, and eliminated the harm affecting the people. In the Shang period (c 1600–1000 BCE) the existence of the king as a powerful, essentially theocratic chief was based a little more in practice than in theory. This man, buttressed by his personal charisma and authority, sustained the ruling structure in the temporal realm, whilst also retaining strong links to the spiritual realm, through the performance of divination and sacrificial rituals. In the following epoch of the Chou, the idea of the 'Mandate of Heaven' was developed. This idea was based on the notion that the cosmos was dominated by an impersonal but all-powerful heaven, which no man ruled, except by the mandate of heaven, and that the ruler (and there could only be one) was entrusted with responsibility for 'all under heaven'.[16]

[14] Kulke, H (1996) *A History of India* (London, Routledge) 44–45.

[15] Thepar, R (1961) *Asoka and the Decline of the Mauryas* (Oxford, Oxford University Press) 96–98, 121–22; de Barry, R (ed) (1958) *Sources of Indian Tradition* (NYC, Columbia University Press) Vol I, 85–86, and Vol II, 72, 139–40; Morgan, P (ed) (2007) *Ethical Issues in Six Religious Traditions* (Edinburgh, Edinburgh University Press) 58–59; Raychaudhuri, H (1999) *Political History of Ancient India* (Oxford, Oxford University Press) 254, 456, 493.

[16] Huai-nan Tzu, as noted in Sawyer, R (2011) *Ancient Chinese Warfare* (NYC, Basic Books) 4–5, 100. See also Bary, T (ed) (1960) *Sources of Chinese Tradition*, Vol 1 (NYC, Columbia University Press) 7.

Post 1000 BCE, the Chou king, and every subsequent ruler, was commonly spoken of as the Son of Heaven, even though there is no implication that the king was actually considered to be a living deity. In later epochs, such as the Qin, the term taken to describe the leader was consciously moved away from 'king' – *Huang-ti* – by combining two terms previously reserved for gods and mythical heroes, which Westerners came to know as 'emperor'. The power of such men was absolute. The regime which stated this most clearly was that of the Legalists, who advanced what was a somewhat totalitarian model of the leader and the absolute power that he held. Scholars such as Kuan Tzu (c 400 BCE) suggested that, if necessary, such a man could do whatever was required with his citizens to achieve the goals that were required to make the state orderly, prosperous and secure.[17] The commentary on the Legal Code of T'ang, c 624 CE, explained:

> The Prince occupies the highest position of the world, and is charged with the Mandate of Heaven above . . . his jurisdiction . . . being the mother and father of all people. The people being his children and subjects at the same time, owe to him the duties of loyalty and filial piety. What a presumption, then, it is to entertain such wicked ideas and to give reign to rebellious intent. This is to turn the heavenly order upside down and to go against human reason.[18]

B. Usurping Power

The history books are overflowing with records of illegitimate or controversial claimants to power, who usurped authority in a manner which was not in accordance with the expected patterns. The first instance of this occurs in the records of the ancient Near East, which note the taking of the throne by a commoner in Lagash around 2340 BCE. It is possible that the great Sargon (2270–2215 BCE) usurped his throne. From this one throne, he subsequently took others, consolidating his rule of the Sumerian city-states by replacing their rulers with his own governors, who were usually members of his own clan. He then orchestrated the handing over of the reins of power to his son Rimush (2278–2270 BCE). Whilst Sargon could keep those who wanted his power at bay whilst alive, he could not prevent his two successors – his children, Rimush and Manishtus (2269–2255 BCE) turning on each other after his death. The Akkadian Empire collapsed around the year 2100, when there appears to have been a civil war in which four kings ruled in only three years (2192–2190 BCE). There are allusions to this in the Sumarian king-list of this period which succinctly summarises 'who was king, who was not king?'[19] Dynastic disputes were also recorded in ancient Syria around the eighteenth century BCE with a sequence of rebellions, all seeking the throne. Similarly,

[17] Kuan Tzu, as noted in Hsiao, K (1979) *A History of Chinese Political Thought* (New Jersey, Princeton University Press) 329; see also 381–89, 400–402; Hucker, C (1994) *China's Imperial Past* (California, Stanford University Press) 42, 92–95.

[18] The Tang code, as noted in MacCormack, G (1996) *The Spirit of Traditional Chinese Law* (Athens, Georgia University Press) 107–10.

[19] See Hamblin, W (2006) *Warfare in the Ancient Near East to 1600 BC* (London, Routledge) 102–103.

within the Hittite kingdom around 1650 BCE, disputes split the country into civil war and even after the great Mursilis I (1620–1590 BCE) had achieved the military conquest of the epoch (taking Babylon) he was murdered by his brother-in-law in a palace coup. The Hittite state then collapsed into quasi anarchy, with several successive coups – after which 'the gods abandoned them'.[20]

A similar fate awaited the Assyrians. The last great Assyrian king, Ashurbanipal (668–627 BCE), ascended the throne upon the death of his father. However, his brother Sinsharishkun (r 627–612 BCE) obtained the throne by forming a military alliance with Babylon, the Elamites, the Arameans, the Arabs and the Egyptians against his sibling. The resulting civil war ripped the country apart, as first the brothers fought each other and then local communities fought for autonomy from both. The result was that by 612 BCE, when a coalition of Medean and Babylonian armies advanced into the region, the Assyrian Empire vanished from history.[21]

The first civil war over kingship and disputes about succession in ancient Egypt may have occurred during the second dynasty (2850–2687 BCE). Similar problems may have occurred at the beginning of the fourth (2649 BCE) and fifth (2513 BCE) dynasties. The fifth dynasty came to an end when Teti (r 2345–2333 BCE), a commoner, replaced the last pharaoh of the dynasty, Unas (2375–2345 BCE), due to the inability of Unas to produce a male heir leaving only females one of whom Teti swiftly married to show legitimacy. Such legitimacy may not have been enough, for it appears Teti was assassinated, being replaced by Userkara for a brief period, before Teti's son, Pepi (r 2332–2282 BCE), took power back (although he too suffered from attempted coups). The death of Pepi II (r 2278–2184 BCE) caused even greater problems, and may have been the catalyst for civil war. In a period of just 20 years, Egypt saw 17 kings come and go, before the seventh dynasty disappeared from history. Egypt was reunified under Mentuhotep (r c 2134 BCE), although within a short period civil turmoil returned to Egypt. This was hinted at when Amenemhat I (1991–1962 BCE) recorded that he was obliged to fight, to save his town 'from the sickening terror of the royal house'. [22] The reliefs in his tomb show unprecedented scenes of Egyptians attacking fellow Egyptians in full-scale urban warfare. Whilst Amenemhat may have won the war, he was, in turn, assassinated by his successor – his son (Senusret I, r 1971–1926 BCE). In such circumstances, it was not surprising that his successor was warned: 'Do not approach them [your subjects] when you are alone! Trust no brother! Know no friend.'[23]

Trust or not, the desire for ultimate power created an endless line of potential or real usurpers. The thirteenth dynasty saw 50 kings in 150 years, before Sobekhotep III (c 1680 BCE) – another military man of non-royal lineage – seised the ultimate prize,

[20] Hamblin, W (2006) *Warfare in the Ancient Near East to 1600 BC* (London, Routledge) 63, 73–74, 79, 80, 259, 294, 295, 301–302.

[21] Gabriel, R (2005) *Empires at War*, Vol I (London, Greenwood) 199–200.

[22] Amenemhat, noted in Wilkinson, T (2010) *The Rise and Fall of Ancient Egypt* (London, Bloomsbury) 161. Also Hamblin, W (2006) *Warfare in the Ancient Near East to 1600 BC* (London, Routledge) 322–23, 331–35, 368–70.

[23] The warning after Amenemhat, Hamblin, W (2006) *Warfare in the Ancient Near East to 1600 BC* (London, Routledge) 414. See also Wilkinson, T (2010) *The Rise and Fall of Ancient Egypt* (London, Bloomsbury) 92–94, 106–107, 119–23, 129–31, 138–39, 161, 170–71.

and attempted to hand it on to his heirs. At other times, when the dynastic line came to an end, the pharaoh peacefully passed the throne to the military leader. Amenhotep, for example, (who had no male heir) passed the throne to Thutmose (r 1493–1481 BCE). There appears to have been a period of uncertainty, if not attempts to grab the throne, when Akhenaten died in 1334 BCE, before Tutankhamun was placed on the throne (c 1333–1322 BCE). At his death, his replacement by Horemheb – a military general of commoner background – may have amounted to a military coup that sealed the end of the eighteenth dynasty. In turn, Horemheb placed another military general on the throne – Ramses – before his demise. Ramses then promptly readopted the hereditary approach (thus establishing the nineteenth dynasty), passing the throne to his son, Seti, upon his death. Ramses II (1303–1213 BCE) combined longevity with extraordinary fecundity – fathering at least 50 sons and probably as many daughters. Although the passing of power to Merenptah was relatively straightforward, when his reign ended in 1204 any number of royal grandchildren came forward to claim the throne. The claims were eventually narrowed down to a conflict between two rival claimants Seti II (r 1203–1197 BCE) and Amenmesse (r 1202–1199) BCE). Egypt was then fought over by the rival contenders, as coup followed coup, and purge was followed by counter-purge. This only ended when Ramses III (1186–1155 BCE) brought back stability, although towards the end of his time there was another attempted palace coup. Under Ramses IX (r 1129–1111 BCE), following a civil war caused by the unauthorised elevation of an outsider to the office of High Priest, the general acting for Ramses, Paiankh, placed two army generals in the position of absolute power. In time to come, the generals would not wait to be given ultimate power. For example, although the pharaoh Wahibra (589–570 BCE) successfully repulsed an attempted Babylonian invasion in 582, he found his power stripped from him when one of his generals, Ahmose II (r 570–526 BCE), took the throne, capturing and killing Wahibra and establishing the twenty-sixth dynasty.[24]

Conflicts to seise absolute power were also part of the history of Israel. After the monarchy had been established, problems that led to conflict can be traced to the appointment of David after the death of Saul. The problem was that whilst the Jewish God may have wanted David, the generals of Saul's armies wanted the son of Saul, Ish-Bosheth, to be king. War then broke out between the two kingdoms of Judah and Israel, before Ish-Bosheth was assassinated. After this problem was resolved, David had to battle his own son, Absalom, who rebelled against the rule of his father. Similarly, Rehoboam, the son of David, inherited the kingdom (upon his father's death) but faced a low-level civil war after 10 northern tribes rebelled in 932/931 BCE to form the independent kingdom of Israel. Part of the justification for this split may have been the harshness with which the new king ruled, which was unpopular with the other tribes.[25]

Although Israel and Judah would be pulled back together again under the influence of Omri (r 886–885 BCE), the relationship was inconsistent, and in the next generation the

[24] Wilkinson, T (2010) *The Rise and Fall of Ancient Egypt* (London, Bloomsbury) 185, 188, 298–99, 311, 315, 319, 345–50, 363, 378–82, 441–44; Spalinger, A (2005) *War in Ancient Egypt* (London, Blackwell) 172–75.

[25] 1 Kings 12:13–14, 12:16, 12:24. Note also, generally, 2 Samuel 3 and 2 Samuel 18; Herzog, C (1997) *Battles of the Bible* (London, Greenhill) 216.

two kingdoms again crossed swords, as they became sucked into various regional alliances and conflicting religious loyalties. Thereafter, the dynastic ruling house, as represented by Amaziah (r 769–781 BCE) and then his son, Uzziah (r 783–742 BCE), was eclipsed by a succession of men from the military claiming the throne from each other, including Pekah (r 737–732 BCE) and Hoshea (r 732–721 BCE).[26]

In India dynastic disputes were apparent from the earliest written records. The first king to unify all of India, Bimbisara of Magadha (r 540–490 BCE), was killed by his own son, Ajatasatru (r 491–461 BCE), who imprisoned and starved him to death. This pattern was repeatedly followed by other sons who felt they were better suited to ultimate power than their fathers. The first Nanda emperor, Mahapadma (450–362 BCE), lost his power to a commoner who seduced his wife, killed him, and took power under the pretext of being regent to his sons – whom he soon killed. Chandragupta (340–298 BCE), the founder of the great Maurya Empire – perhaps an illegitimate scion of the family – usurped power from the last Nanda emperor in 320 BCE. Aware of such precedents, the adviser to Chandragupta, Kautilya (370–283 BCE), noted that princes are best kept under guard at a safe distance, because 'princes, like crabs, have a notorious tendency towards eating up their begetter'.[27]

Of course, crabs also have a tendency to push aside (if not consume) their siblings, as Asoka came to demonstrate, overthrowing his elder step-brother in a fratricidal struggle so as to secure his place in the Mauryan dynasty. However, such acts could not guarantee the longevity of the dynasty, which was eclipsed by Pushyamitra Shunga (r 185–151 BCE), a general in the service of the Mauryans, who overthrew his master, Brihadratha, (r 187–180 BCE), and established his own dynasty – the Sungas. The last ruler of the Sunga dynasty was murdered by a slave girl, and it is said that this was instigated by the king's Brahmin adviser. The Gupta Empire was challenged by the Pushyamitras, before Skandagupta usurped his father's throne by displacing the legitimate crown prince and triggering a war of succession. In turn, this dynasty, which appears to have been shaken by palace revolutions, was toppled by one of the ministers to the last Sunga ruler, Vasudeva Kanva (r 75–66 BCE). Kanva felt he and his children were better suited to power, which they were, until the year 26 BCE, when they were extinguished by the rival kingdom of Satavahana, which lasted until about 200 CE. This pattern of attempts to usurp power from either families or associated governments continued throughout many parts of India in the centuries that followed.[28]

The same pattern of conflict and usurping of power was also a feature of the nomadic tribes who preyed upon China, and of China itself. In the case of the latter, the history of this problem can be traced back to the legendary king Yu (c 2300 BCE) who was subject to criticism for passing his throne to his son, Ch'i, thus establishing clan rule

[26] 2 Kings 14–15.

[27] Kautilya, *Arthashastra* trans Shamasastry, R (1915) (Bangalore, Government Printer) I:17. For the background to this quote, see Kulke, H (1996) *A History of India* (London, Routledge) 56, 61; Smith, V (1962) *The Early History of India* (Oxford, Oxford University Press) 36, 44–45; Raychaudhuri, H (1999) *Political History of Ancient India* (Oxford, Oxford University Press) 186–87, 204.

[28] Smith, V (1962) *The Early History of India* (Oxford, Oxford University Press) 162–63, 204, 214–19, 415–16, 449, 488–90; Kulke, H (1996) *A History of India* (London, Routledge) 72, 94, 96; Thepar, R (1961) *Asoka and the Decline of the Mauryas* (Oxford, Oxford University Press) 25, 195–98; Raychaudhuri, H (1999) *Political History of Ancient India* (Oxford, Oxford University Press) 268, 320, 351, 353–54.

marked by lineal descent. His admirers rationalised this act by claiming that people voluntarily flocked to his son, and that the mandate was decreed by heaven. The contrary view was that Ch'i usurped the throne, thus throwing the dynasty into its first significant military conflict, as he had to wrestle the throne from Yi – a meritorious official. The death of Ch'i then precipitated internal chaos as his five sons battled for the throne, with each success being followed by military conflict until one of the scions, Shao-k'ang, eventually managed to claim the throne (c 2070 BCE), and place the Hsia dynasty on solid ground. This only lasted until the Shang dynasty, which also became bedevilled by conflict over the throne.[29]

The Warring States period saw seven contenders for the throne of a unified China, before the Qin emerged victorious, and were in turn, swept away by the force of the Han. The Han dynasty was also subject to a series of attempts to grasp the reins of power, following a number of emperors around the years 9 to 23 CE who left no children. This allowed some outsiders to claim power whilst others produced distant relatives from within the Han lineage with whom they battled their way to the top. This era was also overlaid by court coups in which those who were meant to have no interest in their own dynasties – eunuchs – still seised ultimate power when they could. The collapse of the Han dynasty in 220 CE saw the rise of a series of 'great families' within the realms of a multitude of warlords as China fragmented into various regions. During the three centuries from the collapse of the Jin to the reunification of China under the Sui, both north and south gave rise to a bewildering profusion of dynastic regimes. Dynasties replaced one another in rapid succession, sometimes by means of an internal military revolt or coup (the usual pattern in the south) and sometimes by the conquest of one state by another (more common in the north). The 30-year war within one of the southern dynasties known as the 'War of the Uncles and Nephews' at the end of the fifth century was self-explanatory, as was the 'War of the Eight Princes'. Then, in 548, a further rebellion of a frontier general saw him proclaim himself emperor in 551 (in the south), before he in turn was toppled by general Yang Jian (541–604) who seised power from the newly formed Sui dynasty, making himself Emperor Wen in 581. The Song dynasty (960–1279) was seeded in the same manner, as one of the commanders of the Palace Corps, Zhao Kuangyin (927–976), took the reins of power.[30]

[29] Hucker, C (1994) *China's Imperial Past* (California, Stanford University Press) 22–23; Sawyer, R (2011) *Ancient Chinese Warfare* (NYC, Basic Books) 61–62, 82, 88–92, 141; Di Cosmo, N (2002) *Ancient China and its Enemies: The Rise of Nomadic Power in East Asian History* (Cambridge, Cambridge University Press) 185; Lewis, M (2007) *The Early Chinese Empires: Qin and Han* (Massachusetts, Harvard University Press) 137.

[30] Lewis, M (2009) *China Between Empires: The Northern and Southern Dynasties* (Massachusetts, Harvard University Press) 32, 71–72; Graff, D (2002) *Medieval Chinese Warfare* (London, Routledge) 121, 160, 245–47; White, M (2011) *Atrocitology: Humanity's 100 Deadliest Achievements* (Melbourne, Text) 42–48; Lewis, M (2007) *The Early Chinese Empires: Qin and Han* (Massachusetts, Harvard University Press) 37, 38; Hucker, C (1994) *China's Imperial Past* (California, Stanford University Press) 147–48.

C. The Standards of Monarchy

It was a commonly-held view that if a king failed to perform his duties, revolution from within the kingdom, or conquest from outside of it, was legitimate if the goal was the promotion of 'justice'. This theme of promoting freedom and restoring justice as a justification for toppling a king can be traced to around 2,400 BCE in ancient Sumer. At this point it appears that citizens began thinking about their relationship to each other, and not just to the gods. From such musings, moral, soon to be legal, codes developed which valued truthfulness, righteousness, compassion and mercy – all under the rubric of 'justice'. Such considerations became a long-standing tradition, which Sumerian kings repeatedly tried to encompass, boasting that they protected the poor from the rich, abolished iniquity and thus restored justice. King Urukagina of Lagash (r 2380–2360 BCE) recorded that he 'established freedom' by restoring the ancient rights of the people, ridding the city of ubiquitous tax collectors, protecting widows and orphans, and ensuring that the high priest did not treat the gods' property as his own. Conversely, conquering kings could claim their acts were justified as they 'banished malediction, violence and strife'.[31] This practice, whereby the reign of justice, protection of the weak, and promulgation of peace became the standard template for law codes (or practices), was followed in both the Near East and Egypt where pharaohs portrayed themselves as 'the good shepherd' of their citizens bringing order in place of chaos. Part of this order involved them being the 'princes of justice'[32] who would 'cast out evil'[33] and suggested they often spent 'the whole time seeking the welfare of Egypt'.[34] Hammurabi of Babylon could claim:

> I enhanced the well-being of the land, I made the people of all settlements lie in safe pastures, I did not tolerate anyone intimidating them [through theft or threat of invasion]. The great Gods have chosen me, I am indeed the shepherd who brings peace, whose sceptre is just.[35]

The Assyrian leaders also saw themselves as personifications of justice, stability and plenty. Sennacherib and Sargon were both notable in this regard, not only for having such values of justice within their empires, but also for attempting to extend them outside. During military campaigns they recorded freeing various peoples who had been imprisoned 'through no fault of theirs' by their enemies, and returning them to their

[31] Urnammu reprinted in Hamblin, W (2006) *Warfare in the Ancient Near East to 1600 BC* (London, Routledge) 108–109; also Muller, HJ (1961) *Freedom in the Ancient World* (NYC, Harper) 33–35, 37; Kramer, S (1956) *History Begins at Sumer* (Pennsylvania, Philadelphia University Press) 101–10, 262–63; Postgate, J (1996) *Early Mesopotamia: Society and Economy and the Dawn of History* (London, Routledge) 260–70.

[32] Thutmose III reprinted in Breasted, J (ed) (1988 edn) *Ancient Records of Egypt*, Vol II (London, Histories and Mysteries) 269.

[33] Sesostris II reprinted in Breasted, J (ed) (1988 edn) *Ancient Records of Egypt*, Vol 1 (London, Histories and Mysteries) 283; see also 286 and 297. Note also Nomarh's Tomb Inscription reprinted in *Ancient Records* Vol I 126–27, also Vol II, 187, 217, 231, 252 and Vol III 25.

[34] Saggs, H (1989) *Civilisation Before Greece and Rome* (New Haven, Yale University Press) 29; Spalinger, A (2005) *War in Ancient Egypt* (London, Blackwell) 75–79; Asante, M (2000) *The Egyptian Philosophers* (Chicago, African Images) 58, 78–79, 90, 107, 112–14; Kemp, B (2001) *Ancient Egypt: Anatomy of a Civilisation* (London, Routledge) 46–53.

[35] Hammurabi reprinted in Hamblin, W (2006) *Warfare in the Ancient Near East to 1600 BC* (London, Routledge) 178. See also VerSteeg, R (2000) *Early Mesopotamia Law* (North Carolina, Carolina Academic Press).

lands. They would also lift taxes, rebuild infrastructure and implement systems of administration which sought clarity, equity and stability.[36]

The Hindu king, despite being a god in human form, was still expected to meet certain standards. The *Arthashastra* explained the best qualities of the king, but these were mainly to do with character types, such as being truthful, enthusiastic and disciplined. Apart from 'having an assembly of ministers of no mean quality' there was no recognition of consideration for the populace. There was an exception in dealing with conquered territories, when it was recommended that in adopting righteous behaviour the king remit taxes, adopt the local cultural practices and assist miserable, helpless and diseased people. The *Book of Manu* insisted that the king should be conscious of the needs of his citizens. Specifically: 'In the happiness of his subjects lies his happiness; in their welfare, his welfare; whatever pleases himself he shall not consider as good, but whatever pleases his subjects he shall consider as good.'[37] When dealing with newly occupied lands, the king 'should worship the Gods and the priests who are religious; he should grant tax exemptions and proclaim promises of safety'.[38]

The Buddhist kings also left examples of what a good king was supposed to achieve – namely: generosity to the people, the prevention of violence, and generally good government, as opposed to becoming isolated and living off the work of the people. Asoka declared it was important 'to govern by righteousness'. In doing so, the king promised to 'work for the welfare of the whole world . . . [as] . . . all men are my children'.[39] The attributes within such a system (when not continuing the practices of spying, torture and banning festive meetings or gatherings) ranged from good administration through to respect for all life and tolerance for all religious faiths.[40] Indian tradition also left clear records of what was considered to be the practices of a bad king (although these were often prejudiced if the king was of a religious persuasion different to the writer). Legends relating to the end of Kanishka explained:

> The king is greedy, cruel, and unreasonable; his campaigns and continued conquests have wearied the mass of his servants. He knows not how to be content, but wants to reign over the four quarters. The garrisons are stationed on distant frontiers and our relatives are far from us. Such being the situation, we must agree among ourselves and get rid of him. After that we may be happy. As he was ill, they covered him in a quilt, a man sat on top of him, and the king died on the spot.[41]

[36] In Luckenbill, D (ed) (1989) *Ancient Records of Asssyria and Babylonia*, Vol II (London, Histories and Mysteries) 20–21, 35, 57, 63, 71, 115, 247–48, 253.

[37] Kautilya, *Arthashastra* trans Shamasastry, R (1915) (Bangalore, Government Printer) I:19; also I:20, VI:1, VII:16 and XIII:5.

[38] *The Laws of Manu* trans Doniger, W (1991) (London, Penguin) VII:201.

[39] The First and Sixth Rock Edicts and First Separate Kalinga Edict. Both are reprinted in de Barry, R (ed) (1958) *Sources of Indian Tradition*, Vol 1 (NYC, Columbia University Press) 145–46; Thepar, R (1961) *Asoka and the Decline of the Mauryas* (Oxford, Oxford University Press) 163; Raychaudhuri, H (1999) *Political History of Ancient India* (Oxford, Oxford University Press) 164–65; Morgan, P (ed) (2007) *Ethical Issues in Six Religious Traditions* (Edinburgh, Edinburgh University Press) 60.

[40] The Twelfth Rock Edict reprinted in de Barry, R (ed) (1958) *Sources of Indian Tradition*, Vol 1 (NYC, Columbia University Press) 148; Thepar, R (1961) *Asoka and the Decline of the Mauryas* (Oxford, Oxford University Press) 151–52; Smith, V (1962) *The Early History of India* (Oxford, Oxford University Press) 190, 355.

[41] The Kanishka legend reprinted in Smith, V (1962) *The Early History of India* (Oxford, Oxford University Press) 287–88.

Failure to satisfy the needs of the citizens could result in the king being cast as a tyrant, from which overthrow could be a short step. There are many examples within ancient Indian history of kings associated with 'shameless lust, fiendish cruelty and pitiless misrule' meeting their end prematurely. Although obedience was an important consideration within Hindu scholarship, oppressed subjects tormented by the injustice of a ruler were not required to suffer in passive obedience. Early Buddhist thinking reached a similar conclusion and there are several tales of kings being overthrown by popular rebellion. The underlying theme that the holding of the title of king was contingent on him fulfilling his function properly was reiterated. This implied a moral right of revolt against a wicked or negligent king.[42]

The warriors of ancient China also possessed a rich heritage in this area, using a core collection of reasons which justified toppling an emperor or opposing a king, because they were 'tyrannical' and/or 'perverse'.[43] When T'ang (c 1675–1646 BCE) toppled the entire Hsia dynasty and put in place his own (Shang) dynasty, the justification was that the king in opposition had become tyrannical, destroying the welfare of the people. Accordingly:

> It is not I, the little child, who dares practice what can be termed rebellion. Hsia is guilty of numerous offences, so Heaven has ordered that he be destroyed . . . the king of Hsia has utterly exhausted the strength of his masses, everywhere wearing them down in their towns. His masses have all become lazy and will not cooperate with him. They are saying: 'when will this sun expire? we will all perish with you'. The Hsia virtue being so, I must now go there. I pray you will assist, the one man, to bring about Heaven's punishment.[44]

Shang, too, became a brutal theocratic state which was toppled in turn by the Chou. The Chou rebelled against the arrogant and presumptuous behaviour of the king (Hsin), who was accused of being unduly coercive of those around him and of falling out of favour with the people due to his inability to satisfy their welfare and sustenance needs. In so doing, the founding emperors of the later dynasties were reminded 'you may have conquered the empire on horseback, but you cannot govern it on horseback'.[45] Thereafter, the Duke of Chou tirelessly lectured the conquered Shang peoples about the Mandate of Heaven, telling them that the Chou leaders had no selfish wish to aggrandise or glorify themselves by attacking Shang but had no choice in the matter once Heaven commanded him to punish Shang. Similarly, kings who displayed a lack of righteousness in their behaviour towards their own subjects, or were offensive towards other kings (including acts such as not paying the correct amount of tribute owed), risked provoking attacks against themselves. Good kings, as exemplified by T'ai Kung

[42] See de Barry, R (ed) (1958) *Sources of Indian Tradition*, Vol 1 (NYC, Columbia University Press) 125, 129, 133, 182–84; Thepar, R (1961) *Asoka and the Decline of the Mauryas* (Oxford, Oxford University Press) 147; Smith, V (1962) *The Early History of India* (Oxford, Oxford University Press) 388–89; Raychaudhuri, H (1999) *Political History of Ancient India* (Oxford, Oxford University Press) 75, 156–57; Morgan, P (ed) (2007) *Ethical Issues in Six Religious Traditions* (Edinburgh, Edinburgh University Press) 8–9.

[43] Sawyer, R (2011) *Ancient Chinese Warfare* (NYC, Basic Books) 82, 101.

[44] T'ang's Oath reprinted in Sawyer, R (2011) *Ancient Chinese Warfare* (NYC, Basic Books) 106–107. See also pages 108, 111–12.

[45] Hucker, C (1994) *China's Imperial Past* (California, Stanford University Press) 55–57; Sawyer, R (1993) *The Seven Military Classics of Ancient China* (Colorado, Westview) 32.

(c 1100 BCE), had moral worth and personal restraint (especially in lavish displays of riches), and looked after, 'loved' and 'respected' their people, ensuring that they were not harmed or caused to suffer for example, by the imposition of light taxes and by ensuring his officials were not corrupt. The exemplar of the good king also had to ensure that the people's material base – especially agriculture – was adequate. These were believed to be the 'essential cords of benevolence and righteousness'.[46]

Political theory from ancient China mirrored these considerations. Philosophies emphasising the importance of satisfying the needs of the common people and their link to the legitimacy of a ruler were iterated by Lao Tzu (c 450 BCE), Ssu-ma Fa (c 400 BCE), Hsun Tzu (312–230 BCE), Huang Shih-Kung (c 200 BCE) and Huai-nan Tzu (d 122 BCE). Mo Tzu (490–403 BCE), perhaps the most eloquent of this group, would explain:

> The universal ruler . . . when he finds his people hungry he would feed them, and when he finds them cold he would clothe them. In their sickness he would minister them, and upon their death he would bury them.[47]

Confucius (551–479 BCE) suggested that providing nourishment for the people was an absolute duty upon the emperor. Enriching livelihoods, keeping taxes and imposts light, limiting labour service and restricting fiscal expenditures were also deemed important. Confucius added that a great minister 'is one who serves his prince according to what is right, and when he finds he cannot do so, retires'.[48] A student of Confucius, Mencius (385–303 BCE), also placed great emphasis upon the common people in terms of enriching their livelihoods, reducing their taxes and lessening their burdens. He denounced ministers who failed to provide for the people, because 'the people are the most important element of a nation; the spirits of the land and grain are next; the sovereign is the lightest'. He saw failure in terms of the unnecessary pursuit of war, famine or the unjust enrichment of the state. Those implementing such policies were 'the robbers of the people' and no loyalty was owed to them.[49]

An interconnected idea was the considerable amount of Chinese political philosophy (and practice) – as manifested by Confucius, Mencius and Mo Tzu, as well as the Mohists – which argued that rigid social orders were not justifiable, and that social status could be acquired by quality and virtue, not by birth. This idea of equality of opportunity, whereby 'worthy and talented men' could be appointed at all levels within a government, and appointment was not determined by birth, was revolutionary. However, it was not seen (or used) as a system that could upset the social hierarchies,

[46] Sawyer, R (1993) *The Seven Military Classics of Ancient China* (Colorado, Westview) 42–43, 47; Sawyer, R (2011) *Ancient Chinese Warfare* (NYC, Basic Books) 85, 88, 90–92, 115, 199–202; Hucker, C (1994) *China's Imperial Past* (California, Stanford University Press) 55.

[47] Mo Tzu, *Universal Love* 16:3 reprinted in Bary, T (ed) (1960) *Sources of Chinese Tradition*, Vol I (NYC, Columbia University Press) 42–44. For the other philosophers, see Hsiao, K (1979) *A History of Chinese Political Thought* (New Jersey, Princeton University Press) 109–110, 121–22, 157–59, 193, 238–39, 295; Sawyer, R (1993) *The Seven Military Classics of Ancient China* (Colorado, Westview) 118–19, 160.

[48] *Analects*, I:5, IV:2, VI:28, VII:29, XI:23:3-6, XV:8, XV:23, XVII:6. This version of *Analects* is reprinted in Legge, J (ed) (1897) *The Chinese Classics*, Vol II (NYC, Alden).

[49] Mencius, *The Works of Mencius* VII:2:14 reprinted in Bary, T (ed) (1960) *Sources of Chinese Tradition* (NYC, Columbia University Press) 90–95; also Hsiao, K (1979) *A History of Chinese Political Thought* (New Jersey, Princeton University Press) 150–53, 156, 355–56.

and it was certainly not to be envisaged as a society of equals, within the workings of a democracy.[50]

D. Slavery

A final idea to examine in this section, from which justifications for toppling the political status quo may be adduced, is the practice of slavery. However, within all of the societies examined above, unlike in other periods of history, this justification does not appear to have been used. Rather, slavery was an unexamined fact of the ancient Near East, with Egypt, Babylonia, Assyria, the Hittites and the Hebrews all holding slaves – although the extent and limits to slavery differed in each instance. Five of Hammurabi's laws controlled aspects of this institution. Of particular interest was the stipulation that any person sold into slavery for debt could only be held for four years. In addition, owners of slaves could not simply put their slaves to death if they were unhappy with them. Similar restraints existed within the Hittite civilization. Egypt also had restrictions in this area, but not for obvious reasons. That is, Egyptian restrictions on selling foreign slaves were based on the distorting effect that the trade had on the domestic labour force rather than on humanitarian concerns.[51]

The Israelites were also very familiar with slavery, having been taken by the Egyptians who 'set over them taskmasters to afflict them with their burdens [and] build for the Pharaoh treasure cities'.[52] It may have been because of such a history that the Bible contained a series of limitations imposed upon slavery which went beyond the comparable civilizations at this point of history, such as not enslaving fellow Jews, only holding slaves for six years, and having a state-wide manumission every 50 years.[53] In practice, it is questionable whether these rules were applied. Moreover, the overall ethos was for regulating, not prohibiting, slavery. This was clearly in accordance with the rule set down in Leviticus. Thus:

> Moreover of the children of the strangers that do sojourn among you, of them shall ye buy, and of their families that are with you, which they begat in your land: and they shall be your

[50] Confucius, *Analects* II:1–3, III:24, IV:5, IV:11, V:15, VI:4, VII:7, IX:7, XII:17, XIII:17; This version of *Analects* is reprinted in Legge, J (ed) *The Chinese Classics*, Vol II (NYC, Alden). Hsiao, K (1979) *A History of Chinese Political Thought* (New Jersey, Princeton University Press) 5, 30–31, 36, 40–41, 88–91, 98–103, 118, 136–42, 161, 241, 619–27; Lewis, M (2007) *The Early Chinese Empires: Qin and Han* (Massachusetts, Harvard University Press) 18–21; Lewis, M (2009) *China Between Empires: The Northern and Southern Dynasties* (Massachusetts, Harvard University Press) 38–43, 135–37; Hucker, C (1994) *China's Imperial Past* (California, Stanford University Press) 75–79, 129–30, 155–59.

[51] Kramer, S (1963) *The Sumerians: Their History, Culture and Character* (Chicago, University of Chicago Press) 78; see Muller, H (1961) *Freedom in the Ancient World* (NYC, Harper) 59; Wilkinson, T (2010) *The Rise and Fall of Ancient Egypt* (London, Bloomsbury) 173; Meltzer, M (1993) *Slavery: A World History* (NYC, DaCapo) 14–18, 32–36; Neufeld, T (1951) *The Hittite Laws* (London, Luzac) 120; Pareti, L (1965) *A History of Mankind* (NYC, Harper) 188–99; Rostovtzeff, M (1941) *The Social and Economic History of the Hellenistic World*, Vol I (Oxford, Clarendon Press) 321, 342–44.

[52] Exodus 1:11; see also Deuteronomy 15:12.

[53] Exodus 21:1–6; Leviticus 25:10 and 25:44–46; Deuteronomy 24:7; Jeremiah 34:8–11. Cook, SA (1903) *The Laws of Moses and the Code of Hammurabi* (London, Black) 153, 160–63.

possession . . . but over your brethren the children of Israel, ye shall not rule one over another with rigour.[54]

Nevertheless, at least two Jewish groups, namely the Essenes and the Therapeutae, completely rejected the idea and practice of slavery. To condemn slavery as powerfully as these two groups did was extraordinary for the time. This was certainly a more practical step forward than the efforts of the Jewish scholar Philo (20 BCE–50CE), who advanced the argument that slavery was more of a philosophical than social problem. He suggested that being a slave could actually benefit some people. He added, 'for in God's judgement that which is base and irrational is by nature a slave, but that which is of fine character and endowed with reason and better, is princely and free . . . selling does not make the purchaser a master, nor the purchased a slave'.[55]

According to tradition, slavery did not exist in ancient China as there were no citizens of 'inferior' quality. The reality may have been somewhat different. Slavery was a clear part of the social system, dating back to the Hsia dynasty, and played a key role in the downfall of the Shang dynasty when the 170,000 slaves who were armed to defend 'their' kingdom, to no-one's great surprise went straight over to the enemy. The justification for slavery in ancient China was that enslaved people had demonstrated that their conduct was not worthy of a higher status. Despite this approach, later scholars such as Tung Chung-shu submitted a memorial to Emperor Wu-ti (c 100 BCE) advising that 'slavery and the right to execute servants on one's own authority should be abolished'.[56] In some instances, emperors such as Wang Mang (9–23) forbade the buying and selling of slaves and tried to alleviate the conditions of slavery in general. However, such measures were ad hoc and the overall system of slavery was never challenged. This lack of challenge may have been the driving factor from which some Chinese slaves rose to fight against the orthodoxy, such as Shi Le, who with a large band of escaped slaves and brigands plundered his way through north China during the War of the Eight Princes, before becoming its de facto ruler for a short period around 320 CE.[57]

Slaves also existed in ancient India. The law, as stated in Kautilya's *Arthasastra*, suggested that the proper treatment of slaves entailed not defrauding them of their property or privileges, mis-employing them (that is, forcing them to carry corpses), or hurting or abusing them.[58] These last stipulations reflect the irony that a slave could

[54] Leviticus 25:45–46; Deuteronomy 15:15.

[55] *The Works of Philo: Complete and Unabridged* trans Yonge, E (1993) (Oxford, Oxford University Press). The specific works the quotations are from are 'Legum allegoria' 3:88; 'De specialibus legibus' 2.123; and 'De Virtutibus' 209. See also Meltzer, M (1993) *Slavery: A World History* (NYC, DaCapo) 42–45.

[56] Tung Chung-shu in Bary, T (ed) (1960) *Sources of Chinese Tradition*, Vol I (NYC, Columbia University Press) 216–17; MacCormack, G (1996) *The Spirit of Traditional Chinese Law* (Athens, Georgia University Press) 112; Meijer, M (1980) *Essays on China's Legal Tradition* (New Jersey, Princeton) 327; Pareti, L (1965) *A History of Mankind*, Vol II (NYC, Harper) 189–94.

[57] Sawyer, R (2011) *Ancient Chinese Warfare* (NYC, Basic Books) 222, 226–27; Lewis, M (2007) *The Early Chinese Empires: Qin and Han* (Massachusetts, Harvard University Press) 252; Hucker, C (1994) *China's Imperial Past* (California, Stanford University Press) 61, 129; Lewis, M (2009) *China Between Empires: The Northern and Southern Dynasties* (Massachusetts, Harvard University Press) 138–47; Graff, D (2002) *Medieval Chinese Warfare* (London, Routledge) 49, 58–59, 81.

[58] *Arthasastra* III:13 and 14; Singh, NK (ed) (1985) *The International Encyclopedia of Buddhism*, Vol I (New Delhi, Anmol Publishing) 17.

often be given more social consideration than some of the lowest and untouchable classes. It is with this last issue, that of the caste system, that the real essence of inequality appears in India.

The importance of the caste system to the foundational *Veda* of Hindu religion and associated social hierarchy is hard to understate. The four basic classes were set out as Brahmins (or priests – the 'lord of the castes'); warriors and nobles; merchants; and the servile class (the sudras).[59] People in the lowest class were seen as impure, with no possibility of raising themselves above the class into which they were born. Beneath the lowest class were the 'outcastes' or the 'untouchables'. It was believed that any contact, however slight, with a member of the untouchable caste had a polluting influence. The untouchables/outcastes were below slaves in status, with slaves having stronger and clearer considerations under the law. The untouchables performed the most 'impure' work in society (that is, scavenging and disposal of the dead) and merited very little social concern. If a Brahman killed an untouchable, he would face the same penalty as if he had killed a dog. Although later Hindu thought, such as that represented in the *Bhagavadgita*, was more egalitarian, with salvation promised to all members of society, the underlying system of the division remained, with the caste system being deemed both socially desirable and divinely approved.[60]

A challenge to the caste system came with Buddhism. Buddhism began as a struggle against Brahminism, and while not directly a religion of social reform, it had that effect, and it often became involved in struggles to improve social concerns. This was especially so because it denied that claims to superiority could be based on birth. Worth or respect was to be gained by spiritual or moral merit as opposed to being determined by the family a person had been born into. Accordingly, Buddha welcomed all levels of caste to be his monks. However, like Jainism, there was also a tradition that meditation was superior to regulation. In practice, this meant that Buddhism seems to have accepted the existence of a society divided upon class lines and that although Buddhists oversaw a number of legal measures which mitigated harsh social rules, they did not seek to overturn the caste or slavery system. Even the great Asoka, did not abolish the institution of slavery. Rather, he suggested that slaves should be treated properly in accordance with the law.[61]

[59] *The Ordinances of Manu* trans Hopkins, E (1971) (London,Trubner) I:99, I:100, I:105, X:2–4, X:24.

[60] Aubryer, J (1965) *Daily Life in Ancient India* (NYC, Macmillan) 21–32; Hindery, R (1996) *Comparative Ethics in Hindu and Buddhist Traditions* (Delhi, Motilal) 145–48; Kulke, H (1996) *A History of India* (London, Routledge) 40–42, 90; Kautilya, *Arthashastra* trans Shamasastry, R (1915) (Bangalore, Government Printer) III:13; *The Laws of Manu*, ibid, X:24.

[61] See Singh, NK (1985) (ed) *The International Encyclopedia of Buddhism* (New Delhi, Anmol Publishing) Vol II, 286; Vol IV, 83–87; Vol XIII, 1422–38; Vol XVII, 44–49; de Barry, R (ed) (1958) *Sources of Indian Tradition* (NYC, Columbia University Press) 38–41, 88–89, 95–96, 125, 140, 149–50; Corless, RJ (1989) *The Vision of Buddhism* (NYC, Paragon) 54; Thepar, R (1961) *Asoka and the Decline of the Mauryas* (Oxford, Oxford University Press) 89, 104, 142–45; Morgan, P (ed) (2007) *Ethical Issues in Six Religious Traditions* (Edinburgh, Edinburgh University Press) 43–44.

3. THE GREEKS AND THE WARS FOR FREEDOM

The behaviour of the Greeks of antiquity was paradoxical. On the one hand, they came to portray the highest of standards in avoiding conflict between themselves, leaving records of over 81 inter-state arbitrations. The resolution of these disputes, often mandated by earlier agreement in treaty form – which often meant that warfare was avoided – covered everything from religious differences and commercial concerns, through to larger political debates about alliances, sovereignty and autonomy of other states. On the other hand, the Greeks were also able to battle each other to death over questions of political choice, and the right of communities to political autonomy. As Epictetus (55–135) once pithily noted, 'whole cities perish for what the world calls freedom'.[62] What the Greeks understood as 'freedom' was different to the modern understanding of the idea. For the Greeks, it concerned the freedom of each city to adopt its own political system; democracy was only one option. For modernity, freedom and democracy are synonymous. It is for this reason that I will track this idea closely in the following pages.

A. Democracy

The world of Homer was familiar with kings such as Priam of Troy. These men were portrayed as 'big men' who ruled powerful tribal groupings due to a status derived from birth and wealth. In some instances, they appear to have achieved the support of tribal assemblies, rather than the son simply inheriting the office from the father. These early models, as evidenced by the practices of ancient Mycenae, eventually gave way to models of government based on aristocracy that evolved in ancient Greece around the end of the sixth century when communities had acquired enough economic and population growth to be seriously considered as a *polis* (a city with an adequate body of citizens). Only the most conservative of the Greek states, such as Sparta, would continue to have kings; Sparta had two kings at the same time, five 'overseers', a council of 28 elders and an assembly of male citizens in possession of equal rights. Most of the other states moved away from monarchy and towards models where a narrow clique of wealthy landowners, nobles, and/or horsemen or knights, held the reins of power. These men were typically identified by the label 'aristocracy', with *aristio* meaning 'the best men'. The best men tended to base their claim on wealth and military prowess.[63]

The lower classes within these models were often completely exploited. This pattern was well demonstrated in Athens, where from the beginning of the first millennium BCE, the free inhabitants of Attica had moved from a monarchy to a model of government made up of three life-serving archons. One of these was from a predominant aristocratic family, the other two were elected. This system largely continued (although

[62] Epictetus, *Discourses* trans Oldfather, W (1934) (Boston, Loeb) 4.1.171.
[63] Gat, A (2008) *War in Human Civilisation* (Oxford, Oxford University Press) 214–16.

the number of archons was increased to nine) until the seventh century, when the rising poverty and expanding levels of debt among the majority of citizens of Athens brought the city to the brink of violence. The result was a set of laws introduced by Draco (c seventh century BCE). The word 'draconian' originates from these laws which gives a sense of their nature. A subsequent legislative initiative by Solon (638–558 BCE), which attempted to divide power amongst four collective classes of property owners, provoked an extreme reaction in which one individual, Peisistratus (c 600–527 BCE), used violence to seize power. For this act Peisistratus was labelled a *tryannos* ('tyrant'), meaning a sole or absolute ruler.[64]

The tyrant never found philosophical support in ancient Greece. For Aristotle (384–322 BCE), the tyrant was obsessed by riches, rather than honour, as would be the case for an ideal monarch.[65] For Plato (424–347 BCE), the tyrant was the 'greatest enemy of the whole state', who threatened their internal liberties and continually risked war with others. This was because 'the tyrant must be always getting up a war' to distract those in his power from 'having notions of freedom [or] resistance to his authority'.[66] Herodotus (484–425 BCE) simply added, 'there is nothing in the whole world so unjust, nothing so bloody, as a tyranny'.[67] The only work written in antiquity which attempted to justify tyranny was the *Hiero* written by Xenophon (430–354 BCE). In it, Hiero, the tyrant, lamented the route he had taken, justifying his actions because he sought what was best for the country: respect and honour. The price for such a quest was to have no true friends and to constantly live in fear of being replaced, or killed, by more talented or more powerful men. As such, for the tyrant who must continually use terror and mercenaries to hold power, 'the day of peace will never dawn'.[68]

This was certainly the case in Athens, where the attempts of Peisistraus were quickly toppled by the reformation of constitutional order, in which a new lawmaker, Cleisthenes (b 570 BCE) remade the constitution of Athens in an attempt to prevent further outbreaks of violence between the citizens. Specifically, he reorganised the core Athenian political structure, as the stepping stone to the creation of a community in which power was more equitably distributed. The core of this work was a council of up to 500 men, elected from the different geographical regions, as opposed to the power being concentrated in those who had the money, to run the Assembly. From here, a model developed which was first described by Herodotus (484–425 BCE):

> The rule of the multitude has the most beautiful name, *isonomia* [best translated as equality before the law or equal opportunity in politics] . . . it works completely differently to monarchy. Offices are assigned by lot, all the magistrates are held accountable for their actions, and all deliberations take place before the common assembly.[69]

[64] Plutarch, *Lives* trans Stewart A (Loeb, London) 453–70.

[65] Aristotle, *Politics* 15:10 reprinted in *The Complete Works of Aristotle* trans Barnes, J (1984) (Oxford, Oxford University Press).

[66] Plato, *The Republic* 8. See also *Laws* IX. 856. These are reprinted in *Plato: The Complete Works* trans Jowett, B (1965) (Oxford, Oxford University Press).

[67] Herodotus, *The Histories* trans De Selincourt, A (2003) (London, Penguin) 5:92.

[68] Xenophon, 'Hiero' in *The Works of Xenophon* trans Dakyns, M (1890) Vol III (London, Macmillan) 364.

[69] Herodotus, *The Histories* trans De Selincourt, A (2003) (London, Penguin) 5.80.6.

This regime was called democracy (*demokratia*: strength or power in the hands of the *demos* – the population/common people). This system was administered with a view to the interests of the many, not of the few. It rendered its citizens equal before the law in their private disputes and equally free to compete for public honours by personal merit and exertion, or to seek to lead the city, irrespective of their own wealth or social background.[70]

Whilst Athens was the most renowned ancient Greek democracy, it was not the only one. Some of the other communities situated in Iona, which practised democracy, appealed to the wider Greek community when they were threatened by the Persian Empire, under the leadership of Cyrus (600–529 BCE). This threat arose whilst Cyrus was at war with the Lydian Empire in 546 BCE and discovered on its western seaboard, in Ionia (the central coastal region in present-day Turkey), a number of important city-states whose inhabitants were not Lydian, but Greek – and sought to conquer them and their democratic practices, which he considered to be both foolish and deceitful. The Ionians called on the assistance of their Greek brothers under the justification of defending the 'freedom of the Greeks' and the Athenians and Eretrians offered assistance. For offering assistance to the Ionians, and for the longer-term anger against the Athenians for what the Persians considered to be the breach of an earlier treaty, the Persians decided to invade Greece. In the thinking of the Persians, the fact that the Greeks practised democracy was, most probably, one of their lesser crimes. However, for some of the Greek communities fighting the Persians, it would become the most vital spark that went on to create Western civilization.[71]

After the Persian defeat at Marathon in 490 BCE, the Greeks agreed to cooperate in their defence in an agreement that was solidified at the joint Hellenic Proceedings Conference of 481 BCE. The following year the Persians were defeated in one theatre (Salamis) and achieved only a very expensive victory in another (Thermopylae). Thereafter, the Persians were forced to abandon their plans to conquer Greece. Unaware of this development, the Greeks came together under the Confederacy of Delos in 478 BCE to provide a collective defensive arrangement against the Persians. Sparta, despite having played an important role in the original defeat of the Persians, declined to become involved in the Confederacy, preferring to stay with their own Peloponnesian League, in which they had the predominant influence. Accordingly, the Delian League fell under the leadership, if not hegemony, of the Athenians. The Athenians felt vindicated by the democratic systems to which they attributed their victories, as the naval victories were driven by the muscle power of the poor and the tenacity of all who were fighting for their freedoms.[72]

[70] Dunn, J (2005) *Democracy: A History* (NYC, Atlantic Press) 26–27, 30–35. Also Roberts, J (1994) *Athens on Trial: The Antidemocratic Tradition in Western Thought* (New Jersey, Princeton University Press) 26–29; Oslwald, M (1986) *From Popular Sovereignty to the Sovereignty of Law: Law, Society and Politics in Fifth Century Athens* (Berkeley, University of California Press) 414–20; Murray, O (1994) *The Greek City from Homer to Alexander* (Oxford, Oxford University Press) 344–66; Greene, WG (1973) *The Achievement of Greece: A Chapter in Human Experience* (London, Allen and Unwin) 158–64, 198–210.

[71] Holland, T (2005) *Persian Fire* (London, Abacus) 155; Billows, R (2010) *Marathon: How One Battle Changed Western Civilisation* (NYC, Scribe) 176–85; Herodotus, *The Histories* trans De Selincourt, A (2003) (London, Penguin) 5.49.

[72] Herodotus, *The Histories* trans De Selincourt, A (2003) (London, Penguin) 7.104.

The Athenians demanded loyalty from their allies and an ever-increasing tribute in return for being at the forefront of the defensive alliance. In collecting tribute in times of peace, the Delian League was unlike the other Greek organisation lead by Sparta, the Peloponnesian League, which only collected tribute in times of war. The flow of tribute was defended by Isocrates (436–338 BCE) as the price necessary for Athens to 'take command of the seas . . . and maint[ain] their own democratic liberties and protections against the disasters arising from the establishment of oligarchy'.[73] The Athenians also increasingly took to imposing democratic institutions in the homes of their allies if they had to intervene. This was done because 'the Athenians chose what is most akin to themselves'.[74]

The First Peloponnesian War broke out in the year 460 BCE. There were several causes of the war, including the building of strong defensive walls around Athens, the growth of their empire, and the defection of Megara from the Spartan to the Athenian League. In view of these considerations, Thucydides (460–395 BCE) suggested that the quest for dominance (from both sides) was 'compel[ing] them to go to war'.[75] Polybius (200–118 BCE) suggested that the war broke out because both sides refused 'to yield the first place to each other'.[76] Either way, both sides painted themselves as advocates of freedom. Indeed, Sparta's slogan in the first of the conflicts in the Peloponnese was 'freedom for the Greeks'.[77] The Spartans, argued this as they asserted that they gave their allies much more autonomy and, although overseeing the foreign policy of their allies, did not interfere with internal constitutional arrangements – as they suggested the Athenians did, giving aid to pro-democracy elements. The Spartans 'proclaimed they were liberating Greece' from the Athenians.[78] The third Spartan embassy to Athens, on the eve of the Peloponnesian War, asked the Athenians to 'let the Greeks have autonomy'.[79] The accusation of infringing the independence of others was thrown back at the accuser and the Athenians duly replied that they would comply if Sparta would do the same for its allies. Athens and Sparta, and their respective allies, then fell into conflict.[80]

The war yielded victories for both sides but, with a substantive Athenian defeat to the Persians (whom they were also fighting in Egypt) in 454 BCE, the situation began to change when both the Athenians and the Persians reached for a peace agreement. The difficulty was that Athens which had justified a large amount of its heavy-handed actions with its allies, on the need to defend Greece from the Persians, suddenly found its pretext diminished when peace was reached with Persia in 449 BCE. Accordingly,

[73] Isocrates, *Panegyric* reprinted in Saunders, A (ed) (1970) *Greek Political Oratory* (London, Penguin) 67–69.

[74] Thucydides, *History of the Peloponnesian War* trans Finley, M (1984) (London, Penguin) I:23, I:95–99, 3:81–83. Also Kagan, D (2003) *The Peloponnesian War* (NYC, Harper) 64; unknown author, *Polity of the Athenians* reprinted in Botsford, G (ed) (1915) *Hellenic Civilisation Records* (NYC, Columbia University Press) 227, 235, 260; Kagan, D (1989) *Pericles of Athens and the Birth of Democracy* (NYC, Secker) 103–104.

[75] Thucydides, *History of the Peloponnesian War* trans Finley, M (1984) (London, Penguin) I:118, I:23, I:76, III:40, III:44, V:105, VIII:68.

[76] Polybius, *The Histories* trans Waterfield, R (2010) (Oxford, Oxford University Press) V:106.1–5.

[77] Kagan, D (2003) *The Peloponnesian War* (NYC, Harper) 1, 57.

[78] Thucydides, *History of the Peloponnesian War* trans Finley, M (1984) (London, Penguin) II.8.4; see also 1.117; Kagan, D (1989) *Pericles of Athens and the Birth of Democracy* (NYC, Secker) 101, 114.

[79] Thucydides, *History of the Peloponnesian War* trans Finley, M (1984) (London, Penguin) I.139.3.

[80] Thucydides, *History of the Peloponnesian War* trans Finley, M (1984) (London, Penguin) I.144.2.

a number of regions questioned whether it was desirable to stay aligned to the Athenians and the Delian League and to continue to pay tribute to the Athenians for a defensive alliance which was no longer required. This question was particularly important as the Spartans offered a different approach in their Peloponnesian League. Before these questions could be examined any further, an end to conflict between Athens and Sparta was reached in the Thirty Years Peace in 445 BCE. The core of this treaty saw a reconciliation over recently acquired territory and mutual recognition of both the Athenian and Spartan blocs. Supplemental promises of allies not being able to swap sides and of arbitration – as opposed to armed conflict – in cases of further difficulties, were also recorded.[81]

It was in the peace that followed the First Peloponnesian War that Pericles (495–429 BCE), a prominent Athenian statesman and general, rose to prominence. Under his leadership the Athenians strengthened the democratic element of their government, creating mechanisms for poor citizens to fully participate in all elements of the state. Around 430 BCE, Pericles explained and justified this system as one based on equality, not hierarchy and unjustifiable privilege. Thus:

> The constitution by which we live does not emulate the enactments of our neighbors. It is an example to others rather than an imitation of them. It is called democracy because power does not rest with the few, but with the many, and in law, as it touches individuals, all are equal, while in regard to the public estimation in which each man is held in any field, his advancement depends not on mere rotation, but rather on his true worth; nor does poverty dim his reputation or prevent him from assisting the State, if he has the capacity. Liberty marks both our public politics and the feelings which touch our daily life together.[82]

From such considerations, Democritus (460–370 BCE) could confidently assert that poverty under a democracy was better than prosperity under an autocracy. Euripides (480–406 BCE) in his play *The Suppliants* (c 422) would add that democracy was the antithesis of both brute force and the rule of wealth.[83] Conversely, Thucydides would portray this system as one which produced leaders who were dishonest, corrupt, unscrupulous and self-seeking.[84]

B. The Limits of Citizenship

One important point to note is that even when there was democracy – and *ipso facto* equality – this was a very restricted type of equality. The city of Athens was never very large, with perhaps a population of 100,000. Of this number, only about 30,000 would

[81] Thucydides, *History of the Peloponnesian War* trans Finley, M (1984) (London, Penguin) V:18–19; Kagan, D (2003) *The Peloponnesian War* (NYC, Harper) 48–50; Kagan, D (1989) *Pericles of Athens and the Birth of Democracy* (NYC, Secker) 128–29.

[82] Thucydides, *History of the Peloponnesian War* trans Finley, M (1984) (London, Penguin) II:36–39.

[83] Euripides, *The Suppliants* trans Jones, A (2004) (London, Kessinger Publishing) sections 403–408, 430–57. The point from Democritus is found in Roberts, J (1994) *Athens on Trial: The Antidemocratic Tradition in Western Thought* (New Jersey, Princeton University Press) 37.

[84] Thucydides, *History of the Peloponnesian War* trans Finley, M (1984) (London, Penguin) II:65.

have been full citizens – that is, males of Athenian descent for several generations. The other 70,000 were resident aliens, women and children. In addition, there were perhaps 150,000 slaves. Thus, the group that was given full equality and equal rights represented a little less than a tenth of the total population. Women were allowed no place in public life. Citizenship was hereditary and thus aliens were prevented from acquiring it. And above all it was a society resting on the backs of a great many slaves who had no rights at all.[85]

The point about the slaves is worth drawing out a little further, as the division between those with full and equal rights at the top of the social pyramid, and those at the absolute bottom of the social pyramid, was large. This was not, however, an inconsistency to the Athenians. The Athenians were merely following the long-standing tradition in Greece that slavery was an acceptable practice with deep roots in its Homeric past. Indeed, although Herodotus suggested that slavery was originally unknown in ancient Greece, by the time of the *Odyssey* slavery was an uncontested part of the cultural landscape.[86] This part of the landscape grew as the numbers of slaves increased and the divisions between the free and the enslaved became more pronounced – even though it was obvious that this could lead to violence. Nevertheless, the acceptance and support for slavery was so strong that traditional enemies, such as Athens and Sparta, were more likely to cooperate in the suppression of uprisings of slaves, as actually mandated in treaties, than to suggest that slavery was wrong. Thus, 'if the slaves rebel, the Athenians shall aid the [Spartans] with all their might and to the utmost of their powers'.[87] This agreement was necessary due to a long history of slave uprisings, which began in the middle of the seventh century BCE when the *Helots* (the enslaved population) of Sparta revolted, and it took Sparta 17 years to crush the uprising. In 464 BCE, also in Sparta, a further uprising occurred, which was so strong that Sparta had to call on the help of Athens to defeat it.[88]

Such support for slavery was a reflection of the prevailing view that although it may need to be regulated, it was not, prima facie, a bad practice. For as Aristotle, a man who owned 14 slaves, asserted, slavery was both natural (due to the irrational nature of the enslaved people) and often of benefit to the slave. 'It is clear, then, that some men are by nature free, and others slaves, and that for these latter slavery is both expedient and just.'[89] He added that barbarians 'on account of their customs [are] more slavish by nature' than Greeks and are therefore 'less suited to liberty'.[90]

[85] Dunn, J (2005) *Democracy: A History* (NYC, Atlantic Press) 35.

[86] For Herodotus, *The Histories* trans De Selincourt, A (2003) (London, Penguin) VI:137. For the *Odyssey* see sections XIV:3–4 and XIV:64–65.

[87] Thucydides, *History of the Peloponnesian War* trans Finley, M (1984) (London, Penguin) V:23.

[88] Thucydides, *History of the Peloponnesian War* trans Finley, M (1984) (London, Penguin) V:18–19; also Meltzer, M (1993) *Slavery: A World History* (NYC, DaCapo) 87.

[89] The quote is from *Politics* I:2–5; see also sections 1252a31–32, 1254a4–18, 30–32, and b21; 1255a2, 22–32, b6–8; 1260a12. Also *Rhetoric* I.12 1373b18, both reprinted in *The Complete Works of Aristotle* trans Barnes, J (1984) (Oxford, Oxford University Press). For some background, see Levin, M (1997) 'Aristotle on Natural Subordination' *Philosophy* 72:241–57; Dobbs, D (1994) 'Natural Right and Aristotle's Defence of Slavery' 56(1) *Journal of Politics* 69, 70; Garver, E (1994). 'Aristotle's Natural Slaves and Incomplete Human Beings' 32 *Journal of the History of Philosophy* 173–95.

[90] *Politics* 1285a19–22. See also section 1255a22–29.

The opposing view, as articulated by Alkidamas (and later reiterated by Philemon, 362–262 BCE), was that 'the deity gave liberty to all men, and nature created no one a slave'. This view never found popular support.[91] The best that could be achieved for slaves was that these 'living tools' (akin to draught animals) were treated fairly by their owners and, if they were lucky, later manumitted. Such goals, as advocated by Plato (who owned four slaves and believed slavery to be a good thing) and lawgivers like Lycurgus (820–730 BCE) and Solon (638–558 BCE), would filter down to the rule that slaves could not be killed by their masters outright. However, if they were killed, the owner needed to be 'purified' – rather than prosecuted. More substantive restraints focused on not enslaving other Greeks because of debt, because they were Greeks from the same polis, or simply because they were Greeks. Some of these restraints, especially in terms of commitments not to enslave specific Greek people, were the subject of reciprocal bilateral treaties in 260 and 251 BCE.[92]

C. Autonomy, Monarchy and the Rise of Rome

Thirteen years into the Thirty Year Peace, an Athenian ally (Potidaea) attempted to swap sides from Athens to a third party, Corinth. Sparta, after refusing to arbitrate in the matter, was drawn into defending the rights of its Corinthian ally. The Second Peloponnesian War was underway. This war, in addition to the further sacking of cities, saw thousands of men go head to head in battles. At Pylos in 425 BCE some 800 hoplites (and 2,000 support troops) from Athens clashed with 420 hoplites from Sparta. A year later at Delium, 7,000 Athenian hoplites fought 7,000 Boetian hoplites, whilst 10,000 light troops and cavalry attacked the sides of phalanxes that were 25 ranks deep.[93]

This second period of carnage ended with the Peace of Nicias of 421 BCE. This followed the earlier precedent, with an exchange of recently acquired territory and the independence of a number of areas. A mutual defence obligation was also agreed. This peace could not hold when Athens made an alliance with some newly-democratised states on the Peloponnese – which Sparta attacked. Athens was then torn between helping new allies, or honouring the peace treaty and coming to Sparta's aid in mutual

[91] Quoted by Aristotle, *Rhetoric* 1373b18.

[92] Slavery and the question of debt was dealt with by Solon. On enslaving fellow Athenians, see Plutarch, *Moralia* 842:A. On the question of not enslaving other Greeks, see Plato, *The Republic* 469.b–c; and Euripides, *Fragment* 831, and his play *Iphigenia* in Buckley, T (1880) *The Tragedies of Euripides* (London, Bohn) 1400–1401. The question of restraints in the behaviour of slave owners is covered by Plato in *Laws* 776b–778a; *Statesman* 289c and 309a. Even Aristotle suggested they had some rights. See *Politics* 1255b19-14, 1260b5-7, 1278b33, 1339a32; *Rhetoric* 1380b16-20. The 260 BCE Treaty was Between Milestus and the Cretan Cities Against the Purchase of Citizens and Slaves reprinted in Austin, M (ed) (1992) *The Hellenistic World from Alexander to the Roman Conquest: A Collection of Readings* (Cambridge, Cambridge University Press) 158–59. The 251 Treaty was between Pellana in Achaea and Delphi. This is discussed in Rostovtzeff, M (1941) *The Social and Economic History of the Hellenistic World*, Vol 1 (Oxford, Clarendon Press) 197–99. For the manumission records at the Delphi, see Austin, at 220–22.

[93] Kagan, D (2003). *The Peloponnesian War* (NYC, Harper) 48–50; Kagan, D (1989) *Pericles of Athens and the Birth of Democracy* (NYC, Secker) 128–29; Grant, R (2005) *Battle* (London, Dorling Kindersley) 63.

defence against the nascent democracies. Athens chose to defend its new democratic allies, taking up arms against Sparta at the battle of Mantinea – and losing the battle and ending the Peace of Nicias. Undeterred, the Athenians then attempted to invade Sicily. This decision may have been linked to a broader plan to use it as a base from which to expand into North Africa and attack Carthage directly. This was certainly in line with the argument raised by the Athenian statesman Alcibiades (450–404 BCE):

> We cannot fix the exact point at which our empire shall stop; we have reached a position in which we must not be content with retaining what we have but must scheme to extend it for, if we cease to rule others, we shall be in danger of being ruled ourselves.[94]

The pretext was to help the city of Lentini. The people of this polis believed their autonomy was being directly threatened by the oligarchs, turned democrats, turned military junta, of Syracuse. The orders of the Athenians were to restore the peoples of Segesta and Lentini to their cities if possible 'and to order all other matters in Sicily as they should deem best for the interests for Athens'.[95] This was not to be. The peoples of Syracuse, with direct assistance from the enemies of Athens, namely Sparta and Corinth, prevented the 50,000 Athenian and associated troops from achieving their objective of taking Syracuse and then proceeded to systematically destroy the Athenian expedition to such an extent that only a handful of the men ever made it back home. This disaster marked a collapse in the fortune of Athens and, in the next eight years, the Athenians suffered a succession of losses, culminating in the Spartan victory at Aegospotami in 405 BCE, at which the Athenians lost 190 of the 200 ships with which it tried to defend itself. In this turmoil, the Athenians opted for an oligarchy of 400 men, but this was short-lived and full democracy was quickly returned. Despite their resolve, in 404 BCE Athens was forced to submit when the city was exhausted, starved and besieged (during which time 80,000 people died of plague). The surrender stripped Athens of its defensive walls, its fleet and all of its overseas possessions. Athens was also obliged 'to have the same friends and enemies'[96] as Sparta. Finally, democracy was removed from Athens. However, the imposition of the 'Thirty Tyrants' was short-lived, as in 403 BCE the Athenians, with the support of one of the Spartan kings, overthrew these rulers and restored their democracy.[97]

It was in this climate that the famous trial (and execution) of Socrates occurred. The trial was held under the jurisdiction of one of the prizes of democratic Athens – the courts. It was this context that drew Plato to make his critique of democracy which would delight those who distrust democracy throughout the ages. Plato saw democracy as 'an agreeable form of anarchy with plenty of variety and an equality of a particular kind for equals and unequals alike'. He argued this system was guided by a public which was ignorant and susceptible to rhetoric rather than reason. The decisions of democratic populations could therefore be irrational and thus could not command respect. It was, he suggested, a dissolution of value, decency and good judgement.

[94] Thucydides, *History of the Peloponnesian War* trans Finley, M (1984) (London, Penguin) VI.18. See also V:18–19.

[95] Thucydides, *History of the Peloponnesian War* trans Finley, M (1984) (London, Penguin) VI:8.

[96] *The Works of Xenophon* trans Dakyns, M (1890) *Hellenica*, Vol I (London, Macmillan) 2:2.20.

[97] Champion, J (2010) *The Tyrants of Syracuse: War in Ancient Sicily* (London, Pen and Sword) 42, 54–61, 91.

It was foolish, viscous and potentially brutal, destroying everything from families to nations. It was also the road to inequality as 'when equality is given to unequal things, the result will be unequal'.[98] This made democracy a frontal assault on the possibility of a good life, lived with others in an ideal community. This situation was juxtaposed against an ideal society (described in *The Republic*) where the most capable (the wisest), not the most numerous, ruled. These wise persons, the Guardians, should make the decisions for all. The other people 'must follow the leader'.[99] From these divisions within the Republic considerations of justice were to be determined in accordance with the social position of individuals and the optimum advantage to the polis. Until this was achieved 'the human race will not see better days'.[100]

Aristotle had similar views. For him, democracy was not itself one of the good forms of rule, since it amounted to government of the poor. He considered it to be a regime of naked group interest, unapologetically devoted to serving the many at the expense of the wealthier, the better, the most elevated, the more fastidious or the most virtuous. He concurred with Plato in considering it to be violent, unstable and menacing. However, he did not suggest that democracy should be completely abandoned, as he realised that 'inequality is a cause of revolution'. To remove this threat, Aristotle suggested that the best political model was a mixed one, in which democracy was part of the governing structure but existed in conjunction with an oligarchy.[101] Very similar views were recorded by the author of *The Constitution of Athens* around 330 BCE, the 'Old Oligarch' (possibly Xenophon, Aristotle, or one of their students). This work suggested that the democratic constitution of Athens did not deserve applause. The author argued that it gave power to the poor, the unsavoury and the unabashedly popular, and did so quite deliberately at the expense of those with wealth, nobility of birth or social distinction. The democrats were ignorant, disorderly and vicious, with no respect for justice or decorum.[102]

Undeterred by such criticisms, democratic Athens survived both internally and externally. It survived the latter through a series of defence agreements by which a coalition of independent areas (including non-democracies) joined together to counter rivals such as Sparta, before the Peace of Antalcidas (also known as 'the Kings Peace') in 387 BCE came into being. This triparte peace treaty between Persia, Sparta and Athens, set down the cities of Asia belonged to Persia, as well as Cyprus, whilst, 'the other Greek cities, both small and great, should be left independent, except Lemnos, Imbros and Scyros; and these should belong, as of old, to the Athenians'. This recognition of independence for the vast majority of areas was a heavy loss to Athens.

[98] *Gorgias* 765E–75B. Note also the earlier sections in this work, 459 A–B, 515D–516E, 518–519; and *The Republic* 558C, 564a; *Crito* 46B–48A; also Dunn, J (2005) *Democracy: A History* (NYC, Atlantic Press) 44–47. For the actual trial, see Stone, I (1988) *The Trial of Socrates* (London, Picador).

[99] Note, although this point is from *The Republic* 474.b, it is supplemented by his writings in *The Laws*. See sections 334c–d, 690b, 722d, 746a–c, 875 c–d, 951c–d, 961a–c.

[100] The quote is from Epistle 7 in *Thirteen Epistles of Plato*. See also *The Republic*, sections 407, 433–34 and 443 c–d.

[101] *Politics* 1253a31, 1256–58, 1269b, 1274b41, 1275b18–20, 1278a20, 1279a32–34, 1292a, 1294b, 1318b, 1328a36, 1329a. Note also *Magna Moralia* I.xxxiii.15–16, and *Ethics* 9.6.3–4.

[102] Old Oligarch, *The Constitution of Athens* trans Bowersock, G (1968) (Cambridge, Harvard University Press) 1:1–1:8 (474–79).

Conversely, it was a strong gain for Sparta which had made a deal with Persia to recognise Persian sovereignty in the given areas in exchange for Persia keeping Athens, now clearly the foremost political power in Greece, in check.[103] This peace was soon eclipsed by the Second Athenian Confederacy of 377 BCE, under which Athens and its friends began to square off first against Sparta and then against Macedonia. This confederacy was based on the objective of collective defence, and the promise to enable each city 'to live in quiet [security], to possess their respective territories in security [to] preserv[e] their freedom and autonomy, using the form of government that they desire'.[104] The conflict which followed saw Sparta losing first to Thebes (who broke free from its Spartan alliance when some 8,000 of their men clashed with 12,000 Spartans, and became the leading power among the Greek city-states) in 371 BCE, and then to Athens, when 50,000 men clashed on the battlefield of Maninea in 362 BCE. At the same time Athens took care to create a new series of defence agreements, in which allies promised to support each other's democratic institutions, not allowing power to be usurped by tyrants or oligarchies. The Alliance of 362 BCE between Athens, Arcadia, Achaea, Elis and Phlius stated:

> If any one goes against Attica or overthrows the people of Athens or sets up a tyrant or an oligarchy, the Arcadians [et al] shall go in support of the Athenians . . . [or] . . . overthrows the people Philus or overthrows or changes the constitution of Achaea [et al] the Athenians shall go in support of these with all their strength as called on by those who are being wronged as far as possible.[105]

Whilst the Spartans were humbled, it soon became apparent that an even greater threat to the autonomy of Greek cities was arising in the form of Macedon. Isocrates may have exaggerated with his assertion that the Athenians were righteous leaders of their Greek neighbours who were not obsessed by overseas conquests nor were tyrants or slave-masters. However, Demosthenes (384–322 BCE) may have assessed the risk correctly in stating that the monarchy of Macedon, as represented by Philip II (382–336 BCE), had ambitions that were 'rooted in greed and violence'.[106]

The Macedonian Empire expanded rapidly through a combination of diplomacy, bluff, and the build up of a highly professional, and overtly rewarded, military. Philip II eventually came to blows with Athens over the Athenian's refusal to hand over

[103] *The Works of Xenophon* trans Dakyns, M (1890) *Hellenica*, Vol I (London, Macmillan) 5:1:31. For the inter-related agreements, see Rhodes, P (ed) *Greek Historical Inscriptions 404–323 BC* (2007) (Oxford, Oxford University Press) 234, 238, 244, 255. Note also the Alliance Between Boetia and Athens as reprinted in Ferguson, J (ed) *Political and Social Life in the Great Age of Athens: A Sourcebook* (1978) (London, Open University Press) 74.

[104] The Founding of the Second Athenian Confederacy 377 BC reprinted in Botsford, G (ed) (1915) *Hellenic Civilisation Records* (NYC, Columbia University Press) 391. See also the Oaths of the Allies (377 BC) also in Botsford at 396.

[105] Reprinted in Rhodes, P (ed) *Greek Historical Inscriptions 404–323 BC* (2007) (Oxford, Oxford University Press) 212–13. See also the Alliance between Athens and the Thessalians of 361 BCE, also in Rhodes, at 221. The figures for the battle are found in Grant, R (2005) *Battle* (London, Dorling Kindersley) 25.

[106] Demosthenes. The key works of Demosthenes are reprinted in Saunders, A (ed) (1970) *Greek Political Oratory* (London, Penguin). See his *Olynthiac II, Philippic I and III*. The pages in Saunders are 188–89, 190, 206–207, 221. The point about democracies and peace can be found in *On the Chersonese* at 40–43. The works of Isocrates are in the same volume, 24, 72, 80, 91, 104–106.

Philip's half-brother (to whom they had given asylum, holding him as a possible successor to the Macedonian crown). An additional pretext was Philip's failure to honour his promise to lease to Athens gold mines within a disputed region. The final provocation was the conquering of communities under the Athenian auspice on the Thracian coast. To make matters worse, Philip II persuaded a number of Athens' allies, including Chios, Rhodes, Cos and Byzantium, to rebel against their Athenian overlords. Philip's siding with the anti-Athenian forces in the Sacred War of 355–346 BCE strengthened him even further. When Philip finally declared war on Athens in 341 BCE, Athens had few allies and little food – as Philip had captured the entire corn supply. When 50,000 Athenians and Thebans were defeated by some 32,000 Macedonians at Chaeronea in 338 BCE, the result was significant.[107]

The battle of Chaeronea changed ancient Greece forever. It made Philip absolute master of a Greece that had previously been composed of autonomous states. As one ancient source soberly put it, 'for the whole of Greece this day marked the end of its glorious supremacy and of its ancient independence'.[108] Undisputed leadership in the Hellenic world passed to Macedon. This transfer was codified in the Common Peace/League of Corinth of 338 BCE. Under this peace, the signatories agreed 'nor shall I overthrow the kingdom of Philip or his descendants, nor the constitutions existing in each State when they swore the oaths concerning the peace'.[109] In practical terms, although some Greek areas (such as Thebes) were occupied and lost local autonomy, others, including Athens, were treated leniently and were allowed to retain their democratic institutions. They did, however, lose their ability to set their own foreign policy goals and had to accept the hegemony of Philip – and ultimately his vision, which was implemented by his son Alexander the Great (356–323 BCE) – of 'panhellenism', which would lead to the invasion of Persia.[110]

Alexander held similar views to his father on the question of constitutional type. The only rule he insisted upon was his absolute authority. Accordingly, when some cities (such as Thebes) attempted to throw off Macedonian rule upon the death of his father, he had them crushed to such a degree 'that the Greeks would be so struck by the magnitude of the disaster that they would be frightened into submission'.[111] Once his overall authority was assured, he did not have any preferred type of political order, allowing communities to be democracies with relative degrees of autonomy, provided they acknowledged him as overlord. His only rule seems to have been that if a community was not loyal to him he would impose the political system of the opposition.

[107] Worthington, I (2008) *Philip II of Macedonia* (New Haven, Yale University Press) 29–34, 40–43, 130–35. Also Philip's War Upon Olythus reprinted in Botsford, G (ed) (1915) *Hellenic Civilisation Records* (NYC, Columbia University Press) 401.

[108] Justin, *Epitome of the Philippic History* trans Heckel, W (1994) (Oxford, Oxford University Press) IX:3.11.

[109] Reprinted in Rhodes, P (ed) (2007) *Greek Historical Inscriptions 404–323 BC* (Oxford, Oxford University Press) 375–76, also reprinted in Barker, E (ed) (1959) *From Alexander to Constantine: Passages and Documents Illustrating the History of Social and Political Ideas* (Oxford, Oxford University Press) 68.

[110] See Rhodes, P (ed) (2007) *Greek Historical Inscriptions 404–323 BC* (Oxford, Oxford University Press) 375–76; also Barker, E (ed) (1959) *From Alexander to Constantine: Passages and Documents Illustrating the History of Social and Political Ideas* (Oxford, Oxford University Press) 65–68. Also the Agreement with Priene and Alexander at 420.

[111] The quotation is from Plutarch, 'Life of Alexander' in *Greek Lives* trans Waterfield, R (2009) (Oxford, Oxford University Press) IX:6–11.

For example, when a pro-Persian oligarchy of Chios betrayed the city, Alexander imposed democracy after he had regained control.[112]

Despite this tolerance of limited forms of local authority and democracy in some instances, the essence of power in Greece at this time was monarchy. Monarchies were not new to the political theories or practice of Persia or parts of Greece. In Macedonia Philip II bequeathed to his son Alexander an established dynasty where 'only the name' of the king and the size of the kingdom changed. For whilst Philip was Lord of Greece, Alexander was Lord of Asia, coming to hold all of the Persian lands in addition to the Greek lands already within his hands. He (and his successors, especially Seleucid (358–281 BCE) and Ptolemy (367–283 BCE)) believed that his rule was divinely inspired and, through the mixing of the best parts of Greek and non-Greek culture, and through absolute and autocratic rule he could hold together a large and diverse empire. In this setting, monarchies became dynasties. This was unlike the more constitutional types of monarchy in Macedon in which succession depended on birth into the royal house, nomination by the outgoing king (if he had time), the agreement of the king's inner circle, and the approval of the assemblies of either the citizens or the army.[113]

This position was only reached with the fragmentation of Alexander's empire. This happened soon after his death as he left no obvious or legitimate heir. His half-brother, Arrhidaeus, suffered from a mental condition that made him unsuitable to rule. There was a child, Heracles, by a former mistress, Barsine, but Alexander had never married her, nor acknowledged the boy as his own. Finally, there was his son by his wife Roxanne (343–310 BCE), Alexander IV (323–310 BCE), who was born after Alexander's death. This left the question of who would act as regent for the baby Alexander (IV), and in the interim, how the newly conquered and barely pacified empire which consisted of about three million square miles, would be governed. The solution was a power-sharing agreement, reached at the Partition of Babylon in 323 BCE, in which the territories of Alexander were assigned to his various generals. The gathering at which the partition occurred included all seven of his bodyguards. Of these men, five would strive to become kings in their own right, but only two would succeed – Ptolemy and Lysimachus (360–281 BCE) – and only one would establish a dynasty. Other senior men present who were not bodyguards included Seleucus (commander of one of the crack regiments) and Antipater (397–319 BCE), the most powerful man in the empire after Alexander. The position was reached whereby the empire was divided up among 12 different men, in the interim, as a type of trust for the future king Alexander IV – who was born around September 323 BCE. Perdiccas (d 320 BCE), one of his bodyguards and leader of the companion cavalry, assumed the

[112] The Agreement Between Alexander the Great and Chios reprinted in Rhodes, P (ed) *Greek Historical Inscriptions 404–323 BC* (2007) (Oxford, Oxford University Press) 420, 433. Note also reprinted in Austin, M (ed) (1981) *The Hellenistic World from Alexander to the Roman Conquest* (Cambridge, Cambridge University Press) 14–15; Diodorus *Library of History* trans Wells, B (1963) (Boston, Loeb) XVII:14.3.

[113] Diodorus *Library of History* trans Wells, B (1963) (Boston, Loeb) XVII:2.2; Barker, E (ed) (1959) *From Alexander to Constantine* (Cambridge, Cambridge University Press) 82–89; also Austin, M (ed) (1992) *The Hellenistic World from Alexander to the Roman Conquest: A Collection of Readings* (Cambridge, Cambridge University Press) 66–67; Waterfield, R (2011) *Dividing the Spoils: The War for Alexander the Great's Empire* (Oxford, Oxford University Press) 9.

regency of the infant, while Roxanne eliminated the last female members of the Persian royal house, including Alexander's two Persian wives. The only problem was that almost immediately the successors, to quote Plutarch (46–120), began to 'carve up his empire like the carcass of some great slaughtered beast'.[114]

The first attempt to carve up the beast was with the treaty of Triparadisus in 321 BCE, through which 21 generals were granted territory, and a further three were granted positions such as collector of the tribute, the king's bodyguard and commander of the horse. This division was a complete failure as there were four brutal wars between 321 and 301 BCE. These were, in essence, civil wars as they involved Macedonian successors fighting each other – but they were also world wars in which battles were fought in, inter alia, Greece, North Africa, Asia Minor, the Middle East and Iran, as a plethora of successors recognised themselves as divinely appointed monarchs. All of these men became kings as a result of war. Their royal status was gained and maintained by war and a never-ending cycle of bloodshed, and the possession of territory and wealth. The situation was one whereby 'they were perpetually at war, because plots and jealousies were part of their natures, and they treat the two words, war and peace, like current coins, using whichever happens to be for their advantage, regardless of justice'.[115]

The First War of the Successors involved the overtly bold Ptolemy, who had already claimed the treasury of Egypt and hijacked the corpse of Alexander as it was making its way back to Macedon, clashing with the ambitious Perdiccas en-route. However, before full conflict could erupt, Perdiccas was murdered by his own troops. This resulted in a further conference of the Successors at Triparadeisus in 320 BCE, which saw another reorganisation of the territory. Antipater was the new regent. Antigonus held most of Asia, whilst Ptolemy retained Egypt and was granted 'any lands further west from Egypt that he may acquire by the spear'.[116] Meanwhile, in Greece, rebellions broke out soon after Alexander died, in the Lamian War – or what the Athenians and Aetolians referred to as the War for Greek Freedom – of 323 to 322 BCE. This was a disaster for those challenging Macedonian hegemony. Following the Battle of Crannon in Thessaly, Antipater (397–319 BCE) imposed a pro-Macedonian oligarchy upon Athens. In addition, the ringleaders who espoused freedom and democracy, including in particular, Demosthenes, were either deported or sentenced to death.

The spark for the Second War was the choice of succession by Antipater, who appointed Polyperchon (394–303 BCE) over his son Cassander (350–297 BCE) to rule after his death in 319 BCE. Thereafter, Cassander attempted a coup which Antigonus (382–301 BCE) was happy to join on the grounds that Antipater had no right to select his own successor. Antigonus added that 'all Greeks should be free, exempt from

[114] Waterfield, R (2011) *Dividing the Spoils: The War for Alexander the Great's Empire* (Oxford, Oxford University Press) 16–29, 142–43; Diodorus (1963) *Library of History* trans Wells, B (Boston, Loeb) XVII:117; Plutarch, 'Life of Demetrius' in *Greek Lives* trans Waterfield, R (2009) Oxford, Oxford University Press) 30.

[115] Plutarch, 'Life of Pyrrhus' in *Greek Lives* trans Waterfield, R (2009) (Oxford, Oxford University Press) 12.

[116] Arrian *Anabasis of Alexander* trans Brunt, P (1983) (Boston, Loeb) 'After Alexander' fragment. I:34; also Waterfield, R (2011) *Dividing the Spoils: The War for Alexander the Great's Empire* (Oxford, Oxford University Press) 65–73.

garrisons and autonomous'.[117] Similarly, Polyperchon (394–303 BCE) wrote an open letter to all the Greek cities, urging them to reopen their battle for freedom by overthrowing the oligarchic administrations installed by Antipater – which most of the Peloponnesian cities, including Athens, agreed to do. However, such democratic revitalisations were short-lived, with the Athenians surrendering in 317 BCE, and having a dictatorship foisted upon them.[118]

The Third War of the Successors began in 314 BCE when Antigonus repeated his cry that all Greek cities should be free, autonomous and ungarrisoned. Ptolemy (367–283 BCE) responded with a proclamation of his own, affirming his commitment to the freedom of the Greek cities. Others within the alliance opposing Antigonus, such as Cassander, did not even pretend to hold such views but rounded up and killed rebels promoting democracy. Cassander could do this as his power was growing exponentially. He had become the de facto regent of Alexander IV, before having him and his mother Roxanne murdered during the Third War. The third conflict, despite much battling between Antigonus and Polyperchon, on one side, and Cassander, Ptolemy, Lysimachus and Seleucus, on the other, was a stalemate. Accordingly, they all agreed to the Peace of the Dynasts in 311. This peace more or less recognised the status quo from before the war. Cassander was recognised as General of Europe. Lysimachus kept Thrace, Ptolemy kept greater Egypt (but renounced his claims to Palestine and Phoenicia) and all of Asia was explicitly reserved for Antigonus.[119]

While peace was being negotiated, the Babylonia War (311–309 BCE) began and it continued as Antigonus and his son, Demetrius I: the Besieger (337–288 BCE) opposed Seleucus, and later Cassander. After Ptolemy and Cassander invaded Greece in 309 BCE Ptolemy joined the conflict against Antigonus and his son in what became known as the Fourth War of the Successors. The rhetoric of the banner of 'freedom for the Greeks' was now adopted by Demetrius I who justified his wars as being waged by 'the liberator of Greece'. His most notable success was that of freeing Athens in 307 BCE and restoring their democratic constitution. He further justified the war with the creation of the Hellenic League of 302 BCE. This appears to have been based upon the League established by Philip in 337 BCE, through which the independent Greek cities could combine, in a federal structure, to regain their traditional status (albeit subservient to an overlord who controlled foreign policy). Opposing him, Ptolemy tried to advance his way through the Greek territories, battling Demetrius and Antigonus, portraying himself as having 'liberated the cities, restored their laws, re-established to all their ancestral constitutions and remitted their taxes'.[120] When the two opposing

[117] Diodorus, *Library of History* trans Wells, B (1963) (Boston, Loeb) XIX:61–62.2.

[118] Waterfield, R (2011) *Dividing the Spoils: The War for Alexander the Great's Empire* (Oxford, Oxford University Press) 82–92, 110–14, 123–24. See Pausanias, *Description of Greece* I.25.3–6.

[119] Diodorus, *Library of History* trans Wells, B (1963) (Boston, Loeb) XIX:61–62.2. *The Library of Photicus* trans Reese, F (1923, 2010) (London, Nabo) 35–37. See also the fragment of Arrian reprinted in Austin, M (ed) (1992) *The Hellenistic World from Alexander to the Roman Conquest: A Collection of Readings* (Cambridge, Cambridge University Press) 45–46; Waterfield, R (2011) *Dividing the Spoils: The War for Alexander the Great's Empire* (Oxford, Oxford University Press) 82–92, 110–14, 123–24.

[120] Decree of the League of Islanders on the Acceptance of Ptolemaieia reprinted in Austin, M (ed) (1992) *The Hellenistic World from Alexander to the Roman Conquest: A Collection of Readings* (Cambridge, Cambridge University Press) 359–60.

sides met at the Battle of Ipsus in 301 BCE an army of 65,000 men swept the opposing force of 80,000 men from the battlefield. Antigonus met his end in this battle under a shower of javelins. Demetrius survived, only to be rejected by Athens, who he then went on to battle, without success.

At the same point, new contenders, such as the young prince Pyrrhus of Epirus (319–272 BCE), emerged, moving as a hostage between Ptolemy and Demetrius, before successfully seising the throne of Epirus (after being invited to be a joint ruler), but failing to seise the throne of Macedon (after being invited into the country through a dynastic dispute) as Demetrius got there first. Undeterred, Pyrrhus formed an alliance with Ptolemy against Demetrius through which they jointly invaded Macedonia and divided it between themselves. Demetrius escaped, only to be captured by his old ally, Seleucus, who allowed his prisoner to die in captivity in 282 BCE. Pyrrhus would die a decade later, attempting to steal the crown of Sparta, after years of fighting both Sicily and Rome and only ever achieving hollow victories. Whilst Pyrrhus was grinding his men into the dirt elsewhere, Seleucus would go on to battle for Lysimachus's Asian provinces. These wars consumed not only their men, but also their leaders. Their last war in 281 BCE saw the armies of the 77-year-old Seleucus and the 80-year-old Lysimachus clashing in Lydia. The 80-year-old lost the battle and died fighting with a sword in his hand with his empire about to collapse like a house of cards. Seleucus took the spoils and added them to his empire, which now included central Anatolia, the Levant, Mesopotamia, Persia, today's Turkmenistan, Pamir and parts of Pakistan. He came the closest of any of the successors to emulating the acquisitions of Alexander. However, his power could not prevent him from being murdered by the political refugee Ptolemy Ceraunus (319–285 BCE) to whom he had been giving shelter.[121]

The two remaining surviving sectors of Alexander's empire, Ptolemy and Seleucid, now locked horns. The battleground for these protagonists was Syria. Ptolemy would invade, and be forced to retreat from, Syria four times. This conflict over the ownership of Syria and other remaining parts of the empire of Alexander, involving questions about imperial succession and territory, would continue to cost the lives of tens of thousands of people in the forthcoming century as the rival dynasties consumed citizens and soldiers alike. Once again, the patterns of the fathers were repeated by their dynastic children. Peace treaties, such as that of 279 BCE, attempted to set the spheres of influence and were glued together with inter-dynastic marriage alliances which disintegrated as the children tried to reclaim the glory and rule the undivided empire of Alexander.[122]

If anything, the tendency towards inter-dynastic marriages added to the mix of usurpers, as blood lines split and fought each other (as in the Second and Third Syrian Wars) and regions such as Bactria and Parthia sought outright independence from

[121] Appian, *Roman History III. Fragment 10* reprinted in Lewis, N and Reinhold M (eds) (1955) *Roman Civilisation: Records*, Vol 1 (Columbia, Columbia University Press) 76–77; Waterfield, R (2011) *Dividing the Spoils: The War for Alexander the Great's Empire* (Oxford, Oxford University Press) 129, 150–54, 178–79, 184–85, 196; Champion, J (2009) *Pyrrhus of Epirus* (London, Pen and Sword) 12–18, 34–35, 98–99, 130–39; Grant, R (2005) *Battle* (London, Dorling Kindersley) 30; Regan, G (2006) *Battles that Changed History* (London, Carlton) 21–23.

[122] Cook, S (ed) (1954) *The Cambridge Ancient History VII: The Hellenistic Monarchies and the Rise of Rome* (Cambridge, Cambridge University Press) 100–101.

around 250 BCE, before they too devolved into dynastic self-destruction. The one leader of note who climbed to the top of this morass was Antiochus III (241–187 BCE), who, despite inheriting a disorganised state, went on to launch a series of attacks against Ptolemaic Syria. The greatest of these was in 217 BCE, at the battle of Raphia, when he directed 70,000 of his men against a slightly larger army under the rule of Ptolemy IV (r 221–205 BCE). This battle aimed at taking control of the area which is, roughly, modern-day Israel, Lebanon, Jordan and Syria. Whilst this adventure was a failure, Antiochus III was successful in retrieving Parthia and Bactria, before venturing out into India and the Arabian coast. This occurred around 206 BCE, when Antiochus III crossed the Hindu Kush mountains, forcing the surrender of a local chief in the Kabul valley. After this surrender the upper north-west corner was reoccupied and held until around 130 BCE by various Greek successors from Bactria, before it disappeared from history.[123]

The background to the next engagement in Greece was the conflict between the Aetolian and Achaean Leagues. In the classical Greek tradition, these two leagues represented opposing blocs linked by defensive agreements. The Achaean League was a large federal-based institution, mainly driven by the goal of freeing all Peloponnesus from despots, and annexing the individual states by negotiation or force. Its ideal was, 'equality and absolute freedom – in a word – democracy among the Achaeans'.[124] By 229 BCE, the League had acquired Corinth, Megalopolis and Argos. Such expansion found the League running into difficulties with Sparta. These difficulties resulted in the Achaean League calling on the aid of the king of Macedonian, Philip V (238–179 BCE). Aid was given, and Macedonia soon regained control over much of the region – including Athens, which ended up losing all vestiges of independence and being garrisoned by Macedonian troops until 229 BCE. No sooner was this contract concluded than, in 220 BCE, the Achaean League entered into a war against the Aetolian League. The Aetolian League was a separate confederation of tribal communities and cities centred on Aetolia in central Greece, with an alliance with Athens, which also shared antipathy to the power of Macedonia. When the members of the Aetolian League struck out, Philip then called for a Panhellenic conference at which the Aetolian aggression was condemned, and action undertaken in what became known as the Social War. Philip, preferring not to fight under the flag of Achaean League, had the league rebranded as the Hellenic League. This league fought the Aetolians because of their sacking of temples, ravaging of territory, and possession of the land of others. By the end of the conflict Philip controlled most of Greece (but not Athens, Rhodes or

[123] Polybius, *The Histories* trans Waterfield, R (2010) (Oxford, Oxford University Press) V:67. Note also Smyrna under Seleucus II reprinted in Austin, M (ed) (1992) *The Hellenistic World from Alexander to the Roman Conquest: A Collection of Readings* (Cambridge, Cambridge University Press) 297–304; Smith, V (1962) *The Early History of India* (Oxford, Oxford University Press) 234–38. Grant, R (2005) *Battle* (London, Dorling Kindersley) 30; Appian, *The Roman Histories* trans White, H (1912) (Boston, Loeb) 55; Raychaudhuri, H (1999) *Political History of Ancient India* (Oxford, Oxford University Press) 338–45, 376–79; Smith, V (1962) *The Early History of India* (Oxford, Oxford University Press) 254.

[124] Polybius, *The Histories* trans Waterfield, R (2010) (Oxford, Oxford University Press) II:37.7–44. Note also the Decree of Chrenmonides on the Alliance between Athens and Sparta reprinted in Austin, M (ed) (1992) *The Hellenistic World from Alexander to the Roman Conquest: A Collection of Readings* (Cambridge, Cambridge University Press) 94–96 and the Hellenic League of 302; also in Austin, 76–78.

Pergamon), and through the Peace of Naupactus in 217 BCE, which brought conflict between Macedon and the Greek leagues to an end. Here, all the parties agreed that 'above all the Greeks should never go to war against each other'.[125]

Philip V then attempted the same trick as his predecessors in seeking to channel all the Greek energy against a common external enemy. His only mistake was that he chose the wrong enemy – Rome. After first linking with Carthage, he managed to avoid a near brush with death through the Treaty of Phoencie with Rome. While this allowed Philip to hold most of his empire intact, he reverted to a traditional pattern of imposing political systems on communities under his auspice – which were the opposite of those in power if they had rebelled against him. In this case, it meant that Philip took a pro-democratic line, generally siding with the democrats within his broad empire against the aristocrats, whom he felt had been insufficiently supportive of his campaigns. Elsewhere, such as in his alliance with Antiochus III, he attempted to try to gain the territories that the successors of Ptolemy still held.

In the case of both Philip V and Antiochus III, the Romans either threatened to, or actually did, stop their advances, while at the same time they came to offer real autonomy to Greek cities. This was achieved by making Antiochus agree to 'stay out of Europe and withdraw from all of Asia on this side of the Taurus mountains'[126] and 'keep away from autonomous [Greek] cities'.[127] Similarly, in the Treaty of Tempe in 196 BCE, Philip had to give up Macedonia's possessions in Greece and Asia and agree that all of these cities were 'to be free and enjoy their own laws'.[128] The Romans demonstrated their sincerity on this point at the Isthmian Games of 196 BCE, when Titus Quinctius Flamininus (c 229–174 BCE) proclaimed that, thanks to Rome, Greece had been liberated and Rome would guarantee its future freedom. Macedonian garrisons were evacuated and their control over the Greek mainland ended. Next Sparta was humbled by Roman military might. Flaminius remained true to his word, as Rome took no territory and by 194 BCE had evacuated her armies from mainland Greece. In doing so, it was declared that having conquered King Philip, eight separate Greek regions were to be 'free, exempt from tribute, and subject to their own laws'.[129] With this move, Rome not only forced Philip to respect the freedom and independence of all Greeks, but implicitly guaranteed their freedom, thus constituting itself as the protector of Hellenic freedom. At the same point, Flamininus returned to the Greeks all of the property that the Romans had seised. As he explained in a letter to some disbelieving Greek authorities:

[125] Polybius, *The Histories* trans Waterfield, R (2010) (Oxford, Oxford University Press) V:103. Also sections II:37; IV:25 and XII:10–12; Waterfield, R (2011) *Dividing the Spoils: The War for Alexander the Great's Empire* (Oxford, Oxford University Press) 110–14, 123–24, 129, 150–54; Grant, R (2005) *Battle* (London, Dorling Kindersley) 30. Also Cook, S (ed) (1954) *The Cambridge Ancient History. VII: The Hellenistic Monarchies and the Rise of Rome* (Cambridge, Cambridge University Press) 66–71, 101.

[126] Livy, *The Early History of Rome* trans De Selincourt, A (1960) (London, Penguin,) XXXVII:45.10–21.

[127] Polybius, *The Histories* trans Waterfield, R (2010) (Oxford, Oxford University Press) XVIII:49.1.

[128] Polybius, *The Histories* trans Waterfield, R (2010) (Oxford, Oxford University Press) XVIII:44–45.1; also Livy, *The Early History of Rome* trans De Selincourt, A (1960) (London, Penguin) XXXIIII.xii–xiii, xxiv. 5–7.

[129] Livy, *The Early History of Rome* trans De Selincourt, A (1960) (London, Penguin) 33.32.4–10; also Polybius, *The Histories* trans Waterfield, R (2010) (Oxford, Oxford University Press) XVIII:44.

> Now therefore, all landed property and buildings belonging to the public domain of the Roman state which are still in its possession, we give to your city, so that in this too you may learn our character and the fact that we are determined to seek absolutely no financial profit, esteeming good will and reputation above all others.[130]

Despite this remarkable gesture of allowing the Greek communities to govern themselves, this situation could not continue in the face of the actions of the son of Philip V, Perseus (212–166 BCE), who drew on the dispossessed in the oligarchies and the poor in the democracies to purse the Third Macedonian War of 171 BCE. The conclusion of this war ensured that the balance of power in Greece was turned conclusively towards Rome, with Macedonia and her allies, although still free, being deprived of their associated territories; both these and the original centres were divided at the end of the conflict and were settled upon by Roman veterans, bolstered by the propertied classes who had generally been opposed to the views of Perseus. Such acts marked the effective end of Hellenistic Macedonia and the monarchy of the Antigonid dynasty.[131]

The Fourth, and final, Macedonian War began in 150 BCE and ended two years later, when a pretender sought to claim the throne of Macedon. The Romans dealt with this quickly, before moving onto the Achaean War in 146 BCE, when the Achaeans erupted in open revolt, before being comprehensively crushed in a series of direct and pre-emptive acts. Not only were the cities of the defeated that had the potential to cause problems in the future destroyed, but so too were their political institutions. After the sack of Corinth, the Achean league and the democracies of the region were disbanded and new governments were established 'based on property qualifications' – rather than equality of citizenship.[132]

The last Greek attempt at retrieving the freedom of Greek communities and the democracy that resided within some of them occurred with Mithridates VI (134–63 BCE). Mithridates, like many of the Greek super monarchs before him, sought to find good reasons for Greek communities to flock to his banner and fight against Roman imperialism. The three conflicts which made up the Mithridatic wars resulted in the deaths of at least 400,000 people. This began with the First Mithridatic War (89–85 BCE), in which a multitude of Greek cities, including Athens and Sparta, which already resented Roman rule (and taxes), were happy to follow the leadership of Mitrhidates. The speech which persuaded the Athenians to become involved in this conflict was recorded in the following terms:

> Athenians! We must not bear this state of anarchy any longer, imposed by the Roman Senate whilst it controls our government. The Romans have closed our temples and let our

[130] Letter of Flamininus reprinted in Lewis, N and Reinhold M (eds) (1955) *Roman Civilisation: Records*, Vol 1 (Columbia, Columbia University Press) 309; also Matyszak, P (2009) *Roman Conquests: Macedonia and Greece* (London, Pen and Sword) 56–57.

[131] See the 171 BCE Letter of the Romans to the Delphic Amphictyony Concerning Perseus reprinted in Austin, M (ed) (1992) *The Hellenistic World from Alexander to the Roman Conquest: A Collection of Readings* (Cambridge, Cambridge University Press) 140–41; Barker, E (1959) *From Alexander to Constantine: Passages and Documents Illustrating the History of Social and Political Ideas* (Oxford, Oxford University Press) 80–82; Matyszak, P (2009) *Roman Conquests: Macedonia and Greece* (Pen and Sword, London) 124–25; also Livy, *The Early History of Rome* trans De Selincourt, A (1960) (London, Penguin) XLII.30; XLV.26–33; Livy XXXIV.51. 4., XLII.xxix.i–xxx.7; Grant, R (2005) *Battle* (London, Dorling Kindersley) 31.

[132] Pausanias. *Description of Greece* trans Wycherly, S (1969) (Boston, Loeb) VII:xvi.7–10.

> schools fall to dust. Our theatres are off limits and our courts of justice and schools of philosophy are silenced. They have even taken the Pnyx, our sacred place of Assembly away from the people![133]

The Athenians then restored democracy and killed the leading oligarch who had allied himself with Rome. This choice was a bad one for Athens and the other Greek allies of Mithridates. From the beginning, although Mithridates could take Delos, his forces could not advance very far. When the Romans struck back under the leadership of Sulla (138–78 BCE), Mithridates lost the battle for Piraeus Athens was taken, and Mithridates then faced defeat at the battle of Orchomenus. The concluding Treaty of Dardanos in 85 BCE was built around a return to the status quo, as it had existed before the war. This meant that Greece belonged to Rome and the rebellious cities such as Athens were forced to play huge indemnities, which accompanied the losses of any residual liberties that they had once possessed.[134]

The complete assimilation of the other regions of the successors to Alexander continued in the remaining parts of the world under Greek control. Antiochus IV Epiphanes (215–164 BCE) attempted to repeat the glories of his father and tried to take all of the Ptolemy territories (using the choice of favourites in dynastic disputes as the stepping stone), from Egypt to Cyprus. His adventures were forbidden by Rome, which warned him not to step outside his circle of influence in Syria. This was difficult as provinces of his empire asserted their independence, with corners such as Parthia again breaking free under what became the dynasty of Mithridates. Thereafter, the Seleucid dynasty began to splinter into many pieces, as various claimants to the throne asserted they were the 'the true king' (as opposed to other contenders), and family feuds resulted in the empire shrinking to a small section of land around Damascus, which saw claimants moving from any display of moderate kings to 'lawlessness of tyrants . . . [which] . . . involved [their] subjects in disasters beyond remedy'.[135] The last Antiochus, XIII, spent his time seeking support from Rome as a client ruler of Syria. This lasted until 64 BCE, when Pompey decided to end the dynasty, having Antiochus deposed and killed by a Syrian chieftain. The same situation occurred within Judea, where it was Rome who approved the appointment of favourable clients, such as Herod (74–4 BCE), and then his children. However, their government was so poor that they were banished, and Judea was made into a Roman province, governed by an imperial curator.[136]

The Greek royal family of Ptolemy ruled an empire in Egypt for 275 years, from 305 to 30 BCE. Their reign ended with the suicide of Cleopatra VII Philopator (69–30 BCE). This dynasty, which reached its geographical peak under Ptolemy III Euergetes, (r 246–222 BCE), thereafter slowly declined, as the country tried to split under the

[133] Athenaeus, *The Learned Banquet* trans Olsen, J (2007) (Boston, Loeb) 5.213–15; also Mayor, A (2010) *The Poison King: The Life and Legend of Mithradates* (New Jersey, Princeton University Press) 177–79. The figures are from White, M (2011) *Atrocitology* (NYC, Norton) 34–35.

[134] Mayor, A (2010) *The Poison King: The Life and Legend of Mithradates* (New Jersey, Princeton University Press) 208–13, 218–22.

[135] Diodorus *Library of History* trans Wells, B (1963) (Boston, Loeb) XXXIII:4.

[136] Polybius, *The Histories* (2010) trans Waterfield, R (Oxford, Oxford University Press) XI:34, XXIX:27, XXXI:2; Cook, S (ed) (1969) *The Cambridge Ancient History. Rome and the Mediterranean*, Vol VIII (Cambridge, Cambridge University Press) 529–30; Scullard, H (1982) *From the Gracchi to Nero* (London, Methuen) 248–51.

reign of Ptolemy IV (r 221–205 BCE) – from which the laws on the Rosetta Stone emerged – before falling victim to the efforts of Antiochus III (and his son) and Philip V of Macedon, to divide the country between themselves. As noted above, these efforts were only prevented from succeeding by the threats from Rome. Although Rome would not allow Egypt to be taken by external forces, it had less success with the internal rebellions and dynastic disputes that plagued the dynasty. For example, on the death of Ptolemy VI in 145, his younger brother took the throne, married Ptolemy VI's widow (who was his own biological sister) and had her and his brother's child murdered during the wedding ceremony. He then began a relationship with his new queen's daughter from a previous relationship – who then, as his lover, became a fierce rival of her mother, the queen. These complications only increased when the Cleopatra line entered the scene.[137]

Even when Rome intervened to place favoured contenders, such as Ptolemy IX (143–81 BCE), on the Egyptian throne, the dynastic disputes and associated palace coups or civil wars did not cease. Ptolemy IX became king of the dynasty three times, as various other contenders took and then lost power. It was only around 55 BCE, when an explicitly supported Ptolemaic king (who was paying half of Egypt's revenue in return for the benefits of being the friend of Rome) was toppled without the approval of Rome, that Pompey authorised the invasion of Egypt and the restoration of Ptolemy XII. This move was consistent with deliberations in Rome about the formal annexation of the region over the previous 20 years, following the alleged bequest of the region by a grateful Ptolemy IX in 80 BCE. This bequest may have been consistent with a similar, also disputed, bequest by Ptolemy VII of the kingdom of Cyrene (modern-day east Libya) to Rome.[138]

Before his death, Ptolemy XII chose his daughter, Cleopatra VII Philopator, as his coregent. Upon the death of her father, Cleopatra was joined by her brother, Ptolemy XIII, who promptly turned on his sister in yet another civil war in Egypt, and attempted to ingratiate himself with the Romans by killing Pompey when he fled to the country in 48 BCE. When the force hunting Pompey entered Egypt, Cleopatra met Julius Caesar (100–44 BCE), who quickly sided with her in her dynastic dispute, in both principle and arms. She consummated a relationship with Caesar that solidified her grip on the throne, as he abandoned plans to annex Egypt. The Roman forces then battled the army of Ptolemy XIII to defeat, after which Ptolemy XIII was drowned in the Nile and Caesar restored Cleopatra to her throne. She stayed loyal to the party of Caesar after his assassination, which continued to recognise her throne, and consummated another relationship with one of the triumvirs, Mark Antony (83–30 BCE). To keep her throne even more secure, she had Antony order the death of her sister (Arsinoe). Such acts, combined with the power-vacuum that developed in the wake of Caesar's death, and a belief that Cleopatra was conspiring with Antony to become 'Queen of Kings', eventually lead to the invasion of Egypt by the forces of Octavian (later known as Augustus) (63 BCE–14 CE). Following defeat at the battle of Actium in

[137] Wilkinson, T (2010) *The Rise and Fall of Ancient Egypt* (London, Bloomsbury) 480–83, 486–88, 492–94.

[138] Cook, S (ed) (1966) *The Cambridge Ancient History. The Roman Republic*, Vol IX (Cambridge, Cambridge University Press) 104–107; Mayor, A (2010) *The Poison King: The Life and Legend of Mithradates* (New Jersey, Princeton University Press) 58–59.

30 BCE, both Antony and Cleopatra committed suicide and Cleopatra's son to Caesar, Ceasarion, was captured and killed. This ended not just the Hellenistic line of Egyptian pharaohs, but the line of all Egyptian pharaohs.[139]

4. ROME AND THE POLITICAL QUESTION

Within the world of Rome, the broad principle was that the system of law, predicated on a broad principle of equality, was consistently applied across the Empire. From such considerations, scholars such as Aelius Aristides (117–181) could suggest that 'everything is set out in the open for everyone to enjoy; nobody is a foreigner who is worth of office or trust . . . there is no divide between Greeks and Barbarians, [instead they are divided into] Roman and non-Roman'.[140] Tactius (56–117) also reflected this view when he suggested 'all else is common between us . . . Love and cherish peace and the city in which we enjoy an equal right, conquered and conquerors alike'.[141] Aristides added that this unique civilization was represented by the fact that walls were placed around the empire, not around individual cities within it. Within these walls, Rome offered many areas and cities limited forms of self-government under the guiding and benevolent eye of Rome, whilst also stepping in to arbitrate between cities and regions when disputes arose, rather than allowing disputes to be settled by violence.[142]

Pliny the Elder (23–79 BCE) called this world the one in which the 'awesome majesty of the Roman Peace' applied.[143] Such pacification involved the giving of limited – or 'moderate' – amounts of liberty in exchange for peace, prosperity, freedom from tyranny and concord. Such ideals were buttressed by the philosophy of Stoicism and the belief of a bond existing with all people under the auspice of Rome, due to their shared social and philosophical values. This type of thinking was most strongly displayed by Marcus Aurelius (121–180) who tried to deliver a state 'based on uniform law and governed on the principles of equality and free speech, and of a monarchy which prized the liberty of the subject above all other things'.[144] Although Aurelius was not talking of monarchy in the sense of 'kings' and 'queens', he was talking in terms of absolute power held by one man, in the form of an emperor. This idea, which was the dividing line between the Roman Republic and the Roman Empire, was the cause of

139 Suetonius, *The Twelve Caesars* trans Graves, R (1989) (London, Penguin) 29, 63; Gelzer, M (1968) *Caesar* (Oxford, Blackwell) 248–50, 256.

140 Aelius Aristides, *The Sacred Tales* reprinted in Barker, E (ed) (1959) *From Alexander to Constantine: Passages and Documents Illustrating the History of Social and Political Ideas* (Oxford, Oxford University Press) 325. Also Glover, T (1927) *Democracy in the Ancient World* (London, Macmillan) 162; Buchan, J (1937) *Augustus* (London, Hodder) 205–206; Frank, T (1914) *Roman Imperialism* (London, Macmillan) 33–34.

141 Tacitus, *Histories* IV:lxxiv.

142 Aristides is reprinted in Lewis, N and Reinhold M (eds) (1955) *Roman Civilisation: Records*, Vol II (Columbia, Columbia University Press,) 411. For the examples of autonomy, see 'Delphi Granted Autonomy By Roman Senate' in Lewis and Reinhold Vol II, at 311. For the arbitrations, see 332–37 and 365–66.

143 Pliny, *Natural History* trans Rackham, T, (1953) (Boston, Loeb) I:1.3 and XXVII:1.1; also Cook, S (ed) (1969) *The Cambridge Ancient History. The Imperial Peace*, (Cambridge, Cambridge University Press) 440–75.

144 Aurelius, *Meditations* trans Collier, J (1964) (London, Penguin) D.ix.23. *cf* Tacitus, *The Annals of Imperial Rome* trans Grant, M (1989) (London, Penguin) IV:32–34.

hundreds of thousands of deaths, as Italians fought Italians over the best model of political governance.

A. Monarchy

Although the traditional date of the foundation for Rome is 753 BCE, before the Roman entry into the Latin League in 493 BCE, it is difficult to find certainty in the political landscape. This is especially so with the seven kings from which Rome evolved. The last of these kings was Targuinius Superbus (535–496 BCE). Although Tarquinius pursued the traditional wars of the Roman kings, fighting the neighbours, it was the devolution of his kingship into tyranny, where his own family attempted to act above the laws which bound everyone else. This descent into tyranny was so total, that on key issues for the early Romans, he usurped all power. Thus, 'in questions of war and peace he was his own sole master'.[145]

Such absolute power was the final reason for the decision of the Romans to abolish monarchy, and chase Tarquins and his family from the capital, in fear of their lives. This abolition of monarchy was despite the long-standing Roman practice of electing their king. In itself, this was not a surprise as the deficiencies of this system, in terms of the quest for power that it generated, were obvious from the outset. The lethal fight between the twin founders of Rome around 750 BCE, Romulus and his brother Remus, over who was best suited to govern the Romans, was only the first in a series of dysfunctional and/or abusive acts associated with the early monarchs of Rome. Mithridates argued that the Romans developed their intense dislike for monarchy due to the character of these kings, 'lowly latin sheepherders, Sabine soothsayers, exiles from Corinth, [and] slaves from Etruria'.[146] Questions of succession and the suitability of candidates for king (such as whether they had a penchant for justice and what background they came from) continued over the following 250 years, before the Roman Republic came into being in 509 BCE. At this point, the leaders of the military uprising declared, 'never again will I let them or any other man be King in Rome'.[147] This was, as Dionysius of Halicarnassus (60–7 BCE) suggested, 'the beginning of [their] liberty'.[148]

Despite their very clear repudiation of monarchs, the Romans did not do away with the idea of specific men being given absolute power in times of emergency. In 501 BCE, they created the position of dictator, whereby one man was appointed by the senate (and possibly approved by the plebs) for a limited period of time. This man was given 'full authority over war and peace and every other matter, possessed of absolute power and subject to no accounting'.[149] Zonaras (c 120 BCE) explained of this

[145] Livy, *The Early History of Rome* trans De Selincourt, A (1960) (London, Penguin) I:50.

[146] Justin, *Epitome of the Philippic History* trans Heckel, W (1994) (Oxford, Oxford University Press) 38.3–7.

[147] The quote is from Livy, *The Early History of Rome* trans De Selincourt, A (1960) (London, Penguin) I:59. See also the earlier sections I.6 and I.32.

[148] Dionysius of Halicarnassus, *Roman Antiquities* trans Cary, E (1937) (Boston, Loeb) IV:84.

[149] Dionysius of Halicarnassus, *Roman Antiquities* trans Cary, E (1937) (Boston, Loeb) V:70.

position: 'No one, not even the tribunes, had the power to make any complaint against him or to take any action hostile to him, and no appeal could be taken from him'.[150]

B. The Senate and the Plebs

Aside from the possibility of creating dictators in times of emergency, the Romans had also long been aware that there were three possible forms of government. These were 'a just and wise king, or a select number of leading citizens, or even the people themselves'.[151] Looking over the waters, the Romans were aware that their largest competitor, Carthage, operated a system which was a mixture of all three. This system was achieved by the election of a king who was placed in position by a powerful oligarchy of merchant princes. The authority of the king was not absolute but was circumscribed by tradition and legal limitations, including the possibility of his removal by the same oligarchy that elected him. By the fourth century BCE the oligarchy had evolved into a republican regime, based on annually elected magistrates; a permanent committee of 30 elders; a high court of 104 judges elected for life; and a popular assembly comprising all citizen who were able to meet the minimum property requirements. Rome was clearly influenced by this model, as it arrived at a similar, mixed, form of government. This was originally a mixture of a democracy and an aristocracy, although it was later expanded to include a person holding absolute power in the same way as a king. This allowed what was known as 'proportionate equality', whereby although people may have been judged to be morally equal, they were not necessarily politically equal.[152]

Before the emperor came to take all the power, the orders which constituted Republican Rome, continually vied for position. The seeds of divisions of political power in Rome can be traced to the period of the kings. At this point, a popular assembly existed – the *Curiate* – to deal with basic legal issues and help choose each king. This assembly acted in conjunction with the senate. The senate was originally a body of experienced men, and first the kings, and later the magistrates, would listen to their advice without being bound by it. From the beginning, the most distinguished citizens formed its membership. The senate was not a hereditary assembly, nor did members receive payment. Membership was filled annually by the principal magistrates of the year, who were entitled to seats for life. Since only those of senatorial family or of equestrian rank were entitled to stand for election to the higher magistracy, the senate was the citadel of the wealthy and propertied. With this composition, Plutarch went so far as to suggest the senate was actually 'a council of many kings'.[153]

Unlike the popular assemblies, the senate could not pass laws. It could only pass motions and resolutions. By constitutional convention it was, however, consulted on

[150] *The History of Zonaras* trans Banchich, T (2009) (London, Routledge) VII:13.

[151] Cicero, *The Republic* trans Powell, J (1977) (Oxford, Oxford University Press) I:xxvi.42.

[152] Polybius, *The Histories* trans Waterfield, R (2010) (Oxford, Oxford University Press) VI:12–14; also Gelzer, M (1969) *The Roman Nobility* (London, Blackwell) 4–8.

[153] Plutarch, 'Life of Pyrrhus' in *Greek Lives* trans Waterfield, R (2009) (Oxford, Oxford University Press) 19.

important questions. It also controlled access to the treasury and dealt with most questions of foreign affairs. Although all citizens had some voice in the running of Rome, the senate was the only genuinely deliberative body in the Roman system of government. Members of the senate held power and rights which other Roman citizens did not.[154]

Echoing Plato, Cicero (106–43 BCE) argued that this was the best possible system because 'equality of legal rights . . . is really most inequitable' as men of both the highest and lowest orders cannot really be compared. Accordingly, 'this very "fairness" is most unfair'. He suggested that citizens should be 'weighed' rather than counted. Therefore, 'the greatest number should not have the greatest power'. He argued for a 'moderate and balanced form of government' whereby the 'best men' were entrusted with the substantive matters of state. Conversely, the state, if run in the same way as ancient Athens, could not be safeguarded as policy would be decided by 'the undisciplined shouting of an inflamed mob'. Such an assembly of totally inexperienced men would not only represent an inequity between the citizens, but would also be dangerous to the existence of the state, as the democracy would 'decide on harmful wars, put troublemakers in charge of public affairs and expel from the city the citizens that served it best'.[155]

Accompanying the senate was a bewildering multitude of economic and social classes, as well as legislative assemblies through which citizens of the Republic attempted to influence policy. These divisions began following the expulsion of the kings, after which governmental authority had been exercised by magistrates, in particular by the two *Consols*. These magistrates were elected annually by all the people according to a system weighted in favour of the affluent middle class. For a century, only *patricians* were elected. Entry into either of these, or other, bodies in Rome was determined by economic wealth. The roots of this division lay in the need to call up men who would be able to arm themselves in times of military need. The men of the sixth class were known as *proletarii* – 'offspring givers'. Above them reached a series of levels based upon how much property each man held, arranged in 'classes'. From 300 BCE onwards, the elimination of age-old *patrician* privileges cleared the last significant obstacle to the merger of the patricians with the rich plebians into a new patrician–plebeian ruling class, the *nobiles*. In the following century, the wealthy *nobiles* were joined by a new emerging class – the *equites* – or calvarymen, who were also moneyed but were not members of the senatorial governing aristocracy. Over time, the amounts required for entry into each class changed but the divisions were always clear. For example, by the time the empire was at its height, a man had to be worth at least one million *sestereces* to become a senator. The next class down, the equestrian, was also determined by wealth with the buy-in price being 400,000 *sestereces*.

The legislative bodies that accompanied the senate were often held in low esteem as they were synonymous with corruption, mob rule and anarchy. They included the

154 Syme, R (1960) *The Roman Revolution* (Oxford, Oxford University Press) 15–31.

155 The quotes are from Cicero, *The Republic* trans Powell, J (1977) (Oxford, Oxford University Press) I:xxvi.42, I:34 and II:22, I:36, I:43, I:69, II:57, III:45, VI:1. Also the *Offices* III:6. Finally, note particularly blunt considerations in *Pro Flacco*. This can be found in Cicero, *Orations* trans Macdonald, C (1924) (Harvard, Loeb Classic Library) sections 14–19.

Comitia (the Committee), which was open to all citizens, and from which laws were made, magistrates elected, and legal cases heard. The second body was the *Concilium* (the Council). This was an assembly of a specific group of citizens. For example, the 'Plebian Council' was an assembly that elected plebian magistrates, and from 449 BCE passed laws known as *plebicisita* (plebicites). As Livy explained, these 'provided the tribunes with a very sharp weapon'.[156] By 287 BCE, it was understood that plebiscites were binding on the whole people. The other substantive power that the tribunes held was their authority to veto military levies. The *Concentio*, by contrast, was an unofficial forum for communication where citizens gathered to debate matters of importance, including the election of *Consuls*, *Praetors* and *Censors*, and – most importantly – had the authority to declare war. There was always strong competition for non-senate authority within the Republic. These contests reached their peak in the century leading up to the fall of the Republic, under the leadership of the Gracchus brothers, who, in essence, created an 'anti-senate' movement. The senate's recourse to lynching the Gracchus brothers (due to its fear that the brothers would completely overthrow the entire senatorial concept of oligarchical government) established a precedence of violence which ultimately became its own undoing. Some commentators from this period, such as Cicero, came to divide the Republic into the '*Optimates*', or senatorial blocs, made up of good, sober, respectable and important citizens; and the '*Populares*', made up of agitators and revolutionaries who fed on 'civil discord and insurrection'.[157]

The *Optimates* and *Populares* clashed on many topics, but the primary ones were those of the courts, debt and – most importantly – land. The question of land and the link to the political order was, most commonly, dealt with by providing land to the soldiers who supported the military objectives of the senate. This debate was about the land acquired by military conquest, and the overt concentration of this land inside and outside Italy in the hands of wealthy landowners – as opposed to those who fought. The pressure of this question increased in the next century, as the Gracchus brothers brought the debate about land ownership to the fore. The eldest brother, Tiberius (163–133 BCE), argued that there should be a limit on the amount of land that any individual could take from the public domain. He added that the proceeds from some of the foreign wars, together with public lands, should be distributed to poor citizens in Rome, rather than the land continuing to accumulate 'to the men of wealth and property'. He added:

> [T]he men who fight and die for Italy enjoy nothing but the air and light; without house or home they wander about with their wives and children . . . they fight and die to protect the wealth and luxury of others; they are styled masters of the world, and have not a clod of earth to call their own.[158]

[156] Livy, *The Early History of Rome* trans De Selincourt, A (1960) (London, Penguin) III:4.

[157] Cicero, *In Defence of Sestius* XLIV:96.

[158] Plutarch, 'Life of Tiberius Gracchus' in *Roman Lives* trans Waterfield, R (2009) (Oxford, Oxford University Press) VIII:7–ix. Also Appian, *The Civil Wars* trans Carter, J (London, Penguin) I:i.9; Livy, *The Early History of Rome* trans De Selincourt, A (1960) (London, Penguin) IV:30, VI:35, VIII:38, XXI:63 and XXXI:11; Cook, S (ed) (1954) *The Cambridge Ancient History. The Hellenistic Monarchies and the Rise of Rome*, Vol VII (Cambridge, Cambridge University Press) 473; Polybius, *The Histories* trans Waterfield, R (2010) (Oxford, Oxford University Press) I:17–18; Wood, N (1988) *Cicero's Social and Political Thought* (California, California University Press) 90–97, 148–50.

Tiberius' solution to this problem in 133 BCE was the *Lex Agraria*, which was a simple measure to provide allotments for the poor. These were to be provided from land taken, but for which compensation would be paid (using money from the treasury), from members of the senatorial class who held land in excess of a maximum fixed by law. Tiberius' proposals were so threatening to the propertied classes that he was driven from the senate (on matters related to constitutional questions) before he was lynched. This was the first time that the senate had solved a political problem by violent means. Undeterred, Tiberius' brother Gaius (154–121 BCE), continued this line of work, passing laws to benefit the poor (such as breaking up the monopoly of the nobility in the courts), and including the division of public lands amongst poor citizens, by planting a colony of 6,000 Roman colonists on the site where Carthage once stood. Despite the popularity of these moves, the Roman poor were unable to protect Gaius and he met the same fate as his brother, killed by senate agents who could not tolerate the idea of such redistribution of lands – especially if it was taken from land they already owned. The core of their argument, as later expressed by Cicero, was that private property was sacrosanct and was the basis for society (and vice versa). With his unique emphasis on economic individualism, Cicero, and the senate, had no desire to equalise property ownership, and spent much of their time arguing against property redistribution.[159]

Any hope that the killing of both the brothers would make matters better was quickly dispelled. The pressure on the state to find more land to distribute to the deserving poor increased rapidly. The difference was that 'the deserving' of land were no longer the independent peasantry but members of the armed forces. The point at which this occurred was in 107 BCE when the Roman army (under the leadership of Marius (157–86 BCE)) began to accept conscripts who owned no property but volunteered for the war against Jugurtha on the promise of land after their military service ended. This meant that the majority of the men in the legions were no longer peasant conscripts anxious to return to their farms. Rather, the majority of the military forces was composed of landless men who hoped to make money out of war and to receive allotments of land upon their discharge. The senate, although unable to prevent such developments, viewed them with disdain. The soldiers, who were aware of this dislike, then looked to their military commanders for support, and in return would fight for them whenever necessary. This mutually reinforcing bond formed the root of the rise of the Roman dictator for, as Caesar noted, 'there were two things that procured, protected and increased power – soldiers and money – and these depended on each other . . . and if one was lacking the other would fall'.[160]

[159] Plutarch, 'Life of Gaius Gracchus' in *Roman Lives* trans Waterfield, R (2009) (Oxford, Oxford University Press) III:9; Wood, N (1988) *Cicero's Social and Political Thought* (California University Press) 76–77, 114–17, 130–33; Cook, S (ed) (1966) *The Cambridge Ancient History. The Roman Republic*, Vol IX (Cambridge, Cambridge University Press) 22–35.

[160] Caesar, noted in Champion, J (2009) *Pyrrhus of Epirus* (London, Pen and Sword) 22; also Sallust, *Jugurtha* trans Woodman, A (1985) (London, Penguin) 84, 86.1–2.

C. Slavery

Slavery was an intrinsic part of most of the societies surrounding Rome.[161] It was also an intrinsic part of the Roman world. Cicero was notable for his assertion that some forms of subjugation, such as slavery, were just and in accordance with nature – where people were incapable of governing themselves. Some even argued that slaves had an advantaged position, as the slave had none of the anxieties the owner suffered.[162] Although such arguments were used to justify the institution of slavery, other philosophers preferred more nuanced approaches, which divided slavery into both physical and moral domains. Epictetus (55–135) and Dio Chrysostom (40–120) argued that whilst the body could be enslaved, the mind could not.[163] Ulpian (170–228 BCE) and Seneca (4 BCE–65 CE), both wealthy slaveholders themselves, whilst concurring that slavery only existed in the physical and not the spiritual world, still appealed to slave owners to show restraint in their actions.[164]

No evidence exists for slavery during the period of the early kings (753–510 BCE). The first clear evidence of slavery in Rome can be found with the first recorded auction of slaves, which occurred in 396 BCE. The first slave market in Rome was established in 259 BCE, just after the outbreak of the First Punic War. Between tens and hundreds of thousands of slaves were acquired following each victory by the Roman armed forces, and were then quickly sequestered into all aspects of Roman society. A considerable number of men were also enslaved by pirates who raided 'barbarian' regions and sold their victims in Rome. When the slaves procreated, their children were also enslaved. Estimates suggest that more than 2 million enslaved aliens were transported to Italy between 80 and 8 BCE alone and by 180 CE, the slave population of the empire was between 7 and 10 million individuals (equating to perhaps one in six of all inhabitants), with at least half a million living in Rome. These numbers were so large that the senate refused a proposal that slaves be given a uniform to help identify them, because 'it became apparent how great would be the impending danger if our slaves began to count their number'.[165] This was an advance on earlier times when many slaves had Latin words crudely tattooed across their foreheads to identify them as Roman property, or to display how much they cost.[166]

[161] For slaves of the Germanic tribes, who would 'often be killed… on the impulse of passion', see Tacitus, *Germania*, ch 25.

[162] For those arguing that slavery was an easy life, see Libanius, *Orationes* 25:66–67; also Theodoret, *On Divine Providence* 7:677B–680B. For the work of Cicero, see *The Republic* 1:51 and 3:38.

[163] Dio, *Orations* 14 and 15 and, the *Manuel of Epictetus* paragraphs 1, 17 and 29. See also *Discourses*. 4.1:33–37.

[164] See Cooper, J (ed) (1995) *Seneca: Moral and Political Essays* (Cambridge, Cambridge University Press) 149–50. See also *On Benefits* 3:20, 3:28; and *Epistles*. 47:1.10, 47:2–5, 47:11–13 reprinted in Saunders, JL (ed) (1966) *Greek and Roman Philosophy After Aristotle: Readings in the History of Philosophy* (New York, Free Press). Note also Seneca's *Letters on Morals* 80.3–4 trans Gummere, R (1920) (London, Loeb Classical Library). The words of Ulpian are in the *Digest*.50.17.32. See also 1.5.4 in the Digest. Note finally, Ulpian's *On the Duties of a Proconsul* 3.3.1–6.

[165] Seneca, *On Clemency* I:xxiv. For the debate on numbers, see Meltzer, M (1993) *Slavery: A World History* (NYC, DaCapo) 127–30.

[166] Mayor, A (2010) *The Poison King: The Life and Legend of Mithradates* (New Jersey, Princeton University Press) 20.

The fact that slaves had no standing in civil law did not equate to a carte blanche for owners to treat their slaves without restraint. By the end of the Republic, a more humane attitude appears to have developed. Augustus (63 BCE–14 CE) regulated against senseless brutality and collective punishments imposed upon slaves. Additional rules removed the right of owners to send their slaves to the arena as victims. However, Augustus did not seek to upset the principle of slavery, or try to stem the extraordinarily high rate of manumissions. Emancipation (*manus* meaning hand and *capere* meaning to take – a Roman master could 'place them out of hand') was seen as being too easy to achieve. Accordingly, he limited the rights that former slaves could acquire by tightening the conditions for manumission through age limits and the requirement of a reasonable cause which had to be examined by a council. Nevertheless, the fact remained that manumission, by which slaves could acquire their freedom, was a common practice in Rome and slaves could become full citizens: at least one emperor, Diocletian (244–311), was born a slave. Additional protections for slaves came from Claudius (10 BCE–54 CE), who stripped masters of their right to arbitrarily kill or discard sick slaves, whilst Vespasian (9–79) forbade the selling of slaves for the purpose of prostitution. Domitian (51–96) forbade the castration of slaves for commercial purposes.[167]

Although such humane considerations were welcome, none of these laws, or the emperors who oversaw them, attempted to completely reject the practice of slavery. Whilst Antonius Pius (86–161) made it an offence for a master to kill his slave without just cause or to treat his slave with 'intolerable cruelty', the law set relatively high thresholds for these offences. Chaining or beating in the ordinary way of correction for offences, even if the slave subsequently died, did not justify any inquiry into the master's intentions or any charge against him. Even Marcus Aurelius (121–180), although in favour of correctly carried out manumission, was a hardliner when it came to matters pertaining to the control of slaves who attempted to run away.[168]

In some instances, the enlistment of slaves was a practice that occurred in some of the conflicts of the period. In the wars with Mithridates (134–63 BCE), slaves owned by Rome were liberated in such a way as to both weaken the enemy and strengthen their own forces. As a result of such acts, around 88 BCE about 6,000 former Roman slaves joined Rome's forces. This followed an earlier precedent in which Aristonicus (c 130 BCE), also in a revolt against the Romans, created an army by, inter alia, freeing all slaves. However, the slaves in these wars did not fight for the abolition of the institution of slavery – only for the manumission of their own individual status. Even then, their hopes were rarely fulfilled, as not only did these individuals lose their wars against Rome, but after the wars ended their repatriation was normally part of the peace treaty.

[167] See the Fufian and Aelian laws reprinted in Lewis, N and Reinhold M (eds) (1955) *Roman Civilisation: Records*, Vol II (Columbia, Columbia University Press) 52–55, 268–69; Buchan, J (1937) *Augustus* (London, Hodder) 207–208; Suetonius, *The Twelve Caesars* trans Graves, R (1989) (London, Penguin)185; Tacitus, *The Annals of Imperial Rome* trans Grant, M (1989) (London, Penguin) 14:42-5; Meltzer, M (1993) *Slavery: A World History* (NYC, DaCapo) 185–87; Thomas, J (1976) *Textbook on Roman Law* (Amsterdam, North-Holland) 389–97.

[168] McLynn, F (2010) *Marcus Aurelius* (London, Vintage) 182–83; Carlyle, A (1936) *A History of Medieval Political Theory in the West: The Second Century to the Ninth*, Vol 1 (Blackwood, London) 48–49; Gwatkin, H (ed) (1955) *The Cambridge Medieval History: The Rise of the Saracens and the Foundation of the Western Empire*, Vol II (Cambridge, Cambridge University Press) 62–63.

For example, when peace was made between the Roman Republic and Aetolia in 189 BCE, it was stipulated that 'the Aetolians shall surrender . . . runaway slaves'.[169] In the peace treaty with Mithridates of 85 BCE, the return of runaway slaves was part of the deal. Similarly, after Pompey, who had promised freedom to the thousands of slaves who flocked to fight for him, was defeated by Octavian, the recaptured slaves found themselves either returned to their original owners, or sold at public auction.[170]

In addition to fighting wars for others to gain their freedom, slaves also fought in wars for themselves for the same purpose. There were three such wars between 134 and 71 BCE, in which the slaves of Rome individually attempted to throw off the yolk of being owned by another human being (that is, they were not fighting against the institution of slavery as such). Some one million people would die in these conficts.[171]

The first Slave War in Sicily began in 134 BCE and involved an estimated 70,000 slaves. The second slave uprising in Sicily raged between 104 and 100 BCE. This second uprising appears to have been due to the Roman Governor refusing to implement the decree passed by the senate that provincial governors should seek out and release all citizens of allied states that were kept as slaves, many of them having been taken by the activity of pirates. The last of this series of uprisings was the Revolt of the Gladiators, led by Spartacus (c 109–71 BCE) during the years 73–71 BCE. Over 100,000 slaves are believed to have died in this third and final uprising. Diodorus recorded that these men wanted 'the complete destruction of their masters as the goal of their power'. These acts were justified by the slaves by a combination of the 'vastly extravagant wealth of their owners and the masters' and their 'cruelty towards their slaves'. Thus, 'oppressed by the grinding toil and beatings, maltreated for the most part beyond all reason, the slaves could endure it no longer'.[172] Despite the implicit appeal of this type of action when viewed from a contemporary perspective, it is important to note that Spartacus did not cast himself as a liberator of those entrapped by slavery everywhere. He was not a political theorist, but a courageous individual who fought for personal liberty – not for the abolition of slavery.[173]

D. The End of the Republic

Lucius Cornelius Sulla Felix (138–78 BCE), better known as Sulla, was the first absolute dictator of Rome. It was the fact that his rule was absolute, without restraints of time, which made his dictatorship at the end of the Republic different from the dictatorships of the earlier centuries, in which absolute power was given in times of emergency to one man – but only for a set period of time. The last dictatorship that

[169] Polybius, *The Histories* trans Waterfield, R (2010) (Oxford, Oxford University Press) XXI:32.

[170] Mayor, A (2010) *The Poison King: The Life and Legend of Mithradates* (New Jersey, Princeton University Press) 20–21, 58–59, 220; Meltzer, M (1993) *Slavery: A World History* (NYC, DaCapo) 189.

[171] White, M (2011) *Atrocitology* (NYC, Norton) 27–28.

[172] Diodorus, 'Fragments' *Library of History* trans Wells, B (1963) (Boston, Loeb) xxxiv.

[173] Champion, C (2004) *Roman Imperialism* (London, Blackwell) 154–57; Garnsey, P (1996) *Ideas of Slavery from Aristotle to Augustine* (Cambridge, Cambridge University Press) 9; Scullard, H (1982) *From the Gracchi to Nero* (London, Methuen) 53–54.

ran for a limited time period, had been during the wars against Hannibal, over 100 years earlier. Sulla first tussled with the senate after he was given command to lead the First Mithridatic War. However, while he was away battling in Greece, his supporters were killed (in 86 BCE) and Flaccus was appointed by the senate as Sulla's replacement in the war. Flaccus was sent to Greece with two legions, with orders to make war on Sulla if he refused to give up his command. Sulla, having won the essential battles against Mithridates and almost coming to blows with the Roman armies of Flaccus (the Roman soldiers refused to fight each other), decided to return to Italy.[174]

Sulla then became the first Roman general to march six legions (36,000 men) into the city limits of Rome. He did this to restore his position on the ground that the senate had acted unconstitutionally in removing his command. No sooner had Sulla left Italy after having his command reinstated than his actions were condemned in the senate and he was officially exiled during the entire time in which he was abroad fighting Rome's enemies. When he returned to Italy a second time, landing at Brundisium in 83 BCE, his forces advanced quickly through the country. This time he was opposed by armed forces which were authorised by the senate. He smashed his way through with a combination of promises to reward those who fought for him and threats to crush those who stood in his way. In the end, over 50,000 combatants lost their lives, and Sulla stood alone as the master of Rome. The terrified senate then granted his wish and declared him dictator, for an unlimited time period, for the purpose of reorganising the constitution. Sulla began this job by drawing up lists of potential opponents, including at least 40 senators and 1,600 *equites* (although this number may have been nearer to 9,000) to be outlawed, with a price put on their heads.[175]

Sulla then introduced a conservative programme of reform aimed at strengthening senatorial power and curtailing the popular political role. His first step was to double the membership of the senate to 600. His second step was to weaken the power of the tribunes of the plebs, limiting their right of veto and forbidding them to propose legislation without the prior assent of the senate. He virtually abolished the role of the popular assembly in judicial settings. He was, however, very loyal to the men in his armed forces, ensuring that each of his 120,000 soldiers was granted a parcel of land. Then, surprising everyone, he resigned as dictator and went back to being an ordinary citizen.[176]

E. Caesar

As a young general of undisputed military brilliance, Gnaeus Pompeius Magnus (106–48 BCE), more commonly known as Pompey, married the step-daughter of Sulla at the suggestion of the dictator. Pompey would fight over vast areas of the Roman Empire, from Sicily to Jerusalem, involving warfare against pirates, slaves, and people seeking self determination. His military conquests, which were supplemented by

[174] Mayor, A (2010) *The Poison King: The Life and Legend of Mithradates* (New Jersey, Princeton University Press) 210–12, 224–27.

[175] Scullard, H (1982) *From the Gracchi to Nero* (London, Methuen) 77–78.

[176] Appian, *The Civil Wars* trans Carter, J (London, Penguin) I:96.1–5, 98–100.

unprecedented powers granted by the senate, were so great that he was compared to Alexander. However, he was not alone in being ambitious. There were two others of similar stature and ambition within the Roman Empire. These were Julius Caesar (100–44 BCE) and Marcus Licinius Crassus (115–53 BCE) – the latter being a former lieutenant of Sulla. These three men formed the First Triumvirate (a political regime governed by three individuals), which held together from 60 to 55 BCE, during which time they at first secretly, and later openly, exercised power over the senate. Together, the 'three constituted an irresistible power with which they overthrew the government of senate and people'.[177] They came to this point after the senate had refused to cooperate with all three of them. Backed by armed force, the urban populace and many of the *equites*, they took complete control of senate, granting each other armies, provinces, land for their soldiers to settle on, and public triumphal parades. Plutarch suggested that this arrangement suited them all, as Pompey had 'an unbounded love of power' and Crassus 'added to his old disease of covetousness a new and ardent passion for trophies and triumphs'.[178]

The First Triumvirate was cemented by the marriage between the daughter of Julius Ceaser (Julia) and Pompey. This arrangement came to an end when Julia died in childbirth in 54 BCE and Crassus died in 53 BCE after a failed attempt to invade and subdue Parthia. The death of Crassus precipitated a rupture to an already strained relationship between the remaining two of the original Triumvirate. The two men could not work together – or as Lucian (125–180 BCE) suggested: 'Caesar could brook no superior. Pompey no equal.'[179] Both Caesar and Pompey sought to gain predominance by winning the support of those who had previously supported Crassus. When it became apparent that Caesar was becoming more popular, Pompey and Cato the Younger (95–46 BCE) joined forces.

The crisis came to a head in 49 BCE, when the pro-consular power of Caesar came to an end. The conquest of Gaul completed, Caesar was set to return to Italy. However, he feared that if he reverted to his private-citizen status he would expose himself to easy prosecution by his political enemies for any illegal activities he may have undertaken in Gaul. He therefore decided to stand in the re-election for the pro-consulship, whilst he still had an army. Then, at the end of 50 BCE, a resolution in the senate called on both Pompey and Caesar to resign their commands in the interests of avoiding a civil war. Caesar offered to do so if Pompey did the same. The following day, attempts were made to condemn Caesar as a public enemy if he refused to lay down his command by a given date. These attempts were vetoed by the two tribunes – Mark Antony and Quintus Cassius. Two days later, these two men were warned to leave the senate house if they wished to escape violence. It was this threat of force against the tribunes who had attempted to veto the senate's decree that Caesar should disband his forces 'which became Caesar's pretext for launching the civil war'.[180]

[177] Plutarch, *Roman Lives* trans Waterfield, R (2009) (Oxford, Oxford University Press); 'Life of Crassus' xiv and 'Life of Pompey' at xlvi.

[178] Plutarch, 'Life of Crassus' in *Roman Lives* trans Waterfield, R (2009) (Oxford, Oxford University Press) xv.

[179] The quote is from Lucian's 'Pharsalia' I. 125–26 in *The Works of Lucian* trans Fowler, H (1905) (London, Forgotten Works) 338.

[180] Suetonius, *The Twelve Caesars* trans Graves, R (1989) (London, Penguin) 27.

Martial law was then declared and Pompey was asked by the senate to save the Republic and assume command of all forces in Italy. Caesar responded by haranguing his troops and leading 40,000 of them across the Rubicon River, the boundary between Italy and Cisalphine Gaul. The first battle of the civil war at Dyrrachium in July 48 BCE (after which 1,000 of Ceasar's men and 2,000 of Pompey's remained dead on the battlefield) was followed a few months later by the battle of Pharsalus. At the latter battle, some 15,000 of Pompey's men (out of an army of 52,000) were left dead or wounded on the battlefield, having been defeated by Caesar's smaller force of 23,000. When Caesar fought Scipio at Thapsus in 46 BCE, he left 30,000 men of his opponents dead on the field. This was only the beginning, as it is estimated that just under 2 million people were killed in the conflict which raged over vast sections of the Roman territories for the next five years.[181]

Caesar justified the war to his soldiers by recounting the wrongs done to him, urging them to 'avenge the wrongs of their commanders and of the tribunes of the plebs'. Specifically, whilst using rhetoric to urge freedom for the Roman people from oppression by a small clique, he also:

> [C]omplained that Pompey, whose honor and dignity he had always favored and supported, had been misled and alienated from him by their invidious attacks on his [Caesar's] glorious achievements. He complained that an unprecedented change had been introduced into the constitution, in that the tribunician veto . . . was being curbed and crushed by armed force . . . Pompey had taken away the rights [the tribunes] had always possessed . . . he urged them to defend from his enemies the reputation and dignity of the commander under whose leadership they had for nine years served the republic well.[182]

Whilst Pompey was on the conservative side of the senate and Caesar was on the more liberal side, it is debatable whether the troops themselves saw this as a conflict about high principles, or whether they were merely showing loyalty to their commander, with an expectation of personal reward. Even for the leaders, it is questionable whether there really were principles at stake which could not have been upheld without violence. Essentially, it appeared to be a struggle for personal power, prestige and honour, with little real regard for the *libertas* of others. The only unshakable principle that Caesar appears to have held was that he would never let go of the power he had won – and, although he adopted the symbols of the Etruscan kings of old, he was careful not to have himself described as a king, or to fulfil the most basic requirement of monarchs, namely, to ensure dynastic planning for succession.[183]

Caesar was not oblivious to the political issues that were preoccupying Rome before the Republic fell. He continued to show his *popularis* slant, but he was not a radical democrat. On the question of enfranchisement, he gave full rights to parts of Gaul and certain provincial towns (such as Lisbon and Cadiz), but he did not grant it every-

[181] The figure given by Pliny is 1,192,000 excluding civilians in *Natural History* trans Rackham, T (1953) (Boston, Loeb) VII:92. Compare, Grant, R (2011) *1001 Battles that Changed the Course of History* (London, Penguin) 77.

[182] Caesar, *The Civil War* trans Gardner, J (1976) (London, Penguin) I:7; also Gelzer, M (1968) *Caesar* (Oxford, Blackwell) 199–204.

[183] Suetonius, *The Twelve Caesars* trans Graves, R (1989) (London, Penguin) 48; Gelzer, M (1968) *Caesar* (Oxford, Blackwell) 278–80; Appian, *The Civil Wars* trans Carter, J (1978) (London, Penguin) V:ii.12–13, 17.

where. On the topic of debt, of which he must have been keenly aware following the attempted Cataline coup (of which debt cancellation was used as a central justification), he only went so far as to remit the rent of one year to the poorest Italian tenants and would not agree to cancellation of all debt. On the question of the distribution of land, he assigned properties to his veterans, but was careful not to dispossess existing owners and thus upset the interests of the aristocracy. He also settled many of his veterans in overseas colonies, with an overall 80,000 colonists sent to Spain, Africa and Greece. He also made plans to settle the surviving veterans of the opposition along similar lines. This was in the tradition of the overt largess he gave to his soldiers. After his wars in Gaul, he gave a war-gratuity of 240 gold pieces to every man in his legions, in addition to the extra 20 gold pieces he had given at the outbreak of hostilities in Italy – and a farm. Despite all of these actions, the fundamental point is that it was Caesar, not the senate, making the decisions. By now, 'the Republic was nothing, a mode of expression, without form and substance'.[184]

Although Caesar was now the sole dictator of Rome, he was still not safe. A group of senators, including idealists and convinced republicans such as Marcus Junius Brutus (85–42 BCE), stabbed him at least 23 times, before leaving him to die on the floor of the building in which the senate met. Caesar was executed because, unlike Sulla, he appeared to have no intention of restoring the senate to its former position. Cicero argued that Caesar deserved his fate as he had tried to be 'king of the Roman people and master of the whole world' destroying 'law and liberty'.[185] With such a tyrant 'we have no ties of fellowship . . . but rather the bitterest feud . . . a man whom it is morally right to kill'.[186] The following day, the senate voted itself a 'general amnesty and reconciliation' although it promised to be faithful to Caesar's measures; it also voted him divine honours. To Brutus and his followers it distributed provinces and other suitable rewards. Cicero attempted to re-enter the political life of the senate, and was quick to play off the senate against the obvious contender for power – Mark Antony – who, as both *Consul* and Caesar's right-hand man, had no intention of respecting the amnesty for Caesar's killers.[187]

F. Augustus

Antony had expected to be named Caesar's heir. This was not to be the case. Caesar's heir was named as Octavian – or, as he became known, Gaius Julius Caesar Augustus. Augustus was the son of the niece of Caesar. Caesar had overlooked his child by Cleopatra. Despite this, Antony, as the leader of Caesar's faction, quickly assumed the powers of the dead dictator, disregarding Octavian, whom he regarded as politically

[184] The quote is from Suetonius, *The Twelve Caesars* trans Graves, R (1989) (London, Penguin) 47. The figures are from pages 30–33. Also Cicero, *Catiline* xxxvi.4–xxxix.3. Note finally, Gelzer, M (1968) *Caesar* (Oxford, Blackwell) 262–64.

[185] Cicero *On Duties* trans Atkins, E (1911) (Cambridge, Cambridge University Press) III:21.82–83.

[186] Cicero, *Offices* (1955) trans Warrington, J (London, Penguin) III:6.32.

[187] Plutarch, 'Life of Caesar' in *Roman Lives* trans Waterfield, R (2009) (Oxford, Oxford University Press) lvii, lxiii–lxvii.

insignificant. The young Octavian was then used by the senate, in an arrangement organised by Cicero, to defeat Antony – who was declared 'an enemy of the State'.[188] Although Antony was defeated by Octavian at Mutina in early 43 BCE, the conflict ended in a truce. At this point the senate expected that Octavian would be 'praised, honoured and removed'.[189] This did not happen. After Octavian had been offended by the senate, Octavian and Antony, together with Marcus Lepidus (89–12 BCE), reconciled in late October, in the form of Second Triumvirate. The Second Triumvirate divided the power and possessions of Rome. Before undisputed power could be enjoyed, there were both external and internal enemies to be dealt with. The external enemies were Brutus and Cassius, with the remnants of their Republic-authorised forces which remained in power in some provinces.

With respect to the internal enemies, the senate agreed that it was not 'safe . . . to leave the rest of our enemies here behind us . . . we must put them one and all out of the way'.[190] The first victim of this arrangement was Cicero. Cicero was guilty of attempting to vilify Antony as a tyrant in a series of speeches known as the *Philippics.* In these works Cicero had tried to warn that Antony wanted to attack the Republic with unmitigated fury and 'to destroy the Senate, that is to say, the council of the whole world'.[191] Whilst Caesar had treated Cicero with both clemency and kindness despite his intrigues and manipulations on the part of the senate, Antony had him executed along with a number of other enemies and potential rivals (some 300 senators and 2,000 *equites*). On Antony's instructions, the hands and head of Cicero were removed and brought to him. Antony's wife, Fulvia, went one step further in final revenge against Cicero's power of speech. As Dio (155–229) recorded:

> Fulvia took the head into her hands before it was removed, and after abusing it spitefully and spitting upon it, set it on her knees, opened the mouth, and pulled out the tongue, which she pierced with the pins that she used for her hair, at the same time uttering many brutal jests.[192]

The forces of Antony and Octavian then proceeded to the East to meet the combined armies of Cassius, who, as governor of the Eastern provinces, had rallied the strength of that part of the Roman world against the Caesarians. Octavian later explained that 'those who assassinated [Caesar] I drove into exile, avenging their crime . . . when they waged war against the State, I conquered them'.[193] This conquering occurred when the forces of two opposing armies – some 100,000 men on both sides – met at Philippi in 42 BCE. When Brutus realised that victory was impossible, he persuaded one of his soldiers to slay him. After the deaths of both Cicero and Brutus, the final extinction of the Roman Republic was achieved. The last general of the Roman Republic to stand against Octavian and Antony was the son of Pompey the Great – Sextus (65–35 BCE).

[188] Cook, S (ed) (1971) *The Cambridge Ancient History: The Augustan Empire*, Vol X (Cambridge University Press, Cambridge) 15.
[189] Cicero, *Letters to Friends* trans Bailey, S (2001) (Boston, Loeb) XI:20.1.
[190] Livy, *The Early History of Rome* trans De Selincourt, A (1960) (London, Penguin) XXII, 57.
[191] Cicero, *Philippics* trans Ker, J (1963) (Boston, Loeb) IV:14.
[192] Dio Cassius, *Roman History* trans Cary, E (1967) (Boston, Loeb) XLVII:8.
[193] *The Res Gestae Divi Augustus: Accomplishment of Augustus* trans Brunt, P (1967) (Oxford, Oxford University Press) 27.

Sextus was initially dealt with via the treaty of Misenum in 39 BCE, which guaranteed him certain territories (Corsica, Sardinia and Sicily). This was in exchange for promises from Sextus that he would not disrupt the food supply to Rome and would not accept runaways or plant colonies in Italy. This peace was short-lived as Octavian reignited the war against Sextus in 37 BCE before defeating him in a sea battle that sunk 28 of his ships (and captured a further 105) at the battle of Naulochus in 36 BCE, and subsequently capturing and executing him in 35 BCE. Antony's orders for the execution of Sextus without trial would later be used as one of the reasons Octavian put forward for Antony's unfitness to govern.[194]

The relationship between Antony and Octavian was cemented with the Treaty of Brundisium. This treaty, which practically eliminated Lepidus by confining his share of power to the province of Africa, gave Octavian the Western part of the Empire, whilst Antony took the East. In addition, a marriage between the families through Antony and Octavian's sister, Octavia (Fulvia had died earlier), was agreed.[195] Two years later in 38 BCE, the Treaty of Tarentum reaffirmed that of Brundisium, extending the period of the Triumvirate for a further five years. In the meantime, Lepidus had been killed after an unsuccessful attempt to reassert himself. This left only Antony and Octavian. Antony, having based himself in Egypt, had not only devoted years to an abortive attempt to crush the Parthians, but had also become infatuated with Cleopatra and the somewhat mystic ways of the East. In 32 BCE, one year after the Treaty of Tarentum had come to its end, Antony divorced Octavia. This gave Octavian the pretext for war that he desired. He represented Antony to the senate as an apostate from Roman ideals and a mere Eastern tyrant, for which reason war was declared. In his own words, 'on my own initiative, I raised an army by means of which I liberated the Republic, which was oppressed by the tyranny of a faction'.[196] Antony saw the matter differently, having his own grievances against Octavian over the uncompromising way he had ended the wars against the forces of the Republic, and his claim of being equal to Caesar.[197]

Despite the fact that 40,000 men fought for Octavian and 22,000 fought for Antony, the resulting conflict at Actium between the two primary protagonists was deeply personal. Knowing Antony's popularity in Rome (at least one-third of the senate fought with him), Octavian painted his successful war as being against Cleopatra – or West against East – rather than a war against Antony. Antony and Cleopatra both met their ends. Just to tidy up any loose ends, Octavian also killed Antony's elder son by Fulvia (Antyllus) and Caesarion, Caesar's son by Cleopatra. This was the final brutal act at the end of a brutal age. Seeing no threat from the children of Cleopatra and Mark Antony, he let these children live. Egypt was then annexed, although not as an

[194] Cook, S (ed) (1971) *The Cambridge Ancient History. The Augustan Empire*, Vol X (Cambridge, Cambridge University Press) 45–47. For the figures, see Grant, R (2011) *1001 Battles that Changed the Course of History* (London, Penguin) 79.

[195] The 40 BCE Treaty of Brundisium reprinted in Axelrod, A (ed) (2001) *Encyclopedia of Historical Treaties and Alliances* (NYC, Facts on File) 7; Cook, S (ed) (1971) *The Cambridge Ancient History. The Augustan Empire*, Vol X (Cambridge, Cambridge University Press) 51.

[196] *The Res Gestae Divi Augustus: Accomplishment of Augustus* trans Brunt, P (1967) (Oxford, Oxford University Press) 25.

[197] Buchan, J (1937) *Augustus* (London, Hodder) 110–13.

ordinary Roman province. Rather, it became the private possession of the emperor. Octavian now went on to rule the Roman Empire alone (without joint emperors or the senate), with the power that 500,000 men acting on his orders gave him.[198]

G. The Principate

The end of all the civil wars based around the different types of political organisation in Rome occurred in 27 BCE. The senate voted Octavian a series of powers which established him as undisputed ruler of the Roman Empire. He accepted the *proconsular* power (a special extended military command) for 10 years, and the consulship, together with the *tribuncian* power (which gave him effective control over the civil government), annually. He was also awarded the honorary title *Augustus* (meaning 'revered' or 'venerable') which, together with the designation *Imperator*, subsequently became a fixed part of the nomenclature of the emperors. The cumulative result of such considerations, as Dio Cassius explained, was that 'the power of both the people and senate passed entirely into the hands of Augustus, and from this time there was, strictly speaking, a monarchy'.[199]

In an obvious contradiction, Dio Cassius also suggested that Octavian, after 'having first briefed his most intimate friends among the senators, restored the Republic'.[200] Officially, the *Principate*, as the new regime became known, was the Republic restored but this was not the case. Octavian, who from this point onwards was known as *Augustus* only, gave the appearance of returning the Republic to its former glory. Apparently, he was twice close to restoring the Republican system, but on both occasions he concluded that 'to divide the responsibilities of government among several hands would be to jeopardize not only his own life, but national security [also]'.[201] In addition he introduced a series of measures which reorganised the senate whereby the 'low-born and ill assorted rabble . . . [who] . . . were wholly unworthy' were removed.[202] Similarly, the popular assemblies continued to meet as in the past, although all independent associations were subject to approval by the emperor. He also instituted censorship in the interests of morality and religion. Tacitus (56–117) explained that the situation was one whereby 'the constitution had been transformed, and there was nothing left at all of the good old way of life. Stripped of equality, all looked towards the directives of the princeps.'[203] Nothing could be done 'that did not please Caesar'.[204] Or, as was later officially explained in somewhat broader terms, the emperor had the power 'to transact and do whatever things divine, human, public and private he deems to serve the

[198] Suetonius, *The Twelve Caesars* trans Graves, R (1989) (London, Penguin) 62–63; Scullard, H (1982) *From the Gracchi to Nero* (London, Methuen) 165–71; Regan, G (2006) *Battles That Changed History* (London, Carlton) 26–30; Gabriel, R (2005) *Empires at War*, Vol II (London, Greenwood) 512–19.

[199] Dio Cassius, *Roman History* trans Cary, E (1967) (Boston, Loeb) LIII:17.

[200] Dio Cassius, *Roman History* trans Cary, E (1967) (Boston, Loeb) LIII:2.

[201] Suetonius, *The Twelve Caesars* trans Graves, R (1989) (London, Penguin) 69.

[202] Suetonius, *The Twelve Caesars* trans Graves, R (1989) (London, Penguin) 74–75, 83–86.

[203] Tacitus, *The Annals of Imperial Rome* trans Grant, M (1989) (London, Penguin) I, II:3.

[204] Dio Cassius, *Roman History* trans Cary, E (1967) (Boston, Loeb) LIII:21.

advantage and overriding interest of the State'.[205] In conformity with these absolute tendencies the great jurist Ulpian (170–223) formulated the principle that 'the emperor is above the laws' in the early third century.[206]

Seneca was notable in this area for, as the adviser to Emperor Nero (37–68 BCE), he wrote as a monarchist, accepting the historical inevitability of the *Principate*. What is striking about his work is its frankness and absolutism. For centuries, the Romans had hated the word 'king'. Caesar had been assassinated because it was thought that he intended to make himself king. Augustus had prudently accepted the modest title of *princeps* or 'first citizen', carefully avoiding any behaviour that smacked of royalty. Seneca showed no restraint about speaking of princes and kings and whatever other title there may be for guardians of public order. Nowhere in his advice to Nero did he advise him to defer to the 'Senate and people of Rome'. He may well watch over himself 'as though the laws . . . will call him to account' – but the operative words were 'as though'. Seneca did not advocate a lack of restraint on the part of the man with absolute power – unlike Nero, who went on to kill his step-brother and then his mother. Rather, Seneca recommended that the ruler exercise mercy, leniency and sound judgement delivered to advance the common good of all the people. With such goals, Seneca could attempt to explain the difference between a king and a tyrant.[207] A good king was 'the bond of the commonwealth . . . the mirror of God . . . the father of his people'.[208] This idea, that the king/emperor acted for the good of all, was also expressed by others, most notably Dio Chrysostom (40–120), who suggested that the king was a 'shepherd' who was 'a copy of the heavenly King and a link in the chain of the universe' who was only concerned 'to secure the greatest good of the greatest number'. He added that the good king was one who 'used his strength for the good of his herd, and one who brought aid to the weak saving the multitude'.[209] Fundamentally, the king/emperor was meant to bring peace, and Augustus received praise for introducing an 'era free of wars'.[210] The Augustan Altar of Peace (*Ara Pacis*) and the Temple of Peace later constructed by Vespasian demonstrated this thinking.

The bringing of peace was also believed to have been achieved internally by stopping civil discord. In both the West (before it collapsed) and the East (thereafter), the theory was that democracy was always 'vexed by sedition, internally divided . . . [and] . . . exposed to extreme danger'.[211] Conversely, the unlimited power of the emperor was actually based on a democratic principle – namely that the people wanted this

[205] This fragment from Egypt is reprinted in Lewis, N and Reinhold M (eds) (1955) *Roman Civilisation: Records*, Vol II (Columbia, Columbia University Press) 89.

[206] Justinian, *The Digest* trans Watson, A (2008) (NYC, Pennsylvania University Press) I:3.31 and XLVII:xxii. Also Muller, H (1961) *Freedom in the Ancient World* (NYC, Harper) 280–83.

[207] See Cooper, J (ed) (1995) *Seneca: Moral and Political Essays* (Cambridge, Cambridge University Press) 121–24, 143, 149.

[208] Seneca, *De Clementia* trans Braund, S (2009) (Oxford, Oxford University Press) I:3.5, I:7.1.

[209] 'Discourse on Kingship' reprinted in Barker, E (ed) (1959) *From Alexander to Constantine: Passages and Documents Illustrating the History of Social and Political Ideas* (Oxford, Oxford University Press) 298–302.

[210] Paterculus, recorded in Barker, E (ed) (1959) *From Alexander to Constantine: Passages and Documents Illustrating the History of Social and Political Ideas* (Oxford, Oxford University Press) 65–68. Note also Horace, *Odes* IV:15; Aritides, *Oration* 26 'To Rome' 70–71; Strabo, *Geography* VI.4.2.

[211] This quote is from the Byzantine philosopher Methochite reprinted in Barker, E (ed) (1959) *Social and Political Thought in Byzantium* (Oxford, Clarendon Press) 175.

situation to occur. As Dio Cassius (150–225) suggested, Romans were 'subjects without being slaves, and citizens of a democracy unvexed by faction'.[212] This was believed to be better than traditional forms of democracy, as citizens could claim many of the benefits of democratic systems without the strife. Philosophers such as Philostratus (170–250) would argue:

> Just as one man who is preeminent in virtue can transform democracy into the likeness of the rule of the one best man, so conversely, the rule of one man, which it provides everything which tends to the welfare of the community, really is a democracy.[213]

This was complete fiction. In reality, all of the processes which could control the power of the emperor had been removed. The last meetings of the masses had occurred at the end of the first century. In Rome, the senate ceased to exist after 282 CE, with their last known decree being in 280 CE. In the East, in Constantinople, despite the formation of a new senate of 2,000 men based on hereditary claims, the principle of imperial power held by one man was absolute. This was made very clear when Justinian explained in his famous code of law that 'the Emperor shall justly be regarded as the sole maker and interpreter of the laws'.[214] To reinforce his absolute position, Justinian also imposed a more exacting code of etiquette upon senators who wished to meet with him. Previously, whenever a senator had entered the imperial presence, he had simply crooked his right knee. Now, the senator was expected to fall flat on his face, stretch out his hands and feet as far as he could, and humbly kiss the slipper of the emperor. This change was supplemented by a constitutional order which demoted the senate to a largely ceremonial role in which 'it was absolutely not allowed for anyone of those assembled there to discuss anything [seriously]'.[215] On the few occasions that the senate in Byzantium attempted to reassert any form of authority it was overruled; for example, Leo VI (886–912) told them only to provide advice when it was asked for.[216]

H. The Emperor in Practice

There was no one model that all emperors followed. Some emperors, such as Trajan (r 98–117), were favourably received as 'a fellow citizen, not a tyrant, one who is our father not our overlord. He is one of us'.[217] Others did not receive such praise. Caligula

[212] Dio Cassius, *Roman History* trans Cary, E (1967) (Boston, Loeb) LVI.100.43.

[213] Philostratus reprinted in Barker, E (ed) (1959) *From Alexander to Constantine: Passages and Documents Illustrating the History of Social and Political Ideas* (Oxford, Oxford University Press) 329–30. Note also Aelius Aristides, 'To Rome' xxxvi reprinted in Lewis, N and Reinhold M (eds) (1955) *Roman Civilisation: Records*, Vol II (Columbia, Columbia University Press) 411. See also Carlyle, A (1936) *A History of Medieval Political Theory in the West: The Second Century to the Ninth*, Vol 1 (London, Blackwood) 63–67.

[214] This part of the Justinian code, on 'imperial authority' is reprinted in Cantor, N (ed) (1963) *The Medieval World 300–1300* (NYC, Macmillan) 89.

[215] Procopius, *Anecdota* trans Dewing, H (Cambridge, Loeb) 170; Holland, T (2012) *In the Shadow of the Sword* (NYC, Brown) 143.

[216] See the comments of Leo VI reprinted in Barker, E (ed) (1959) *Social and Political Thought in Byzantium* (Oxford, Clarendon Press) 99–100.

[217] Pliny, *Letters and Panegricus* trans Radice, I (1969) (Boston, Loeb) II:3–4.

(12–41), Nero, Domitian (51–96), Commodus (161–192) and Elagabalus (218–224) have particularly bad reputations and left poor legacies. These men simply executed and expropriated as they wished, cowing and terrifying senators. The more intelligent emperors liked to obfuscate and camouflage their use of absolute power by humouring and flattering the senate. The less subtle emperors did not waste their time.

The one area on which all of the emperors apportioned their time and resources was the military. Whilst it is correct that all the emperors continued to distribute largess to the people in terms of occasional debt relief and social assistance, coupled with an ongoing supply of what Juvenal (c 100) called 'bread and circuses'[218] it was to the military that the emperors were most attentive. In the early years of the Empire, Augustus, like Sulla, Pompey, Caesar and Antony before him, was very aware that he had achieved his position of power through the support of his armed forces. Their loyalty was handsomely rewarded. Augustus rewarded them by a combination of exempting many of his soldiers from various forms of taxation and the distribution of 'bonuses of cash' given after the completion of their terms of service. Finally, he initiated a large-scale programme of overseas colonisation as a regular means of providing for the veterans as a reward for service. Augustus boasted of settling more than 300,000 Roman citizens in the army in colonies in, inter alia, Africa, Sicily, Macedonia, Spain, Achaea, the province of Asia, Syria, Southern Gaul and Italy. The planting of veterans in distant colonies was politically astute especially when dealing with the defeated armies of his enemies, such as Antony's armies, which were broken up and scattered throughout the Empire. They also served the useful purpose of keeping an eye on the locals. Such rapid and forthright colonialism was facilitated by the powers of the emperor, as agreed from Augustus onward, inter alia, 'to extend and advance the boundaries of the *pomerium* [the lands which Rome possesses] whenever they deem it to be the interest of the State'.[219]

After 6 CE, although military colonies were still occasionally established, the veteran normally received his discharge in cash. All of the emperors after Augustus were careful to reward the armed forces, in a policy known as *donativum*, by which the legions and Praetorian Guard in particular (10,000 highly trained and well-paid men kept in and around Rome as the Imperial bodyguard) were directly gifted money. The money, given under the pretext of rewards or favours required, was ultimately a clear bribe to those with the weapons not to overthrow the man in power – or, to overthrow the man in power. For example, when the general Galba (3 BCE–69 CE) snatched the power from Nero, the usurper promised the Praetorian Guard ten times their annual pay.[220]

What developed in the centuries that followed was a competition for the control of power between the emperors and their attempts to control and pass on their power to

[218] Juvenal, *Satires* trans Braund, S (1993) (Cambridge, Cambridge University Press) X:80. For the social laws, see Lewis, N and Reinhold M (eds) (1955) *Roman Civilisation: Records*, Vol II (Columbia, Columbia University Press) 344–45.

[219] Augustus, as noted in Barker, E (ed) (1959) *From Alexander to Constantine: Passages and Documents Illustrating the History of Social and Political Ideas* (Oxford, Oxford University Press) 227–28; *The Res Gestae Divi Augustus: Accomplishment of Augustus* trans Brunt, P (1967) (Oxford, Oxford University Press) 31. Note Lewis, N and Reinhold M (eds) (1955) *Roman Civilisation: Records*, Vol II (Columbia, Columbia University Press) 89, 274–75, 392.

[220] Morgan, G (2006) *69 AD The Year of Four Emperors* (Oxford, Oxford University Press) 29.

whoever they wanted, and the military forces, who sought to control the power for themselves. Initially, this process went the way of the emperors. Augustus, who had no biological heir, adopted Tiberius (42 BCE–37CE) as his successor, and upon the death of Augustus the transfer of power proceeded without incident. There was no thought about revolution or a return to the old Republican order. In large part, this was because Augustus had left money to the Praetorian Guard in his will and Tiberius was equally generous to them. He was generous to them because he was aware of the extreme risk they represented for, as he remarked, handling the armed forces was 'like holding a wolf by the ears'.[221]

For half a century after the death of Augustus, while there were still members of the Julio–Claudian (that is, Augustan–Tiberian) family, the succession to the *Principate* remained within that family. The power of the armed forces was apparent from the start, when the prefect of the Praetorian Guard was the first after the *consols* to swear allegiance to Tiberius, and it was not long before the military intervened openly in emperor-making. The Praetorian prefects were the leaders in the assassination of Caligula, and while the senate debated who should succeed Caligula the Praetorians applied their interpretation of dynastic succession and proclaimed the late emperor's uncle, Claudius, their ruler. A guardsman found Claudius hiding behind a curtain in the palace and had him carted to the Praetorian camp. In the year 68 CE the doom of Nero was sealed by the disaffection of legions under the rallying cry of 'freedom from the tyrant'.[222] With Nero's death, the Julio-Claudian line was extinct and in the following year four generals in different parts of the empire were proclaimed emperor by their respective forces. Thus, as Tacitus explained, 'a secret of the imperial power' was revealed, namely 'that the emperor could be created elsewhere than at Rome'.[223]

Vespasian emerged the victor at the end of the civil wars, in which the senate had expressed no support for any of the commanders. This was unlike the legions, who supported opposing contenders – each seeking the *diadem* – who fought repeatedly for one commander or another in the so-called 'year of the four emperors'. The year ran from the death of Nero in the middle of 68 CE, through to the triumph of Vespasian at the end of 69 CE. In the interim, three other emperors held power, if only for a few months. Galba was officially declared emperor in the middle of 68 (after proclaiming that he was acting as 'lieutenant of the senate and people of Rome') and was assassinated in the middle of January 69. Otho (32–69) was responsible for his murder, yet having seised power by a coup in Rome, he committed suicide in the middle of April in the hope that his death would end the bloodshed. Vitellius (15–69) was hailed emperor by his troops in early 69 and was recognised by the senate in Rome once they heard of the death of Otho. He was then cut down by Vespasian partisans at the end of that year, following the two pitched battles of Bedriacum between the armies of Vespasian and Vitellius.[224]

[221] Suetonius, *The Twelve Caesars* trans Graves, R (1989) (London, Penguin) 113.

[222] See Morgan, G (2006) *69 AD The Year of Four Emperors* (Oxford, Oxford University Press) 18–19.

[223] Tacitus, *The Annals of Imperial Rome* trans Grant, M (1989) (London, Penguin) I:iv. See also Lewis, N and Reinhold M (eds) (1955) *Roman Civilisation: Records*, Vol II (Columbia, Columbia University Press) 28.

[224] See Morgan, G (2006) *69 AD The Year of Four Emperors* (Oxford, Oxford University Press) 1, 21.

Vespasian, who adopted an openly dynastic policy, was succeeded by his two sons, Titus (39–81) and Domitian (51–96). This dynasty, the Flavian, ended with Domitian's assassination in the year 96. Thereafter, a series of emperors without sons of their own put into practice the policy introduced by Galba (3–69) in 69, when the emperor adopted the ablest man available as his son, chief aid and successor. Marcus Aurelius, the last of what is known as the 'Good Emperors', reverted to the dynastic principle, designating his son Commodus (161–192) as his successor – without any recourse to the views of the senate. Commodus was later slain and the throne once again became the plaything of armies. The conclusion of this period was the Praetorians auctioning the right to be Roman Emperor in 193. Septimius Severus (r 193–211), who secured the role of emperor at the end of 193 after much bloodshed, is reported to have said to his sons upon his death: 'Live in harmony, enrich the soldiers, scorn all others.'[225] True to his advice, he had doubled the amount given to soldiers when the title of emperor had first been auctioned in 193. His eldest son, Caracalla (188–217), continued to follow this advice closely destroying all contenders for the throne (including his own brother, Geta, who was the co-ruler of the Empire) and the communities that supported the opposition (such as the 20,000 rebellious citizens of Alexandria). Only the military forces were lavished with praise and economic rewards.[226]

The Severan dynasty came to an end in 235 with the rebellion of Maximinus (173–238), who gained the support of the military by doubling their wages. This caused another half-century of civil war. From the assassination of Severus Alexander in 235 to the accession of Diocletian (244–311) in 284, 26 soldier emperors were proclaimed (out of more than 50 who claimed the title), and all but one died a violent death – usually at the hands of their own soldiers.

Diocletian brought some stability with his novel idea of the *Tetrarchy* (leadership of four people), whereby the Empire was divided between four men, two senior (*augusti*) and two junior (*caesars*) rulers. This extension to four rulers followed the joint rule by Diocletian and Maximian (250–310) between 285 and 293. When it was extended to four rulers, it was also divided between East and West. In the first instance, these were Diocletian and Maximian, joined by Galerius (260–311) and Constantius (250–306). The only difficulty with this idea was that it was a complete failure. The *Tetrarchy* began to disintegrate after two of the four were no longer in office (Diocletian, in 305 being the only Roman ever to peacefully retire from his position and Maximian committed suicide after retiring in the same year). Constantius died of disease in 306, after passing his part of the empire to his son, Constantine the Great (272–337). When Galerius, the last of the original four, died in 311, all hopes for stability were gone. In reality, this hope had disappeared years earlier, with discord and confusion being the rule between 305 and 313. During this point, the empire was afflicted by five civil wars, and the remainder of the time was not so much a state of tranquility as a suspension of arms between several hostile monarchs. These men viewed each other with fear and hatred, and each strove to increase their respective forces at the expense of their

[225] Dio Cassius, *Roman History* trans Cary, E (1967) (Boston, Loeb) LIX:2, LXXI:3, LXXIV.11, LXXVI:15

[226] Morgan, G (2006) *69 AD The Year of Four Emperors* (Oxford, Oxford University Press) 50–70; Gibbon, E (1926 edn) *The Decline and Fall of the Roman Empire*, Vol I (London, Methuen) 139–51.

subjects. It was from this morass that Constantine, the first Christian Emperor, eventually rose to power.[227] The obvious question that this raises is whether or not Christianity made a difference to the political practices of running the Empire.

5. THE CONTRIBUTION OF CHRISTIANITY

Christianity sought a kingdom which was 'not of this world'.[228] This focus on spiritual rather than temporal goals meant that Christianity became a faith which supported the status quo, rather than aiming to upset political structures. The early theologian Justin (100–165) expressed this position when he suggested 'it is our special care to be the first of all to pay our taxes and dues . . . [although] we adore God alone . . . in other matters we gladly serve you, we acknowledge you as Kings and rulers'.[229] This willingness not to upset the status quo was evident in two areas. The first was in its support for the existing constitutional structures. The second was in its treatment of the question of slavery.

The support for existing political structures was somewhat surprising, given Christianity's strong emphasis on (spiritual) freedom, combined with a core philosophy that the religion was open to all, with a particular emphasis upon the poor, and the broadly democratic principles adopted by the early Church. However, perhaps as a counter-weight to the rebellious Jews who were giving the Romans so much trouble at this point of history, submission – rather than rebellion – to governing authorities was a primary obligation for Christians.[230] Chapter 13 of Paul's epistle to the Romans is clear on this point:

> Let everyone be subject to the governing authorities, for there is no authority except that which God has established. The authorities that exist have been established by God. Consequently, whoever rebels against the authority is rebelling against what God has instituted, and those who do so will bring judgment on themselves. For rulers hold no terror for those who do right, but for those who do wrong. Do you want to be free from fear of the one in authority? Then do what is right and you will be commended. For the one in authority is God's servant for your good. But if you do wrong, be afraid, for rulers do not bear the sword for no reason. They are God's servants, agents of wrath to bring punishment on the wrongdoer. Therefore, it is necessary to submit to the authorities, not only because of possible punishment but also as a matter of conscience.

The first letter of Peter parallels what Paul had to say, with his call to 'submit yourself to every ordinance of man for the Lord's sake . . . honour the king'.[231] Additional

[227] See Lactantius, 'De Mortibus Persecutorum' trans Moreau, J (1954) (Paris, Scribe) 97–99 reprinted in Geanakoplos, D (ed) (1986) *Byzantium: A Sourcebook on Church, Society and Civilisation Seen Through Contemporary Eyes* (Chicago, Chicago University Press) 39.

[228] John 18:36. See also Matthew 4:8–10 and Mark 8:36.

[229] Justin, *Apologia I pro Christianis*. This is noted in Eppstein, J (1935) *The Catholic Tradition of the Law of Nations* (London, Burns and Oates) 32.

[230] The point about spiritual equality is found in Galatians 3:28. See also Muller, H (1961) *Freedom in the Ancient World* (NYC, Harper) 289, 296, 308; Carlyle, A (1936) *A History of Medieval Political Theory in the West: The Second Century to the Ninth*, Vol 1 (London, Blackwood) 96–100.

[231] 1 Peter 2:13–17.

sources on this point can be found in the letter to Titus, in which Christians are exhorted to 'be subject to rulers and authorities, be obedient',[232] whilst in the first letter to Timothy, Christians are told to pray for the kings, so that they may live peaceful and quiet lives.[233]

This promise of a quiet life for the rulers was supplemented by the equally powerful theological justification for kingship which evolved with Christianity. Christianity managed to accommodate the Roman tradition of the ruler cult by making the emperor God's special agent. Although demoted from divine status himself, the emperor (and later the king) maintained a central position in the Christian theory of empire, as with the link to God, the all-powerful sole leader could be considered to be of service to humanity, benefitting man, the Church, and the community they were meant to serve. Gregory of Nazianzus (329–390), who became bishop of Constantinople in 380, argued that the power possessed by emperors was a unique, divine gift and so the emperor was worthy of pubic veneration. Supplemental views, such as those of Themistius (317–390), would suggest that the emperor was the embodiment of law itself – the 'animate' or 'incarnate law'. The conclusion, he suggested, was that 'God sent kings to the Earth to serve men as refuge from an immovable law to the safety of the animate and living law'.[234] Pope Agapetus (d 536) would later suggest around the year 530:

> Having a dignity which is set above all other honors, Sire, you render honor above all to God, who gave you that dignity; inasmuch as He gave you the scepter of earthly power after the likeness of the heavenly kingdom, to the end that you should instruct men to hold fast the cause of justice, and should punish the howling of those who rage against that cause; being yourself under the kingship of the law of justice and lawfully king of those who are subject to you.[235]

Gregory I (669–731) would later add 'the deeds of superiors are not to be smitten with the sword of the mouth, even when they are rightly judged of blame . . . for when we offend against those who are set over us, we go against the ordinance of Him who set them over us'.[236]

In time, this view would be supported by successive Christian scholars, such as Regino of Prum (d 915), who would record the canon that pronounced the anathema of the Church on anyone who dared to try to resist royal power, as this power derived its authority, according to the Apostolic teaching, from God himself.[237]

Successive Byzantine scholars rolled out a large number of 'mirrors' for the princes, in terms of advice given to the emperor. These all recommended to the most powerful man in the empire the basic considerations of piety, upholding the laws,

[232] Titus 3:1.

[233] 1 Timothy 2:1–2.

[234] Themistius reprinted in Maas, M (ed) (2010) *Readings in Late Antiquity: A Sourcebook* (London, Routledge) 8. Gregory is reprinted in the same title at 7. See also Barker, E (ed) (1959) *From Alexander to Constantine: Passages and Documents Illustrating the History of Social and Political Ideas* (Oxford, Oxford University Press) 347, 359.

[235] Agapetus reprinted in Barker, E (ed) (1959) *Social and Political Thought in Byzantium* (Oxford, Clarendon Press) 54–60, 82.

[236] Gregory I reprinted in Cantor, N (ed) (1963) *The Medieval World 300–1300* (NYC, Macmillan) 113–14.

[237] Carlyle, A (1906) *A History of Medieval Political Theory in the West*, Vol II (London, Blackwood) 146.

and the implementation of justice. Although some, such as Synesius (373–410), suggested that emperors who 'fattened themselves' on their own citizens could become tyrants, and others like Procopius (500–565) would become deeply disillusioned over the reign of emperors such as Justinian, no-one suggested that the emperor's power was in any way limited by any earthly force. Thus, even Procopius, with his misgivings due to the behaviour of the court of Justinian, still believed 'the natural course for a high-souled Emperor to pursue is to seek to enlarge the Empire, and make it more glorious'.[238]

The second area where Christianity supported, rather than threatened, the status quo was the question of slavery. Early Christian theologians inherited the problem that the Bible limited, but did not prohibit, slavery. Christians, rather than contradict the earlier rulings in this area, adopted the spiritual metaphor of being slaves of Christ – which they agreed with, as opposed to slaves of other humans, which they avoided. What was important in relation to being owned by other people was the state of the soul in relation to God, rather than the ownership of the body. In terms of restraint, the rule in the Gospels in this area was: 'Masters, treat your slaves justly and fairly, knowing that you also have a Master in heaven.'[239] This restraint should be matched by the obedience of the slaves. Thus:

> [O]bey your earthly masters with respect and fear, and with sincerity of heart, just as you would obey Christ . . . Serve wholeheartedly, as if you were serving the Lord, not people, because you know that the Lord will reward each one for whatever good they do, whether they are slave or free.[240]

The letter to Titus, in attempting to make the instruction of Christianity more attractive to the Roman authorities, advised 'teach slaves to be subject to their masters in everything'.[241] Peter suggested 'slaves, be submissive to your masters with all respect, not only to the gentle and kind, but also to the overbearing'.[242] Finally, the first letter to Timothy added:

> All who are under the yoke of slavery should consider their masters worthy of full respect, so that God's name and our teaching may not be slandered. Those who have believing masters should not show them disrespect just because they are fellow believers. Instead, they should serve them even better because their masters are dear to them as fellow believers and are devoted to the welfare of their slaves.[243]

Such instructions meant that generations of Christian theologians, including Dio Chrysostom (c 100 CE) and Ambrose (337–397), continued to argue that slavery was more of a religious than a social construct. Origen (184–254) argued it was God's will, whilst Augustine (354–430), although advocating a humane approach, continued to

[238] Procopius, *Secret History* trans Williamson, G (1988) (Harmondsworth, Penguin) V:5; also Norwich, J (1988) *Byzantium: The Early Centuries* (London, Guild) 245; also Synerius of Cyrene, *Writings* trans Nichol, J (1967) (NYC, Hodge) Book III.

[239] Colossians 3:22–4:1. Note also Galatians 3:28.

[240] Ephesians 6:5–8. See also Colossians 3:22–24.

[241] Titus 2:9–10.

[242] I Peter 2:18–21.

[243] 1 Timothy 6:1-2; also Romans 6:15–23; I Corinthians 7:20–24; Galatians 3:28–29.

justify the institution of slavery and the benefits that could flow to slaves from having righteous Christian owners. He believed this so strongly that he added that the dictates in the Bible for manumission were not precedents that Christians should follow. He also noted that because Christianity was open to everyone, even free slaves could go on to take up leading positions within the Church, as Callistus – the Bishop of Rome around 190 to 195 achieved. A future pope, Gregory the Great, was so influenced by this view that he bought slaves for the purpose of sending them to Rome to be converted.[244]

Although many theologians spoke of kindness to slaves, only a few, including Gregory of Nyssa (335–394) and Lactantius (250–325) – the adviser to Constantine the Great, took the different view that God created all people equal, whereby 'no one is master, no one slave'.[245] Early church leaders did not appear to exhort congregations to manumit their slaves either selectively or en masse. One of the most notable Christians in power, Bishop Gregory of Nazianzus (d 390), was a slave-owner and did not manumit all his slaves when he died. Rather, the focus of the early Christian Church seemed to have been on acting in accordance with fairness and upholding the letter of the law. Church Councils from the fourth century cautioned against anyone telling slaves to flee, and against using Church property for purposes of sanctuary for runaway slaves.[246]

The result of this lack of condemnation was that until the first millennia the taking and keeping of slaves as a lawful practice, via war, debt or court processes, whereby one person could become the property of another, continued unabashed in the east and west of the Holy Roman Empire and adjoining lands. Reminders of this practice are evident today, in the language the Anglo-Saxons left behind after their invasion of England – inventing the word for a person with no freedom as 'Welshman'.

Although slavery existed in this period, the practice was supplemented by the invention of serfdom. The word 'serf' was a name taken from the Roman word for slave '*servus*', but the difference was that such people no longer lived in complete servitude. That is, they became free tenants who were permanently bound to the land, as were their children, and were under the direct control of their local landlord. Personal freedom was technically theirs, and they still had basic rights (such as not to be wrongfully disinherited from their farms or have extraordinary dues imposed on them), but their condition was now semi-servile. Despite this distinction, the differences between those bound to the land and those who were traditional slaves are often very hard to distinguish.[247]

[244] Augustine *City of God* 19:15–21. See also Book 19 of Chapter XIX; Augustine, *New Sermon* 4:91–93; Dio Chrysostom, *Orationes* 15:29; Ambrose, *De Jacob et vita beata* 2.2.II. The work of Ambrose (*Epistulae* 7.1–13) and Origen (*Homily on Genesis* 16:1) can be found in Garnsey, P (1996) *Ideas of Slavery from Aristotle to Augustine* (Cambridge, Cambridge University Press) 44–52, 168–72, 200–209; Kyrtatas, DJ (1995) 'Slavery as Progress: Pagan and Christian Views of Slavery as Moral Training' *International Sociology* 10:219–34; Ayerst, D (ed) (1971) *Records of Christianity*, Vol I (Oxford, Blackwell) 99.

[245] Lactantius, *Divine Institutes* trans McDonald, M (1992) (NYC, Catholic Universities) section 5.14.15–15.3; Gregory of Nyssa, *Homilies on Ecclesiastes* trans Hall, S (1993) (London, De Gruyter) 74.

[246] Eppstein, J (1935) *The Catholic Tradition of the Law of Nations* (London, Burns and Oates) 414–16. Garnsey, P (1996) *Ideas of Slavery from Aristotle to Augustine* (Cambridge, Cambridge University Press) 32–33, 70–71; Pirenne, H (1939) *Mohammed and Charlemagne* (London, Allen and Unwin). 98; Meltzer, M (1993) *Slavery: A World History* (NYC, DaCapo) 205–208; The Council of Orleans, 511 reprinted in Rosenwein, B (ed) (2006) *Reading the Middle Ages: Sources from Europe, Byzantium and the Islamic World* (Ontario, Broadview) 60.

[247] Herlihy, D (ed) (1970) *The History of Feudalism* (NYC, Harper) 122–23; Meltzer, M (1993) *Slavery: A World History* (NYC, DaCapo) 204–205; Mango, C (1994) *Byzantium: The Empire of the New Rome* (London, Paladin) 43–44.

Serfdom existed in tandem with more traditional types of slavery which continued to flourish. Between 700 and 900 there was a substantive trade in slaves within Europe, with many people captured in remote parts of Europe and transported, to be purchased in either European or Islamic countries. It was only from the eighth century onward that some humane attitudes began to reappear. The only Christian theologian to speak out against the overall institution of slavery was Smaragdus (ninth century). The other restraints that emerged involved recommendations from some Church councils that slaves should not be treated too harshly, and that sales of slaves should not be wrongfully coerced. The other area where change emerged was in relation to slaves who were Christian. The first restraint that emerged around the year 600 involved the forbidding of Jewish people to own Christian slaves. The second restraint involved the transfer of Christian slaves outside of Europe (especially to Muslim countries). In 779 Charlemagne (742–814) promulgated regulations which demanded that any sales of slaves had to be in the presence of a bishop, count or archbishop. Likewise, in 781 he ruled 'let no one sell Christian or pagan slaves . . . outside our kingdom'.[248] The first treaty on this appeared in the following century between Venice and Lothair in 840, forbidding the sale of Christian slaves and of eunuchs. A further treaty between Naples and the Duke of Benevento forbade the Lombards from buying slaves for the purpose of reselling them. This restraint later (in 922) became an overall prohibition of the enslavement of any Christians by other Christians.[249]

6. THE CHRISTIAN EMPERORS OF THE ROMAN EMPIRE

Constantine the Great did not prevent the collapse of the Roman Empire in the west. After his death, the problems of conflict in the pursuit of absolute power continued. The essential difficulty was that there was no simple, clearly defined law or method of succession to the throne, and once on the throne, others were always willing to try to usurp power. Although Constantine managed to keep the throne himself, upon his death it was divided between his three sons, Constantine II (316–340), Constantius II (317–360) and Constans 323–350. This arrangement was short-lived, with two of the brothers – Constantine II and Constans – fighting each other in 340, three years after the death of their father, over what they considered to be inequitable divisions of the western provinces of their father's empire. Constantine II lost these wars, and his life,

[248] The Capitulary of Mantua, 781 reprinted in Loyn, H (ed) (1975) *The Reign of Charlemagne: Documents on Carolingian Government and Administration* (London, Edward Arnold) 50; Herlihy, D (ed) (1970) *The History of Feudalism* (NYC, Harper) 84–86. The restriction on Jewish ownership can be found in Ayerst, D (ed) (1971) *Records of Christianity*, Vol II (Oxford, Blackwell) 260.

[249] Eppstein, J (1935) *The Catholic Tradition of the Law of Nations* (London, Burns and Oates) 416; Pirenne, H (1935) *Mohammed and Charlemagne* (London, Allen and Unwin) 95–100, 179, 182, 259; Carlyle, A (1936) *A History of Medieval Political Theory in the West: The Second Century to the Ninth*, Vol 1 (London, Blackwood) 46–54, 199–209; Brink, S (2012) *The Viking World* (London, Routledge) 49–51; Abels, R (1998) *Alfred the Great: War, Kingship and Culture in Anglo-Saxon England* (London, Longman) 36–38; 'European Slave Exports' in Rosenwein, B (ed) (2006) *Reading the Middle Ages: Sources from Europe, Byzantium and the Islamic World* (Ontario, Broadview) 141–42. For Charlemagne, see the Capitulary of Herstal, 779 reprinted in Loyn, H (ed) (1975) *The Reign of Charlemagne: Documents on Carolingian Government and Administration* (London, Edward Arnold) 48.

leaving his two brothers to re-divide the empire. This was another short-lived reign, as in 350 parts of the army of Constans, under the leadership of one the generals, Magnentius, revolted (due to his objection to Constans' personal lifestyle), and had him assassinated. Soon afterwards, the only surviving son of Constantine the Great, Constantius, had to turn all of his efforts into destroying the forces of the usurper Magnentius, under the banners of revenge for the death of his brother, and the glory that would be achieved in the fight. Constantius then had to fight and defeat two other generals who tried to seise power, before a third – Julian (331–363), was promoted to Caesar by the legions he commanded in the west of the Empire. A further, almost certain, civil war was only avoided because Constantius died a natural death in 361. Realising his death was near, he declared that Julian was his rightful successor.[250]

On the death of Julian, the army declared Jovian (331–364) to be the emperor. At the death of Jovian, a meeting of civil and military officials decided that Valentinian (321–375) was the most appropriate person to be made emperor. In 364, Valentinian, realising that the size of the empire made it difficult to rule gave the eastern half to his brother, Valens, to look after, thereby dividing the east from the west. The only difficulty with this transition was that the one surviving relative of Julian attempted to claim the throne for himself. This attempt only ended in 366 when Valens fought and defeated the armies of the usurper, and then executed the man responsible. This left Valentian free to pass on the empire to his sons, Gratian (359–383) and Valentian II (375–392). In 378, Gratian invited Theodosius (347–395) to take command of the Illyrian army. Gratian's appointment of Theodosius amounted to a de facto invitation to Theodosius to become co-Augustus for the east. When Gratian was killed in a rebellion in 383, Theodosius appointed his oldest son, Arcadius (377–408), as his co-ruler in the east (thus continuing the trend of dividing the empire into east and west). Meanwhile, Valentian II, with the support of the armies of Theodosius, had to defeat the usurper Magnus Maximus (335–388), whose ambitions reached beyond being commander of Britain, to the point that Maximus invaded Italy in 387, where he met his death a year later. When Valentinian II died in 392, Theodosius was elected to rule as sole emperor. However, another usurper, Eugenius (d 394), attempted to grab power in the west, at the behest of the mandarins who had supported Valentinian II. Theodosius stated that Eugenius was an illegitimate usurper, and gave his eight-year-old son Honorius (384–423) the full rank of Augustus in the west. In order to secure this appointment, the forces of Eugenius had to be defeated in combat, which was achieved at the battle of Frigidus in 394, during which Eugenius was captured and executed.[251]

Hororius faced revolts in North Africa (397–398) and Britain. In Britain, the army rebelled three times between 407 and 410. The last revolt was driven by the desire of Constantine III (d 411), the then Roman general in Britain, to become emperor of the west. To achieve this he sent his (Roman) soldiers to invade Spain and Gaul His forces

[250] Gibbon, E *The Decline and Fall of the Rome Empire* ed Bury, J (1929 edn) Vol II (London, Methuen) 420–49; Gwatkin, H (ed) (1957) *The Cambridge Medieval History. The Christian Roman Empire*, Vol I (Cambridge, Cambridge University Press) 61–63.

[251] Gwatkin, H (ed) (1957) *The Cambridge Medieval History. The Christian Roman Empire*, Vol I (Cambridge, Cambridge University Press) 244–47.

ground to a halt and he lost his head – once his own soldiers found another candidate. The new usurper, Priscus Attalus (d 416), who had the support of the duplicitous Visigoth Alaric (370–410), was later betrayed by Alaric for a greater prize. However, so as not to rule alone, towards the end of his reign Attalus gave the title of co-emperor to Constantius III (d 421). Although Constantius III only ruled for seven months before his death, his son, Valentinian III (419–455) was named as emperor by his emperor cousin in the east, Theodosius II (401–450). However, before this title could be claimed, another usurper, Joannes (d 425) had to be dealt with, and this duly occurred.

Theodosius II died of natural causes in 450, but a power struggle developed after his death, in which his sister won the contest against a court eunuch and then placed her husband Marcian (392–457) on the throne, making him emperor of Byzantium. In the west, Valentinian III was murdered by Maximus, a prominent aristocrat who only managed to hold power for two-and-a-half months, before he was killed during the events that culminated in the Vandal sack of Rome in 455. Another Roman aristocrat, Avitus (385–457), held power for a year, before the general Majorian (420–461) deposed Avitus as the western Roman emperor, only to be deposed, in turn, by another general, Ricimer (405–472), who placed his favourite, Libius Severus (420–465), on the western throne. When Liberius Severus died of natural causes, a dispute arose over who would take power next. This initially saw the last capable emperor of the west, Anthemius, attempting to fight against both the Vandals and the Goths. This ended with Ricimer sacking Rome, decapitating Anthemius and enthroning the candidate he preferred – Olybrius (d 472). From this point, the end of the empire came quickly, with Gycerius (420–480), Nepos (430–480) and finally Romulus Augustus (c 460–476) seeing the Western Roman Empire to its conclusion. It was the deposition by the German chieftain Odoacer (433–493) in 476, the first 'barbarian' king of Rome, which is commonly regarded as the end of the Western Roman Empire – the fall of ancient Rome, and the beginning of the Middle Ages in Western Europe.[252]

As the control of the western side of the Roman Empire was lost, the same pattern of war and conflict relating to the quest and the holding of absolute power in the empire by one person continued unabated in the east. This pattern, of attempts within families to change dynasties, was constantly punctuated by those brave enough to seek power from outside the family. Both situations often resulted in civil war. The palace intrigues of the east began when Zeno (425–491) was replaced by Anastasius (430–518). Anastasius, a former palace official, was raised to the throne by Zeno's widow, Adriadne, who preferred him to Zeno's brother. To cement the choice, she married Anastasius shortly before his accession. However, this choice was not accepted by Zeno's brother, who dragged Anastasius through five years of what is known as the Isaurian war, from 492 to 497. Anastasius' successor was the chief of the Guards, Justin I (520–578), who Anastasius chose over his three nephews. Justin I was went on to proclaim the leader of the army, the famous Justinian I (482–565) as the next Emperor. Justinian gave it to his nephew, Justin II (520–578) who in turn gave the title of co-emperor to his favourite general, Tiberius II (520–582). Maurice (539–602) gained the throne after having married the emperor's daughter, but lost it to Phocas

[252] Gibbon, E (1926 edn) *The Decline and Fall of the Roman Empire*, Vol IV (London, Methuen) 47–53.

(r 602–610), a centurion, who led a military coup. Maurice was executed after having been forced to watch the execution of his own sons.[253]

Phocas was overthrown and personally executed by another military man, Heraclius (575–641). Heraclius was succeeded by his sons, Constantine III (612–641) and Heraklonus (626–641), who both only ruled for a short period. The son of Constantine III, Constans II (630–688), had a relatively long period on the throne, before being assassinated and having his crown seised by a military general, Mezezius, before it was seised back by the son of Constans II, Constantine IV (652–685), who held onto power after suppressing another military rebellion within months of his coming to power. To ensure that he retained power and was not threatened by family rivalry, he had both of his brothers mutilated so badly that they were incapable of ruling. This cleared the way for his son (Justinian II (699–711)) to take power when the time was right. Unlike his father, Justinian II could not hold onto power. He survived the first military coup and fought his way back to place his feet on the neck of the ringleader, Tiberius III (d 706), before executing him. In the second coup he lost power to the military and could not recover; his child was executed in front of him, thus eradicating the line of Heraclius. Justinian then had his nose and tongue slit, before being exiled. These acts were carried out by the general Leontios (d 706).[254]

Another general, Bardanes (r 711–713), took the title of emperor after defeating the forces of Leontios, and torturing and then publically executing their leader. The reign of Bardanes ended when the military decided that Anastasius (r 713–719) was a better choice. Anastasius, too, was overthrown (but was lucky enough to live out his days as a monk) by Theodosios III (r 715–717) when the army changed its mind again, and decided that a former tax collector was better suited to rule the empire. The fact that Theodosios III did not want this position, and had to be found and taken from his hiding place in the forest, did not deter the military. With the accession of Theodosius III, the Byzantines could look back on no less than six emperors in the previous 20 years, five of whose reigns had ended violently. The sixth emperor, Theodosius III (r 715–717), was eclipsed (but allowed to live out his days in a monastery) when Leo III (685–741), another man of the military, entered Constantinople at the head of an army. Leo III was succeeded by his son, Constantine V (718–775), who ruled from 741, having defeated his brother-in-law in a civil war for the title. Leo IV (750–800), the son of Constantine V, took over the throne and ruled for five years. His reign, given his intention to pass the throne to his son, Constantine VI (r 776–797), led to a failed uprising by his five half-brothers. Constantine VI, who became emperor at the age of nine, held the position under the regency of his mother Irene (752–803). However, his mother had no intention of relinquishing power to her son when he came of age, and after a struggle for power, he was captured and blinded and died of his wounds. This act allowed Irene to be crowned as first Empress of Constantinople and left her free to rule the empire for five years. She was removed from the throne in the year 802 by the minister of finance, Nikephoros I (d 811), who allowed her to live – but in poverty.[255]

253 Hussey, J (1966) *The Cambridge Medieval History: The Byzantine Empire*, Vol IV(1) (Cambridge, Cambridge University Press) 156–60.

254 Kaegi, W (2007) *Heraclius: Emperor of Byzantium* (Cambridge, Cambridge University Press) 37, 49–51.

255 Luttwak, E (2009) *The Grand Strategy of the Byzantine Empire* (London, Harvard University Press) 137–44.

Nikephoros I (d 811), despite some attempted revolts, managed to hold onto power for his son, Staurakios (d 812). Staurakios, who had been injured in the same battle that killed his father, was deposed by Michael I Rangabes (770–813), who had Staurakios removed from service, due to physical injuries that allegedly prevented him from being able to govern. Michael could not hold onto power, and facing a revolt he could not win he abdicated in favour of the general Leo V the Armenian (775–820). Although Michael was allowed to live out his days in a monastery, his sons were castrated to ensure the end of any future claims from his family. Another general, Michael II (770–829), was toppled and killed by Leo V. Although there were revolts during the reign of Michael II, he managed to pass power onto his son, Theophilos (813–842), who in turn, passed power onto his son, Michael III (840–867). This line came to an end when Basil I (830–886), a peasant who found work in the imperial court, managed to work his way through the administration before usurping the throne himself. His illegitimate son, Leo VI (866–912), was identified and enthroned by Basil I before Basil died to ensure that the dynasty continued. Similarly, the illegitimate son of Leo VI, Constantine VII (905–959) was enthroned by his father when he was two years old, along with his brother, Romanos II (938–963). The children of Constantine VII did not inherit power, as it was taken by the general, Nikephoros Phokas (912–969). His nephew, John I Tzimiskes (925–976), took the throne from his uncle (after marrying a daughter of Constantine VII), before passing on the power to his nephew, Basil II (958–1025).

7. THE RETURN TO MONARCHY IN THE WEST

Whilst the Empire of Byzantium continued to struggle through the centuries up to the first millennium, writing and rewriting legal and philosophical justifications for the absolute power of the emperor, in the west, the scholarship was somewhat thinner. By the time of the collapse of the western section of the Roman Empire, the kings of the west, be they Anglo-Saxon, Frankish, Visigoth, Lombard, Germanic or Viking, held absolute power. Before this time, although no major narratives exist for these groups between the first and fourth centuries of the Common Era, it appears that non-centralised, loose confederations existed, with variations of oligarchy and shared (or delegated) command being common. The Vikings were known for their ability to field Great Armies, which were groupings of up to 20,000 men, serving under 11 different kings, of which there was no overall leader. Other non-Roman groups could elect a single man in times of need. Famously, Tacitus once remarked of Germanic societies of the first century that 'they choose their kings for their nobility, war leaders for their courage'. Even when the king was chosen, his position was often challenged by discontent from within the Empire. Such challenges were often assisted by the assemblies that appear to have been held to decide group policy. Such assemblies continued to meet on an annual basis in the centuries that followed within the Empire of the Franks. However, the influence of the assemblies on the king declined as the years passed.[256]

[256] Heather, P (2009) *Empires and Barbarians: Migration, Development and the Birth of Europe* (London, Pan) 485–90; Gat, A (2008) *War in Human Civilisation* (Oxford, Oxford University Press) 218–20, 230–50. The quotation from Tacitus is in *Germania*, ch 7.

By the fifth century, these loosely organised approaches were becoming much less common in Western Europe, and were being replaced by the practice of an entrenched monarch, as a leading warrior at the epicentre of a highly stratified society (which included nobles and 'freemen'), with the monarch at the apex. Attila the Hun held absolute power by the force of his arms and his ability to convince others (bribed by plunder) to follow him. His power was so unlimited that he believed it was everlasting, and could be handed on to his children. He was mistaken in this. There was no convention that a follower of one king must give allegiance to his children – or continue to support a leader whose luck had deserted him. This only began to change, slightly, when the kings became settled and those who supported them were rewarded with land, titles and influence, the retention of which was dependent upon loyalty to the next generation. Although, on occasion, kings were selected in some parts of Europe by a diet of selected members of the aristocracy, this was becoming increasingly rare (except in times of emergency), as was any suggestion that the power of the king was anything but absolute as models of governance moved from being petty-states to becoming much larger, integrated, and all together more powerful, models.[257]

Despite the absolute power of the king, the king needed a structure which could support his kingdom. This structure evolved from a system of vassals to feudalism. Vassals were people who had a personal service obligation to their master. Feudalism was a more advanced version of this system, as represented by a highly integrated pyramid system of dependence, with the king at the top and relationships of various types of social power beneath him, woven together by an intricate combination of land tenure (typically as fiefs), military organisation, personal rights, patronage, obligations, service and subjection.[258]

Among non-clergy, towards the top of the social pyramid, the nobles acted as somewhat soft political power. It was these nobles that would cause many of the difficulties for kings in all parts of Europe during the centuries to come. Supplementing this pyramid was the structure of the Church, which legitimised and reinforced the position of the king over secular matters – whilst the king reinforced the position of the Church – at least over theological matters. Some theologians, such as Atto of Vercelli (924–961), believed that since the king was appointed by God, it was impious to resist him, even if he were unjust or wicked.[259]

Western kings of this period also used non-religious rhetoric to justify their position. The most important thing a king of this period could do was provide peace for his subjects. Bede's description of the reign of King Edwin of Northumbria, when 'a

[257] Stenton, F (1985) *Anglo Saxon England* (Oxford, Clarendon Press) 35–39.

[258] Carlyle, AJ (1910) *A History of Medieval Political Theory in the West*, Vol III (London, Blackwood) 20–25; Gwatkin, H (ed) (1955) *The Cambridge Medieval History: The Rise of the Saracens and the Foundation of the Western Empire*, Vol II (Cambridge, Cambridge University Press) 133–34, 151; Herlihy, D (ed) (1970) *The History of Feudalism* (NYC, Harper) viii–ix, 81–84, 86–87, 104–107.

[259] Bede, *The Ecclesiastical History of the English Nation* trans Jane, L (1910 edn) (London, Dent) III:24; Heather, P (2009) *Empires and Barbarians: Migration, Development and the Birth of Europe* (London, Pan) 38–39, 43–46, 66–70; Morris, J (2004) *The Age of Arthur: A History of the British Isles* (London, Phoenix) 488–91; Pirenne, H (1939) *Mohammed and Charlemagne* (London, Allen and Unwin) 57, 266–67; Abels, R (1998) *Alfred the Great: War, Kingship and Culture in Anglo-Saxon England* (London, Longman) 28–29, 34–35; Carlyle, AJ (1910) *A History of Medieval Political Theory in the West*, Vol III (London, Blackwood) 116–18.

woman could carry her new-born babe across the island from sea to sea without any fear of harm',[260] was the highest praise possible. Thus, the Roman title *domitor gentium* ('pacifier of nations') came to be used to praise great rulers of this period. In addition, the ability of a king to rule wisely, providing justice and stability for his people as well as protecting the Church and the poor was seen as valuable. To achieve such goals, the great monarchs of the age often left detailed legal codes behind them, through which their virtue was displayed. For example, Charlemagne specified that 'concerning the oppression of poor free men . . . they should not be unjustly oppressed by men more powerful than themselves for any evil purpose, to the point of being compelled to sell or hand over their property'.[261] Despite such considerations, not everyone was equal before the law. The Carolingians legislated vigorously against the formation of horizontal social bonds and insisted on the primacy of vertical bonds of obligation of sworn fidelity and lordship. 'Men of good family' were tried before the king, whilst 'lesser men' were tried before their local lord.[262]

In practice, the kings of the west behaved in exactly the same way as all of the monarchs before them, battling both internal and external enemies who wished to take the throne. In Continental Europe this pattern began with the rise of Charles Martel (686–741), an illegitimate son of a duke, who roused the support of disgruntled nobles in France, and then began the civil war in France of 715 to 718. Martel defeated Chilperic II (672–721) – the last Merovingian dynast to exercise any real authority. Although Martel did not hold the title of king (choosing to decline it when offered it by the pope), he held power over all of the Frankish kingdoms. This was the beginning of the Carolingian dynasty, which came to full power with Martel's son Pepin (714–768). Pepin disposed of the last of the Merovingian contenders, Childeric III (717–754), who claimed the right to rule based on the claim that his dynasty had precedence. When the advice of Pope Zackarias (679–752) was sought, the pope replied that 'it would be better that he who actually had the power should be called king'.[263] Zackarias was wise to adopt this approach, for when a Byzantine envoy approached Pepin, offering him huge rewards for the former imperial possessions he had taken in Italy, he replied that he had presented these lands to Saint Peter and that nothing would induce him to give them back. By so doing, he was effectively informing Constantinople that he had

[260] Bede, *The Ecclesiastical History of the English Nation* trans Jane, L (1910 edn) (London, Dent) II:16.

[261] See 'Imperial Administration' reprinted in Rosenwein, B (ed) (2006) *Reading the Middle Ages: Sources from Europe, Byzantium and the Islamic World* (Ontario, Broadview) 181, 185; Carlyle, AJ (1910) *A History of Medieval Political Theory in the West*, Vol III (London, Blackwood) 107–108.

[262] Carlyle, A (1936) *A History of Medieval Political Theory in the West: The Second Century to the Ninth*, Vol 1 (London, Blackwood) 214–18, 223–28; Gwatkin, H (ed) (1963) *The Cambridge Medieval History: Germany and the Western Empire*, Vol III (Cambridge, Cambridge University Press) 82; Halsall, G (2003) *Warfare and Society in the Barbarian West, 450–900* (London, Routledge) 18–19, 32; Costambey, M (2012) *The Carolingian World* (Cambridge, Cambridge University Press) 190.

[263] Zackery, as noted in the Annals of Lorch reprinted in Oliver, J (ed) (1905) *A Source Book for Medieval History*, (New York, Scribners) 37–38. See also Costambey, M (2012) *The Carolingian World* (Cambridge, Cambridge University Press) 31–34. The treaty of Andelot is in Gregory of Tours, (1974) *History of the Franks* trans Lewis Thorpe (Baltimore, Penguin) III:15, IV:14, VI:31, VII:2, IX:20. See also Halsall, G (2003) *Warfare and Society in the Barbarian West, 450–900* (London, Routledge) 14–15, 17, 22, 71, 74, 76, 85, 87, 89, 136; Gwatkin, H (ed) (1967) *The Cambridge Medieval History: The Rise of the Saracens and the Foundation of the Western Empire*, Vol II (Cambridge, Cambridge University Press) 122–23.

severed parts of Italy from the Byzantine Empire, and that a pontificate state had been created.[264]

Charlemagne inherited the throne from his father. Yet even this greatest monarch of the early middle ages was not immune from the plotting of discontented men, as in 792 his eldest son, Pippin (the Hunchback), felt himself being marginalised and attracted enough support to attempt to topple the king. Afterwards, when Pippin was defeated Charlemagne rewarded those who had not rebelled and made it known that Pippin was illegitimate and physically unsuitable to rule, before shipping him off to a monastery. This still left three other legitimate sons. Cognisant of the difficulties that competition between his children could cause upon his death, Charlemagne had, on paper, divided his kingdom into three parts, so that his children could be 'co-rulers' and:

> [E]ach of them shall be content with his portion as we have assigned it, and shall with God's help strive to defend the boundaries of the kingdom which border on foreign land, and to remain at peace and in charity with his brother.

It was added that none of them were to harbour those causing dissent towards any of the others; they should subject their disputes to 'truthful inquiry'; and in 'no case . . . should ever be settled by a struggle of any kind or on the field of battle'.[265]

Charlemagne's plan never came into force, as Louis the Pious (778–840) was the only adult son to survive him. This meant there was no internal struggle between the children for the power and territory that their father had possessed. However, when it was time for Louis to pass on the power that he held to his sons, the regime was poisoned to the core by a series of viscous civil wars. The contemporary chronicler, Regino of Prum (d 915), explained the situation as one whereby each area had made a prince 'out of its own bowels'.[266]

The result of this discord would be the disappearance of the Carolingian Empire within a century of Charlemagne's coronation as the most powerful man in the western world. The catalyst for these acts was the second marriage of Louis and his intention to add his son from his second marriage, Charles the Bald (823–877), into his succession plans. This meant that his three sons from his first marriage were not set to inherit as much as Louis had originally envisaged in his Partition of Aachen. The original plan was that a unified empire would be ruled jointly by his three sons, Lothair I (795–855), Pepin of Aquitaine (797–838) and Louis the German (806–876), and his nephew Bernard of Septimania (795–844) – who were all to be given specific territories. The re-division caused by the inclusion of Charles the Bald caused Lothair (with the support of some of the bishops in 'his' area) to rebel against his father in 830. However, Louis out-maneuvered him, rewriting the succession plan in 831, promising greater shares to his other sons thus leaving Lothair without enough support to continue the conflict.

[264] Hussey, J (1966) *The Cambridge Medieval History: The Byzantine Empire*, Vol IV(1) (Cambridge, Cambridge University Press) 76–77.

[265] The Division of the Kingdoms, 806 reprinted in Loyn, H (ed) (1975) *The Reign of Charlemagne: Documents on Carolingian Government and Administration* (London, Edward Arnold) 91, 94; Costambey, M (2012) *The Carolingian World* (Cambridge, Cambridge University Press) 196–97.

[266] Regino of Plum, as noted in Heather, P (2009) *Empires and Barbarians: Migration, Development and the Birth of Europe* (London, Pan) 368.

Underterred, Lothair increased his offer to Pepin and Charles, and in 832 took the fight back to his father. However, the barons supporting Louis remained firm, and Louis managed to keep the throne from his children, and drew up yet another succession plan for the division of the Empire of the Franks. This plan lead directly to the third civil war during which Frank armies continued to roam the empire in a game of armed chess whose top prize was the control of the Carolingian heartlands. The final war saw Louis the German and Charles the Bald fighting against their father, who this time was allied with his other son, Lothair, who pledged his support in return for a larger portion if the inheritance was, again, divided. This final division remained in place when Louis the Pious died in 840.[267]

On the death of his father, Lothair disregarded all of the previous partitions and claimed the entire empire for himself. For three years he was opposed by his brothers, Charles the Bald and Louis the German, who made a military alliance which promised mutual friendship and loyal assistance and was sealed with the Strasbourg Oath.[268] This formal alliance followed the battle of Fontenoy in 841 – in which commentators of the period were shocked by the breach of the peace in which the armies of the Christian siblings fought each other. All four of the Carolingians survived Fontenoy and, realising that no side could win, agreed to negotiate a settlement. The result was the 843 Treaty of Verdun. This treaty ended the dream of a united Europe dividing the Empire amongst the three Carolingian brothers. The treaty gave Charles the Bald the western portions of the Empire (most of what eventually became France: East Francia) as far as Spain. Louis the German took (and went on to rule) the eastern portion of the Empire, consisting of the land to the east of the Rhine and to the north and east of Italy (which became Germany: West Francia). Lothair received the central portion of the Empire, known as Middle Francia (consisting of the Low Countries, Lorraine, Alsace, Burgundy, Provence and the Frankish Kingdom of Italy). [269]

Externally, the division broadly held, with a further refinement in the 870 Treaty of Mersen. This treaty set the shape of eastern and central Europe until the eighteenth century. Territory was roughly divided along the Meuse and Ourthe rivers, allocating the land to the west to Charles, whilst the Rhineland and former Duchy of Alsace went to Louis. Internally, within this division, Louis the German soon found himself fighting his son Carloman (830–880) in 861 and then his other sons Louis the Younger (835–882) and Charles the Fat (839–888). The peace was achieved at the cost of further divisions and fragmentations within East Francia. When Louis the German died in 876, the last remaining brother of Louis the Pious – Charles the Bald – opened warfare against the inheritor of East Francia, Louis the Younger. Although Charles could not

[267] Costambey, M (2012) *The Carolingian World* (Cambridge, Cambridge University Press) 216–19; Gwatkin, H (ed) (1968) *The Cambridge Medieval History: Germany and the Western Empire*, Vol III (Cambridge, Cambridge University Press) 14–20.

[268] The Strasbourg Oath reprinted in Thatcher, O (ed) (1905) *A Source Book for Mediaeval History. Selected Documents Illustrating the History of Europe in the Middle Age* (London, Brown) 70.

[269] The 843 Treaty of Verdun reprinted in Laffan, R (ed) (1929) *Select Historical Documents: 800–1492* (NYC, Holt) 8–9; Wallace-Hadrill, J (1962) *The Barbarian West: The Early Middle Ages AD 400–1000* (NYC, Harper) 7, 124–28; Gwatkin, H (ed) (1968) *The Cambridge Medieval History: Germany and the Western Empire*, Vol III (Cambridge, Cambridge University Press) 25; Costambey, M (2012) *The Carolingian World* (Cambridge, Cambridge University Press) 379–87.

achieve his goal, upon his death Louis the Younger responded in kind to the inheritors of Charles (Louis III and Carloman), who were busy trying to hold together West Francia. The resultant military losses were cemented in the year 880 through the Treaty of Ribemont. This was the last treaty of partition of the Frankish Empire. In exchange for his neutrality, Louis the Younger was given the Low Countries and the western Rhineland. When Louis died without an heir, all his territories reverted to his brother, Charles the Fat (the youngest child of Louis the German). Charles the Fat became the last Carolingian emperor to hold (880–887) all of the parts of the Carolingian jigsaw of East and West Francia, as well as Italy. However, he could not hold this position and was deposed around 877. Although the details of how this happened are not clear, the results were. The Empire splintered, not to be reunited for over a thousand years.

One of the other elements that became apparent from this period was that while the kings were trying to keep those without dynastic lineage from power, the nobles were becoming increasingly influential in the choice, if not the election, of the monarchy. This became evident in West Francia, with the selection of Odo (860–898) as king, due to his skill in dealing with the Vikings. In East Francia, Henry I – the Fowler (876–936) followed his father to become Duke of Saxony. Then from 919 he became the king of East Francia. He was known as 'the Fowler' because of his hunting of birds at the time he was informed that he was to be king. Henry was appointed following the recommendation of the dying Conrad I (890–918). Conrad I had himself been placed on the throne by agreement of the dukes of East Francia, who did not want Charles the Simple (879–929) to become king of West and East Francia. In Henry's case, the dukes of East Francia agreed with Conrad's recommendation and then the crown be offered to 'the Fowler'. This recommendation from civil authority, rather than a religious anointing was very important to the early German understanding of kingship.[270]

Otto I (912–973), the son of Henry the Fowler inherited the kingship of the Germans on the death of his father in 936. In this case there was no question of nomination or support from the nobles. Nor, unlike in the past, was there any suggestion that the kingdom be divided up between children. Rather, Otto was given all the power through an act of individual succession to the throne. Otto continued the unification of all the German tribes into a single kingdom. However, this became a much more hierarchical and authoritarian system than the one in place under his father, in which all were subjects under the king's authority. There was no pretence of equality with the nobles. Otto was not 'first among equals'. He was first. Key appointments were directed by the king (and loyalty was directly rewarded with land and titles). In addition, the position of the Church, also brought under the authority of the king, was enhanced. The link to the Church was particularly important for Otto, as through his Church anointment, he demonstrated that he held divine power, not power allowed by his nobles. This was useful to him as a number of nobles twice rebelled against his

[270] Carlyle, A (1936) *A History of Medieval Political Theory in the West: The Second Century to the Ninth*, Vol 1 (London, Blackwood) 249–50; Gwatkin, H (ed) (1968) *The Cambridge Medieval History: Germany and the Western Empire*, Vol III (Cambridge, Cambridge University Press) 42–46, 66–70; Costambey, M (2012) *The Carolingian World* (Cambridge, Cambridge University Press) 418–25.

absolute supremacy. Both rebellions resulted in losses to the nobles and an increase in both the territory and authority of the king.

Whilst Otto could defeat the nobles, he could not defeat his own family members. A third revolt, brought about and led by his son and nephew (as well as disgruntled nobles, Slavs and Hungarians) over the question of who was to be heir apparent to power led to a two-year civil war which was only concluded after two monumental clashes of opposing armies. Peace was only achieved when Otto's son, Liudolf (930–957), was promised regency over Italy, and his other rebellious family members were given, inter alia, command of armies against common enemies, dukedoms, appointments within the Church and/or personal domains. Such reconciliations could not ensure peace in the long term and subsequent rebellions by the great landed magnates (and cousins), such as those in Bohemia and Bavaria, also had to be dealt with by the heir to Otto I, as did an attempted revolt by his half-brother Thankmar (908–938).

8. ISLAM AND THE POLITICAL QUESTION

A. Authority

Although the peoples of Islam could not agree on the leadership system of the overall community, they could agree that whichever model was chosen, the authority had to be strict. The difficulty was that Islam began speaking against absolute forms of power. As a universal religion, the people, it is believed, are bound together by faith and justice. What mattered is not tribe, race or gender but godliness. Islam often appeared hostile to pharaohs, kings and emperors, as to call a human being an absolute ruler was considered to be a trespass upon the divine prerogative. This trespass held, even if it involved Muslim communities. Thus, the Umayyads came undone because of accusations that they had become a monarchy, and that such kingship was an illegitimate form of human self-aggrandisement which Muslims had come to eliminate.[271]

Despite this dislike for monarchy, only a small minority of Muslims, namely the Kharijites, came to the conclusion that rulers of Islamic communities should be based on merit rather than genealogical lineage; very influential within most of the Islamic tribal organisations. The Kharijites also held that elevation to ultimate power should be through communal participation in decision-making. This was not the practice of the Abbasid or Umayyad dynasties, which had little time for considerations of participation or consensus, preferring models of autocratic rule by one man. In this respect, Muslim rulers drew from the the Old Testament stories of David and Solomon in which religious and political authority could be concentrated in one man. They also tapped into Greek ideas – and Plato's view in particular – of the philosopher-king,

[271] Black, A (2011) *The History of Islamic Political Thought* (Edinburgh, Edinburgh University Press) 14–15; Crone, P (2004) *God's Rule: Government and Islam* (NYC, Columbia University Press) 6–7, 46, 66–67.

which were taken to support views of spiritual enlightenment and leadership based on the holding of particular forms of knowledge.[272]

Strong rule was necessary, as it was commonly believed by most (if not all) Islamic scholars that people were fallible and in need of guidance, just as communities had to be kept on 'the right path'.[273] Otherwise, the people would cause the destruction of both the community and justice. Although strict, the rulers always liked to portray themselves as fair and as fulfilling both the spiritual and temporal needs of their people. This interaction did not go so far as allowing the people a voice in government. Muslim scholarship of the period was clear that God had reserved his right in all matters to those who held power, or, as Ibn Muqaffa (d 756) explained, 'the people have . . . no other [right] than to give counsel when consulted, to reply when appealed to, and to give sincere advice in secret'.[274]

The removal of power from Islamic communities was furthered in the ninth and tenth centuries with a greater focus on tribal armies, and/or slave soldiers by which the personal fidelity of specific groups could be assured. This removal of influence by peasants who could become a military force directly threatening the rulers, reduced the threats the rulers faced. A further sign of separation was that the landed aristocracy did not generally have military power or political influence. Theoretically, all land belonged to the ruler, and it could be redistributed as necessary. Tenure was not hereditary. There was thus no feudal system and no representation of landed interests as such. When local notables did emerge, they tended to be men tied into the religious network, rather than as men of property or hereditary power, as was the Western way.[275]

B. Slavery

Although there were significant differences between countries and epochs, between the seventh and nineteenth centuries the Muslim world acquired somewhere between 10 million and 25 million slaves to serve them.[276] Although the Islamic ending of slavery was different from that adopted by non-Muslim countries, its beginning was very similar. This similarity can be seen particularly in terms of accepting the overall institution of slavery while trying to mitigate its impacts.

[272] Black, A (2011) *The History of Islamic Political Thought* (Edinburgh, Edinburgh University Press) 58–59, 61–63, 67–69, 76; Crone, P (2004) *God's Rule: Government and Islam* (NYC, Columbia University Press) 10–11, 165–96.

[273] See the works of Al-Farabi reprinted in Rosenwein, B (ed) (2006) *Reading the Middle Ages: Sources from Europe, Byzantium and the Islamic World* (Ontario, Broadview) 231–34.

[274] Ibn Muqaffa, as noted in Black, A (2011) *The History of Islamic Political Thought* (Edinburgh, Edinburgh University Press) 24, also 27–30, 33–34, 41–42, 47, 56; Crone, P (2004) *God's Rule: Government and Islam* (NYC, Columbia University Press) 60, 96–97, 148–64.

[275] Black, A (2011) *The History of Islamic Political Thought* (Edinburgh, Edinburgh University Press) 51; Crone, P (2004) *God's Rule: Government and Islam* (NYC, Columbia University Press) 146–47.

[276] White, M (2011) *Atrocitology: Humanity's 100 Deadliest Achievements* (Melbourne, Text) 82–87; Clarence-Smith, W (2006) *Islam and the Abolition of Slavery* (Oxford, Oxford University Press) 9–14.

The acceptance of the institution of slavery can be seen through the taking of slaves during religiously sanctioned wars. From such conflicts, the slaves could be held and afterwards either ransomed or freed. Muhammad and his direct followers left precedents of this type of practice. The procurement of slaves through peaceful means was not mentioned within the *Quran*. Peaceful acquisition of slaves through tribute, trade or purchase was a question that was often bypassed by the traditional belief that Muhammad (who may have personally owned between 30 and 70 slaves) exchanged some of his slaves for his essential needs. This silence on the topic of enslaving peaceful peoples of other faiths (especially if they were 'those of the book' – Christian, Jewish or Zoroastra) was problematic. So too was the injunction in the *Quran* to ransom or release the captives at the end of the conflict. When civil wars broke out, and the question of what constituted legitimate Holy Wars (from which enslavement could proceed) was raised, the difficulties multiplied, as the Muslims in opposition due to their theological differences were often classified as 'pagans' who could be enslaved, as they were not people of Islam. These theological splits, coupled with varying degrees of political indifference, meant that the idealised rule (dating back to Umar) of non-enslavement of fellow Muslims (let alone peaceful non-Muslims) was not always followed.[277]

The rule that fellow Muslims could not be enslaved was only one aspect of Islamic law, which, although suggesting that slaves were similar to livestock in many respects, granted them carefully circumscribed rights, arising out of their undeniable humanity. This followed from Islamic belief, which was borrowed from other traditions, that slavery could be seen in both spiritual and temporal terms. Tradition has it that Muhammad started this process, trying to treat his slaves not as chattels but as his children, to whom kindness should be shown. This kindness ranged from the prohibition of mutilation and the freeing of all slaves at set periods (akin to the recommendation in the Bible), through to the encouragement of manumission. Manumission was particularly encouraged if the slaves converted to Islam. Due to such practices, some Muslim philosophers, such as Abu al-Basr Muhammad al-Farabi (870–950), came to justify slavery as 'the best and most advantageous status in the world'.[278]

Aside from the premise that slavery was not condemned as an institution within Islam, an additional difficulty which became apparent was that some Muslim communities adhered to the humane rules while others considered them only as recommendations which they did not necessarily need to follow. For example, in some instances, because it was feared that slaves would pretend to accept Islam to gain their freedom, conversion came to be seen as its own reward, with enslavement portrayed as a golden opportunity to learn and practice the true faith. Others even banned or discouraged their slaves from converting because of the customary exemption it provoked.[279]

[277] Clarence-Smith, W (2006) *Islam and the Abolition of Slavery* (Oxford, Oxford University Press) 16–21, 24, 27, 32-36, 38, 45–46, 74–79, 86–87; Roberts, R (1925) *The Social Laws of the Quran* (London, Curson) 54.

[278] As quoted in Clarence-Smith, W (2006) *Islam and the Abolition of Slavery* (Oxford, Oxford University Press) 54.

[279] Roberts, R (1925) *The Social Laws of the Quran* (London, Curson) 56–60; Clarence-Smith, W (2006) *Islam and the Abolition of Slavery* (Oxford, Oxford University Press) 3, 22–24, 40–41, 50–53, 63–65, 69, 82; Karsh, E (2006) *Islamic Imperialism: A History* (London, Yale University Press) 25.

It may have been the lack of humane standards that found the early centuries of Islam in a particularly difficult position in relation to slaves. This was demonstrated by individual slaves rebelling (Umar was assassinated by a slave in 644) through to significant slave uprisings. Two such slave uprisings broke out in Southern Iraq in the seventh century. The first occurred around 689 to 690, and a more serious uprising took place around 694 to 695. The third and greatest rebellion was the Zanj rebellion in Iraq in the ninth century. This was among the most impressive of slave insurrections in world history and lasted for 14 years. This last rebellion, led by Ali b Muhammad, was unique, as it was led by a man who was not a slave, but who saw the opportunity to link together disquiet with the Abbasid rulers, a large number of poor Muslims and slaves in a common cause which placed a great value on shared common property. However, even here, the goal was not the abolition of slavery, but rather the reversal of who were the slaves, and who were the slave owners.[280]

9. CONCLUSION

The question which this chapter sought to examine is the extent to which wars occur over political choices. Politics (from the Greek *politicos*, 'of, for, or relating to the citizens') is a term generally applied to the art or science of running governments and/or state affairs. Within the context of this chapter the issue of politics was seen to cover the options of running the state, which ranged from monarchy through to democracy. The particular questions it sought to examine were which were the more common practices, which were most closely linked to warfare, and whether there were any particular patterns that became apparent.

The findings suggest that within the given period of study, roughly from 3000 BCE to 1000 CE, the holding of all power in the hands of one person was the overwhelming political choice. The title of this person ranged from pharaoh, to king, to emperor, to pope or caliph. This was evident in all societies. However, so too was the idea held in many of these regimes that more collective forms of governance were at times a better choice. This notion was never strong, and the trend was typically towards the concentration of power in the hands of one person. In ancient history, this was the pattern of the ancient Near East, from Egypt to Persia. It was also replicated in India and China. In all of these societies, those who held absolute power were legitimised by religion, and only rarely (as in the case of the Greek tyrants) was the quest for absolute power not buttressed by a theological faith.

All of those who held absolute power, no matter where they were, lived in constant fear that they could be killed and their position taken by someone else. There were many reasons that might cause them to lose the throne. These included revolutions which came from the bottom up, when those governed felt that the monarch failed to live up to certain standards, such as the provision of justice – and peace – to the people. Failure to achieve these goals could result in the loss of their throne from below.

[280] Clarence-Smith, W (2006) *Islam and the Abolition of Slavery* (Oxford, Oxford University Press) 5, 63–65.

However, there were few grass-root rebellions particularly among those who had absolutely no power – slaves, who were generally obedient throughout this period of history. Although every regime attempted to limit the overtly inhumane treatment of slaves, none attempted to abolish the practice. This was despite the fact that all of the major regimes – Greek, Roman and Islamic – had to deal with wars caused by slaves seeking to establish their own freedom. Note, however, that none of these wars was about trying to abolish slavery completely.

More commonly, civil war would break out when either a contender from outside the ruler's family, or someone from within their family (especially when there was more than one child and only one throne), or most likely of all, someone in the military, would try to take the throne. This became a pattern from China to Rome once Caesar had taken absolute power. This pattern held in both pre and post Christian times of influence. In all instances, the pattern was the same – the holding of absolute power attracted others who wanted it. This incessant desire meant that dynasties were often short-lived, lasting no more than a few generations. In best-case scenarios, transitions could be made with minimal bloodshed beyond a palace coup. A large number of transitions in Egypt and Byzantium followed this pattern, although in both cases a number of civil wars still occurred. In worst-case scenarios, entire empires could be split apart. Assyria, the western side of the Roman Empire, and its successor, the realm of Charlemagne, all provide examples of this. This was especially likely if the disputes about who held absolute power were mixed with external pressures. The history of China is a textbook example of this problem. In all cases, the root cause was the quest by one person to take the absolute power of another.

The exceptions to the overwhelming dominance of one person governing the state were the options of government by an aristocracy or a democracy. The democratic tradition was one which existed only in pockets – of ancient Greece – most notably Athens. Democracy, the equality of (a limited) citizenship, was born as a reaction against all the power being held by one man as a tyrant or a monarch, or the power being held by a few, as in an aristocracy. Democracy survived in a tide of wars in which Greek communities, and later Roman, fought for the autonomy of cities to decide their own political choices. In the Roman era, although a number of Greek communities were allowed to retain their own democratic institutions, they had no ability to commit to an independent foreign policy. Democracy in Greece was eventually extinguished by Rome after a series of failed uprisings in which the people had been attracted to complete autonomy. Rome was, in essence, acting under an aristocracy through its senate. The rule of the aristocracy of Rome was no more peaceful than a democracy. The aristocracy continually struggled both with those beneath them in the social order and those who sought to rise above it. When Caesar and his successors rose above the aristocracy, the pattern reverted to one of absolute control in the hands of one man.

V

Religion

1. INTRODUCTION

THIS CHAPTER ORIGINATED from an idea put forward by Richard Dawkins, who once suggested that 'religious faith deserves a chapter to itself in the annals of war'.[1] This is that chapter. The chapter examines a number of questions. What was the influence of religion upon warfare? How constant and common was this influence in the years leading up to 1000 CE? What were the nuances by which it was displayed? Most importantly, did the influence of religion on warfare change?

2. MESOPOTAMIA, EGYPT, ASSYRIA, ISRAEL AND PERSIA

From the beginning of written history, religion has provided the intellectual foundation that justified monarchy. To rebel against god-given leaders was seen as tantamount to apostasy, as rebels were seen as fighting against the entire cosmological universe and all of the deities within it. In such conflicts, the gods were fierce entities that could either join the fighting or keep the peace. Vengeful gods were seen as the ultimate guarantors of treaties; all sides believed that the gods would enforce compliance by raining down vengeance if oaths were broken. For example, in the important treaty of 1269 BCE between Egypt and Hatti, the text concluded with an oath before 'a thousand gods' who were requested to 'destroy' the 'house, land and servants' of anyone who breached the agreement.[2] Conversely, those who honoured the treaty were promised 'health and life' from the gods.[3]

[1] Dawkins, R (2004) *The Selfish Gene* (Oxford, Oxford University Press) 66.

[2] This treaty is reprinted in Breasted, J (ed) (1988 edn) *Ancient Records of Egypt*, Vol III (London, Histories and Mysteries) 171–72.

[3] For examples of inscriptions on this point, see Luckenbill, D (ed) (1989) *Ancient Records of Assyria and Babylonia*, Vol II (London, Histories and Mysteries) 14, 33, 46, 83, 91–92, 200–201, 294–95, 301, 315, 318, 335, 337, 384–85; Parpola, S (1987) 'Neo-Assyrian Treaties from the Royal Archives of Nineveh' 39(2) *Journal of Cuneiform Studies* 161, 167; Bederman, D (2001) *International Law in Antiquity* (Cambridge, Cambridge University Press) 150; Spalinger, A (2005) *War in Ancient Egypt* (London, Blackwell) 75–77; Postgate, J (1996) *Early Mesopotamia: Society and Economy and the Dawn of History* (London, Routledge) 34, 46, 109–36, 257; Kramer, S (1956) *History Begins at Sumer* (Pennsylvania, Philadelphia University Press) 256–57; Hamblin, W (2006) *Warfare in the Ancient Near East to 1600 BC* (London, Routledge) 38, 42, 79, 82, 186–90.

In addition to enforcing compliance with treaties, gods were also called upon to help in the battles of their chosen people. Recorded requests and/or boasts that gods were giving a helping hand on the battlefield can be traced back to around 3500 BCE in ancient Mesopotamia. One inscription from Assur, probably from around 2300 BCE, called upon the relevant (Sumerian) god to 'hate the enemies' of the king and 'overthrow' the rule of his enemies, bringing 'violence and destruction' to their lands.[4] The gods also gave (directly to the king and/or priest) both the authority and clear instructions to pious combatants to attack and rule over others. At other times, the gods would tell subjects that they should rebel against the existing status quo. For example, Ishbi-Irra of Isin (2107–1985 BCE) explained in a letter to one of his rivals that he was usurping the kingship of Mesopotamia, because: '[The God] Enlil, my king, by his command, has given me the kingship of Sumer. Enlil commanded me to . . . carry off spoils, and to conquer cities. Why do you resist me?'[5]

The Egyptians displayed similar rhetoric in which their gods empowered the rulers and directed them to fight. This was often an easy instruction to acquire, as many of the pharaohs claimed a direct relationship to the gods, as their earthly incarnations. Whilst some claimed a lineage to Ra (the Sun God), a greater number claimed a close relationship with Horus (the falcon deity), the God of War. Such gods could, through the pharaoh, achieve wondrous military victories, unifying Egypt or crushing powerful neighbours. Some of the greatest pharaohs who unified Egypt, such as Narmer (c 3100 BCE) and Montuhotep I (2061–2011 BCE), could claim their direction and power from the god Horus. The *Coffin Texts* (written around 2055–1650 BCE) reiterated a similar line. 'I have assaulted and conquered the horizon by my own hand . . . The kingship on the thrones of Horus is given to me, he shoots down the slaughterers for me.'[6] Ramses II (1303–1213 BCE) claimed that Ptah (the Egyptian God at the birth of creation) had given him such power that 'the throne of every land is under my authority'. Moreover, he suggested that Egypt had divine protection 'for the eye of every God is behind him who would violate her'.[7] Similarly, divine help gave Ramses III (r 1186–1155) the authority and ability 'to destroy' invading armies.[8]

Other pharaohs obtained their power, and the right to perform a coup to gain power, from different gods. Amenemhet founded the twelfth dynasty (1991 BCE) because Atum (the god who completed creation) had demanded that he lead a revolt to 'restore what he had found in ruins [in Egypt]'.[9] This type of justification for conflict

[4] In Luckenbill, D (1989) *Ancient Records of Assyria and Babylonia*, Vol 1 (reprinted by Histories Ltd, USA) 14, 17.

[5] Letter of Ishbi-Irri, reprinted in Hamblin, W (2006) *Warfare in the Ancient Near East to 1600 BC* (London, Routledge) 160. See also Kramer, S (1963) *The Sumerians: Their History, Culture and Character* (Chicago, University of Chicago Press) 65; Hamblin, W (2006) *Warfare in the Ancient Near East to 1600 BC* (London, Routledge) 302; Postgate, J (1996) *Early Mesopotamia: Society and Economy and the Dawn of History* (London, Routledge) 251.

[6] The *Coffin Texts*, reprinted in Hamblin, W (2006) *Warfare in the Ancient Near East to 1600 BC* (London, Routledge) 413. See also 313–15, 319, 353, 354, 412–13; Wilkinson, T (2010) *The Rise and Fall of Ancient Egypt* (London, Bloomsbury) 46, 94, 280–81.

[7] Ramses II, reprinted in Breasted, J (ed) (1988 edn) *Ancient Records of Egypt*, Vol III (London, Histories and Mysteries) 180 and 261.

[8] Ramses III, reprinted in Breasted, J (ed) (1988 edn) *Ancient Records of Egypt*, Vol IV (London, Histories and Mysteries) 52.

[9] Amenemhet, noted in Hamblin, W (2006) *Warfare in the Ancient Near East to 1600 BC* (London, Routledge) 413.

– namely warfare to ensure that correct religious protocols were followed – had a lineage going back to Ankhtifi of Hierakonpolis (c 2130 BCE), who based his justification for seising power on the restoration of the proper ritual order of the gods. Similarly, Sesostris III (1887–1849 BCE) portrayed himself as one who 'overthrew the enemies of Osiris'.[10] Likewise, Piankhi (d 721 BCE) reunited Egypt under the primary justification of reintroducing religious orthodoxy, thereby purifying the country. Warfare was also justified by the need to advance certain religious practices. For example, when Thutmose I (r 1506–1493 BCE) invaded the kingdom of Kush, he took with him not just battalions of Egyptian soldiers, but also the High Priest of Amun to convert the heathens to the 'true religion'.[11] To the same end, Thutmose III built a great temple to Amun at the foot of Upper Nubia's holiest mountain. This was in accordance with his view that Amun had given him the right to 'lead all the living' and also the right to 'set the boundary as far as the breadth of heaven'.[12]

The Assyrians, too, recognised a strong relationship between warfare and religion. Ashur, who reigned at the top of the Assyrian pantheon, decreed that Assyria should rule all peoples and should expand its borders to his glory. The Assyrians freely called upon their gods to overthrow their enemies (via an 'evil curse') and deliver floods, storms, confusion, famine and destructive lightning upon the lands of their enemies. Adad-Nirari (1307–1275 BCE) and Tiglath-Pileser I (1114–1076 BCE) believed that Assur gave them their sovereignty and Ishtar (the Assyrian God of War) had enlarged their kingdoms. Such backing enabled some Assyrian rulers, such as Tukulti-Urta I (c 1250 BCE), to proclaim themselves 'king of the universe . . . king of the four quarters [of the world]'.[13] Tukulti-Urta II (r 890–884 BCE) and Shalmaneser III (858–824 BCE) also built on these religious traditions, seeing themselves as 'conqueror[s] of the faithless'.[14] The Assyrians would often (but not always) dispatch people to teach those they had conquered, in the words of Sargon (r 722–705 BCE), 'how to fear God'.[15] Sargon's successor, Sennacherib (705–681 BCE), went out of his way to smash and destroy the gods of opposing cities (such as Babylon), whilst Esarhaddon (680–669 BC) assured those under his power that the gods supported his campaigns.[16]

[10] Sesostris III, reprinted in Breasted, J (ed) (1988 edn) *Ancient Records of Egypt*, Vol 1 (London, Histories and Mysteries) 300.

[11] Wilkinson, T (2010) *The Rise and Fall of Ancient Egypt* (London, Bloomsbury) 411–21; Hamblin, W (2006) *Warfare in the Ancient Near East to 1600 BC* (London, Routledge) 371.

[12] Reprinted in Breasted, J (ed) (1988 edn) *Ancient Records of Egypt*, Vol II (London, Histories and Mysteries) 81, 92, 117, 328.

[13] In Luckenbill, D (ed) (1989) *Ancient Records of Assyria and Babylonia*, Vol 1 (London, Histories and Mysteries) 50. For the quotations from Adad and Tiglath, see Luckenbill, at 72 and 109.

[14] In Luckenbill, D (ed) (1989) *Ancient Records of Assyria and Babylonia*, Vol 1 (London, Histories and Mysteries) 236.

[15] In Luckenbill, D (ed) (1989) *Ancient Records of Assyria and Babylonia*, Vol II (London, Histories and Mysteries) 57.

[16] Quotations from all of these kings on this subject can be found in Luckenbill, D (ed) (1989) *Ancient Records of Assyria and Babylonia* (London, Histories and Mysteries) Vol I, 53, 134; Vol II, 185, 200–201. See also Dawson, D (2001) *The First Armies* (London, Cassel) 132, 176; Kelle, B (2007) *Ancient Israel at War* (Oxford, Osprey) 67; Ferrill, A (1988) *The Origins of War* (London, Thames and Hudson) 77; Saggs, H (1989) *Civilisation Before Greece and Rome* (New Haven, Yale University Press) 186–89; Edwards, I (ed) (1975) *The Cambridge Ancient History. History of the Middle East and Aegean Region 1380–1000 BCE*, 3rd edn, Vol II(2) (Cambridge, Cambridge University Press) 296–97.

The Old Testament contains many of the same themes reflecting the Near Eastern context from which it emerged. It is not a document that advances pacifism, clearly recognising that violence, in some settings, is acceptable. Although the Garden of Eden was created as a peaceful utopia, discord quickly developed between the first couple, and within one generation of Creation, Cain had killed his brother. The Old Testament foresaw a time when peace would reign supreme. At this point: 'They will beat their swords into plough-shares and their spears into pruning hooks. Nation will not take up sword against nation, nor will they train for war anymore.'[17] Until this point was reached, war and violence was expected to be the pattern. The Hebrew God, sometimes represented as a warrior, was clearly part of this schema. He encouraged the Jewish people in warfare, promising victory against overwhelming odds. He helped them in their wars and was recorded as joining the conflicts, driving out earlier inhabitants to deliver the lands into the hands of the people of Israel.[18] Fundamentally, as summed up in Deuteronomy 20:1–4, this God would not abandon his people. Thus:

> When thou goest out to battle against thine enemies, and seest horses, and chariots, and a people more than thou, be not afraid of them: for the LORD thy God is with thee, which brought thee up out of the land of Egypt. And it shall be, when ye are come nigh unto the battle, that the priest shall approach and speak unto the people, And shall say unto them, Hear, O Israel, ye approach this day unto battle against your enemies: let not your hearts faint, fear not, and do not tremble, neither be ye terrified because of them; For the LORD your God is he that goeth with you, to fight for you against your enemies, to save you.[19]

The Persians also emphasised the importance of religion as a justification for conflict. Zoroaster (c 600 BCE) sought to convert 'all living men' without discrimination between communities or ethnicities. This revolutionary theology fitted the polyglot empire of the Persians closely, as it was a religion without national preference. Zoroaster articulated a vision where people were free to choose their own destiny, but they had to choose between the 'Right and the Lie', the latter ultimately destined to be vanquished in an apocalyptic conclusion. Fighting in conflicts related to this conclusion was considered 'just'. Adherents of this faith, such as Darius (550–486 BCE), preached 'holy war' as he saw himself as fighting 'false Gods and demons' when fighting some of his enemies. To bolster his credentials, he promised 'divine blessings' to those who died in battle, and he attributed his victories to his devotion to the Zoroastrian faith which was central to the identity of the state: 'Church and State were born of the one womb, joined together and never to be sundered.'[20] At other times the Persian kings were instructed by their high priests to destroy the religious practices and buildings of other faiths within the Persian realm. In this regard, Xeres (519–465)

[17] Isaiah 2:4.

[18] Exodus 14:14 and 15:3; Ecclesiastes 3:1–8; 1 Samuel 14:47; Deuteronomy 1:30; I Chronicles 22:7–8; 2 Chronicles 20:17–22; Leviticus 26:7–8; Judges 4:23; Isaiah 10:5–7 and 10:22–25; Joshua 11:20; Judges 4:13.

[19] For commentary on this question within the Old Testament, see Carrol, R (1995) 'War in the Hebrew Bible' in Rich, J (ed) *War and Society in the Greek World* (London, Routledge) 22; Walzer, M (1996) 'War and Peace in the Jewish Tradition' in Nardin, T (ed) *The Ethics of War and Peace* (New Jersey, Princeton University Press) 95–98, 115–16; Morgan, P (ed) (1996) *Ethical Issues in Six Religious Traditions* (Edinburgh, Edinburgh University Press) 164–65; Kelle, B (2007) *Ancient Israel at War* (Oxford, Osprey) 26.

[20] This quotation is from a letter by the priest Tansar, from the third century CE. It is reprinted in Boyce, M (1990) *Zoroastrianism* (Chicago, University of Chicago Press) 109–10.

proudly recorded the destruction of a number of sanctuaries of opposing faiths. This pattern became particularly pronounced when the theology of Mazdak (d 528), pursuing a vision of a reformed and purified version of Zoroastrianism, came to challenge orthodox views within Persia. The outcome of the theological dispute between conservative and liberal views of Zoroastrianism ended up being a justification for civil war in Persia. Afterwards, the Persian king, Kavadh (449–531), continued the violence, designating Mazdak and his followers as heretics. The penalty was death, and thousands are believed to have been tortured and executed.[21]

Despite their embrace of Zoroastrianism, the Persians seem to have been – at times – tolerant of different local customs and religious traditions and they did not attempt to impose their own customs or religion on those they had conquered. Zoroaster was considered to be a national, rather than a universal prophet. This meant that different practices were allowed and the return of both peoples and cultural/religious property – when removed by previous overlords – was encouraged. These practices had made the Persians welcomed by the communities they conquered in Assyria, Jerusalem and Babylon. Even Xeres, after having the Acropolis sacked, ordered the surviving locals to go and make peace with their local gods when the killing stopped.[22]

3. CHINA AND INDIA

The link between religion, authority and warfare in ancient China reaches back thousands of years. The gods were believed to both guarantee treaties between countries and legitimise rulers within them. This key idea was known as 'The Mandate of Heaven'. The mandate was given at the start of a dynasty to a worthy ruler, and represents, in essence, the legitimacy of a ruler to govern his own people and to wage war against others. For example, in facing down a rebellion, the son of Yu, Ch'i (c 2000 BCE), explained:

> Heaven is about to employ force to end his mandate. Today I am just respectfully implementing Heaven's punishment . . . Those who follow my edict will be rewarded at the ancestral temple.[23]

Similarly, Mo-tzu (c 470–391 BCE) reflected this approach when he wrote of an earlier war and its justification:

> The San Miao were causing great disorder, Heaven mandated that they be put to death . . . lightning and thunder suddenly arose, a spirit with a human face and the body of a bird held a jade tablet to repress the Miao's auspicious power. The Miao forces were thrown into chaos and thereafter fell apart.[24]

[21] Boyce, M (1990) *Zoroastrianism* (Chicago, University of Chicago Press) 30–31, 50–52, 84–97, 104–105; Bozeman, A (1994) *Politics and Culture in International History* (London, Transaction) 46–51; Holland, T (2005) *Persian Fire* (London, Abacus) 56; Billows, R (2010) *Marathon: How One Battle Changed Western Civilisation* (NYC, Scribe) 108–11; Holland, T (2012) *In the Shadow of the Sword* (NYC, Brown) 78–81, 101–103, 115.

[22] Fowden, G (1993) *Empire to Commonwealth: The Consequences of Monotheism in Late Antiquity* (New Jersey, Princeton University Press) 19–20, 24, 33; Roux, G (1964) *Ancient Iraq* (NYC, Pelican) 340–42; Holland, T (2005) *Persian Fire* (London, Abacus) 12–13, 24.

[23] Sawyer, R (2011) *Ancient Chinese Warfare* (NYC, Basic Books) 88–89.

[24] Mo-tzu, as noted in Sawyer, R (2011) *Ancient Chinese Warfare* (NYC, Basic Books) 86–87.

In practice, this meant that the emperor needed to ensure that he had a monopoly on all of the important divination procedures and on links to bygone ancestors. This link to forces that were believed capable of affecting every aspect of personal and public life was fundamental in empowering and sanctifying the king. This was particularly important in matters of warfare, when the people were expected to go forth and fight in a kind of religious service in accord with the will of Heaven. If a ruler betrayed Heaven's trust and failed to deal justly with the people Heaven could withdraw its mandate from that dynasty and present it to the founder of the next.

Exactly how sincere those presenting the theological justifications for warfare in ancient and medieval China were is a matter of debate, particularly since religion was perceived as being less relevant to those doing the fighting. The sincerity of the rulers on religious matters was not in question when the Han Empire distintegrated between 169 and 220 CE following two substantial religious uprisings with strong, personalised and apocalyptical Taoist influences. Here, although the dissident groups at the forefront of the conflict known as the Yellow Turbans, and later, the Five Pecks of Grain, did not directly cause the collapse of the dynasty, they and their strongly religious justifications were fundamental in undermining it.[25]

The most dominant religious influence in ancient India was Hinduism. The beginning of this faith is described in the *Rig Veda*, which was composed between 1200 and 900 BCE, and this work was supplemented with a cascading body of works over the following thousand years, including, inter alia, the *Upanishads* and *Sutras* and *Bhagavad Gita* (also considered to be an *Upanishad*). From these original Hindu sources emerged a world born of warfare, in which the god Indra defeated and destroyed his enemies. Hindu teaching came to recognise that killing may be both inevitable and necessary in order to follow *dharma* (the moral law that upholds the balance of the universe) providing there is a just cause (such as defending the caste system). A further principle that originated in Hinduism was that to fight and die in the pursuit of a just war would bring extra-temporal rewards. This point was drawn out in the *Bhagavad Gita*, which described how Krishna had to convince soldiers to fight in a war in which they would probably end up killing men they knew. Krishna explained:

> You should not grieve for any being. Further, having regard to your own *dharma* you should not falter . . . Blessed are [those] who get such a war, which being, as it were, the open gate to heaven . . . if you do not fight in this battle which is enjoined by *dharma*, you will have given up your own *dharma* as well as glory, and you will incur sin . . . all beings will recount your eternal infamy . . . infamy is worse than death . . . either being slain you will attain heaven or you will enjoy [the rule on] earth. Therefore arise . . . intent on battle.[26]

[25] Lewis, M (1990) *Sanctioned Violence in Early China* (NYC, State University of New York Press) 17, 22–26, 137–63; Sawyer, R (2011) *Ancient Chinese Warfare* (NYC, Basic Books) 204, 208–209; Lewis, M (2009) *China Between Empires: The Northern and Southern Dynasties* (Massachusetts, Harvard University Press) 32–33, 199; Lewis, M (2007) *The Early Chinese Empires: Qin and Han* (Massachusetts, Harvard University Press) 21, 28, 62, 185–86; Graff, D (2002) *Medieval Chinese Warfare* (London, Routledge) 8–9; Gascoigne, B (2003) *The Dynasties of China* (London, Robinson) 81–82.

[26] *The Bhagavad Gita*, sections 2.11–2.37 reprinted in de Barry, R (ed) (1958) *Sources of Indian Tradition*, Vol 1 (NYC, Columbia University Press) 279–81. For other references to the paragraph above this, see Griffiths, R (1897) *The Hymns of the Rigveda* (London, Benares) sections I.32, I:104, VI:26, VI:47, VII:5. See also Hindery, R (1996) *Comparative Ethics in Hindu and Buddhist Traditions* (Delhi, Motilal) 118, 133–34, 145; Kulke, H (1996)

From similar texts within the *Arthashasstra*, Kautilya went so far as to provide the exact religious wording from the *Vedas* for the king and his priests to use before battle. The priests were to promise the assembled army that 'brave men, losing life in good battles, are destined to attain [heaven] immediately . . . [and] . . . a man who does not fight . . . for his master . . . is destined to go to hell'.[27] *The Laws of Manu* would later iterate a similar theme, suggesting that: 'Kings who try to kill one another in battle and fight to the utmost of their ability, never averting their faces, go to heaven.' [28]

The other two dominant religions in this epoch are Jainism and Buddhism. Of the two, only Buddhism held a strong appeal in India as well as China, Korea and Japan. Despite Jainism being the 'lesser' of the two faiths, the similarities between them on the question of violence are noticeable. The emphasis on non-violence within Jainism originated directly from its founder, Mahavira (d 468 BCE), the son of the chief of a warrior clan. Mahavira taught that 'all things breathing, all things existing, all things living, all beings whatever, should not be slain or treated with violence, or insulted, or tortured, or driven away'.[29] Such harm to any other living being, no matter how humble or small, was believed to harm, through karma, the person inflicting the injury. Violence was to be avoided not so much because it harms other beings, as because it harms the individual who commits it. With regard to warfare, the instruction was 'when men rise up in enmity and wish to fight, it is not cowardice, say the wise, to refuse the challenge. Even when your enemies do the utmost evil, it is right to do no evil in return'.[30] This was not an absolute injunction, as Jain scholars came to believe that killing others was permissible if there was no alternative. This was a useful exception, as the Indian emperors who adopted Jainism, such as Chandragupta (c 340–298 BCE), Kharavela (193–170 BCE) and, later, Kumarpal (1143–1172), could all continue to govern and be directly involved in military conflict.[31]

Gautama Buddha (563–483 BCE) was born at a time when the approximately 16 kingdoms of northern India were battling for dominance. Despite being surrounded by violence, Buddha suggested that 'never in this world is hate appeased by hatred; it is only appeased by love – this is an eternal law. Victory breeds hatred for the defeated lie down in sorrow. Above victory or defeat, the calm man dwells in peace'.[32] Building on such precepts, the early (Theravada) Buddhists suggested that killing was always wrong and would bring very serious karmic consequences in this or another life, even when the intentions behind the killing were taken into account. Thus, there could be no theory of just war for Theravada Buddhists. Later (Mahayana) Buddhists would

A History of India (London, Routledge) 34; Morgan, P (ed) (1996) *Ethical Issues in Six Religious Traditions* (Edinburgh, Edinburgh University Press) 5.

[27] Kautilya, *Arthashastra* trans Shamasastry, R (1915) (Bangalore, Government Printer) X:3.

[28] *The Laws of Manu* trans Doniger, W (1991) (London, Penguin) VII:87–88.

[29] 'The Book of Good Conduct', reprinted in de Barry, R (ed) (1958) *Sources of Indian Tradition* (NYC, Columbia University Press) 58.

[30] 'The Four Hundred Quatrains', reprinted in de Barry, R (ed) (1958) *Sources of Indian Tradition* (NYC, Columbia University Press) 53, 66–67.

[31] For the supporting primary sources for this section, see de Barry, R (ed) (1958) *Sources of Indian Tradition* (NYC, Columbia University Press) 42–43, 86, 87; Smith, V (1962) *The Early History of India* (Oxford, Oxford University Press) 153–63, 185, 190; Kulke, H (1996) *A History of India* (London, Routledge) 100.

[32] 'The Way of Righteousness' reprinted in de Barry, R (ed) (1958) *Sources of Indian Tradition*, Vol I (NYC, Columbia University Press) 118–19.

take a different view in which the motive for killing could be taken into account, and if it was carried out completely unselfishly and with a willingness to accept all the negative karmic consequences, it may not be wrong.[33] Such views were profoundly influential both inside India and further afield, for example in China. At the national level, although Buddhism was never made an official state religion, a number of emperors in both India and China were involved in the intricacies of the faith. In India, this was largely restricted to trying to resolve theological differences, while in China, some emperors allowed themselves to be presented as an incarnation of Buddha. Arguably, the foremost of all the Buddhist kings was Asoka (c 304–232 BCE). As a prince, Asoka oversaw the reconquest of a number of provinces which had rebelled. As an emperor, Asoka oversaw the conquest of a neighbouring region – Kalinga. In a response which was unique in the age, despite achieving victory, in 262 BCE, he recorded his feelings of 'remorse, profound sorrow and regret'.[34] These feelings were documented in his *Thirteenth Rock Edict*, in which he recorded that in his eight-year war with Kalinga some 150,000 people were deported and 100,000 (or more) were killed. The 'violence, murder and separation from their loved ones . . . [left Asoka] very painful and grievous'. From this pain, Asoka swore to pursue 'universal conquest' and 'victories' through 'righteousness' as opposed to further military conquest. Nevertheless, Asoka did *not* disband his armed forces, renounce war, nor allow Kalinga to regain its autonomy.[35]

Asoka's reaction was consistent with the then solidifying Buddhist position that, in theory, some wars could be legitimate whilst others such as for territorial aggrandisement were wrong. In practice, a number of Buddhist emperors in India and Sri Lanka fought wars in exactly the same manner as their Hindu contemporaries, with many of them going on to become renowned conquerors – although they expressed regret once they had gained what they wanted. Kanishka (r 120–160) had a strong predisposition to Buddhism and, like Asoka, may also have felt remorse for all the blood he caused to be shed during his wars. Similarly, Samudragupta (r 335–375) eschewed military conquest after his successful adventures in war. Harsha (606–647) adopted a similar remorseful stance after 37 years of warfare.[36]

A similar situation occurred within China, where the Buddhist teaching of non-violence and avoidance of killing appears to have had very little influence in mitigating

[33] Morgan, P (ed) *Ethical Issues in Six Religious Traditions* (Edinburgh, Edinburgh University Press) 88–89; Smith, V (1962) *The Early History of India* (Oxford, Oxford University Press) 35.

[34] Smith, V (1962) *The Early History of India* (Oxford, Oxford University Press) 164–65.

[35] The *Thirteenth Rock Edict* is reprinted in de Barry, R (ed) (1958) *Sources of Indian Tradition*, Vol 1 (NYC, Columbia University Press) 143–44. See also Thepar, R (1961) *Asoka and the Decline of the Mauryas* (Oxford, Oxford University Press) 21–22, 36–37, 41–49, 159–60, 168–69, 191; Smith, V (1962) *The Early History of India* (Oxford, Oxford University Press) 168–70, 178, 186–88, 198; Kulke, H (1996) *A History of India* (London, Routledge) 67; Raychaudhuri, H (1999) *Political History of Ancient India* (Oxford, Oxford University Press) 270–72, 288–89, 291, 396–97, 420; Draper, G (1995) 'The Contribution of the Emperor Asoka Maurya to the Development of the Humanitarian Ideal in Warfare' 305 *International Review of the Red Cross* 192–205; Lewis, M (2009) *China Between Empires: The Northern and Southern Dynasties* (Massachusetts, Harvard University Press) 102–105, 159, 203–17.

[36] 'The Blessings of Peace', reprinted in de Barry, R (ed) (1958) *Sources of Indian Tradition*, Vol 1 (NYC, Columbia University Press) 126, 181; Kulke, H (1996) *A History of India* (London, Routledge) 80–81; Smith, V (1962) *The Early History of India* (Oxford, Oxford University Press) 280, 352, 357–58, 413–14; Raychaudhuri, H (1999) *Political History of Ancient India* (Oxford, Oxford University Press) 485–86.

the frequency of fighting. At the national level, Emperor Wen (541–604), the most powerful of the Sui dynasty, was a devout Buddhist who sought to present himself as a divinely ordained Buddhist ruler – while establishing tight control of Buddhist clergy and overseeing the subjugation of north China and the invasion of Korea. At the local level, some of the uprisings of the period were led by Buddhist monks, who in some instances participated in the combat. Once a conflict was over, the Buddhist faith was often enlisted by the state to help bring about closure. For example, in 628 the emperor held a Buddhist memorial service for those who had perished in a recent conflict, and ordered the construction of monasteries on the sites of his battles so that monks would be able to offer prayers for all of the dead.[37]

Buddhism was generally tolerant of other faiths. Such tolerance appears to have been the general trend in ancient India and China, but this was not always the case. In India, Dharmapala of Bihar and Bengal (770–810) may have been unique in being a Buddhist who was willing to wage war on unbelievers.[38] There were also instances of other groups rebelling against Buddhism. This was most evident with the nomadic groups that attacked both India and China such as the Northern Nomads (the Eastern Turks/Toba, a half-Sinicised Turko-Mongol horde) who came to occupy much of central Eurasian steppe and north China and actively persecuted Buddhism in the fifth century CE. This overlapped with the practices of the White Huns, who appear to have exhibited extreme ferocity against the Buddhists during their invasion of India, sacking monasteries, destroying fine works of art and killing the monks.

Direct attacks on Buddhism within the country (as opposed to attacks by foreign invaders) occurred in both India and China. In India, the first noticeable violence occurred when the Maurya empire came to an end and Pushyamitra Sunga (r 185–151 BCE), reputedly a Brahmin, took charge and destroyed a number of Buddhist monasteries. Sasanka of the Gupta dynasty also allegedly hated Buddhism. According to legend he burnt the holy Bodhi tree at Bodh Gaya, broke the stone marked with the footprints of Buddha at Pataliputra, and destroyed monasteries, scattering the monks to the wind. Conflict was also apparent in the Northern Wei, where in 446 the Daoists and Confucians combined to persuade the emperor that Buddhist temples and images should be destroyed and the monks executed. The tide flowed the other way when another northern emperor became a fervent Buddhist and ordered the destruction of all Daoist temples. The most serious attack occurred in 854, when the Daoists and Confucians again combined forces. At this point more than 4,000 monasteries and 10 times as many temples and shrines were destroyed. Over a quarter of a million Buddhist monks and nuns were forced to return to lay life and the monasteries' lands were seised. At the same point, the nascent Christian communities that had been seeding in China (from the end of the eighth century) were also destroyed, being caught up in the conflict as a foreign, non-Chinese faith. The succeeding emperor reversed the

[37] Graff, D (2002) *Medieval Chinese Warfare* (London, Routledge) 138–39, 185.

[38] See de Barry, R (ed) (1958) *Sources of Indian Tradition*, Vol 1 (NYC, Columbia University Press) 126; Kulke, H (1996) *A History of India* (London, Routledge) 80–81; Smith, V (1962) *The Early History of India* (Oxford, Oxford University Press) 280, 352, 357–58, 413–14; Raychaudhuri, H (1999) *Political History of Ancient India* (Oxford, Oxford University Press) 485–86.

policy of persecution, re-established many of the monasteries and executed a dozen of the Daoist advisers who had most influenced his predecessor.[39]

4. GREECE AND ROME

Compared with other civilisations, it is striking how rarely warfare was linked to religion for the classical Greeks and Romans. This is not to suggest that there was not a strong religious background in both Greece and Rome. Before the Greek wars with Persia, the epics of Greece are rich in stories of how their gods personally engaged in combat alongside mortals. Similarly, it was not unknown for the Roman gods to make favourable appearances at times of critical military need. Despite these actions, the Greek – like the Roman – gods were not interested in conquest and in being worshipped by foreign handmaidens, and neither civilization attempted to export their own cults. In both societies, the priests of the temples never became powerful castes, tyrannising the community in their own interests, nor were they able to silence voices raised against religious beliefs. Tolerance and freedom of speech around religious questions was the rule (although there were exceptions) in both Greece and Rome. This was especially so in Rome, which came to style itself as a cosmopolitan city, in which all of the world's faiths could be represented – and tolerated. Tiberius (42 BCE–37 CE) exemplified this view when he suggested 'if the Gods are insulted, let them see to it themselves'.[40]

Nevertheless, the civil authorities in both Greece and Rome kept the general control of public worship in their hands, using religion to perform the function of social cohesion and rituals in which the gods came to play roles more suited to figureheads than soldiers. For example, in Greece the gods threatened against the breach of treaties.[41] The Romans also retained the belief that the gods were responsible for ensuring compliance with treaties. The Romans went one step further in using religious protocol to ensure that any war declared was just. This process, traceable to the (fourth) Roman king, Ancus Marcius (r 640–616 BCE), involved placing considerations of whether or not to go to war in the hands of the *fetials* – special religious officials who oversaw aspects of inter-state relations. The obligation for the first 'formal demands for justice'

[39] Gascoigne, B (2003) *The Dynasties of China* (London, Robinson) 104–105, 108–11; Kulke, H (1996) *A History of India* (London, Routledge) 71, 92–93, 102; Smith, V (1962) *The Early History of India* (Oxford, Oxford University Press) 123, 221–22, 312–16, 320; Grousset, R (2010) *The Empire of the Steppes: A History of Central Asia* (New Jersey, Rutgers) 63, 70; Ayerst, D (ed) (1971) *Records of Christianity*, Vol II (Oxford, Blackwell) 86–87.

[40] Tiberius, as noted in Bury, J (2007 reprint) *Freedom of Thought: A History* (NYC, Prometheus) 34; Fowden, G (1993) *Empire to Commonwealth: The Consequences of Monotheism in Late Antiquity* (New Jersey, Princeton University Press) 46–49. For the intervention of the Roman Gods, see the episode of the 'miracle rain' which helped Aurelius when fighting the Germans, see Ferris, I (2009) *Hate and War: The Column of Marcus Aurelius* (Gloucestershire, Mill) 81–96.

[41] Herodotus, *The Histories* trans de Selincourt, A (London, Penguin) IX:65; Hedreen, G (2004) *Capturing Troy* (USA, University of Michigan Press) 84–85, 170–71. For the religious influence in the treaties, see for example, the Oaths of the Allies (377 BC) reprinted in Botsford, G (ed) (1915) *Hellenic Civilisation Records* (NYC, Columbia University Press) 396.

by which the gods would judge whether the cause was 'righteous' fell on these men.[42] This need for religious support for a cause was never lost, for as the pragmatic Onasander (c 100 CE) explained:

> It should be evident to all that one fights on the side of justice. For then the gods also, kindly disposed, become comrades in arms to the soldiers, and men are more eager to take their stand against the foe . . . [The General] should call heaven to witness that he is entering upon war without offence.[43]

Religious zeal dropped out of the world view of Classical Greece when the Greeks acknowledged that the principal gods had been absent during their conflict with Persia, at the time that they were needed most. It was recognised that it was men and not gods who won battles at Marathon and Salamis. Accordingly, when the Athenians returned to their city after it had been sacked by the Persians, they first rebuilt their defences and only later rebuilt the religious shrines. This is not to suggest that religious influences were not evident in future conflicts, but rather that they were only a small part of the mix. Thus, in the Peloponnesian war, although both sides claimed religious support as they were fighting sacrilegious opposition, they believed that the reason the enemy was disliked by the gods had more to do with their political views.[44] A change occurred with the ascendency of Alexander the Great (356–323 BCE), and the successor empires of the Ptolemies and the Seleucids, whereby the leaders associated themselves with a god-like status, as a type of religious cult which had roots in the religious practices of the defeated. This approach allowed the rulers to portray themselves as a harmonious lynchpin between the newly-conquered populations and those they sought to subject. Antiochus I (d 261 BCE) recorded:

> I am Antiochus, the great king, the legitimate king, the king of the world, king of Babylon, king of all countries, the caretaker of the temples, the first born son of King Seleucus, the Macedonian, king of Babylon . . . [after addressing Babylonian gods, he requests] . . . and may I personally conquer all the countries from sunrise to sunset.[45]

At the end of the Roman Republic, the tutelary spirit, if not the body, of the emperor was subject to religious worship in a manner which complemented the existing religious practices. This process became clear with the role of both Julius Caesar (100–44

[42] This language is taken from Livy, *The Early History of Rome* trans De Selincourt A (1960) (London, Penguin) I:24, I:32, VIII:39; XXXVI:2. For the example of the oversight of the gods of the Roman treaties, see the 509 BC Treaty Between Rome and Carthage reprinted in Lewis, N and Reinhold M (eds) (1955) *Roman Civilisation: Records*, Vol 1 (Columbia, Columbia University Press) 73; Dawson, D (1996) *The Origins of Western Warfare* (NYC, Westview) 114–16; Elton, H (1997) *Warfare in Roman Europe* (Oxford, Oxford University Press) 176–79; Watson, A (1993) *International Law in Archaic Rome* (NYC, John Hopkins Press) 6–7, 23–34, 51–56.

[43] *Aeneas Tacitus, Asclepiodotus, and Onasander* trans Illinois Greek Club (Loeb Classical Library) 4.1–3.

[44] Thucydides, *History of the Peloponnesian War* trans Finley, M (1984) (London, Penguin) I:118 and 127, IV:92 and V:53; also Zimmern, A (1962) *The Greek Commonwealth* (Oxford, Oxford University Press) 182.

[45] Antiochus I as King of Babylon reprinted in Austin, M (ed) *The Hellenistic World from Alexander to the Roman Conquest: A Collection of Readings* (1992) (Cambridge, Cambridge University Press) 310–11. See also the inscriptions in Barker, E (1959) *From Alexander to Constantine: Passages and Documents Illustrating the History of Social and Political Ideas* (Oxford, Oxford University Press) 101–102; 357–59. For Alexander, see Diodorus *Library of History* trans Wells, B (1962) (Boston, Loeb) XVIIII:56.2; Arrian, *Anabasis of Alexander* trans Brunt, P (1956) (Loeb, Boston) IV.C.9. Also Waterfield, R (2011) *Dividing the Spoils: The War for Alexander the Great's Empire* (Oxford, Oxford University Press) 7–9.

BCE) and Gaius Octavius Thurinus – Augustus (63 BCE–14 CE). In the first instance, Caesar persuaded the senate to honour him as a god and claimed that, like a god, his influence was everywhere and everlasting. He held the posts of tribune, censor, consol and dictator simultaneously and collectively. He put his fingerprints on all aspects of Roman society and culture. He even worked on reforming the Roman calendar, in which the seventh month was replaced – and remains – *Julius*. In the second instance, in the eastern provinces Augustus was regarded as the successor to the divine monarchs of the earlier dynasties. Upon his death he was deified, being declared immortal by the senate. When these matters were concluded, the senate voted Augustus his own month, similar to Caesar – but with a differentiation in the number of days each was allocated. Subsequent emperors, including Caligula (12–41) and Commodus (161–192), introduced the concept of the emperor as God on Earth, whilst Domitian (51–96) insisted on being addressed as *dominus et deus* (master and god). Obediance in the presence of the emperor came into vogue, and the appellation *dominus noster* (our lord and master) became standard.[46]

Despite this change, the extent to which the worship of the emperor and the associated Roman gods was for the purpose of unifying the empire and galvanising the political elite, as opposed to being integral to religious doctrine, is an open question. Indeed, whilst it is correct that the Romans could take actions in some provinces to remove the power of those with religious authority (such as the druids), the more common approach was one whereby local traditions were broadly tolerated and were allowed to exist in the shadows of all the manifestations of the power of Rome.[47]

A. The Jewish People

Although the Romans and Greeks may not have predicated their justifications for warfare on religion, many of those they fought did. This was most obvious with the Jewish people in Palestine. The issue first became clear when Antiochus IV (215–164 BCE) in his attempts consolidate his empire and strengthen his hold over the region, decided to override the earlier policy of the Ptolemies which had allowed the Jewish people to largely regulate their own affairs and practise their own rites. Antiochus decided to outlaw Jewish religious rites and traditions and ordered the worship of the Hellenistic gods. When there was a rebellion against this by the group known as the Maccabees, Antiochus ordered his general to destroy the forces of Judah by the use of any and all means at his disposal and 'to uproot and destroy the strength of Israel and the remnant of Judea, to blot out all memory of them from the place, to settle strangers in the territory and allot the land to the settlers'.[48] The resulting rebellion that began in 167 BCE cost the lives of perhaps 80,000 Jewish people before it was finally subdued. Antiochus IV died before the problem of the Maccabees was concluded, and it fell to his son Antiochus V (r 163–161 BCE) and the regents of his son, to moderate a peace with the

[46] Dio Cassius, *Roman History* trans Cary, E (1967) (Boston, Loeb) LI:20 and LVI:46.
[47] Morley, N (2010) *The Roman Empire: Roots of Imperialism* (London, Pluto) 122–25.
[48] 1 Maccabees 3:35–36.

Jewish people. The core of this agreement was to 'guarantee them rights to follow their laws and customs as they used to do, for it was our abolition of these very customs and laws which aroused their resentment and produced all these consequences'.[49]

When Judah accepted this proposal, Antiochus V was able to reorientate his efforts to secure other parts of the Seleucid empire, in which he was successful. He had less success in trying to survive the internecine struggle that followed when his cousin Demetrius I (185–150 BCE) seised power, killing Antiochus V and reasserting a strong authority in Jerusalem – which included the execution of many Orthodox Jews who were suspected of Maccabean sympathies. Unwilling to allow the suppression of their faith again, the Jewish people revolted once more. At the same time they sent an embassy to Rome, requesting a military alliance. Rome agreed to this alliance and warned Demetrius that if the Jews appealed to them in relation to the 'heavy yoke' laid upon them, it would 'defend their rights and fight you on sea and on land'.[50] The extent to which Rome directly supported Jerusalem in the coming decades is questionable, as Demetrius was able to crush the rebellious Maccabean forces in 160 BCE when approximately 24,000 Seleucid troops overwhelmed 3,000 Jewish soldiers.[51]

Although the Seleucids regained control of Jerusalem, they quickly lost control of their empire, and Rome came to control the region and appoint client kings. Notably, Mark Antony (83–30 BCE) appointed the heavy-handed Herod (73–4 BCE) as the monarch of Judea, who managed to offend both religious and nationalistic sensibilities. His sons continued in the same patterns, leading the Jews and the Samaritans to cooperate in a request to Rome that the monarchy should be abolished. The Romans listened, and in 6 CE Judea was made into a Roman province, governed by an imperial curator. Thereafter, ironically, the Romans – who were initially drawn into the issue by volunteering to defend the cultural and religious practices of the Jewish people – would go on to make exactly the same mistakes as the Seleucid dynasties. When they tried to force the Jewish people to meet their obligations to the Roman Empire – as required of all other groups within the Empire – they ended up, instead, creating two nationalistic, religion-based rebellions between 66 and 74 CE, and 132 and 135 CE. The final death toll was roughly 350,000.[52]

The imperial Roman authorities were tolerant in many areas. The Jewish religion was officially permitted by the Roman emperors both before and after the Jewish rebellions – but not at the time of rebellion. This was in accordance with the general Roman principle of not tolerating any form of military dissent. Dissent arose when the Jewish landowning aristocracy (whom the Romans supported) ignored those who held religious authority within the Judean faith, and a number of Jewish groups rebelled against the Romans and their supporters. Vespasian (9–79) ordered his son Titus (39–81) to stifle the core of the rebellion in Jerusalem. He did this in the year 70 but the last

[49] 1 Maccabees 6:58–39.

[50] 1 Maccabees 8:31–32 and 8:18–19; 15:1–9. Herzog, C (1997) *Battles of the Bible* (London, Greenhill) 292–95.

[51] 2 Maccabees 5:11–14 and 6:1–12. Also Herzog, C (1997) *Battles of the Bible* (London, Greenhill) 265, 294–95; Scullard, H (1982) *From the Gracchi to Nero* (London, Methuen) 248–51.

[52] White, M (2011) *Atrocitology* (NYC, Norton) 50–51. Note, early historians put the figure much higher, at about 2 million. See Lewis, N and Reinhold M (eds) (1955) *Roman Civilisation: Records* Vol II (Columbia, Columbia University Press) 414.

embers of the revolt did not die down until the mass suicide of the defenders at the fortress of Masada in 73. The end result of a destroyed Jerusalem, the loss of large amounts of land, and the abolition of the Jewish religious authorities only served to push the Jewish resentment into other parts of the Levant. For example, in 115, Jewish and Greek communities, the latter being firmly connected to Imperial government, went head-to-head. This conflict was particularly brutal. The Jews both destroyed the non-Jewish populations and drove out the Roman forces. Five bloody years followed during which Jews were banished from Cyprus and largely vanished from the Egyptian and Cyrenian provinces as well as from Alexandria. This was in accordance with the order of Trajan (53–117) to 'clean them out'.[53]

Further uprisings occurred in 130. The Jews were already under a regime which was trying to Hellenise them in many ways, ranging from destroying their built heritage, through to forbidding circumcision (as originally outlawed by Domitian and Nerva (30–98) and followed through by Hadrian (76–138)). The pretext for the uprising in 130 had been Trajan's decision to build a new Roman colony with 'Greek' settlers on the site of Jerusalem, which Titus had destroyed earlier. In the place of the old temple of Jehovah, he ordered one to be erected to Jupiter Capitolinus, to be built on the ruins of Herod's temple, in which he himself was to be honoured. Hadrian continued this policy of rebuilding Jerusalem as a Roman settlement. When the tomb of Solomon was breached by a building accident during the construction of the *Aelia Capitolina*, revolt broke out and quickly became full-blown war. The Romans soon gained control of the situation, taking and securing every hill and strongpoint they encountered before advancing. By the year of 134, 985 villages had been taken, 50 mountain forts destroyed, and tens of thousands of fighting men slaughtered. Tens of thousands more were taken prisoner and sold as slaves. The result was that Judea was largely depopulated of Jews. The building of the *Aelia Capitolina* proceeded and an equestrian statue of Hadrian and other pagan shrines were erected on the land of the disputed site. In addition, Judea ceased to exist as a territorial entity when it was added to Galilee and the enlarged province known as Syria Palestina. Although they lost local political power, under Emperor Antoninus Pius (86–161) the Jews were restored to their ancient privileges and they once more obtained permission to circumcise their children.[54]

B. Christians

The other religion which Rome inadvertently ran into, but was subsequently overrun by, was Christianity. The Romans had been aware of Christianity since the time of

[53] Eusebius, *Church History* trans Maier, J (1943) (London, Penguin) 4:2–5; Everitt, A (2009) *Hadrian and the Triumph of Rome* (NYC, Random House) 159–62; Morley, N (2010) *The Roman Empire: Roots of Imperialism* (London, Pluto) 58–59.

[54] Dio Cassius, *Roman History* trans Cary, E (1967) (Boston, Loeb) LXIX:xii; Suetonius, *The Twelve Caesars* trans Graves, R (1989) (London, Penguin) Claudius 25, Nero 16, Domitian 12, 15 and 17; Cook, S (ed) (1968) *The Cambridge Ancient History: The Augustan Empire*, Vol X (Cambridge, Cambridge University Press) 862–65; Cook, S (ed) (1965) *The Cambridge Ancient History: The Imperial Peace*, Vol XI (Cambridge, Cambridge University Press) 250–51, 314–16.

Nero (37–68). Around this time Peter (c 1–67) established a Church in Rome; the primacy of this location would prove significant for many people for thousands of years to come. This was the subject of immediate difficulty, as this little known community of Christians was blamed by Nero for the fire that destroyed much of Rome around the year 65. For this alleged act, the Christians suffered their first persecution, with Peter and Paul, amongst others, being executed. This first persecution dissipated after the death of Nero, with more reasonable approaches being advocated by administrators such as Pliny (61–112), who saw Christians as law-abiding citizens. When Pliny asked the Emperor Trajan how to deal with such peoples, Trajan replied 'nothing can be laid down as a general ruling involving something like a set form of procedure. They are not to be sought out, but if they are accused and convicted, they must be punished.'[55]

This type of approach, where all communities were obliged to perform Roman rites in public, but were largely allowed autonomy in private, continued in the years that followed. Toleration of Christianity was possible, because although some early Christian theologians had taken the command to love your enemy literally, ending up at points very close to non-violent resistance, other theologians such as Tertullian (160–220) supported the emperor, and it appears that a number of early Christians served in the Roman forces without difficulty. Tolerance dissipated when another difficulty arose. This problem was not the killing of others in military conflict, but the fact that Roman soldiers had to sacrifice to Roman idols as part of the state religion. A number of Christian soldiers refused to do this. Such disobedience forced the emperors to demand that all citizens and soldiers conform fully with the practices of state religion in public (for which they would be granted a certificate), irrespective of what they practised in private. Following these demands, systematic persecutions began, particularly under Diocletian (244–311), in which hundreds, if not thousands of people were executed and/or lost their property because they would not perform the acts required to earn their 'certificate of conformity'.[56] This persecution only ended in 313 when Constantine the Great (272–337), who at this point held one quarter of the Tetrarchy, agreed with Licinius (263–325), who held another quarter, what was known as the Edict of Milan. This stated:

> We . . . give to both Christians and all others free facility to follow the religion which each may desire, so that by this means whatever divinity is enthroned in heaven may be gracious and favorable to us . . . for the sake of peace in our time a similar public and free right to practice their religion or cult is granted to others, so that every person may have free opportunity to worship according to his own wish. This has been done by us to avoid any appearance of disfavour to any one religion.[57]

[55] Trajan, noted in Perowne, S (1962) *Caesars and Saints: The Evolution of the Christian State* (London, Hodder) 84. See also Letters 10, 96 and 97 of Pliny, reprinted in Ayerst, D (ed) (1971) *Records of Christianity*, Vol I (Oxford, Blackwell) 14–15. The point about the location of Rome is found in Matthew 16:18.

[56] See the 'Certificate of Conformity', reprinted in Ayerst D (ed) (1971) *Records of Christianity*, Vol I (Oxford, Blackwell) 123. Note also the 'Acts of Marcellus' reprinted in Maas, M (ed) (2010) *Readings in Late Antiquity: A Sourcebook* (London, Routledge) 105; Stephenson, P (2009) *Constantine* (London, Quecus) 52–58, 104–109; Perowne, S (1962) *Caesars and Saints: The Evolution of the Christian State* (London, Hodder) 93. For the pacifist early theologians, see Ignatius (c 50–98) and Origen (185–254) as discussed in Cahill, L (1994) *Love Your Enemies: Pacifism and Just War Theory* (NYC, Cahill) 41–55.

[57] The Edict of Milan, reprinted in Rosenwein, B (ed) (2006) *Reading the Middle Ages: Sources from Europe, Byzantium and the Islamic World* (Broadview, Ontario) 3; Lactantius *On the Deaths of the Persecutors* trans Creed, T (1984) (Oxford, Oxford University Press) 48:1.

This principle of freedom of religion split the Tetrearchy in two. Licinius went on to battle successfully against Maximinus Daia (270–313), who had continued the persecution of Christians, seeing them as disloyal, mischievous and offensive to the pagan gods. Constantine decided upon a pre-emptive attack on Maxentius (the last holder of the Tetrarchy) under the justification that he was freeing Rome from 'tyranny' by a man involved with black magic and human sacrifice. Whether Constantine identified himself as a Christian before – or during – the conflict that followed, when some 125,000 men clashed for the control of Rome, is a matter of debate. The popular account suggests that during the battle of Milvian Bridge in 312 Constantine had his famous 'vision of a Cross of Light in the Heavens at midday, with an inscription admonishing him to "conquer by that"'.[58] The difficulty is that the inscription commemorating the war only recorded Constantine as 'being instinct with Divinity and by the Greatness of his spirit avenged the State in a just war on the Tyrant and all of his party'.[59] Although Constantine omitted to mention Christ, posterity recorded Constantine as the 'Christian victor' who came to possess the entire Roman Empire. This possession was made secure by Constantine putting to death the two sons of Maxentius.[60]

Before Constantine could claim complete control, he had to deal with the last remaining member of the Tetrarchy – Licinius. Despite a peace treaty between the two of them over the division of the Roman Empire in 317 and the entrenchment of their respective dynasties, conflict broke out. Constantine had incited conflict by portraying Licinius as a tyrant who disobeyed his own laws and was covetous of the resources of his own citizens. When Licinius appeared to have reneged on the promises of the Edict of Milan in 320, oppressing Christians, destroying their property and reinvigorating pagan rituals, the drift towards war could not be stopped. 'Constantine was stirred in behalf of the Christians in danger of persecution'. Following these acts war broke out, and, according to Eusebius, Licinius' actions were the same as 'carry[ing] arms against God himself'. [61] Although Licinius was allowed to retire after losing the final conflict, both he and his son were later accused of plotting against Constantine, and were executed.[62]

[58] Eusebius, *The Life of the Blessed Emperor Constantine* trans anon (2009 reprint of 1854 edn) Vol 8 (London, Bagster, Christian Roman Empire Series) I:28, I:37; Grant, R (2005) *Battle* (London, Dorling Kindersley) 50.

[59] Inscription, reprinted in Norwich, J (1988) *Byzantium: The Early Centuries* (London, Guild) 231. See also the letter addressed to Maximinus, reprinted in Stephenson, P (2009) *Constantine* (London, Quercus) 132–38, 159. Also Gwatkin, H (ed) (1957) *The Cambridge Medieval History: The Christian Roman Empire and the Foundation of the Teutonic Kingdoms*, Vol I (Cambridge, Cambridge University Press) 3–6; Eusebius, *The Life of the Blessed Emperor Constantine* trans anon (2009 reprint of 1854 edition) Vol 8 (London, Bagster, Christian Roman Empire Series) I:26, 35, 36; Lactantius, *De Mortibus Persecutorum* trans Creed, T (1984) (Oxford, Oxford University Press) 44:4.

[60] Stephenson, P (2009) *Constantine* (London, Querus) 88, 172–82; Norwich, J (1988) *Byzantium: The Early Centuries* (London, Guild) 39, 43–44.

[61] This quotation is in two parts. Both are from Eusebius, *The Life of the Blessed Emperor Constantine* trans anon (2009 reprint of 1854 edn) Vol 8 (London, Bagster, Christian Roman Empire Series). The first part is from section II:2 and the second from section I:49.

[62] Stephenson, P (2009) *Constantine* (London, Quercus) 228; Gibbon, E (1926 edn) *The Decline and Fall of the Roman Empire*, Vol I (London, Methuen) 466–67.

5. CHRISTIANITY

Before the final victory of Constantine, there was little question about the relationship between the state and the Church. At this point, the Church was not merely separate; it was a threat to the status quo. After Constantine, everything changed. Christianity was unlike the traditional Roman religion, which was more a department of the state. Christianity was a religion which was not based upon the lofty and abstract ideals of Stoicism. Rather, it was something which every individual had the capacity to grasp in a very personal and powerful way. Nor was Christianity about the worship of the emperor as a deity. Under Christianity, God was an important part of the state, and the emperor was just another mortal man (albeit a remarkably powerful one) at the forefront of a religion which was strongly universalist in vision, under which both he and all other Christians were instructed to go and 'make disciples of all nations; baptise them in the name of the Father and of the Son and of the Holy Spirit'.[63]

All of these changes unified the state in a previously unforeseen way, and forced those in charge to radically rethink the way things worked. This was often difficult as the answers to pivotal questions were not always clear. For the purposes of this book, the most obvious unresolved question concerned the relationship between Christianity and war and violence. The difficulty is that Christianity is ambiguous on this issue. One the one hand, the Bible can be interpreted as a pacifist document. The central portion of the Sermon on the Mount states:

> Ye have heard that it hath been said, An eye for an eye, and a tooth for a tooth, But I say unto you, That ye resist not evil: but whosoever shall smite thee on thy right cheek, turn to him the other also . . . Love your enemies, bless them that curse you, do good to them that hate you, and pray for them which . . . persecute you.[64]

Additional text in the Gospels records how Jesus instructed Peter: 'Put your sword back into its place. For all who take the sword will perish by the sword.'[65] It was, he said, the peacemakers who were blessed. In practical terms, it is notable that Jesus was not associated with the Zealots, who during his lifetime were busy trying to start an armed uprising against the Romans.[66]

An alternative view in which violence could be seen as legitimate can also be read from the Gospels. In practice, Jesus had already shown that he vigorously opposed evil. He denounced people he believed to be hypocrites, and used a whip of cords to drive animals (and perhaps people) from the temple when he believed they were defiling it. [67] The Book of Matthew adds: 'Think not that I am come to send peace on Earth: I came not to send peace, but a sword',[68] whilst the Book of Luke adds 'but

[63] Matthew 28:19. See also Fowden, G (1993) *Empire to Commonwealth: The Consequences of Monotheism in Late Antiquity* (New Jersey, Princeton University Press) 91–96.

[64] Matthew 5:38–48. See also Luke 3:14; Matthew 8:5–13; Romans 13:1–4; Timothy 2:1–2; Peter 2:13–17.

[65] Matthew 26:52.

[66] Matthew 5:9. Also Morgan, P (ed) *Ethical Issues in Six Religious Traditions* (1996) (Edinburgh, Edinburgh University Press) 206–210.

[67] Matthew 23:13 and John 2:13–17.

[68] Matthew 10:34.

those of mine enemies, which would not that I should reign over them, bring hither, and slay them before me' (although this was spoken in a parable of a king).[69] Christians are also urged to 'fight the good fight'[70] in a passage from the Book of Timothy from which countless generations of Christian soldiers have drawn inspiration. Thus:

> Thou therefore endure hardness, as a good soldier of Jesus Christ. No man that warreth entangleth himself with the affairs of this life; that he may please him who hath chosen him to be a soldier.[71]

The message of the last book in the Bible, the Book of Revelation, suggests a conclusion which is far from peaceful, as armies pour from heaven:

> And out of his mouth proceedeth a sharp two edged sword; that with it he may strike the nations. And he shall rule them with a rod of iron; and he treadeth the winepress of the fierceness of the wrath of God the Almighty.[72]

From such scripture, and no doubt whilst the memories of the military victories of Constantine were still fresh, and large numbers of non-Christian, non-Roman barbarians were beginning to attack the Empire, a number of theologians started to look for ways in which Christianity, citizenship and violence could be reconciled. The first to attempt this balancing act was Ambrose (339–397). He warned the newly anointed Christian emperor that 'in matters of war one ought to see whether the war is just or unjust'. War was not something to be scared of, and he recounted how figures in the Old Testament, such as Abraham, David, Joshua, Samson and even Deborah, had all achieved great victories after fighting in justified wars. 'Courage in war,' he explained, 'preserves one's country from the barbarians, or at home defends the weak, or comrades from robbers, [and] is full of justice'. He recalled the military successes of Moses, who 'put on one side the thought of his own safety so as to give freedom to the people'. This example was matched by his discussion of the Book of Maccabees, 'which bears no light impress of what is virtuous and seemly upon it, for [the oppressed] prefer death to slavery and disgrace'. In terms of what was not just, he advised the emperor 'to take care not to stir up war one with the other by allowing thoughts and cares about the belongings of others to take hold of them'.[73] Synesius of Cyrene (373–414) largely reiterated such views. Whilst he agreed that God was always on the side of the good, he advised that the Christian Roman emperor still had to be 'a craftsman of wars, just as the cobbler is a craftsman of shoes'. Such a craftsman needed to be prepared for war, for if he is not 'he will certainly be warred against'.[74]

Augustine of Hippo (354–430) put down his thoughts on this topic whilst an army of Vandals was trying to break into the city within which he was besieged. Augustine held that the teachings of Christ were not contrary to the actions of the Roman Empire and

[69] Luke 19:27.
[70] 1 Timothy 1:18.
[71] 2 Timothy 2:3–4.
[72] Revelation 19:14 and 15.
[73] Ambrose, *On the Duties of the Clergy* trans Romestin, H (2010) (London, Black) I:13, I:24, I:27–29, I:35, I:41.
[74] Synesius, *On Imperial Rule*, 14–16. This is reprinted in Bregman, J. (ed) (1982) *Synesius of Cyrene: Philosopher-Bishop*. (California, California University Press) 18-20.

that it was possible to serve both the military and God, arguing that Christ did not tell soldiers to throw their weapons away, but to serve with integrity. For Augustine, and generations of Christians afterwards, it was agreed that 'wise men only fight just wars. If they are not just, they are not obliged to fight them'.[75]

The question was, therefore: what made a just war? Augustine concluded that a war could be just if the methods and causes were sufficient. In terms of methods, the decision about whether or not to resort to violence had to be made 'under the control of a leader'. Once this decision was made, it followed that a soldier could be excused from killing if he were following orders and if the violence were not excessive (such as that based on the desire to harm, or revenge or on lust for domination). In terms of causes, it was specified that, in addition to being necessary, and all other means of redress exhausted, 'the desired end of war is peace'. With these caveats in mind, Augustine suggested that a war may be just if it was waged to repel an unjust aggressor, defend an ally, secure a legitimate right of passage, or rescue victims of oppression in a country other than one's own. It would not be just if the objectives were the achievement of glory and/or to gain the possessions of others. Indeed, 'he who desires glory and is avid for domination is worse than the beasts in the vices of cruelty and extravagance'. [76] He went on to suggest, in one of his better-known passages, that the pursuit of the property or territory of others is the defining characteristic of pirates and emperors:

> Set justice aside then, and what are kingdoms but fair thievish purchases? For what are thieves' purchases but little kingdoms, for in thefts the hands of underlings are directed by the commander, the confederacy of them is sworn together, and the pillage is shared by the law amongst them? And if those ragamuffins grow up to be able to keep forts, build habitations, possess cities, and conquer adjoining nations, then their government is no more thievish, but graced with the eminent name of a kingdom, given and gotten, not because they have left their practices, but because now they may use them without danger of law. Elegant and excellent was that pirate's answer to the great Macedonian Alexander, who had taken him: the king asking him how he dare molest the seas so, he replied with a free spirit: 'How darest thou molest the whole world? But because I do it with a little ship only, I am called a thief: thou, doing it with a great navy, art called an emperor'.[77]

Even where no theological teachings remain, it should be noted that a number of the great religious leaders of the age, in the form of popes, had direct relationships with warfare in a practical – not just theoretical – sense. For example, when Rome was threatened after the Emperor Honorius (384–423) had fled, it fell to Pope Innocent (r 401–417) to negotiate directly with Alaric (370–410), just as Leo I (c 391–461) had to negotiate directly with the other barbarian warlords Attila (d 453) and Geiseric (389–477). Subsequently, Gregory (540–604), unable to secure Byzantine assistance, would be forced to defend Rome by himself from the Lombards – who were, until their conversion in 653, notoriously anti-Christian, destroying nearly all religious establishments within their reach. In this latter instance, Gregory found himself acing as civil

[75] This quotation is from Augustine's *City of God*, chapter 7 reprinted in Augustine, *Political Writings* trans Tkacs, M (1994) (NYC, Hackett) 149, xiii, 189, 204, 209, 219.

[76] These quotations, in sequence, are from *City of God* chapter 21, and *Against Faustus*, XXII, and *Letter 189 to Boniface*. All are in Augustine, *Political Writings* trans Tkacs, M (1994) (NYC, Hackett) 10, 150, 220, 222–23.

[77] Augustine, *The City of God* trans Healey, J (1946) Vol I (London, Dent) Book IV:3.

and military governor of virtually the whole of central Italy, organising supplies and directing troop movements as well as paying wages (often from Church funds) and shouldering responsibility for the defence of both Rome and Naples.[78]

6. ORTHODOXY, HERESY AND INTOLERANCE

It was always hoped that there would be an agreed and shared theological unity within Christendom. This hope was so strong that, despite repeated warnings from theologians for political leaders not to get involved (as the temporal and spiritual realms were meant to be separate), a number of emperors continued to try to encourage theologians to come to an agreement. The emperors were attracted to the idea of a unified theology binding the empire together, for as Constantine explained, a theological uniformity would result in a 'common harmony of sentiment' which would encompass the servants of God and the general community. For this reason, many emperors called religious councils in order to find definite answers to theological questions that had not been settled (including debates about, inter alia, Arianism, Miaphysitism, Monophysitism and Monothelitism) and to end the bickering that the authorities believed threatened not only the Church, but the unity of the empire. This unity was important not only as the glue that held everything together within the empire's borders, but also as the propellant that helped expand the perimeter of the borders. The theologian and archbishop of Constantinople, Nestorius (386–451), made this very clear when he called for the emperor's support for a further ecumenical council in 451: 'Help me destroy the heretics, and I will help you destroy the Persians.'[79]

A. Arians and Paulicians

In some instances, although the Church within Constantinople could not accept differing theological views, some emperors could. The primary example was the Monophysite

[78] Norwich, J (2011) *Absolute Monarchs: A History of the Papacy* (NYC, Random House) 20–26, 41–45; Wallace-Hadrill, J (1962) *The Barbarian West: The Early Middle Ages A.D 400–1000* (NYC, Harper) 49, 58–59; Ayerst, D (ed) (1971) *Records of Christianity*, Vol II (Oxford, Blackwell) 23–25.

[79] Nestorius, as noted in Holland, T (2012) *In the Shadow of the Sword* (NYC, Brown) 185; Eusebius, *The Life of the Blessed Emperor Constantine* trans anon (2009 reprint of 1854 edn) Vol 8 (London, Bagster, Christian Roman Empire Series) II:67; Carlyle, A (1936) *A History of Medieval Political Theory in the West: The Second Century to the Ninth*, Vol 1 (London, Blackwood) 175–78; Barker, E (ed) (1959) *Social and Political Thought in Byzantium* (Oxford, Clarendon Press) 86–87, 90, 107–108; Gwatkin, H (ed) (1967) *The Cambridge Medieval History: The Rise of the Saracens and the Foundation of the Western Empire*, Vol II (Cambridge, Cambridge University Press) 44–45. For some of the decrees attempting to settle theological questions, see the 'Decree of the Council of Chalcedon' reprinted in Ayerst, D (ed) (1971) *Records of Christianity*, Vol I (Oxford, Blackwell) 520. Also the 'Fifth Ecumenical Council Decrees' reprinted in Geanakoplos, D (ed) (1986) *Byzantium: A Sourcebook on Church, Society and Civilisation Seen Through Contemporary Eyes* (Chicago, Chicago University Press) 150–52. Also 'the Henotikon of Zeno' reprinted in Maas, M (ed) (2010) *Readings in Late Antiquity: A Sourcebook* (London, Routledge) 138–39.

faith, for which, for the sake of peace (often in the provinces further removed from the centre of the Byzantine Empire), a soft tolerance emerged. In other instances, war rather than tolerance was the preferred option of the emperors. Open warfare arose owing to theological differences between Christians in at least two groups, the Arians and the Paulicians, before the year 1000.

The Arians drew their inspiration from Arius (250–336), an influential theologian who questioned the relationship of the Trinity and the precise nature of the Son of God, whom he considered to be a subordinate entity to God the Father. Arius was condemned and labelled as a heretic at the Council of Nicea in 325, for holding views differing from what became the (still current) Nicene/Catholic Creed.[80] Nevertheless, his views were highly influential. In the first instance, the children of Constantine (Constantine II (316–340) and Constans (323–350)) almost came into military conflict over their differences about Arianism. Despite this near clash, within the Byzantine Empire the Arians were slowly rooted out and their wealth confiscated. Although many of the adherents of this faith were killed or made destitute in the process, the suppression of this heresy did not involve outright warfare.[81]

Outside the Empire, the situation was harder to control. This was because the German tribes of the Vandals and the Goths were both sympathetic to the Christian teaching of Arius, although the orthodox Christian Church (the Catholics, claiming both universality and direct lineage to Christ) were not. Whilst some of the leaders of these groups, such as Alaric, were relatively tolerant of the opposing Nicene Creed, others, like Geiseric, were not, and were more forthright and discriminatory (although not to the point of military justification) in their pursuit of the primacy of Arianism over the Nicene Creed. The Ostrogoth king, Theodoric (471–526), despite showing a tolerance towards Jews, became increasingly intolerant of the Nicene world view, going so far as to execute one of the most notable theologian-philosophers of the age – Boethius (480–525).[82]

The Franks, and especially Clovis (466–511), were happy to fight for the (Catholic) Christian God against heretics, as they believed that God gave them military victories. Thus, when Clovis went to war against the Arian Visigoths, he justified the war as being fought for religion, to free Gaul from Arian heretics. He addressed his people in the following terms: 'I take it very hard that these Arians hold part of Gaul. Let us go with God's help and conquer them and bring the land under our control.'[83] When Clovis later saw smoke rising from the churches of his enemy, he took it as a sign of God's support. This type of military pressure on the borders of Visigoth Spain was also replicated inside its borders. A civil war broke out a little later against the Arians when

[80] 'We believe in one God . . . and one Lord Jesus Christ . . . that is of the substance of the father . . .'. The Nicene Creed can be found in Schaff, P (ed) (1976) *A Select Library of Nicene and Post Nicene Fathers of the Christian Church*, Vol 2 (Michigan, Grand Rapids) 10–12.

[81] Ayerst, D (ed) (1971) *Records of Christianity*, Vol II (Oxford, Blackwell) 83–84.

[82] See the 'Policies of Theodoric the Ostrogoth' reprinted in Cantor, N (ed) (1963) *The Medieval World 300–1300* (NYC, Macmillan) 76.

[83] Gregory of Tours, *History of the Franks* trans Thorpe, L (1974) Vol II (Baltimore, Penguin) 27, 30, 31. Also Davies, N (2011) *Vanished Kingdoms: The History of Half Forgotten Europe* (London, Penguin) 24–26.

a Catholic community tried to break free – just before King Leoviglid adopted Catholicism and abjured the Arian faith in the year 580.[84]

The most notable opponents of the Arians, the Byzantines, did not use their religious differences as the primary justification for their conflicts, although some of their foremost leaders, like Justinian (482–565), were not shy to utilise them when to their advantage. Thus, when arguing why it was necessary to invade and retake North Africa from the Arian Vandals, he would cite dreams in which God commanded him to go to war in this area because it was necessary to 'release the Christians . . . from the Usurpers'.[85] He would also subsequently attribute his victories to the active support of the Catholic God who abjured the administration of the Arian Christians. Similarly, when Justinian invaded Italy with the goal of pushing the Arian Ostrogoths out of the formerly Byzantine territories, he appealed to the Franks to help him on account of their shared 'orthodox faith, which rejects the opinion of the Arians'.[86]

The Paulicians were a second Christian group that ran into military conflict with the orthodox position. This group, who rejected the Old Testament and many parts of Catholicism, flourished for over 200 years between 650 and 870. Both the founder and the subsequent leader of the sect were killed on the orders of the Byzantine state, but the religion continued to grow in strength until it was favourably received by Leo the Isaurian (685–741). Later emperors, such as Nikephorus (802–811), tolerated their beliefs, on condition that they were willing to serve the Empire, but had them moved to Armenia and other parts of the eastern frontier. This tolerance lasted as long as the life of the emperor. Whilst some emperors were mildly intolerant, others were markedly so. This was most obvious from 856 onwards under the reigns of Leo V and Michael III, when military expeditions were sent to set the East in order – the people had to renounce their faith or be killed. In the last great battle of the conflict in 872, some 100,000 people were reported to have perished, by hanging, drowning, the sword and even crucifixion. Because of this persecution, many Paulicians fled into Muslim territories and joined forces with the Muslims in fighting the Byzantines. Whilst some eventually returned to Byzantine territories and continued to exist in scattered communities experiencing periods of freedom and of persecution, by the end of the tenth century they had all but disappeared.[87]

[84] Jordanes, *The Origins and Deeds of the Goths* trans Miero, C (2009 reprint of 1910 edn) (London, Theophania) LX; John of Biclaro, *Chronicle* reprinted in Wolf, K trans (1999) *Conquerors and Chroniclers of Early Medieval Spain* (Liverpool, Liverpool University Press) 68. Also Isidore of Seville, *History of the Kings of the Goths*, also in Wolf at 101; Gregory of Tours, *History of the Franks* trans Thorpe, L (1974) (Baltimore, Penguin) II:7. See the Donatist Sermon reprinted in Rosenwein, B (ed) (2006) *Reading the Middle Ages: Sources from Europe, Byzantium and the Islamic World* (Ontario, Broadview) 17–18; Gwatkin, H (ed) (1967) *The Cambridge Medieval History: The Rise of the Saracens and the Foundation of the Western Empire*, Vol II (Cambridge, Cambridge University Press) 169; Gibbon, E (1926 edn) *The Decline and Fall of the Roman Empire*, Vol IV (London, Methuen) 88–90.

[85] *The Chronicles of Theophanes Confessor* trans Mango, C (2006) (Oxford, Clarendon Press) 288; Wallace-Hadrill, J (1962) *The Barbarian West: The Early Middle Ages AD 400–1000* (NYC, Harper) 36–41; Gibbon, E (1926 edn) *The Decline and Fall of the Roman Empire*, Vol V (London, Methuen) 143–44.

[86] Procopius, *History of the Wars* trans Dewing, H (1919) (Massachusetts, Harvard University Press) Book V:5.

[87] Hastings, J (1972) *Encyclopedia of Religion and Ethics*, Vol IX (NYC, Scribner) 665–70; Gibbon, E (1926 edn) *The Decline and Fall of the Roman Empire*, Vol VI (London, Methuen) 120–26; Norwich, J (1992) *Byzantium: The Apogee.* (NYC, Knopf) 57–58; Hussey, J (1966) *The Cambridge Medieval History: The Byzantine Empire*, Vol IV(1) (Cambridge, Cambridge University Press) 119–22, 713–15.

B. Jews

As the people of the Old Testament, the Jews acquired a significance in Christian theology and subsequent management of the state which allowed them to be tolerated – although they were discriminated against as second-class citizens. This differed from the fate that befell the theologically-related Samaritans, 20,000 of whom were killed or taken into slavery during and after the failed uprisings in Jerusalem at the end of the fifth century. For the Jews who did not physically rebel, the situation was different. After an initial period in which Christians who destroyed synagogues were not punished because they were 'stirred by wrong done to God or insult offered to the Church',[88] the situation stabilised and laws were passed to prevent synagogues from being burnt down or converted into churches. However, although old synagogues could be renovated, new synagogues could not be built. Jews were also excluded from both the armed forces and the civil bureaucracy, and were subject to a strong strain of anti-Semitic writings from the year 400 onwards.[89]

In time, the discrimination increased in intensity. The most obvious example was the enforced baptism of Jews (who were enslaved if they refused) – this was a pattern which emerged in Byzantium, Spain and France from the fifth century onwards. Such oppressive practices often led Jewish communities to be sympathetic to new rulers, be they Persian or Muslim. This lack of resistance to, if not actual support for, incoming overlords always ended badly for any Jewish populations that were subsequently recaptured. Heraclius (575–641) allowed a massacre of Jews around Jerusalem and the mountains of Galilee to take place as his forces regained the area. Similarly, in 694, when the Jewish population in Spain was accused of plotting with Muslims against Christians, all Jews within the area were reduced to slavery and had their goods confiscated.[90]

[88] For the history of the Callinicum affair, see Maas, M (ed) (2010) *Readings in Late Antiquity: A Sourcebook* (London, Routledge) 205–206. See the correspondence between Theodosius and Ambrose, reprinted in Ayerst, D (ed) (1971) *Records of Christianity*, Vol I (Oxford, Blackwell) 220–22; Gibbon, E (1926 edn) *The Decline and Fall of the Roman Empire*, Vol V (London, Methuen) 143–44.

[89] See the Theodosian Code, sections 16.8, 16.9, 3.7, 16.8, 2.1; Maas, M (ed) *Readings in Late Antiquity: A Sourcebook* (London, Routledge) 200–206; Sypeck, J (2006) *Becoming Charlemagne: Europe, Baghdad and the Empires of AD 800* (NYC, Harper) 91–96; Ayerst, D (ed) (1971) *Records of Christianity*, Vol II (Oxford, Blackwell) 257–58; *The Chronicles of Theophanes Confessor* trans Mango, C (2006) (Oxford, Clarendon Press) 459, 554; Kaegi, W (2000) *Byzantium and the Early Islamic Conquests* (Cambridge, Cambridge University Press) 220–25.

[90] Marcus, J (ed) (1938) *The Jew in the Medieval World: A Sourcebook* (New York, Jewish Publication Society) 20–23; Gwatkin, H (ed) (1967) *The Cambridge Medieval History: The Rise of the Saracens and the Foundation of the Western Empire*, Vol II (Cambridge, Cambridge University Press) 174, 181; Pirenne, H (1939) *Mohammed and Charlemagne* (London, Allen and Unwin) 82–85; Kaegi, W (2007) *Heraclius: Emperor of Byzantine* (Cambridge, Cambridge University Press) 204–205, 216–17; Kaegi, W (2000) *Byzantium and the Early Islamic Conquests* (Cambridge, Cambridge University Press) 116–18; anon 'The Chronicle of 754' reprinted in trans Wolf, K (1999) *Conquerors and Chroniclers of Early Medieval Spain* (Liverpool, Liverpool University Press) 115; Ayerst, D (ed) (1971) *Records of Christianity*, Vol II (Oxford, Blackwell) 258–60.

C. Pagans

Inside the Roman Empire, discriminatory laws against pagans were introduced after the death of Constantine. The only emperor to attempt to prevent favouritism towards Christianity after this point was Julian (331–363), who tried to return to the principle of equal freedom for all religions. This lasted only as long as Julian's reign. Under the reign of Theodosius (347–395), Nicene/Catholic Christianity became the state religion in 380, thus ending any form of state support – or toleration – for other forms of worship. Theodosius enforced this supremacy in 394 at the battle of Frigidus, when he saw off a challenge from Eugenius (d 394), who had seised power in Rome and had attempted to reinstate the traditional pagan rituals. Thereafter, all such rituals, from the ancient Olympic games through to gladiator contests, were ended. Theodosius' famous code contains no fewer than 66 laws directed against heretics. These included denial of freedom of assembly, confiscation of their property, prohibition of the appointment of pagan officials, burning of their books and even a prohibition against pagans burning incense or candles. Theodosius also ordered the destruction of the *Serapeum* (a famous Hellenistic/Egyptian religious temple). Thereafter, many pagan places of worship, practices and people, were eradicated from the Empire. Even the famous schools of philosophy within Athens were caught up in these practices, with the philosophers fleeing from the influence of Byzantium to the relative safety of Persia. When the philosophers decided to return home, Justinian promised that they could live in peace in their homeland 'without being compelled to alter their traditional beliefs or to accept any view which did not coincide with them'.[91] It is not known whether this promise was kept, as there was no resurgence of philosophy in Athens because all of the independent schools/universities which were not in Christian hands had been closed down in 529.[92]

Outside the Empire, the eradication of paganism occurred more slowly. This was because the spread of Christianity was not seamless, and a number of communities did not want it introduced. In at least two instances in the fourth century, a number of Germanic tribes expelled Roman missionaries from their territory. The first occurrence, in 348, passed without incident; in the second, in 369, a number of Christians were martyred in the process. Although not used as a pretext for war, such acts were not easily forgotten, although retribution could not be gained until the successor states emerged from the wreckage of the western side of the Roman Empire. At this point, paganism was eliminated by the use of military, rather than legal, force.[93]

[91] Justinian, as noted in Holland, T (2012) *In the Shadow of the Sword* (NYC, Brown) 193. For the attack on paganism within Christendom, see Maas, M (ed) (2010) *Readings in Late Antiquity: A Sourcebook.* (London, Routledge) 186–91, 195–96; Carlyle, A (1936) *A History of Medieval Political Theory in the West: The Second Century to the Ninth*, Vol 1 (London, Blackwood) 178–81; Ayerst D (ed) (1971) *Records of Christianity*, Vol I (Oxford, Blackwell) 227; Gibbon, E (1926 edn) *The Decline and Fall of the Roman Empire*, Vol III Bury, J (ed) (London, Methuen) 205–14.

[92] See Geanakoplos, D (ed) (1986) *Byzantium: A Sourcebook on Church, Society and Civilisation Seen Through Contemporary Eyes* (Chicago, Chicago University Press) 127–28. The works of Julian in this area are reprinted in Ayerst, D (ed) (1971) *Records of Christianity*, Vol I (Oxford, Blackwell) 178–79. The influence of Justinian in this area is also seen in the *Records of Christianity*, Vol II 83–85.

[93] Heather, P (2009) *Empires and Barbarians: Migration, Development and the Birth of Europe* (London, Pan) 60.

In the case of Britain, although the Romans left in 410 CE, Christianity survived. It appears that most, if not all, of the seven kingdoms of England were Christian by the seventh century. Before this point, some of the early kings, such as Vortigern (fifth century), used imported Christian Irish forces to combat heretics. This was consistent with wars of religion in Ireland being traceable to the same period. For some historians, such as Bede (672–735), the victories that were achieved, such as at the Battle of Mount Badon in the Briton–English war around 500, were directly attributable to the fact that the Britons had become Christian. It was, Bede asserted, as if 'Christ Himself commanded in their camp'.[94] For Bede, good Christian kings, replete in their faith, could not fail to win and increase the size of their kingdoms (of which property would then go to the Church and its followers), for their wars against non-Christians, or lapsed Christians, were legitimate. They were deemed legitimate if built around considerations such as what King Oswald (604–642) called 'a just war for the safety of our nation'.[95] A similar pattern was evident in Spain, where some scholars recorded the Christian God actually intervening in some battles to protect his people, whilst others, such as Isodore (560–636), suggested that the new Catholic kings 'gloriously waged war against hostile people'. Isodore added that 'the name of the King is held by doing right, by sinning, it is lost'.[96] This approach was consistent with what became a dominant theme of the age, best exemplified by Sedulius Scottus (c 850) that religious faith was the foremost weapon with which to defeat enemies in time of war.[97]

The wars of the Franks against their pagan neighbours to their north and east, the Saxons, also included a strong religious element. Frankish claims for tribute from some of the adjoining Saxon lands dated back at least a century to the high Merovingian era, and continued thereafter. Charles Martel (686–741) waged war in Saxony in 718, 720, 724, 728 and 738. These wars were not of conquest, unlike the wars of Charlemagne (742–814) in the same areas, which raged from 772 until 804. Charlemagne was intent on safeguarding border churches and monasteries while further spreading Christianity. He also wished to punish the pagans who had assassinated key Christian missionaries of the time, such as Boniface (680–755), who was martyred whilst attempting to spread Christianity in Frisia (in modern-day Germany/Netherlands). According to Einhard (775–840), 'no war ever undertaken by the Frankish people was more prolonged, more full of atrocities or more demanding of effort'.[98] This assertion was made after angels were reported to have been seen on the battlefield helping secure victory for the forces

[94] Bede, *The Ecclesiastical History of the English Nation* trans Jane, L (1910 edn) (London, Dent) I.20, II:6, 14, 15, III:4, 7, 21, 22; IV:13; Collingwood, R (1958) *Roman Britain and the English Settlements* (Oxford, Oxford University Press) 291–301, 422–23; Morris, J (2004) *The Age of Arthur: A History of the British Isles* (London, Phoenix) 64–67, 158–59.

[95] Bede, *The Ecclesiastical History of the English Nation*, trans Jane, L (1910 edn) (London, Dent) III:1 and 2, I:32, II:20, III:18–24.

[96] Isidore of Seville, *Etymologies* IX:iii. See also *History of the Kings of the Goths* reprinted in trans Wolf, K (1999) *Conquerors and Chroniclers of Early Medieval Spain* (Liverpool, Liverpool University Press) 101–103; John of Biclaro, *Chronicle* reprinted in trans Wolf, K (1999) *Conquerors and Chroniclers of Early Medieval Spain* (Liverpool, Liverpool University Press) 68, 70–71, 74–75.

[97] Sedulius Scottus, *On Christian Rulers and the Poems* trans Doyle, E (1906) (NYC, Medieval Texts) 69–73.

[98] Thorpe, L (ed) (1969) *Einhard and Notker the Stammerer: Two Lives of Charlemagne* (London, Penguin) 61; Sypeck, J (2006) *Becoming Charlemagne: Europe, Baghdad and the Empires of AD 800* (NYC, Harper) 14–16.

of Charlemagne. To ensure that the uprisings were never repeated, Charlemagne had 4,500 Saxons decapitated on a single day in 782 when they refused to convert to Christianity. Conversion to Christianity and the renunciation of Saxon national ceremonies was a key part of the subsequent peace treaty. Although the Saxons agreed to baptism, harsh new laws followed to ensure that there were no relapses to paganism. Saxons were forbidden to gather in public, and paganism – in fact, any visible contempt for Christian customs – carried a death sentence.[99]

In other instances, religious victory was achieved at the conclusion of military campaigns through a peace treaty which required the leader of the opposition to adopt Christianity. This requirement was evident in a number of treaties or peace settlements from the end of the eighth century onwards. Some of the Avar leaders seem to have accepted baptism after their defeat by Frankish forces in 796. A similar pattern occurred with the Vikings from the ninth century onwards. This was a rather ironic situation, as it was the conversion to Christianity of Harold Bluetooth (932–986), the king of both Norway and Denmark, (rather than the worship of their traditional pagan gods) that forced many of the Northmen to abandon their country and invade other parts of Europe. King Olaf Trygveson (r 995–1000) of Norway went a step further, forcing Christianity upon his chiefs by the sword. With such foundation, great Viking leaders, such as Cnut (985–1035), could go on to promise to 'honour one God and steadfastly hold one Christian faith . . . and diligently avoid every heathen practice'.[100]

There was a similar pattern in the Byzantine's dealings in the ninth and tenth centuries with both the Bulgars and the Rus. In the latter case, in around 955 Princess Olga of Kiev (890–969) was probably the first Rus of noble status to be converted to the Orthodox Christian faith. This was followed by the conversion of Vladimir the Great (958–1015) in about 988 – as part of a peace deal with Byzantium. In an age and place where freedom of religion was not a recognised concept, Vladimir had all of the people in his Kievan state baptised in the Dnieper river.[101] Likewise, within five years of their defeat by the Germans at Lechfeld, the Magyars accepted the Christian Stephen

[99] The Capitulary of Paderborn reprinted in Loyn, H (ed) (1975) *The Reign of Charlemagne: Documents on Carolingian Government and Administration* (London, Edward Arnold) 51–52. See also Thorpe, L (ed) (1969) *Einhard and Notker the Stammerer: Two Lives of Charlemagne* (London, Penguin) 63; Sypeck, J (2006) *Becoming Charlemagne: Europe, Baghdad and the Empires of AD 800* (NYC, Harper) 55–58; Costambey, M (2012) *The Carolingian World* (Cambridge, Cambridge University Press) 48–50, 72–75; Ayerst, D (ed) (1971) *Records of Christianity*, Vol II (Oxford, Blackwell) 60–63.

[100] The Laws of Cnut reprinted in Baker, D (ed) (1982) *The Early Middle Ages* 33, 35 and 67; The 911 Treaty of St Clair-Sur-Epte reprinted in Laffan, R (ed) (1929) *Select Historical Documents 800–1492* (New York, Holt) 13; Abels, R (1998) *Alfred the Great: War, Kingship and Culture in Anglo-Saxon England* (London, Longman) 29, 112–15, 136, 164–65; Gwatkin, H (ed) (963) *The Cambridge Medieval History: Germany and the Western Empire*, Vol III (Cambridge) 59–62; Rosenwein, B (ed) (2006) *Reading the Middle Ages: Sources from Europe, Byzantium and the Islamic World* (Ontario, Broadview) 266–67; Brink, S (2012) *The Viking World* (London, Routledge) 230–32.

[101] Mango, C (1994). *Byzantium: The Empire of the New Rome* (London, Paladin) 55; Moss, W (2005) *A History of Russia* (London, Anthem) 28–30, 42–46; Luttwak, E (2009) *The Grand Strategy of the Byzantine Empire* (London, Harvard University Press) 113, 120–23, 156; Heather, P (2009) *Empires and Barbarians: Migration, Development and the Birth of Europe* (London, Pan) 465; Costambey, M (2012) *The Carolingian World* (Cambridge, Cambridge University Press) 72–73; 'Letter to the Bulgar Khan' reprinted in Rosenwein, B (ed) (2006) *Reading the Middle Ages: Sources from Europe, Byzantium and the Islamic World* (Ontario, Broadview) 143–47; Norwich, J (2011) *Absolute Monarchs: A History of the Papacy* (NYC, Random House) 74–76; Norwich, J (1992) *Byzantium: The Apogee* (NYC, Knopf) 8–13; Grant, R (2005) *Battle* (London, Dorling Kindersley) 65.

(967–1038) as the king of Hungary, and his kingship was legitimised by Pope Sylvester II (946–1003) in the year 1000.[102]

7. THE RISE OF THE PAPACY AND THE EAST–WEST TENSION

In retrospect, it is surprising that debates on the theological differences between the eastern and western branches of the Holy Roman Empire did not result in violence before the year 1000. The relationship between the two branches was already worsening by the end of the fifth century, with squabbles over the election of popes, emperors and patriarchs, and, later, debates over which Church had primacy. The debate intensified in the following centuries, especially when the Byzantine Emperor Leo III (685–741) sought to prohibit the worship of religious icons within his realm. This decision provoked near civil war in parts of his own empire (in Greece and Italy) when subjects rebelled. The rebellions followed acts of state which decreed punishments for those who defied the ruling, including mutilation, flogging, exile and/or execution of leading iconophiles. Within a short period of time this policy became a catalyst for a dispute between Constantine V (718–775) and his brother-in-law, who became opposing contestants for the throne and adopted opposite sides on the question of the restoration of icons. Constantine, upon victory, emphasised his religious purity by reiterating the banning of icons and expanding the list of prohibited acts to include the burning of incense and the lighting of candles.[103]

The attack on icons also caused a rupture with the west, when councils under the guidance of Popes Gregory II (669–731) and Gregory III (d 741) anathematised and excommunicated the iconoclasts, thus effectively detaching the western side of the Empire from the east. Despite the renunciation of this policy by successive Byzantine leaders and the Acclamation of Orthodoxy in 843, an east–west breach remained. Thereafter, until the year 1000, the two sides broadly tolerated each other, albeit with some double-dealing and positioning for the acquisitions of allies and Byzantine territory.[104]

Although the east and the west, the two major sides of the Christian faith, were expert at antagonising each other, actual conflict did not occur, probably because the western branch had nothing to fight with (or, at least, did not have armies to fight its part), until towards the end of the ninth century. It took several centuries of hard work to reach this point during which time the papacy had to learn how to control and manipulate kings to achieve its goal. This process began in the west with the rise of the

[102] The Grant of the Kingdom of Hungary reprinted in Laffan, R (ed) (1929) *Select Historical Documents: 800–1492* (New York, Holt) 16–18; Norwich, J (2011) *Absolute Monarchs: A History of the Papacy* (London, Random) 92.

[103] Hussey, J (ed) (1966) *The Cambridge Medieval History: The Byzantine Empire*, Vol IV(1) (Cambridge, Cambridge University Press) 65–72, 79–81; Pirenne, H (1935) *Mohammed and Charlemagne* (London, Allen and Unwin) 213–16, 485–88.

[104] The Acclamation of Orthodoxy reprinted in Geanakoplos, D (ed) (1986) *Byzantium: A Sourcebook on Church, Society and Civilisation Seen Through Contemporary Eyes* (Chicago, Chicago University Press) 115, 152–57; Rosenwein, B (ed) (2006) *Reading the Middle Ages: Sources from Europe, Byzantium and the Islamic World* (Ontario, Broadview) 81.

Merovingian kingdom, and one man in particular – Charles Martel. Martel was of particular interest to the papacy because of his defeat of the advancing Muslim armies at the Battle of Poiters in 732, which left 10,000 invaders dead on the field, a mere 180 miles from Paris. Consequently, Pope Gregory II came to recognise Martel as his paramount defender. This recognition coincided with the fact that when Rome was looted by the Lombards in 739, it was clear that neither the forces that the pope could scrape together, nor the supplementary efforts of Byzantium, were sufficient to defend the western church. Accordingly, the pope asked Martel to abandon his traditional alliance with the Lombards, and to help secure the Italian political boundaries to the satisfaction of the papacy, which Martel duly did.[105]

His reward was approval by Pope Zachary (679–752) for the succession of his son, Pippin the Younger (714–768), to the throne of the Franks on the death of his father. Two years later, the following pope, Stephen II (715–757), travelled to Paris to anoint Pippin in his new position. To further cement the relationship, Stephen II told him 'be sure that by the battle you fight for the Church [of St Peter], your spiritual mother, the Prince of the Apostles will remit your sins'.[106] Pippin responded as expected, going to war against the Lombard king Aistulf (d 756), forcing the Lombards to return land they had 'illegally' seised from the Church and to formally recognise the Pippin as overlord. Pippin followed this up with his *Donations* in 754 and 756, which provided the legal basis for organising the papal states and inaugurated papal temporal rule over civil authorities. This situation allowed the pope to reign for the first time as a temporal ruler, exercising effective sovereignty – in essence – independent from Byzantium. When the Lombards rebelled again, going so far as to capture Rome in 772, Pepin's successor – Charlemagne – continued the partnership his father had created with the papacy, and entered Italy and conquered the Lombards. Charlemagne had no intention of allowing the situation to recur, and moved from being overlord of the Lombards to taking complete control and becoming their king. Charlemagne's assumption of the title 'King of the Lombards' (*rex langobardorum*) in the summer of 774 was an act without parallel. No west European king had taken another's kingdom and title by force for over 200 years. The papacy classified this as a just war, absolving Charlemagne and his armies from the bloodshed that resulted from this war and his other battles against pagans elsewhere.[107]

Charlemagne did not subordinate himself to the pontiff as Pippin had done earlier. In 796, the new pope, Leo III (715–816), sent Charlemagne gifts that included the

[105] Norwich, J (2011) *Absolute Monarchs: A History of the Papacy* (NYC, Random House) 25–26, 30–35, 45, 52–53; Costambey, M (2012) *The Carolingian World* (Cambridge, Cambridge University Press) 60–63. For the figures, see Grant, R (2011) *1001 Battles that Changed the Course of History* (London, Penguin) 116.

[106] Stephen II noted in Contamine, P (1984) *War in the Middle Ages* (Oxford, Blackmore) 270.

[107] Thorpe, L (ed) (1969) *Einhard and Notker the Stammerer: Two Lives of Charlemagne* (London, Penguin) 160–62. The Annals of Lorch reprinted in Oliver, J (ed) (1905) *A Source Book for Medieval History* (New York, Scribners) 37–38; Norwich, J (2011) *Absolute Monarchs: A History of the Papacy* (NYC, Random House) 52–56; Pirenne, H (1935) *Mohammed and Charlemagne* (London, Allen and Unwin) 216, 228–32; Costambey, M (2012) *The Carolingian World* (Cambridge, Cambridge University Press) 65–69; Gwatkin, H (ed) (1967) *The Cambridge Medieval History: The Rise of the Saracens and the Foundation of the Western Empire*, Vol II (Cambridge, Cambridge University Press) 216, 586–87; Halsall, G (2003) *Warfare and Society in the Barbarian West, 450–900* (London, Routledge) 18, 89, 110–11, 144–45; Sypeck, J (2006) *Becoming Charlemagne: Europe, Baghdad and the Empires of AD 800* (NYC, Harper) 19–21.

symbolic keys to the tomb of Saint Peter and the banner of the city of Rome. Charlemagne, sending back gifts of a portion of treasure he had recently taken, wrote to the new pope that he wished to reaffirm the bonds of friendship between the papacy and the Franks, and promised that the papacy would 'always, by God's gift, be defended by our devotion'. Charlemagne then went one step further, changing the terms of the friendship, linking the defence of the Church with acceptance from Leo that he was the subordinate of Charlemagne. This subordination was important as Charlemagne saw himself as 'lord and father, king and priest, chief and guide to all Christians'.[108] Charlemagne went on to explain their different roles:

> It is for us, in accordance with the help of divine goodness, outwardly to defend by force or arms the Holy Church of Christ in all places from the incursions of pagans and the ravages of infidels, and inwardly to fortify her with our confession of the Catholic faith. It is for you, most holy father, reigning your hands to God with Moses, to aid our armies, to the end that with you as intercessor with God [so that we] in all places have the victory over the enemies of its holy name, and that the name of Our Lord Jesus Christ may be renowned throughout the world.[109]

This configuration of papal interest and policy was demonstrated on Christmas Day in the year 800, one year after the people of Rome had forced Leo III from the city due to a number of alleged crimes and the forces of Charlemagne had intervened to reinstate him. Clearly beholden to Charlemagne, Leo then went to great lengths to increase Charlemagne's status by crowning him 'Roman Emperor'. At the point of coronation, the congregation in one voice exclaimed three times: 'To Charlemagne, pious Augustus crowned by God, great and peaceful emperor, life and victory.'[110] Then Leo knelt before the new emperor – just as the patriarch of Constantinople would have done when conferring power on an emperor in Byzantium. In western eyes, the (entire) empire had now been transferred to the Franks by the authority of the pope. Although this act bestowed a great honour on Charlemagne, it conferred an even greater one on the papacy – namely, the right to appoint, and to invest with crown and sceptre, the Emperor of the Romans. Here was something revolutionary. No pontiff had ever claimed such a privilege, which not only established the imperial crown as his own personal gift but simultaneously granted himself implicit superiority over the emperor whom he had created.[111]

Leo justified this act because the Roman throne was empty because it lacked a male occupant (as Irene (752–803) was governing Byzantium at the time). To the Byzantines, Leo's claims appeared ridiculous and were in direct conflict with the fundamental

[108] Charlemagne, as noted in Pirenne, H (1935) *Mohammed and Charlemagne* (London, Allen and Unwin) 230.

[109] Letter of Charles the Great to Pope Leo III, 796 reprinted in Loyn, H (ed) (1975) *The Reign of Charlemagne: Documents on Carolingian Government and Administration* (London, Edward Arnold) 117–19. See also Cantor, N (ed) (1963) *The Medieval World 300–1300* (NYC, Macmillan) 145–46.

[110] The chant of the coronation, as noted in Sypeck, J (2006) *Becoming Charlemagne: Europe, Baghdad and the Empires of AD 800* (NYC, Harper) 152. Also Ayerst, D (ed) (1971) *Records of Christianity*, Vol II (Blackwell, Oxford) 287–88.

[111] Wright, R (1930) *Medieval Internationalism: The Contributions of the Medieval Church to International Law and Peace* (London, Norgate) 34–51; Norwich, J (2011) *Absolute Monarchs: A History of the Papacy* (NYC, Random House) 57.

Byzantine belief in the inalienable unity of the Roman Empire. Although Irene tried (but failed) to negotiate her way through the situation by marrying herself to Charlemagne or her children to those of Charlemagne, it was seen as a serious insult to both Byzantium and the Eastern Orthodox Church. However, it was an insult they learnt to live with following Charlemagne's conquests in Italy, and the subsequent peace treaty of 811 between the Franks and Byzantium which recognised, inter alia, the division of eastern and western Christendom. It was agreed that Venice, Istria, the Dalmatian coast and South Italy would be assigned to the east, whilst Ravena, Pentapolis and Rome were placed within the western realm. This split sovereignty between east and west. The difficulty posed by the fact that Venice and southern Italy had been conquered and taken from Byzantium by the forces of Charlemagne in the recent conflict was resolved with their return on the condition of the payment of an annual tribute. An additional cost to the Byzantines was their recognition (after years of denying that this was possible) of Charlemagne's title of Emperor of the West. In subsequent allegiances, although the two sides watched each other cautiously, if any of their proxies changed allegiance, war would be deemed justified. For example, when Bulgaria swapped from the Orthodox Christianity offered by Byzantium to the Catholic type offered by Rome, the Byzantine armies invaded and forced a reconversion.[112]

The question of whether emperor or the pope had primacy was discussed in the teachings of Ambrose and the beliefs of Gelasius I (r 492–496). In both cases, the men of religion argued that because the pope would, on Judgement Day, have to answer for the sins of all, including the king, on divine affairs, all kings had to bow their head.[113] The fuller theological theory, as described by Hincmar (806–882), was that 'the dignity of the pontiffs is above that of the kings: for the kings are consecrated by pontiffs, while the pontiffs cannot be consecrated by kings'.[114] The political reality was somewhat different. When emperors felt strong, they dispensed with the legitimisation of the pope. For example, when Charlemagne passed the imperial crown to his son, he did so himself, without the involvement of the pope. The strength of the emperor increased as the papacy appeared to go to great lengths to discredit itself, beginning at the turn of the ninth century, with the first recorded papal assassination (of John VIII (d 882)) by priests. This was followed by a succession of men, ranging from nobles to clerics, seising power by deposing or murdering the pontiffs. Those murdered included Stephen VI (d 897), Leo V (d 903) and possibly Christopher (d 911). Unsurprisingly, such problems at the head of the Church were replicated many times over at the local and national levels, as problems of simony and other forms of corruption within the Church multiplied during the tenth century. This was particularly apparent with the monarchies' control of the appointment of bishops, where the consistent trend throughout Europe was to move away from elective processes within the community

[112] The 811 Treaty Between Charlemagne and Michael I Rangabe reprinted in Axelrod, A (ed) (2001) *Encyclopedia of Historical Treaties and Alliances*, Vol I (NYC, Facts on File) 14; Costambey, M (2012) *The Carolingian World* (Cambridge, Cambridge University Press) 165–68; Luttwak, E (2009) *The Grand Strategy of the Byzantine Empire* (London, Harvard University Press) 140–42, 166–70.

[113] For Ambrose and Gelasius, see Cantor, N (ed) (1963) *The Medieval World 300–1300* (NYC, Macmillan) 15, 96–97.

[114] Hincmar, noted in Pirenne, H (1939) *Mohammed and Charlemagne* (London, Allen and Unwin) 269.

and/or the Church, to hand-picked men, installed at the behest of the crown. This came about despite a succession of decrees in the eighth and ninth centuries that had anathematised anyone contesting an election among priests, prelates and the whole clergy of the Roman Church.[115]

At the highest level, these situations became increasingly messy as various popes or papal candidates requested outside assistance to enforce their authority and/or claims – promising divine favour to their benefactor as well as appropriate titles, such as emperor. Having been granted such titles, these benefactors developed a personal interest in that pope staying in place, and would often have to battle into Rome to ensure his stability. This pattern began with Popes Stephen V (d 891), Formosus (d 896) and John X (d 928) – and with those seeking national and imperial honours, notably Arnulf (850–899) and then Berengar I (845–924). The last decades of the 900s then repeated the pattern, with Otto the Great (912–973) having to go under the weight of arms to Rome three times to ensure that the popes that he approved of were not removed from office. His successors, Otto II (955–983) and Otto III (980–1002), were locked into the same cycle, having to ensure that the man who crowned them Emperor of the Holy Roman Empire was not toppled.[116]

8. THE RELIGIOUS QUESTION BETWEEN ROME AND PERSIA

The Christian Roman Emperor Constantine inherited Rome's wars with Persia, which reached back hundreds of years. The difference was that now there was an additional religious context to the relationship between Rome and Persia. The background to the clashes during this period was the conversion to Christianity of Armenia, Mesopotamia and the land around modern-day Georgia. These were the traditional areas of conflict between the two empires. These lands, which also contained large numbers of Zoroastrians, were of direct concern to Persia. In 334, the Persian leader, Shapur (309–379), who was suffering a loss of trade in raw materials provided by Rome to manufacture weapons, sent troops into Armenia to remove the Christian king and install a Zoroastrian in his place. Constantine wrote to Shapur to make clear that he was in the business of disposing of tyrants, wherever they were, in the service of the Christian God. He also recorded his 'anxiety for the general welfare of that country also, as one whose aim it was to care for all alike in every nation'.[117] This anxiety, essentially based on the considerations of Christians in a non-Christian area, devolved into at least nine major recorded battles during the periods 337 to 350 and 358 to 363.

[115] Gwatkin, H (ed) (1963) *The Cambridge Medieval History: Germany and the Western Empire*, Vol III (Cambridge, Cambridge University Press) 14–20; Tanner, J (ed) (1957) *The Cambridge Medieval History: Contest of Empire and Papacy*, Vol V (Cambridge, Cambridge University Press) 4–7, 36; Norwich, J (2011) *Absolute Monarchs: A History of the Papacy* (NYC, Random House) 76–80.

[116] Norwich, J (2011) *Absolute Monarchs: A History of the Papacy* (London, Random) 81–84, 89; Ayerst, D (ed) (1971) *Records of Christianity*, Vol II (Oxford, Blackwell) 290–95.

[117] Eusebius, *The Life of the Blessed Emperor Constantine*, Vol 8 trans anon (2009 reprint of 1854 edn) (London, Bagster, Christian Roman Empire Series) III:8 and III:9.

These wars of the fathers then became the wars of the sons, involving Constantius (317–361) and Shapur II (309–379).[118]

Although some successive Roman emperors who were not Christian, such as Julian, continued to battle Persia, as the decades passed and the Christian influence over the Roman Empire became more pronounced, the religious catalyst for the conflict with Persia came to the front. The primary solution for the problem in the areas of conflict involved both Persia and Rome adopting a neutral stance, allowing the locals in the disputed territories, such as Armenia, to select their own king. However, the superpowers continued to become involved whenever a king unsympathetic to their religion was installed. In the most obvious example, Shapur began enticing discontented Armenians to overthrow the (Christian) king, Arsakes II (d 367), and reintroduce Zoroastrian orthodoxy back into Armenia. The Roman response (after they had initially left Asakes to face the Persian forces alone) was to support Arsakes's son. Such meddling by both sides resulted in further warfare, as a result of which Armenia fell squarely within the Persian realm of influence. Rather than perpetuate a perennial problem, Shapur III (r 383–388), simply partitioned Armenia in a treaty with Rome in 387. This treaty held until the war of 421 to 422, which was caused by the persecution of Christians by the Persian king Bahram V (r 421–438), who sought to uphold the traditional religion, causing many Christians to flee the Persian territory. This – in addition to concerns about holding some Roman civilians captive – allowed Theodoius II (401–450) to declare war. Although the war ended in stalemate, the peace treaty that followed was unique as it recorded not only promises not to accept defectors from each other's territory, but also agreement on allowing freedom of religion in the disputed provinces.[119]

The great wars between Byzantium and Persia in the sixth century demonstrated that a lasting reconciliation between the two sides was very hard to maintain. The wars which took up the first decades of the century revolved around many issues, involving allegiances with third parties, tribute, militarisation and the attempts of some provinces to swap sides. Religion does not appear to have been a driving concern externally, although it was clearly gaining power internally. In Persia, interest in religion was increasing, following a civil war over questions of religious orthodoxy, and the completion of the first canon of Zoroastrianism around the middle of the sixth century. In terms of external relationships, for example in the peace treaty of 561 with Byzantium, it was a lesser issue. Nevertheless, the status of Christians in Persia was an outstanding matter of concern. In this regard, as part of the overall peace package, it was agreed that the Christians could build their churches and worship freely in accordance with their customs. This freedom appears to have been granted as part of a broader recognition of the importance of religious tolerance within the Persian Empire. Specifically:

[118] Hussey, J (ed) (1966) *The Cambridge Medieval History: The Byzantine Empire*, Vol IV(1) (Cambridge, Cambridge University Press) 595–601.

[119] See the Inscription of Kirdir reprinted in Maas, M (ed) (2010) *Readings in Late Antiquity: A Sourcebook* (London, Routledge) 334; Gwatkin, H (ed) *The Cambridge Medieval History. The Christian Roman Empire*, Vol 1 (Cambridge, Cambridge University Press) 240; Hussey, J (ed) (1966) *The Cambridge Medieval History: The Byzantine Empire*, Vol IV(1) (Cambridge, Cambridge University Press) 599–602.

> Even as our royal throne cannot stand upon its two legs without the back ones, so also our government cannot stand and be secure if we incense the Christians and adherents of other religions, who are not of our faith. Cease, therefore, to harass the Christians, but exert yourselves diligently in doing good works . . . [so that they] . . . feel themselves drawn to our religion.[120]

Whilst the Persians tried to practise tolerance within their realm, it was expected that, as the 561 treaty stipulated, the Christians in Persian territory would not seek to convert the followers of Zoroaster. This pattern, in which religion was a secondary consideration, reappeared when war broke out again in 572, as the traditionally-disputed territories of Armenia were again being pressured to swap sides. A further peace agreement in 591 reiterated the split of Armenia between Persia and Constantinople.[121]

Religion ceased to be a secondary consideration in the last war between Persia and Byzantium in which the Persians experienced unprecedented victories as the Byzantine armies virtually collapsed between 609 and 615. Starting out with victories in the territories of Armenia and Mesopotamia, the Persian forces advanced to a high-water mark that submerged the Caucasus, Syria, Palestine and Egypt. Whilst some regions and cities barely resisted the Persian forces, others, such as Jerusalem, were the subject of intense fighting and subsequent sack, resulting in the deaths of tens of thousands. It was at this point of crisis for Byzantium that the issue of religion came to the fore. Emperor Heraclius introduced a strongly religious element into the justification for continuing the fight. With his back against the wall, he told his army that it was their privilege to be the chosen instruments of God which would destroy the forces of the Antichrist. They were fighting not just for the empire but also for their faith. In galvanising his troops Heraclius argued:

> You see, O my brethren and children, how the enemies of God have trampled upon our land, have laid out cities to waste, have burnt our sanctuaries and have filled with the blood of murder the altars . . . Let us keep in mind the fear of God and fight to avenge the insult done to God. Let us stand bravely against the enemy who have inflicted many terrible calamities on the Christians. Let us respect the sovereign state of the Romans and oppose the enemy who are armed with impiety. Let us be inspired with faith that defeats murder . . . the danger is not without recompense; nay, it leads to the eternal life. Let us stand bravely, and the Lord our God will assist us and destroy the enemy.[122]

Although many of those conquered had not originally objected to the Persian invasion, they soon discovered that their new overlords were not as desirable as they expected. The occupied lands and peoples were diverse and more numerous than their Persian occupiers. The Persians themselves were over-extended and often lacked resources, direction and cohesiveness. There were also traditional religious tensions with Persian

[120] Letter from Hormizd IV (579–90) reprinted in Boyce, M (1990) *Zoroastrianism* (Chicago, University of Chicago Press) 115.

[121] See *The History of Menander the Guardsman* trans Blockley, R (Liverpool, Cairns) 75–77; Kaegi, W (2007) *Heraclius: Emperor of Byzantine* (Cambridge, Cambridge University Press) 65–70, 74–75, 77–79, 85; Boyce, M (1990) *Zoroastrianism* (Chicago, University of Chicago Press) 113–15.

[122] *The Chronicles of Theophanes Confessor* trans Mango, C (2006) (Oxford, Clarendon Press) 437, 439. See also Kaegi, W (2007) *Heraclius: Emperor of Byzantine* (Cambridge, Cambridge University Press) 146–47; Regan, G (2001) 'The First Crusader' in *BBC History* November 45–48.

Zoroastrianism, especially in the parts of the Byzantine Empire where there were zealous Christians. Such tensions were also reflected at the highest levels. When Heraclius sent out ambassadors seeking peace, Khosrau II (r 590–628), after boasting that the Christian God could not protect him or his possessions, replied: 'I shall not spare you until you renounce the Crucified one, whom you call God, and worship the sun.'[123] Such rhetoric only helped to inflame Heraclius, who marched out of Constantinople under the banner of Christ, and urged his soldiers to take revenge for the holy alters which had been profaned by those who worshipped Zoroaster. He galvanised his troops with speeches about fighting godless enemies who were attempting to destroy their faith and with the promise that God was on their side. Combining elements of revenge and religious and patriotic sentiment, he argued:

> My brothers, let us keep fear of God in mind and let us struggle to avenge the divine sacrilege. Let us stand courageously against the enemy who have perpetrated so many dreadful acts against Christians. Let us honour the independent empire of the Romans, and let us stand against the impiously armed enemy . . . Let us avenge the rape of our virgins . . . danger is not unrequited, but the way to eternal life. Let us stand courageously, and the Lord God will help us and will destroy our enemies.[124]

The results were staggering. Heraclius reclaimed many of the lost territories, before advancing deep into Persian lands, destroying a number of Persian palaces and threatening to attack the capital Ctesiphon. At this point, the Persian army overthrew Khosrau, in a coup led by his own son, Kavadh II (590–628). Kavadh II at once sued for peace, seeking to live 'in peace and love' with the Roman emperor and his empire.[125] Heraclius agreed and the subsequent peace treaty settled on, inter alia, the Persian withdrawal from all occupied Byzantine territories and a restoration to the borders agreed in the treaty of 591.[126] Although Persian and Byzantine soldiers stopped killing each other, it was a futile victory, for as a Persian envoy had warned, decades of conflict had reduced them both 'to a wretched and miserable condition'.[127] Kavadh II only survived a few more months and Persia descended into several years of further dynastic disputes, civil wars, economic decline, religious unrest and lack of control of its own provinces. The conditions were perfect for the germination of the new religion which would quickly bring an end to the Persian Empire.

[123] *The Chronicles of Theophanes Confessor* trans Mango, C (2006) (Oxford, Clarendon Press) 433. See also the Letter from Khosrau reprinted in Norwich, J (1988) *Byzantium: The Early Centuries* (London, Guild) 284.

[124] Heraclius, as quoted in Kaegi, W (2007) *Heraclius: Emperor of Byzantine* (Cambridge, Cambridge University Press) 126. See also his speeches on pages 113–14 and 129. Note also *The Chronicles of Theophanes Confessor* trans Mango, C (2006) (Oxford, Clarendon Press) 435.

[125] The Persian Memorandum reprinted in Kaegi, W (2007) *Heraclius: Emperor of Byzantine* (Cambridge, Cambridge University Press) 178.

[126] *The Chronicles of Theophanes Confessor* trans Mango, C (2006) (Oxford, Clarendon Press) 453, 455. See also Maas, M (ed) *Readings in Late Antiquity: A Sourcebook* (London, Routledge) 342–43; Kaegi, W (2007) *Heraclius: Emperor of Byzantine* (Cambridge, Cambridge University Press) 168–69, 175.

[127] Persian envoy, noted in Kaegi, W (2000) *Byzantium and the Early Islamic Conquests* (Cambridge, Cambridge University Press) 32; Luttwak, E (2009) *The Grand Strategy of the Byzantine Empire* (London, Harvard University Press) 202–204.

9. ISLAM

Muhammad was born into an era which was fundamentally different to the one that Jesus had lived in. Jesus was born within the *pax Romana*, which had an established and relatively tolerant basis. This allowed the new Christian religion to flourish within safe borders, albeit with periods of persecution. Although it was turned on its head when Christian rulers came to power, the ideal that the Christian kingdom was 'not of this world' was long-standing. This certainly helped to forge the theoretical division between Church and State. The situation was very different for Muhammad, who gave rise to an empire which diametrically reversed this assumption, that is, the community that he founded had, at its heart, the assumption that all military and political power would be transferred from the worldly empire to the Prophet (and later, to the religious community). There was to be no division of power, and religious texts were to form the spine of any future constitution.[128]

Muhammad was born into the bloodbath and no-man's land that resulted from wars between Rome and Persia that had raged for over 500 years. Whilst it is true that Arabia knew religious turmoil and conflict during the early parts of the sixth century, as in the overthrow of Himyraite kingdom (110 BCE–520s CE) and its Jewish/Arab king, Yusuf As'ar Yath'ar (d 520), on the whole the Arabs, who had a historical legacy of around 1600 years at this point, were minor players in much larger conflicts. When the Byzantine–Persian wars came to an end, the people of Muhammad were freed from their now bankrupt, or defeated, former employers. The land was socially, economically, militarily – and religiously – exhausted. The timing was perfect for a man who had personally fought in (27) battles to proclaim a new religion of Islam/peace.[129]

It may have been because Muhammad was personally so familiar with military violence that he was clear that his people should 'not kill except for a just cause'.[130] This question of what was a just cause became connected with the related debate of *jihad* – and the idea that warfare, based on religious considerations, could be justified. The term *jihad* is derived from the verb *jahada*, which means 'exerted'. Its juridical–theological meaning is exertion of one's power in the path of *Allah* ('the God'), that is, the spread of the belief of *Allah*. This definition is based on the Quranic injunction which runs 'believe in *Allah* and His Apostle and carry on warfare (*jihad*) in the path of *Allah* with your possessions and your persons'.[131] *Jihad*, in the broad sense of exertion

[128] Black, A (2011) *The History of Islamic Political Thought* (Edinburgh, Edinburgh University Press) 9–10; Crone, P (2004) *God's Rule: Government and Islam* (NYC, Columbia University Press) 12–15.

[129] The word *islam*, which denotes the existential 'surrender' of one's whole being to God which Muslims are required to make, is related to *salam* meaning 'peace'. For commentary, see Morgan, P (ed) (1996) *Ethical Issues in Six Religious Traditions* (Edinburgh, Edinburgh University Press) 255–57; *The Chronicles of Theophanes Confessor* trans Mango, C (2006) (Oxford, Clarendon Press) 466–67; Kaegi, W (2000) *Byzantium and the Early Islamic Conquests* (Cambridge, Cambridge University Press) 47, 52–53, 60–62, 89–91, 108–10; Holland, T (2012) *In the Shadow of the Sword* (NYC, Brown) 3–5, 241–47, 280–85; Perowne, S (1962) *Caesars and Saints: The Evolution of the Christian State* (London, Hodder) 55–58.

[130] *Quran* trans Dawood, N (1990) (London, Penguin) 25:68.

[131] *Quran* trans Dawood, N (1990) (London, Penguin) 61:10.

– which is meant to be a permanent obligation with universal applicability – does not necessarily mean war or fighting in the physical sense, since exertion in *Allah's* path may also be achieved by peaceful means. Thus, it can be contended that the root of *jihad* involved more than a 'holy war' and signified a physical, moral, spiritual and intellectual effort. There are plenty of Arabic words denoting armed combat – such as *harb* (war), *sira'a* (combat), *ma'araka* (battle) or *qital* (killing) – which could have been used in the *Quran* if war was to be the Muslim's principal way of engaging in this effort. Instead, a vaguer, richer, word of wider connotations – *jihad* – was used. *Jihad* is not one of the five pillars of the religion; nevertheless, it was, and remains, a duty for Muslims to commit themselves to a struggle on all fronts – moral, spiritual and political – to create a just and decent society. Tradition has Muhammad say on his return from a battle, 'we return home from the little *jihad* to the greater *jihad*'.[132]

Muhammad's introduction to warfare appears to have started with his authorisation of raids on caravans carrying commercial merchandise to Mecca. Such attacks were so familiar in this period that the owners of the caravans and/or the cities they were trying to reach would go to great lengths to defend themselves. In the case of Muhammad, he may (there are two versions of the same story) have authorised attacks during a period of agreed non-violence but what is not in dispute is his decision not to keep the booty that was taken from the raid. He argued that, although the attack was an offence, there were greater offences (such as 'debar[ing] others from the path of God, to deny Him, and to expel His worshippers from the Holy Mosque') – of which those attacked were guilty. [133] This ruling was prefaced by the instruction that 'fighting is obligatory for you, much as you dislike it'.[134] Additional considerations pertaining to the justification of war suggested that Muslims should not pre-empt war. Accordingly, 'fight for the sake of God those that fight against you, but do not attack them first. God does not love the aggressors'.[135] Or, 'permission to take up arms is hereby given to those who are attacked, because they have been wronged'.[136] It was added:

> If they keep away from you and cease their hostility and offer you peace, God bids you not to harm them . . . If the[y] do not keep their distance from you, if they neither offer you peace nor cease their hostilities against you, lay hold of them and kill them wherever you find them. Over such men We give you absolute authority.[137]

The Battle of Badr in 624 followed the raids on the caravans. Here about 400 Muslims fought around 1,000 men from the *Quraish* (the merchant tribe that controlled Mecca, and possibly the most powerful tribe in Arabia at that point). The Muslims attributed their success to the fact that God helped them. This idea that God directly supported the righteous is repeated a number of times in the *Quran*. This idea was supplemented

[132] As quoted from Armstrong, K (2001) *Muhammad: A Biography of the Prophet* (London, Phoenix) 168; also Khadduri, M (2006) *War and Peace in the Law of Islam* (New Jersey, Law Book Exchange) 56–57; Mayer, A (2001) 'War and Peace in the Islamic Tradition and International Law' in Kelsay, J (ed) *Just War and Jihad* (New York, Greenwood) 195–210.

[133] *Quran* trans Dawood, N (1990) (London, Penguin) 2:217.

[134] *Quran* trans Dawood, N (1990) (London, Penguin) 2:216.

[135] *Quran* trans Dawood, N (1990) (London, Penguin) 2:190.

[136] *Quran* trans Dawood, N (1990) (London, Penguin) 22:39.

[137] *Quran* trans Dawood, N (1990) (London, Penguin) 4:191.

by another, that those who died fighting would be rewarded in heaven, as: 'God has prepared for them gardens watered by running streams, in which they shall abide forever.'[138] The *Quran* was supplemented by the *Hadith* (sayings ascribed to Muhammad) on this point:

> Paradise is in the shadow of the swords . . . swords are the keys to paradise . . . He who dies fighting on the frontier in the path of God, God protects him . . . A day and night of fighting on the frontier is better than a month of fasting and prayer . . . The best thing a Muslim can earn is an arrow in the path of God.[139]

Unjust conflicts were seen as those related to tribal warfare, akin to the petty squabbles which existed among the Arabian tribes prior to Muhammad. Feuds and raids were also seen as characteristic of primitive people. Just conflict was against peoples who were pure unbelievers (polytheists, primarily pagans). Violent *jihad* against apostasy (those who had turned their back on Islam after being part of the community), those dissenting against the rulings of the imam (the leader of the community), or those who were highway robbers, was also seen as legitimate. Moreover, as Muhammad's Treaty of Hudaibia of 628 with the people of Mecca showed, it was possible that 'conditions of peace' (truce) and cooperation could be reached for certain periods.[140]

The answer to the question of whether it was legitimate to fight for religion was ambiguous. On the one hand, it was stated that 'there shall be no compulsion in religion'.[141] On the other hand, it was recorded: 'Believers, make war on the infidels who dwell around you';[142] 'fight for the cause of God'[143] and 'fight against them until idolatry is no more and God's religion reigns supreme. But if they desist, fight none except the evil-doers.'[144] Furthermore:

> When you meet unbelievers in the battlefield strike off their heads and, when you have laid them low, bind your captives firmly. Then grant them their freedom or take ransom from them, until War shall lay down her burdens . . . And for those who are slain in the cause of God, He will not allow their works to perish.[145]

A. Tolerance towards Non-Muslims

Tradition has it that Muhammad instructed 'let there be no compulsion in religion'.[146] This rule meant that, assuming they were not rebellious (which could lead to severe

[138] *Quran* trans Dawood, N (1990) (London, Penguin) 9:87, 2:154, 3:13, 3:169, 8:9, 8:17, 9:26, 9:100, 9:111. For the figures, see Grant, R (2011) *1001 Battles that Changed the Course of History* (London, Penguin) 104.

[139] Sayings ascribed to Muhammad in Lewis, B (ed) (1987) *Islam: From the Prophet to the Capture of Constantinople*, Vol I (Oxford, Oxford University Press) 210–12.

[140] The Treaty of 628 reprinted in Gibbon, E (1926 edn) *The Decline and Fall of the Roman Empire*, Vol V (London, Methuen) Appendix 19, 571.

[141] *Quran* trans Dawood, N (1990) (London, Penguin) 2:256.

[142] *Quran* trans Dawood, N (1990) (London, Penguin) 9:123.

[143] *Quran* trans Dawood, N (1990) (London, Penguin) 22:78.

[144] *Quran* trans Dawood, N (1990) (London, Penguin) 2.191.

[145] *Quran* trans Dawood, N (1990) (London, Penguin) 47:4.

[146] *Quran* trans Dawood, N (1990) (London, Penguin) 2:257.

and fatal consequences),[147] respect was the expected attitude to be shown to the fellow 'people of the book' that is, Jews, Christians and Sabians – the latter being a monotheistic Abrahamic religious group – people who all shared a belief in God – albeit an imperfect one. If they were not people of the book, tolerance could not be expected. For example, the Caliph Mu'awiya (661–680) was known to destroy Zoroastrian temples and places of worship and replace them with mosques – and to offer direct financial incentives for non-Muslims to come and worship within Islam. Conversely, for people of the book (to which Zoroastrians, Sikhs and Hindus would later be added) tolerance and peace was possible, and they could stay within the Muslim community if they paid a *jizyah* (a poll tax on non-Muslims). This approach was clearly reflected by Muhammad, who in agreement with the pact of Medina (622), held that the Jewish community was to have equality with Muslims. Specifically:

> The Jews who attach themselves to us shall be protected from insults. They shall have equal rights with our people to our assistance . . . they shall practice their religion . . . [and] . . . enjoy the same security and freedom.[148]

Apparently, Muhammad also granted a charter to the Christians at Najran, in which he undertook to protect them, their churches and the residences of their priests. Nevertheless, there were restrictions, such as no building of new churches, no proselytising of Muslims, and a generally second-class status for Christians in Muslim societies. Christians were also obliged to show respect to Muslims 'and rise from [their] seats when they wish to sit', and not, inter alia, use saddles, carry weapons, or build houses overtopping the houses of Muslims. In some places, both Christians and Jews had to be marked on their hands. They also had to pay an additional tax.[149]

If the non-Muslims paid the *jizyah*, they were allowed to live with a freedom of conscience with equal protection of person and property to that enjoyed by Muslims. This type of tolerance was considered very favourably by a number of groups, ranging from Jewish communities through to non-orthodox Christians (such as the Paulicians), who were suffering under an intolerant Byzantine state and its orthodox religious principles. Many of these persecuted communities were willing to swap allegiances, even though they would be discriminated against as non-Muslims. The advantage (aside from lower taxes) was that Christians of all types were now treated equally. These new allegiances made some Muslim communities, such as the

[147] This was most obvious after the Jewish people within his community had attempted a failed uprising against Muhammad following the Battle of Badr. Seven hundreds of the defeated were executed. Muhammad then turned his attention to the affluent Jewish community in the oasis of Khaibar, some 90 miles north of Medina. Surrender after a month of siege saw the Jews stripped of their possessions and granted free passage with their women and children away from the conquered territory.

[148] The Pact of Medina printed in Levy, R (1922) *The Sociology of Islam* (London, Macmillan) 275; Karsh, E (2006) *Islamic Imperialism: A History* (London, Yale University Press) 26; Boyce, M (1990) *Zoroastrianism* (Chicago, University of Chicago Press) 116.

[149] The Pact of Umar reprinted in Maas, M (ed) (2010) *Readings in Late Antiquity: A Sourcebook* (London, Routledge) 396. For the instructions for the invasion of Egypt, see Geanakoplos, D (ed) (1986) *Byzantium: A Sourcebook on Church, Society and Civilisation Seen Through Contemporary Eyes* (Chicago, Chicago University Press) 337. Also the 'Tax Demand in Egypt' reprinted in Rosenwein, B (ed) (2006) *Reading the Middle Ages: Sources from Europe, Byzantium and the Islamic World* (Ontario, Broadview) 93; *The Chronicles of Theophanes Confessor* trans Mango, C (2006) (Oxford, Clarendon Press) 465, 550, 594, 616.

Moorish kingdoms in Spain in the ninth and tenth centuries, the most cosmopolitan beacons of the age.[150]

B. Inter-Muslim War

The early Muslim communities were not always tolerant of those who had different interpretations of their common faith. For example, on a number of occasions the Abbasids made it clear that they did not agree with the Shiites' interpretation of Islam by persecuting leading Shiites and destroying shrines. Such provocations, supplemented by deeply held views on inter-religious difference, led to a number of civil wars within Islam, overlapping with political questions about leadership (and legitimacy).[151]

This problem arose after the death of Muhammad in 632. Although his spiritual and prophetic mission was considered to be complete, the task of maintaining and defending the faith and the law of Islam and bringing the faith to the rest of humanity remained. It was assumed that someone must succeed him in his role as leader (imam) of the community, as his deputy (caliph). This was a difficult task as Muhammad left no surviving sons and had not designated a successor or even indicated what type of leadership should replace him. Consequently, the most active and able among the inner group of Muhammad's followers chose one of their number to rule. The first four of those chosen are known as the 'Rightly Guided' ones, and are commonly seen to represent a type of golden age in Islam. However, inter-Islamic warfare soon arose. Conflicts within Islam were not, as in Christianity, about the nature of the divine, but about who should lead and how the leader should be appointed. Fundamentally, they were about the exercise of power in a religious community.[152]

The first leader selected to be caliph was Abu Bakr, a veteran of many of Muhammad's campaigns. Bakr was not a universally accepted choice. In the first year of his caliphate, several Arabic tribes revolted against his rule, on the grounds that power should have gone to one of Muhammad's direct descendants. Abu-Bakr would not tolerate this dissent. He drew from a large number of sayings ascribed to Muhammad prohibiting community division, such as 'whoever shall divide my community, strike off his head . . . [and] . . . if anyone comes out against my community when they are united and seeks to divide them, kill them'.[153] Thus, Abu-Bakr entered into the first inter-Muslim conflict in what is known as the Ridda War, to achieve and maintain the unity of the religious community.[154]

[150] Khadduri, M (2006) *War and Peace in the Law of Islam* (New Jersey, Law Book Exchange) 75–81; Karsh, E (2006) *Islamic Imperialism: A History* (London, Yale University Press) 13–15; Boyce, M (1990) *Zoroastrianism* (Chicago, University of Chicago Press) 116–20. Note also references in the *Quran* 9:5, 9:24 and 47:4; Luttwak, E (2009) *The Grand Strategy of the Byzantine Empire* (London, Harvard University Press) 199, 201, 205–11.

[151] Bartlett, W (2007) *Assassins: The Story of Medieval Islam's Secret Sect* (London, Sutton) 19, 23.

[152] Black, A (2011) *The History of Islamic Political Thought* (Edinburgh, Edinburgh University Press) 13–15.

[153] Saying ascribed to Muhammad, reprinted in Lewis, B (ed) (1987) *Islam: From the Prophet to the Capture of Constantinople*, Vol I (Oxford, Oxford University Press) 150.

[154] See 'The Founding of the Caliphate' reprinted in Lewis, B (ed) (1987) *Islam: From the Prophet to the Capture of Constantinople*, Vol I (Oxford, Oxford University Press) 1–5; Gwatkin, H (ed) (1967) *The Cambridge Medieval History: The Rise of the Saracens and the Foundation of the Western Empire*, Vol II (Cambridge, Cambridge University Press) 335.

The Ridda War did not bring lasting theological unity. The second caliph, Umar, was assassinated in 644, and the third caliph, Uthman ibn Affan, had to slow Islam's external conquests in order to focus on halting internal rebellions. Disquiet became clear in Uthman's reign when a split developed between his family and associates, and others who believed they were being denied their fair share of wealth and other benefits accruing from Islam's conquests. Uthman was then assassinated, and his opponents rallied to Ali ibn Abd Munaf (598–661) as the new caliph. The killing of Uthman was a deed similar to the execution of Charles I in the English Civil War or of Louis XVI in the French Revolution. However, in contrast to the European revolutions, the killers did not bring to an end the concentration of power. Instead, they elevated Ali, who was both the cousin and son-in-law of Muhammad. This action did not receive unanimous support and some notables, such as the kin of the assassinated Uthman and Muhammad's widow, who thought that Uthman had been a legitimate leader who had been unjustly killed, demanded a new election by consultation. The degree to which consultation occurred is questionable.

Upon appointment, Ali made it clear that he would not tolerate sedition. Despite the rhetoric, it became clear that his power was not as strong as he had believed, and accordingly, he did not attempt to punish those who had assassinated his predecessor. In addition, some of the governors within the region were reluctant to follow his direction.

This combination of concerns laid the seeds for the first civil war, in which the forces of Ali clashed with those of the widow of Muhammad and Muawiyah I (602–680) – a previous governor of Syria, kinsman of Uthman and brother-in-law to Muhammad. Both had a number of disagreements with the rule of Ali, whilst also desiring that justice be delivered on those who had assassinated the previous caliph. Disentangling the events of this conflict is nearly impossible owing to the differing interpretations of what happened. What is more certain is that, in addition to a disputed attempt at arbitration (a splinter group, the *Khariji*, rejected the idea that Ali would arbitrate on such matters), a number of battles occurred between 656 and 661. Conflicts came to an end upon Muawiyah's assumption of the caliphate, which was assisted by the assassination of Ali (by a *Khariji* who believed he was acting in accordance with the will of *Allah*) in 661. Whilst those loyal to Ali continued to govern from Medina, Muawiyah I went on to establish the Umayyad caliphate, which was to be a hereditary dynasty governing from Damascus. The Umayyads grounded their right to the caliphate in the legitimacy of Uthman. They argued that Uthman had been lawfully elected by consultation and unlawfully killed – indeed martyred. His Umayyad kinsmen and avengers then took over his position as imam of guidance.[155]

This dispute shattered the unity of the Muslim community and set into motion long-term trends that ended in the division of Islam into Shia and Sunni sects. The Sunnis believe that the legitimacy of rulers is determined by representing the wishes of the majority of the community. For the Shia, the question of legitimacy was (and remains)

[155] See 'The Death of Umar' reprinted in Lewis, B (ed) (1987) *Islam: From the Prophet to the Capture of Constantinople*, Vol I (Oxford, Oxford University Press) 6–7; Black, A (2011) *The History of Islamic Political Thought* (Edinburgh, Edinburgh University Press) 15–17; Crone, P (2004) *God's Rule: Government and Islam* (NYC, Columbia University Press) 20–25, 34, 54–55.

one of lineage, wherein power should be handed to a man of sanctity, defined as someone related to Muhammad. The Shia believe that Muawiyah I, the first caliph of the Umayyad dynasty, wrongfully usurped power from Muhammad's true successor – the slain Ali. The problem was, since these people had all now died, power could not be concentrated in any one person beyond what the community agreed. The Shiites subsequently divided into a number of subgroups. This culminated in the emergence of the *Kharijites*, who believed that any Muslim could be the leader of the Muslim community, with the determining criterion being merit. They also held that any ruler who deviated from their interpretation of Islam (or unbelievers in general) did not deserve loyalty, nor life itself. This position was not surprising given that the *Kharijites* were devotees of religious violence. For them, 'holy war' was the sixth pillar of Islam. They advocated indiscriminate killing of all of their opponents on the grounds that they must be polytheists and as such had no rights, including the right to life.[156]

The second civil war within the Islamic empire broke out between 683 and 685, a few years after Muawiyah's death. This was a conflict amongst the Umayyads for the control of the caliphate. By this stage, the Umayyad caliphate was close to a monarchy in terms of both power and dynastic approach. The dispute was between the son of Myaqiyah, Yazid I (645–683), who acquired power through inheritance, and Huasayn ibn Ali (626–680) – the son of Ali and grandson of Muhammad. War broke out over this disputed succession. Specifically, Ali was no longer seen simply as a companion and son-in-law of Muhammad, but rather as the heir of his prophetic spirit, which was believed to live on in his sons. The dynastic pretensions of the Umayyad caliphate, and assertions from the opposing camp that they were not acting in obedience to *Allah*, helped to inflame the situation. In 680 the Battle of Karbala, resulted in the death of Huasayn (and his children). The Umayyads, directing an army of 4,000, were – unsurprisingly – successful against the 70 opponents fighting for Huasayn. Yazid then went on to face down further revolts where local authorities would not swear allegiance to his caliphate. When Yazid and his son died suddenly, widespread revolt broke out within the territories of Islam, especially in the form of Shia reaction against Umayyad rule. This situation was not brought under control until the end of the seventh century, when Abd al-Malik (646–705), the fifth Umayyad caliph, reasserted control over the Islamic empire. The final act of the conflict was the bombardment and sack of the rebel stronghold – Mecca. Although this further tarnished the Umayyad image, it was clear that sanctity and power were very hard to reconcile. Abd declared on coins he had minted, as a warning to all others, that Muhammad had been 'sent with guidance and the religion of truth to make it supreme over all others whether the polytheists like it or not'.[157]

[156] Khadduri, M (2006) *War and Peace in the Law of Islam* (New Jersey, Law Book Exchange) 68–69; Robinson, F (ed) (2010) *The Islamic World* (Cambridge, Cambridge University Press) 18–22. Kennedy, H (2001) *The Armies of the Caliphs* (London, Routledge) 5–10, 64–65; Black, A (2011) *The History of Islamic Political Thought* (Edinburgh, Edinburgh University Press) 16–17.

[157] Coin of Abd al-Malik, recorded in Robinson, F (ed) (2010) *The Islamic World* (Cambridge, Cambridge University Press) 13; Robinson, F (ed) (2010) *The Islamic World* (Cambridge, Cambridge University Press) 13; Holland, T (2012) *In the Shadow of the Sword* (NYC, Brown) 372–74, 379–81, 390; Crone, P (2004) *God's Rule: Government and Islam* (NYC, Columbia University Press) 35–37; Grant, R (2005) *Battle* (London, Dorling Kindersley) 75.

The third inter-religious conflict within the territories of Islam involved the toppling of the Umayyad caliphate by the Abbasids. Rejection of the Umayyads was commonly formulated as an accusation that they had perverted the caliphate by turning it into a kingship. This accusation was linked to violence with the Berber revolt of 740, which led to the first successful split from the established caliphate. This spread through North Africa and across to Spain, and a number of regions claimed political independence. Full-scale war did not begin until 744, when a group of Syrian soldiers killed the caliph al-Walid II (d 744) and enthroned their own candidate, Yazid III (701–744). Refusing to acknowledge the new regime, Marawan II (688–750), the Umayyad governor of Armenia, marched on Syria with his own troops, defeated his rival, and then proclaimed himself caliph. Seeing an opportunity, the *Kharijites* also rebelled, but refused to join the new regime, so Marawan then had to battle with them. Whilst this was a success, a Shiite uprising in 747 could not be defeated and Marawan – and the Umayyad dynasty he was from – lost power in 750 at the battle of the Zab. The victors then decided to enthrone a member of Muhammad's family, Abu l-Abbas (d 754), as the first of the Abbasid caliphs, who were descended from one of the uncles of Muhammad. They believed this lineage, which they aimed to preserve through a dynasty, made them the true successors of Muhammad. There was also a reorganisation of the centres of power during this period, with the capital of the Muslim Empire being moved from Damascus (from which the Umayyads ruled) to the new centre of Baghdad – designed to be 'the crossroads of the universe' – which was founded in 762. This was part of a transition of power towards non-Arabic influence, which was also much more akin to the imperialistic approaches of both Persia and Byzantium.[158]

A fourth civil war broke out at the end of the eighth century, when it was clear that the Abbasid caliphate was having difficulty in holding the total Muslim regime together. By the turn of the century, the Abbasids were losing control of the provinces, which, while remaining nominally under their suzerainty, were in fact governed by independent rulers, as provincial dynasties, caught in a strong drift of separatism. These were flowering in places such as Tunis and Morocco in the early parts of the ninth century. This fragmentation was exacerbated by the dynastic struggle between the two sons of Harun al-Rashid (763–809): al-Amin, (based in Baghdad, r 809–813); and al-Mamum (r 813–833, based in Merv). The civil war ended with the siege of Baghdad in 812, and its eventual conquest, which coincided with the death of al-Amin. The resultant regime demanded strict loyalty, but large areas of the empire, including Syria, Palestine, Egypt and parts of Iran, could only be held by force, as the emergent regimes had no intention of acquiescing. Other groups, such as the *Ismalilis*, which aimed at nothing less than the transformation of all Islam, refused to give even token recognition to the Abbasid caliphs.

This fragmentation of Abbasid power accelerated around the years 865 to 866 with the Caliphal War, in which two rival caliphs, al Musta'in and al-Mu'tazz, fought over Baghdad for the control over the Abbasid caliphate. Whilst al-Mu-tazz emerged victo-

[158] Robinson, F (ed) (2010) *The Islamic World* (Cambridge, Cambridge University Press) 18–22; Kennedy, H (2001) *The Armies of the Caliphs* (London, Routledge) 96–99; Lewis, B (ed) (1987) *Islam: From the Prophet to the Capture of Constantinople*, Vol I (Oxford, Oxford University Press) 120–21; Crone, P (2004) *God's Rule: Government and Islam* (NYC, Columbia University Press) 43–44, 87–89.

rious, his life was cut short when his army failed to receive their pay on time. Another Shia sect, the *Qarmatians*, began their revolt against the Abbasid caliphate at the end of the ninth century, and continued their struggle for another 50 years. In 861, the last Abbasid caliph of any power, al-Mutawakkil, was assassinated by the slave soldiers he had imported to keep him safe, who then took power for themselves. Although remnants of the Abbasid empire would last until 1258, this was the point at which it began to slip into major decline, as regions became autonomous and provincial governors founded hereditary dynasties. The beginning of the tenth century saw the emergence of the *Fatimids*, who held another Shia-based faith and claimed lineage back to Muhammad. This group proclaimed Ubaydallah al-Mahdi (d 934) as imam in Tunis in 909. In pursuit of their goal of reuniting all Muslims under a new caliphate, and to achieve a final victory over the known world, they proceeded to conquer Sicily, North Africa and Egypt. They gained control over Mecca and Medina, to the dismay of the Sunni world. The conquest followed in the footsteps of decades of conflict, in which groups such as the *Qarmatians* had killed thousands of Sunni Muslims, in attacks on their undefended caravans and in the sacking of several major cities, including Kufa, Basra and finally Mecca in 930. In the last instance, not only was the city attacked when it was full of unarmed pilgrims (of which 30,000 were reportedly slain), but the revered black stone that was encased in the *Ka'ba* (the holiest place in Islam) was torn down and carried away. The Fatimids subsequently went from strength to strength. Finally, in 969 an army reported to be in excess of 100,000 men marched across Egypt to take full control of the country. The crowning achievement of this conquest was the building of a great city, named *al-Qahira* – 'The Victorious' – but it would become better known to the West as Cairo.[159]

10. ISLAM AND CHRISTIANITY IN THE EAST

Despite the examples of tolerance cited above, it is believed by some that Muhammad instructed his forces to 'expel the Jews and Christians from the Arabian peninsula'.[160] Possibly consistent with this instruction, in the middle of 629 Muslim and Christian Byzantine forces met for the first time and fought at Mu'tah (in modern-day Jordan). The alleged reason for the conflict was the killing of one of Muhammad's messengers (announcing the arrival of Islam and calling on unbelievers to repent) by a local Arab tribal leader who was allied with Byzantium. This minor clash, which left the Muslims victorious, was followed by the execution of a Muslim convert by some Christian zealots. A month later, the Muslim forces sent an expedition to Tabuk (in the north-west corner of the Arabian peninsula), where, in the year 630, rather than fight, the leading

[159] Kennedy, H (2001) *The Armies of the Caliphs* (London, Routledge) 108–19, 131–35, 140–44, 153–60; Robinson, F (ed) (2010) *The Islamic World* (Cambridge, Cambridge University Press) 28–31; Crone, P (2004) *God's Rule: Government and Islam* (NYC, Columbia University Press) 88–89; Black, A (2011) *The History of Islamic Political Thought* (Edinburgh, Edinburgh University Press) 45–46; Hodgson, M (1974) *The Venture of Islam*, Vol II (Chicago, Chicago University Press) 19–24.

[160] Sayings ascribed to Muhammad reprinted in Lewis, B (ed) (1987) *Islam: From the Prophet to the Capture of Constantinople*, Vol 1 (Oxford, Oxford University Press) 210–12.

official or bishop of Ayla and the Muslim forces made a peace arrangement which protected the Christians' property and freedom of travel, in exchange for payment of the *jizyah* (the tax on non-Muslims).[161]

It is possible that more than one messenger was sent by Muhammad to Byzantine leaders throughout the region, and that these messengers met a similar fate to that of the messenger at Tabuk. Although no definitive answer as to whether or not this was so can be found, what is known is the reaction of the Muslims, who declared war on the Byzantine Empire for the slaying of their messenger and the rejection of his message. This event was not recorded by the most notable historian of the period – Sebos, a seventh century Armenian bishop. Although he did not record the arrival or execution of a messenger, he did record a military clash between the two sides that was clearly predicated upon religious differences. The Muslims asserted: 'God gave that country as the inherited property of Abraham and of his sons after him. We are the sons of Abraham. It is too much that you hold our country.' The emperor replied: 'The country is mine. Your inheritance is the desert. So go in peace to your country.'[162] The Muslims had no such intention, and in 633, once the entire Arab peninsula was under their control, they issued a further letter to the Persians:

> Submit to our authority, and we shall leave you and your land and go by you against others. If not, you will be conquered against your will . . . Become Muslim and be saved. If not, accept protection from us and pay the poll tax. If not, I shall come against you with men who love death as you love to drink wine.[163]

This threat was followed by a series of raids into Persian territory, before the armies of both sides finally collided in full force in 637, when 50,000 Persian soldiers were routed by a smaller force of 30,000 Muslim soldiers at the battle of Qadisiyya (in southern Mesopotamia). The last battle for Persia occurred in 641, when the last remnant of the once-great Persian army was finally extinguished. The peace treaty of the following year, overseen by (the second) caliph Umar (586–644), stipulated:

> You are safe as long as you discharge your obligations, which are: to pay the *jizyah,* which you must pay according to your capacity every year . . . Do not assert your authority over any Muslim. What you owe to the Muslims is your goodwill and payment of your dues; you have safe conduct as long as you comply . . . If anyone insults a Muslim, he will be punished for it. If he strikes a Muslim, we shall kill him.[164]

Umar succeeded in enforcing a decision that all lands taken by force (and subsequent rentals, poll tax and/or other taxes) were to pass into the ownership of all Muslims,

[161] The Treaty of 630 reprinted in Appendix 19 of Gibbon, E (1926 edn) *The Decline and Fall of the Roman Empire*, Vol V (London, Methuen) 571.

[162] Sebeos' *History* trans Thomson, R (1999) (Liverpool, Liverpool University Press) ch 30; Kaegi, W (2000) *Byzantium and the Early Islamic Conquests* (Cambridge, Cambridge University Press) 69, 71; Gibbon, E (1926 edn) *The Decline and Fall of the Roman Empire*, Vol V (London, Methuen) 395.

[163] The Letter to the Persians reprinted in Lewis, B (ed) (1987) *Islam: From the Prophet to the Capture of Constantinople*, Vol I (Oxford, Oxford University Press). 228.

[164] The Surrender of Isfahan reprinted in Lewis, B (ed) (1987) *Islam: From the Prophet to the Capture of Constantinople*, Vol I (Oxford, Oxford University Press) 238. Also Boyce, M (1990) *Zoroastrianism* (Chicago, University of Chicago Press) 115–18. The figures are from Grant, R (2005) *Battle* (London, Dorling Kindersley) 74.

through the state, rather than being distributed among the conquerors. This meant his soldiers were not allowed to occupy and settle on the lands they had conquered. Instead, they were to live off the tax revenues paid by local peoples, which were, in essence, a salary. This removed any social or economic links between the advancing soldiers and the territories they conquered. It also meant that the spoils of victory were re-divided amongst the entire Muslim community, and not just the soldiers at the front. Most of all, it kept the momentum of further conquest rolling forward. According to tradition, this fear of progress being slowed due to the acquisition of territory had preoccupied Muhammad, leading to the warning that 'the survival of my Community rests on the hoofs of its horses and the points of its lances; as long as they keep from tilling the fields; once they begin to do that they will become as other men'.[165]

After defeating in some 15 years the enemy (Persia) that Rome had battled for five centuries, the forces of Islam turned west. They had first turned westward in 634, when the first caliph, Abu-Bakr (c 573–634), had directed some of his forces to prepare for the invasion of Byzantine Syria, in which the town of Areopolis/Ma'ab was the first to fall, followed by Gaza and the city of Damascus. Two years later, in 636, the Byzantine forces regrouped and finally gave battle against the Muslims near the Yarmuk River, along what is today the border between Syria and Jordan. The six-day battle, in which an estimated 40,000 Muslims and 80,000 Roman Byzantines clashed, was a disaster for Byzantium (with perhaps 70,000 men being lost). Byzantium lost both the entire army and subsequently all of the provinces in the area, which were left unable to meaningfully defend themselves. Few, if any, battles in history had consequences that matched this loss. Jerusalem fell next, after accepting peace terms whereby the inhabitants were either allowed safe conduct away from the area, or, if they chose to stay, were given certain protections for their persons and heritage, conditional upon paying the *jizyah*.[166]

The Muslim advances stopped only when short-term truces were agreed. For example, for a set period the Muslims agreed: 'Not to cross the Euphrates, neither peacefully nor in a state of war, as long as the Byzantines pay the [agreed] amount of gold.'[167] Such agreements were always localised, allowing the concentration of military force into other theatres of conflict. By 638, the Muslims had occupied northern Syria, taking, inter alia, the large cities of Antioch and Aleppo. They then invaded Byzantine Mesopotamia, Egypt and Armenia. In the case of Egypt (which was overrun by 642,

[165] Muhammad, noted in Karsh, E (2006) *Islamic Imperialism: A History* (London, Yale University Press) 24. See also Kennedy, H (2001) *The Armies of the Caliphs* (London, Routledge) 59–61, 88–89, 128–29, 139, 160–61, 195–98.

[166] The Peace Terms for Jerusalem reprinted in Lewis, B (ed) (1987) *Islam: From the Prophet to the Capture of Constantinople*, Vol I (Oxford, Oxford University Press) 235; Sebeos' *History* trans Thomson, R (1999) (Liverpool, Liverpool University Press) ch 30; Robinson, F (ed) (2010) *The Islamic World* (Cambridge, Cambridge University Press) 11; Gwatkin, H (ed) (1967) *The Cambridge Medieval History: The Rise of the Saracens and the Foundation of the Western Empire*, Vol II (Cambridge, Cambridge University Press) 342–44; Regan, G (2006) *Battles That Changed History* (London, Carlton) 41–43; Grant, R (2005) *Battle* (London, Dorling Kindersley) 74.

[167] The truce of Chalkis reprinted in Kaegi, W (2000) *Byzantium and the Early Islamic Conquests* (Cambridge, Cambridge University Press) 159; for the Egyptian truce, see 167. See also *The Chronicles of Theophanes Confessor* trans Mango, C (2006) (Oxford, Clarendon Press) 472; Kaegi, W (2007) *Heraclius: Emperor of Byzantine* (Cambridge, Cambridge University Press) 247, 250, 255.

alongside the occupation of Alexandria and the founding of Cairo, following an 11-month truce and wholesale evacuation of the province by the Byzantine forces), the advice given to the commander before advancing was to make no war against those who agreed to peace (and to pay the *jizyah*), but to 'plunder and take as prisoners those that will not consent to this and resist you'.[168] In other instances, where occupation was not deemed necessary, Umar allowed greater degrees of autonomy, as a way to encourage a region to switch allegiance. For example, in Armenia, where a large number of non-Orthodox citizens had already experienced difficulties due to theological differences with Byzantium, an agreement allowed (largely Christian) Armenia to reach a peace with the Muslims in which there would be no occupation and no tribute demanded (for three years) in return for agreeing not to ally themselves with Byzantium.[169] The only place where the tide of Muslim advance was halted was against (Christian) Nubia in 652, where a treaty of non-aggression was agreed, providing an annual exchange of slaves for wheat and lentils.[170]

In 647 the military forces of the new caliph, Uthman ibn Affan (579–656), took Cappadocia, before moving on to maritime expeditions against Crete, Cyprus and Rhodes. Constans II (630–668), despite paying for expensive short-term truces, could not hold these areas, which fell by 649. In 653, the general, and future Caliph Muawiyah I recognised Armenia as an autonomous tributary state, at the same time that Iberia accepted Muslim suzerainty. The cumulative impact on Constantinople was massive, as within a few short decades it had lost between two-thirds and three-quarters of its economic capacity – not to mention manpower – within these regions. In 655 Constans II, at the head of some 500 vessels (of which 400 were lost), fought – and held an Arab navy at the Battle of the Masts, off south-west Anatolia.[171] Pressure from Islamic forces only eased when they were at war with themselves. Thus the first civil war allowed Constans II to reach a peace with the Muslims in 659, before warfare broke out again. A particularly belligerent Muawiyah I wrote to Constans II in 668:

> If you want to spend your life in peace . . . abandon that foolish faith which you learned from childhood. Deny that Jesus and turn to the great God whom I worship, the God of our father Abraham. . . . how can that Jesus whom you call Christ – who was unable to save himself from the Jews – possibly save you from me?[172]

Despite his rhetoric, all of the attacks by Islamic forces against Carthage, Sicily and even Constantinople itself failed. These unexpected defeats forced Muawiyah I to seek a 30-year truce with Byzantium in 678. This involved the Muslims having to evacuate

[168] Instructions for the invasion of Egypt, as reprinted in Geanakoplos, D (ed) (1986) *Byzantium: A Sourcebook on Church, Society and Civilisation Seen Through Contemporary Eyes* (Chicago, Chicago University Press) 337.

[169] Sebeos' *History* trans Thomson, R (1999) (Liverpool, Liverpool University Press) chs 34 and 35.

[170] The Conquest of Nubia reprinted in Lewis, B (ed) (1987) *Islam: From the Prophet to the Capture of Constantinople*, Vol I (Oxford, Oxford University Press). 232. The peace terms are reprinted in Ayerst, D (ed) (1971) *Records of Christianity*, Vol II (Oxford, Blackwell) 100.

[171] Sebeos' *History* trans Thomson, R (1999) (Liverpool, Liverpool Univesity Press) ch 33; *The Chronicles of Theophanes Confessor* trans Mango, C (2006) (Oxford, Clarendon Press) 437, 479; Heather, P (2009) *Empires and Barbarians: Migration, Development and the Birth of Europe* (London, Pan) 380–82. For the figures, see Grant, R (2011) *1001 Battles that Changed the Course of History* (London, Penguin) 111.

[172] Sebeos' *History* trans Thomson, R (1999) (Liverpool, Liverpool University Press) ch 36.

the Aegean islands that they had recently taken, and having to pay an annual tribute consisting of 50 slaves, 50 thoroughbred horses and 3,000 pounds of gold. This was only agreed by Muawiyah because he had become engaged in the second Islamic civil war, and he was anxious to safeguard himself against a Byzantine attack.[173] Once secure, Muawiyah again attacked the west. A Byzantine resurgence began when Constantine IV (652–685) and Justinian II (669–711) recaptured parts of Cyprus and Armenia. Tiberius III (r 698–705) pushed back into Syria. However, Byzantium could not hold Carthage, which fell in 697, and by 711 all of North Africa was in Islamic hands. A further advance by Emperor Anastasios II in 715 petered out and was followed by a Muslim invasion of Anatolia, before an army of perhaps 180,000 men, supplemented by 2,500 ships, ended up directly beneath the walls of the city of Constantinople for most of 717, attempting to destroy Byzantium once and for all. Under the pivotal guidance of Leo III, this attack (along with further attempts in 726 and 739) was defeated in a campaign in which, according to Arab sources, more than 150,000 men died. This defeat was one of the most decisive battles in history.[174]

Pressure eased with the advent of another Islamic civil war but the distraction was not sufficient to allow Constantine V (718–775) to achieve much when he tried to exploit the situation by invading both Syria and the Balkans. The Muslim reply, under the leadership of the third Abbasid caliph, Al-Mahdi (r 775–785), resulted in the Empress Irene, in 781 and again in 798, agreeing to pay an annual tribute of around 90,000 dinars (in addition to 10,000 silk garments and access to markets) in exchange for truces and the Muslim withdrawal of forces from their recent military acquisitions. Harun-al-Rashid continued this policy, grinding the Byzantines down in no fewer than eight invasions of their territory, and demanding an annual tribute of 70,000 gold dinars per year. When the new emperor, Nikephoros (r 802–811), informed al-Rashid that he had no intention of paying further tribute in exchange for peace, the resultant battle at Krasos in 805 was followed by another Muslim invasion of Asia Minor in 806 with over 135,000 men who took Heraclea, captured a number of forts, and raided Cyprus. Peace was only achieved through a tribute agreement at a cost of 50,000 gold pieces paid immediately and a yearly tribute of 30,000 gold pieces.[175]

War broke out again in the ninth century, with further Muslim advances, including the capture of Crete in around 828 and advances into Anatolia under the leadership of Al-Mamum (786–833) in 830. Attempts to make peace were fruitless, as the war ebbed

[173] *The Chronicles of Theophanes Confessor* trans Mango, C (2006) (Oxford, Clarendon Press) 484. A slightly different list of tribute is recorded in anon, 'The Chronicle of 754' reprinted in trans Wolf, K (1999) *Conquerors and Chroniclers of Early Medieval Spain* (Liverpool, Liverpool University Press) 124; Luttwak, E (2009) *The Grand Strategy of the Byzantine Empire* (London, Harvard University Press) 214–16.

[174] Hussey, J (1966) *The Cambridge Medieval History: The Byzantine Empire*, Vol IV(1) (Cambridge, Cambridge University Press) 62–64; Pirenne, H (1935) *Mohammed and Charlemagne* (London, Allen and Unwin) 157–58; Gwatkin, H (ed) (1967) *The Cambridge Medieval History: The Rise of the Saracens and the Foundation of the Western Empire*, Vol II (Cambridge, Cambridge University Press) 380–85, 406–407; Regan, G (2006) *Battles That Changed History* (London, Carlton) 44–45.

[175] *The Chronicles of Theophanes Confessor* trans Mango, C (2006) (Oxford, Clarendon Press) 629–30; Hussey, J (1966) *The Cambridge Medieval History: The Byzantine Empire*, Vol IV(1) (Cambridge, Cambridge University Press) 81–85, 90–91; Kennedy, H (2001) *The Armies of the Caliphs* (London, Routledge) 105–107; Gibbon, E (1926 edn) *The History of the Decline and Fall of the Roman Empire*, Vol VI (London, Methuen) 36–37; Lewis, B (ed) (1987) *Islam: From the Prophet to the Capture of Constantinople*, Vol I (Oxford, Oxford University Press) 28–29.

and flowed around Mesopotamia, Anatolia and Syria for the following decade. A similar pattern of continual skirmishes occurred in the tenth century, before this turned into a tide of Byzantine victories, with Basil (830–886), Constantine VII (905–959), Nikephoros Phokas (912–969) and John (925–976) all taking turns at reclaiming Armenia and Iberia and advancing into Syria and northern Mesopotamia. Crete was reclaimed in 961; Cyprus in 965. Aleppo was captured in 962, Tarsus in 965, Antioch in 969, and Nisbis was brought back within the Byzantine Empire in 972. By the end of the century, much of the territory from Armenia to Damascus and through to Beirut had been recovered. Had it not been for internal discord within Byzantium, it is quite possible that Jerusalem could have been retaken at this point, and Baghdad sacked. Whilst there were ongoing provocative raids on Muslim cities from Emesa to Tripoli, peace was bought by semi-independent Muslim cities via the annual payment of tribute and promises of military assistance when called upon by the emperor, in return for promises to protect local Muslim rulers. Even the Fatimids of Egypt agreed in 998 to a 10-year truce with Byzantium, in the hope of slowing the advance of the resurgent empire.[176]

In addition to fighting various Islamic groupings, the rulers in Constantinople were also beginning to master a divide-and-rule strategy to exploit the differences between Islamic sects. The first example of this strategy may have been in 928, when Emir Abu Hafs of Melitene (d 928) agreed to a peace treaty with Byzantium, whereby the local Amir was allowed to retain a degree of independence and was given support in breaking away from the fragmenting Abbasid caliphate. In exchange, Abu Hafs promised to provide 12,000 horsemen to support Byzantine military expeditions. Further treaties were agreed around 987 or 988 between Byzantium and the Egyptian caliphs (to the exclusion of their Abbasid rivals). The scant surviving details of these later treaties suggest that the emperor exercised his influence on behalf of the Christian subjects of the caliph, and that the caliph similarly acted as protector of the Muslims within the Byzantine Empire.[177]

When Islam ventured east it ran into the empires of China and India. Some 100,000 men under the flag of Islam clashed with an equal number of Chinese of the Tang dynasty at the battle of Talas in 751. The Muslims had been aware of the power of China for over a century. The background to the conflict with China involved a local king who had been confirmed on his throne by the Muslims, but acknowledged himself to be a vassal of China. When called to make a choice between the two he asked the Chinese for help. The Chinese duly responded, but ended up losing control of the area (and 30,000 men) west of the Pamir Mountains. The Muslims made no attempt to press forward into further unchartered territories, and the Chinese made no attempt to reclaim what was lost. The southern province of Canton, which was popular with Muslim traders, was overrun in 758 (and again in 879) in retaliation for the wholesale

[176] Hussey, J (1966) *The Cambridge Medieval History: The Byzantine Empire*, Vol IV(1) (Cambridge, Cambridge University Press) 71–77, 149–51, 163–70, 614–20, 719–25; Norwich, J (1992) *Byzantium: The Apogee* (NYC, Knopf) 177–78, 248–52.

[177] Tanner, J (ed) (1957) *The Cambridge Medieval History: Contest of Empire and Papacy*, Vol V (Cambridge, Cambridge University Press) 244–47, 250–51; Hussey, J (1966) *The Cambridge Medieval History: The Byzantine Empire*, Vol IV(1) (Cambridge, Cambridge University Press) 139.

killing of those practising the Islamic faith – which was itself the consequence of looting by an Islamic force that had arrived in the region earlier in the same year.[178] The Muslims' restraint in dealing with China stood in contrast to their advances into India, where battles dated back to 644. Muslim armies clashed with Indians under the leadership of Buddhist kings in Sind (part of modern-day Pakistan), and by 710, it had been invaded, conquered and occupied. A slow expansion continued over the centuries, despite repeated attempts by Hindu kings to unite and combat the external threat. In 991, Jalalabad fell to the forces of Islam.[179]

11. ISLAM AND CHRISTIANITY IN THE WEST

The empire of Islam reached its greatest extent under the reign of Al Walid I (688–715). At this point, all of the lands from the Indus Valley through to North Africa and Spain were within his grasp. The invasion of Spain and occupation of the Iberian Peninsula was at the expense of the Christian Visigoth community who were living there. The invasion, which followed at least two earlier attempts in 675 and 694, was carried out by Tariq ibn Ziyad (d 720). It may have been that Zihad was invited into a country which was already riven by civil war to help depose Roderic (d 712), who had, allegedly, wrongfully usurped the crown. Having destroyed the army of Roderic at the battle of Guadalete in 711, Ziyad insisted that 'God shall be exalted in this country and the true religion shall be established here'.[180] This was easily achieved as a nearly wholesale collapse of collective opposition made it possible for Muslim forces to move progressively through the region, both by force of arms and by diplomacy. In a number of instances, rather than risk fighting and losing everything non-Muslim communities accepted limited autonomy with protection for their persons, property and faith, in exchange for payment of *jizyah* and acceptance of Muslim masters. For example, the 713 Treaty of Orihuela, between the invading Muslims and the Christians in the city of Orihuela, recorded:

> In the name of God, the merciful and compassionate. This is a document . . . establishing a treaty of peace and the promise and protection of God and his Prophet . . . We [the Muslims] will not set special conditions for [the Christian leader] or for any among his men, nor harass him, nor remove him from power. His followers will not be killed or taken prisoner, nor will they be separated from their women and children. They will not be coerced in matters of religion, their churches will not be burned, nor will sacred objects be taken from the realm, [so long as] he [the Christian leader] remains sincere and fulfils the [following] conditions

[178] Grousset, R (2010) *The Empire of the Steppes: A History of Central Asia* (New Jersey, Rutgers) 118–20; Graff, D (2002) *Medieval Chinese Warfare* (London, Routledge) 215; Gascoigne, B (2003) *The Dynasties of China* (London, Robinson) 111–13; Grant, R (2005) *Battle* (London, Dorling Kindersley) 76; Warmington, E (1928) *The Commerce Between the Roman Empire and China* (Cambridge, Cambridge University Press) 31–35; Hucker, C (1994) *China's Imperial Past* (California, Stanford University Press) 130–32.

[179] Smith, V (1962) *The Early History of India* (Oxford, Oxford University Press) 369, 377–78, 397, 402–408, 418–19, 451–52.

[180] Al-Maqqari, 'The Breath of Perfumes' reprinted in Horne, E (ed) (1997) *Sacred Books and Early Literature of the East: Medieval Arabic, Moorish and Turkish* (London, Kissenger) 241.

> that we have set for him. . . . He will not give shelter to fugitives, nor to our enemies, nor encourage any protected person to fear us, nor conceal news of our enemies. He and [each of] his men shall [also] pay one dinar every year, together with four measures of wheat, four measures of barley, four liquid measures of concentrated fruit juice, four liquid measures of vinegar, four of honey, and four of olive oil. Slaves must each pay half of this amount.[181]

The Muslim conquest continued to tighten its hold in Iberia (although a series of unsubdued, inter-quarrelsome Christian communities, such as Asturias, Leon, Castile, Navarre, Argon and Catalonia continued to exist in the north) before advancing over the Pyrenees. At this point, four major battles were fought: in 721 (Toulouse, under the leadership of Odo the Great, d 735); in 722 (Covadonga, under the leadership of, possibly, the grandson of Rodrigo – King Pelayo, (716–737)); and in 732 (Poitiers) and in 737 (Avignon, both under the leadership of Charles Martel). At Avignon, armies of perhaps 50,000 on each side clashed head-on. Martel's armies, probably the only effective Christian force in the west, stopped Muslim forces from taking the entire region. A little over 20 years later, Pippin (714–768) retook Narbonne in 759 and pushed the Muslim forces back over the Pyrenees. Pippin's son, Charlemagne (742–814), continued to push the Muslim forces back into Spain. Charlemagne also attempted to take advantage of the existing division within Islam between the Abbasids and the Umayyads by seeking an agreement with the Abbasid caliphate of Baghdad to combat their common enemy – the Umayyad caliphate of Cordova. Within this alliance, it appears that the caliph in Baghdad may have granted a type of semi-feudal jurisdiction of Jerusalem to Charlemagne.[182]

Despite his diplomatic success, on the more immediate question of the reconquest of Spain, Charlemagne found success elusive. As he advanced into the country in 778, he attacked both non-loyal Christian and Muslim communities, with both showing a tendency to change overlords when necessary. Louis the Pious (778–840), the son of Charlemagne, took Barcelona from the Muslims in 801 (it had earlier changed hands in 797 and 799) and asserted Frankish authority over Pamplona and the Basques, south of the Pyrenees, in 812. However, the Franks could not maintain their grip on this region. This fluid situation allowed Muslim forces to strike back in the ninth century. In 838 Marseilles was invaded, and in 842 and 850 they penetrated as far as Arles

[181] The Treaty of Tudmir reprinted in Rosenwein, B (ed) (2006) *Reading the Middle Ages: Sources from Europe, Byzantium and the Islamic World* (Ontario, Broadview) 92. For other commentary on this conquest, see anon, 'The Chronicle of 754' reprinted in Wolf, K trans (1999) *Conquerors and Chroniclers of Early Medieval Spain* (Liverpool, Liverpool University Press) 132–35; Pirenne, H (1935) *Mohammed and Charlemagne* (Allen and Unwin, London) 155; The Conquest of Spain reprinted in Lewis, B (ed) (1987) *Islam: From the Prophet to the Capture of Constantinople*, Vol I (Oxford, Oxford University Press) 111; O'Callaghan, J (2003) *Reconquest and Crusade in Medieval Spain* (Philadelphia, Pennsylvania University Press) 12–13. Also Gwatkin, H (ed) (1967) *The Cambridge Medieval History: The Rise of the Saracens and the Foundation of the Western Empire*, Vol II (Cambridge, Cambridge University Press) 183–84, 370–72.

[182] Sypeck, J (2006) *Becoming Charlemagne: Europe, Baghdad and the Empires of AD 800* (NYC, Harper) 78–81; Pirenne, H (1935) *Mohammed and Charlemagne* (London, Allen and Unwin) 154–60; Thorpe, L (ed) (1969) *Einhard and Notker the Stammerer: Two Lives of Charlemagne* (London, Penguin) 70, 148; Gwatkin, H (ed) (1967) *The Cambridge Medieval History: The Rise of the Saracens and the Foundation of the Western Empire*, Vol II (Cambridge, Cambridge University Press) 128–30, 374–75; Grant, R (2005) *Battle* (London, Dorling Kindersely) 67, 75; O'Callaghan, J (2003) *Reconquest and Crusade in Medieval Spain* (Philadelphia, Pennsylvania University Press) 1, 5, 23; Gibbon, E (1926 edn) *The History of the Decline and Fall of the Roman Empire*, Vol VI (London, Methuen) 13–19, 36–37; Costambey, M (2012) *The Carolingian World* (Cambridge, Cambridge University Press) 40–48.

in France before being repelled. In 852 the Muslims successfully took Barcelona, and the continual sway of attacks and defence continued. Between 791 and 883 the Spanish kingdom of the Asturias was attacked 33 times by the emirs of Corboda. Conversely, on at least seven occasions, when not under assault, the Christians took advantage of the respite to attack the Muslims. In turn, the Muslim forces would push back. One of the last great events of this epoch in Spain occurred when Ibn-Amir al-Mansur (938–1002) united all the Muslim resources in the region to subdue the independent Spanish Christians of the northern fringes of the peninsula. In doing so, he destroyed the famous shrine of Saint James (Santiago), at the furthest north-west extremity of Spain.[183]

Whilst the status quo in Spain consolidated, in other parts of the western Mediterranean the Muslim advance continued. Muslim forces took Crete in 828 and in the following year invaded Sicily although similar to the case of Spain, the Islamic forces insisted that they were invited to enter the country by the local Byzantine commander, who had rebelled against the emperor, Michael II (770–829). Once in Sicily, the Muslim forces fought for complete control for themselves, rather than for the renegade local commander. The invasion slowly progressed through Sicily during the reign of Theophilos (813–842), when an army of 10,000 Muslims seised the city of Palermo in 831. In 843, taking advantage of a fragmented Italian political landscape (that is, Naples aligned itself with both sides, and concluded an alliance with the Muslims in 836), Muslim forces took Messina. Three years later they advanced up the Tiber and tried to attack Rome, but since they could not breach the walls they had to be content with attacking the churches outside the defensive perimeter. Although in 871 Bari, in 880 Taranto and Cyprus were recovered (although the latter was held only for seven years), in 877 Syracuse was lost. By 883 Muslim forces had destroyed Monte Casino, and by 890 they were again just outside the walls of Rome.[184]

In such a situation, it was feared that Italy could be lost and annexed to Islamic territories. The two factors that seemed to galvanise the resistance in Italy were spiritual and political. On the spiritual level, Pope Leo IV (790–855) clearly stated that 'whoever meets death steadfastly in this fight [against the Muslims] the Heavenly Kingdoms will not be closed to him'.[185] Similarly, Pope John VIII (d 882) ranked the victims of holy war as martyrs, and promised that if they died in battle their sins would be remitted. This was a radical development. The remission of sins meant the blotting out of all the sins a knight may have committed up to the point he took up the war authorised by

[183] Hodgson, M (1974) *The Venture of Islam*, Vol II (Chicago, Chicago, Chicago University Press) 28–29; Rosenwein, B (ed) (2006) *Reading the Middle Ages: Sources from Europe, Byzantium and the Islamic World* (Ontario, Broadview) 167–70; Gwatkin, H (ed) (1967) *The Cambridge Medieval History: The Rise of the Saracens and the Foundation of the Western Empire*, Vol II (Cambridge, Cambridge University Press) 604–605; Gwatkin, H (ed) (1963) *The Cambridge Medieval History: Germany and the Western Empire*, Vol III (Cambridge, Cambridge University Press) 8.

[184] Pirenne, H (1935) *Mohammed and Charlemagne* (London, Allen and Unwin) 161, 249; Kennedy, H (2001) *The Armies of the Caliphs* (London, Routledge) 133–34; Gwatkin, H (ed) (1967) *The Cambridge Medieval History: The Rise of the Saracens and the Foundation of the Western Empire*, Vol II (Cambridge, Cambridge University Press) 385; Karsh, E (2006) *Islamic Imperialism. A History* (London, Yale University Press) 66–67; Gibbon, E (1926 edn) *The History of the Decline and Fall of the Roman Empire*, Vol VI (London, Methuen) 38–48; Grant, R (2005) *Battle* (London, Dorling Kindersley) 75.

[185] Leo IV, noted in Contamine, P (1984) *War in the Middle Ages* (Oxford, Blackmore) 270.

the pope. In the past, one may have atoned for a sin by entering a monastery or going on a pilgrimage, but from this time remission could be gained by taking up arms. This idea became central in the fight against Muslims both in Western Europe and, later, in the Crusades. In the interim, to display their piety, some popes took to the battlefield for example, John X (d 928) in 915.

On the political level, the papacy, in conjunction with other local Italian authorities, formed a league to force the people of Naples to end their alliance with the Muslims. The papacy (and forces of the Holy Roman Empire), Byzantium and Naples then united to secure Southern Italy. Progress was slow, as the Muslims declared holy war to protect the territory they already held, and the forces of Christendom (under Otto II) were not always successfully coordinated. In at least one instance Byzantium formed an allegiance with the Fatimids to attempt to defeat the German emperor, whom they believed to be a greater threat to their possessions in Southern Italy. Thus, the Christian forces proved unsuccessful in battle, such as the battle around Calabria in 892, and in 902 the last Byzantine stronghold in Sicily was lost.[186]

12. CONCLUSION

This chapter has demonstrated that religion created common ritual and cult ceremonies whereby intensive social cooperation became more habitual and social as well as political goals more legitimised. This was achieved through the consolidation and legitimisation of power – especially that held by one person. Kings from all epochs claimed their power from gods. In all instances, it was claimed that the gods fought on their side and assured victory. A mutually reinforcing bond between those in power and the religious legitimiser is the pattern found in all the periods examined in this book. The ancient Near East provides numerous stories in this area, from Sumer to Israel. Christianity later picked up and used this idea from the macro level of the empire through to the micro level of individual kings carving out countries in the west during the Dark Ages. The overlap between the papacy and kings, as both used each other to advance their positions, is hard to ignore. India, too, followed this pattern as did China, although in China's case the idea became a question of a given mandate, rather than the gods actually picking up weapons. In India, the Hindu faith was particularly notable for introducing the idea that dying in war could result in religious reward. Both Christianity and Islam would later take up the same theory. Other religions from India, such as Buddhism and Jainism, although not as dogmatic on these questions, came to accept the idea of just wars, and when emperors of these faiths were in power, although remorse over killing was recorded, armies were not disbanded and warfare was not repudiated.

[186] Pirenne, H (1935) *Mohammed and Charlemagne* (London, Allen and Unwin, London) 162, Gwatkin, H (ed) (1963) *The Cambridge Medieval History: Germany and the Western Empire*, Vol III (Cambridge, Cambridge University Press) 169–70; Runciman, S (1954) *A History of the Crusades*, Vol 1 (Cambridge, Cambridge University Press) 84; Finucane, R (2004) *Soldiers of the Faith* (London, Phoenix) 9–10.

In a number of instances, the importance of the domination of religion over enemies can be found. Tolerance of conquered faiths only clearly emerges with the Persians. Buddhists were largely tolerant, although their tolerance was not always reciprocated. Persecution of Buddhism by competing Chinese (Confuciasts and Daoists), Indian (Hindu) and Arabic (Islam) forces is well recorded. Tolerance was also a feature of both the Greek and Roman epochs, during which religion and the state were largely separated. This changed with the rise of the super-rulers, Alexander and Caesar (and their successors), who believed that they were gods on earth. However, even then tolerance of others was largely accepted if the opposing faiths did not challenge the ruling class or the glue that held society together.

Whilst the Romans managed to navigate through their wars with the Jewish people on such questions, they could not manage the same success with Christians. Here, they could not turn a blind eye when the early Christians refused to perform traditional Roman rituals. The oppression that followed created a movement that thrived on martyrdom and created a radical new world view that quickly eclipsed the theological distance and staleness that had become characteristic of Rome. Although Rome came to tolerate Christians, when the Christians were in power they did not reciprocate. Within the Christian empire, paganism was the first belief system to be suppressed. Anti-Semitism was also rife, and clearly rose in tempo from the sixth century onwards. The overt discrimination did not result in warfare, only oppression. However, those who were discriminated against were quick to change overlords when opportunities to do so presented themselves.

The tolerance of Christian Rome towards those of different religious faiths outside the empire – particularly Persia, and then Islam – was more difficult. In the case of Persia, both sides recognised the importance of tolerance of each other's faith within contested territories such as Armenia or at least, the importance of letting the locals choose their own paths. During three centuries of warfare, both sides returned to this conclusion, in which there was a general respect for the other. This was not the case from the end of the fifth century onwards, when the warfare on both sides became more comprehensive. Persia emerged from a civil war over questions of religious orthodoxy with a new fervour which gave its forces unprecedented military success against Byzantium. Byzantium, with its back against the wall, responded with an unprecedented degree of religious rhetoric, as a core theme in its justifications for conflict. The extreme nature of the final phase of the Byzantine–Persian conflict had religious overtones that were without precedent.

The extreme nature of the final clash between Persia and Byzantium provided a perfect precedent for the emerging faith of Islam. Whilst exhibiting a relative tolerance of (most) of the different religious communities that it conquered provided that they paid a poll tax), Islam was rarely at peace with those outside its borders. Aside from the questions of the theory of just war within Islam, the practice during 350 years up to the year 1000 was one of continual expansion. The Islamic conquests of India, the clash with China, and the advances against both Byzantium and western Europe were remarkable. The catalyst for advance was often the unwillingness of opponents to accept the rule of Islam. Aside from the instance of China, peace with external powers was never permanent, and warfare was only slowed when the forces were brought to a standstill or a truce was bought. Usually, the truces – or the retaking of former Christian lands – occurred when Islamic forces turned on themselves.

Toleration of questions within their own faith, in which orthodoxy was challenged and heresy bred, was not a feature of Islam – Christianity, or Persia. In all three cases, there was a grave risk of civil war when the orthodoxy was challenged. In the case of Christianity, the threat of military conflict over different interpretations of Scripture, could be either subtle, as with the Arians, or overt, as with the Paulicians. In the case of Islam, the faith split itself into two branches, Sunni and Shia, over issues related to interpretation and practice on the question of leadership of the Muslim community within a very short period of time. Although this subject would cause untold bloodshed within Islam, it would be the saving of many other countries.

VI

Conclusion

A JUST CAUSE for war can make the difference between war being seen as an act of heroism or as an act of murder. For this reason, hundreds, if not thousands of philosophers and state leaders have recorded justifications for why bloodshed was necessary, and why the loss or acquisition of property that followed was fair. This point about property is an underlying theme that I have identified in this book. That is, in the overwhelming majority of the wars in the period covered by this book, the control and/or ownership of resources was the motivation. Whilst countless scholars throughout the period of this work detested the idea of warfare being driven by base considerations of material (or social) wealth, the fact is that winning wars brought an ability to harness and control resources that losing wars did not.

Despite this primary consideration, it was rare to find justifications for war based purely on material (or social) reward. This was implicit in all of the other four themes that I have identified, which are evident in the the first 4,000 years for which written records exist. The four themes that I can consistently trace *in practice* from the years 3000 BCE to 1000 CE relate to empire, migratory peoples, politics and religion.

During the period 3000 BCE to 1000 CE, the most obvious cause of warfare was the formation and clashing of empires. My reading of history from this period suggests that, as states formed and geographical boundaries, internal peace, economic and social growth, and religious syncretism came together, so cooperation, coercion and conquest matched the process. Quite simply, war made the state, and the state made war. A desire to expand the boundaries of the state, including into areas contested by equally powerful states, appears to have been unavoidable, even if punctuated by a number of peace treaties, as the states from the centre of power expanded outwards – until only one power remained. At the same time, the desire for autonomy was a powerful catalyst for action among many of those under the yolk of another.

India provided a good example of the latter point. India did not really fight other empires: the warfare India experienced during this period had more to do with establishing itself. It dealt with successive waves of migratory peoples, some of whom settled and some of whom were pushed back. Some foreign empires, such as the Greek Empire, took bites out of the north of the country, before divesting themselves of it after a relatively short period of time. Other forces, such as those of Islam, fought their way into north India. Dynasties within India spent the majority of the 3,500 years covered by this book in civil war as multiple leaders sought the ultimate goal of uniting the realm under one ruler. In the course of achieving this goal seven successive dynasties rose and fell, with all failing to fully subdue all areas, for a prolonged period of time. Each dynasty expanded and then collapsed as areas broke free under the flag of autonomy in movements that snowballed into a force greater than that of the ruling dynasty. Accordingly, the geo-political landscape and the goals of the Indian kings of 1000 CE were not radically different to what had been evident 2,500 years earlier.

China replicated the pattern found in India through centuries of warfare as successive dynasties attempted to control larger and larger areas until eventually control at the centre weakened and the empire fragmented into separate parts that each sought autonomy. Sometimes these fragments were in hundreds of parts which would themselves compete for absolute control. The Han dynasty was the first to attempt to expand their empire into Korea and Vietnam, whilst taking tribute from Japan. It failed due to internal revolt and the subsequent lure of autonomy felt in many of the provinces. This coincided with the removal of Chinese influence in Korea and Vietnam, the mass disintegration of North China, and the splintering of the south into large sections following the Lulin rebellion in 23 BCE. This pattern of contradicting pushes towards unity followed by separation and the quest for local automony, was shared by the Sui, Tang and Sung dynasties.

The 2,500-year history of the Middle East – made up of Egypt, Mesopotamia, Canaan, Assyria and Persia – repeated the same pattern. This began with the rise of a king who sought to expand his territory at the expense of neighbouring rulers. This momentum of expansion spread to the wider region. In Egypt, this process brought the country into direct conflict with opposing Empires such as the Hittites, and a number of smaller powers ranging from the Babylonians to the Israelites. When neither side could achieve military victory, they opted for a peace which set a boundary and protected each other's status quo. This was unusual, as the pattern both before and after was that peace was achieved only by victory – or by the submission of one of the parties to the status of a type of vassal. The alternative was destruction. The civilizations of Elam, Assyria, Babylon and even Egypt fell in this way before Persia was left dominant.

Once Persia became dominant, it continued to expand its boundaries until it eventually came up against independent Greek communities. When these communities called for help from other Greeks, the response saw Persia mount a full-scale invasion of Greece. At this point, the autonomous communities of the Greeks stopped fighting each other and joined together in collective defence of their territories. When the threat of invasion passed, they returned to their traditional mutual antagonisms. It was only when the Macedonians managed to defeat and then unite all of the Greek communities that aggressive war against Persia became possible. This was an absolute war of conquest, in which an emergent empire completely overran the original antagonist. This success of Alexander against Persia stood in contrast to the Greek's venture into Sicily against Carthage, where five treaties punctuated the end of each conflict, the majority of which reflected the status quo, with the two sides agreeing to re-divide the island into different spheres of influence. Whilst a divided island was the military reality, the dream for both sides, especially as the centuries wore on, appears to have been complete control of the island, and all the peace treaties were broken to achieve this goal. To avoid being swallowed up, the threatened communities would invite in whoever they felt would best guarantee their survival. Whilst the division of the island between the Greeks and Carthagianians lasted for four centuries, when the emergent Rome was invited in for the same purpose the dynamic quickly changed, concluding with the clash of the two superpowers.

By the time that Rome was ready to fight Carthage, its empire was largely in place. The establishment of the empire, had begun with joint defensive alliances such as that formed with the Etruscans, and had eventually seen Rome emerge at the forefront, continually expanding its boundaries within the Italian peninsular until it had brought the entire area under its authority. Uniquely, even under Roman direction warfare continued, as all within the empire fought for and ultimately achieved equal rights. This demand for equal rights increased as the Roman conquests spread and the resulting benefits accrued. The empire's boundaries expanded both to the north and to the west. The wars against the peoples north of Italy, in Gaul and Germany, marked both the beginning and the end of Roman history. From the outset, Rome was aware of the raw power of Gaul and its covetous intentions towards the assets of Italy. The original success of the Gauls in Italy in 390 BCE was not repeated (despite several attempts) until the middle of the third century CE. Between these points, Rome entered into a series of wars with the intention of pacifying large parts of the north and advancing further to build strong defensive lines against future incursions. Before the eventual collapse of the western arm of the Roman Empire, there was a constant stream of uprisings by communities under the Roman yolk seeking autonomy. Whilst Rome was able to bring these revolts under control, it became increasingly aware that it could not control all of the forces beyond its borders and so developed elaborate systems of support for those in buffer zones to prevent the troubles from reaching too far into Roman territory.

This approach was different from that originally envisaged by the Romans in Greece, where, having first secured the formerly autonomous Greek parts of Italy, Rome's goal had been to keep Greece divided and to prevent the resurgence of a united region as seen under Alexander. In order to achieve this, the Greeks fought two regimes, under Philip V and Antiochus III. Although the Roman rhetoric was about ensuring Greek autonomy, the secondary objective of ensuring that the Greeks were not united under a single monarch. The limits of Roman patience in allowing Greek autonomy were tested when subsequent Greek monarchs, attempted to revive the absolute autonomy of Greek communities and reunite all of Greece. When Rome had dealt with these threats, pro-Roman factions were cemented in place.

The only two – unified – empires that Rome fought were those of Carthage, and then Sassanid Persia (formerly Parthia). War with Carthage broke out after 200 years of peaceful co-existence and collective defence agreements against common enemies. War initially occurred because the Romans were invited into a conflict of a kind which they had traditionally ignored, as it did not consolidate their territory. However, after taking all of Italy, Rome's boundaries and interests changed. The Romans feared the Carthaginians were taking territory, much as they themselves were. Since their treaties with Carthage did not explicitly prohibit Rome's intervention in Sicily, they did just that. Given that this war was largely brought about because the treaties covering which superpower had influence over particular areas were not clear the peace treaties which concluded the Punic War attempted to draw much sharper lines. The problem was that the lines were insufficient to stop Roman interventions to defend their friends (and/or Carthaginian attempts to provoke them), even though they were on the wrong side of the line. The peace treaty which followed the Second Punic War allowed the survival and limited autonomy of Carthage, but stripped it of all of its possessions and foreign policy options. Eventually, when Carthage acted without Roman approval in defending itself against a provocative Roman ally, Rome categorically crushed what remained of the once great empire of Carthage.

Rome also fought Sassanid Persia for over 600 years in wars which raged from the end of the Republic to the middle years of Byzantium, punctuated by four treaties that tried to resolve areas of dispute. Rome's original attacks on Persia appear to have been more concerned with glory than with any substantive considerations. This was not the case in subsequent centuries. The sticking point for both Rome and Persia was the control over disputed areas, particularly Armenia and later Mesopotamia. The mechanisms developed to deal with this issue were promises of autonomy for Armenia, and when neither side could stop meddling in the supposedly autonomous regions a division of Armenia was agreed. Supplementing the split were promises of regional demilitarisation and cooperation against common enemies. When the sincerity of demilitarisation promises were tested, and commitments to provide financial assistance against common enemies were not kept, warfare broke out again. This war, which raged over large areas throughout the sixth century, despite a number of truces and attempts to return to the status quo, was exacerbated when each side became involved in the other's dynastic politics. At this point, the warfare appears to have reached new levels of intensity, fuelled by a much stronger religious background than in the past. The war between the two sides was no longer over disputed provinces, but was for absolute mastery, in which there could be no negotiated outcome.

When the Western side of the Roman Empire eventually collapsed, the tension between groups seeking autonomy and those seeking to re-establish authority over all areas re-emerged. In this instance, the fragmentation of the empire of the west was spectacular. Whilst some areas battled for hundreds of years to achieve absolute dominance over relatively small spaces, such as in Britain, in the case of continental Europe the area was larger, and the conquest was quicker as in the Merovigian and Carolingian dynasties. However, this grasp of the whole area only lasted until the grandchildren of the original conquerors fought and split the core of western Europe into three parts which effectively became France, Germany and Italy.

The second dominant theme I have identified as a cause of warfare in the period 3000 BCE to 1000 CE is migratory peoples who constantly sought the riches of others. The riches would begin as plunder, before becoming tribute, and then territory within an empire, if not the empire itself. These people, who had no settled home and no ideology beyond seeking the riches of others, had a strong military advantage due to their mobility. For thousands of years they learnt how to advance where they wanted, and they could easily disappear when challenged as they possessed no territory that they were attached to.

The threat that these people represented was both universal and constant. It was also potentially cataclysmic, resulting in the downfall of a number of empires – to which they were attracted like parasites. The waves that swept through the ancient Near East toppled everything from the empire of the Hittites to the communities of Achaean

Greece. Only Egypt survived. India and China, were too large to be overrun by the nomadic hordes – but this was not for lack of appetite. In the case of the western side of the Roman Empire, when the breach finally occurred the dam burst with such ferocity that what is euphemistically known as 'the Dark Ages' accurately described the splintering, chaos and warfare that would last for five centuries in Europe. Byzantium survived similar threats, although a number of the threatening peoples' combined into independent countries/communities within what had once been Byzantine territory. In all instances, the attacks by the migratory peoples were most likely to succeed when the empires they targeted were distracted by internal difficulties.

All the regions that had to deal with migratory peoples who were drawn to the riches of established communities worked out the same solutions for dealing with them. These were strategies of divide and rule, in which the best defence was to keep the migratory hordes divided. In order to achieve this, multiple treaties were drawn up in all regions, whereby favoured groups were given benefits. These benefits ranged from tribute and trading rights, through to the ability to settle in certain areas. In exchange, the migrants were expected either to provide troops for the empire, or to battle others – normally other migratory peoples – at the direction of the empire. Those who were not given benefits were fought. The necessity of fighting migratory peoples who were divided, or who were demanding too much, was understood by all empires who recognised the constant need to keep those preying on the fringes of empire subdued. In many instances, it was only when the migratory peoples were denied their requests for benefits, and had been subdued in battle, that peace could be achieved.

Keeping migratory peoples subdued was an issue of management and adaptation, rather than securing a complete and final victory. This was a constant problem due to the almost endless supply of migratory groups who possessed a clear ability to form, mutate and turn on either their fellow migratory allies, or different empires. Awareness of the benefits that one group held could encourage other groups to seek the same rewards, either by threat or demand to the paymaster, or by the destruction of the original recipient. Only as a last resort would an empire give territory and/or acknowledge the legitimacy of the rulers. Even when this occurred and the migratory people settled in lands belonging to others, their position was never secure as the former owners had long memories, and when the time was right would often attempt to retake the land.

The third main reason why warfare occurred between 3000 BCE and 1000 CE was conflict over types of political system, or more commonly over the benefits that they offered to those who were in (or who desired) positions of power. The holding of all power in the hands of one person was the overwhelming political choice of all the civilisations studied within the time periods of this book. The title given to this person varied from pharoah, to king, emperor, or caliph. This system was evident in all societies. However, so too was the acknowledgement in many of these regimes that more collective forms of governance were at times a better choice. This idea was never strong, and the trend was typically towards the concentration of power in the hands of one person. In ancient history, this was the pattern of the ancient Near East, from Egypt to Persia. It was also replicated in India and China. In these societies, those who held absolute power were usually legitimised by religion, and only rarely, in the case of the tyrants who arose in Greece, was the quest for absolute power not supported by a theological faith.

All of those who held absolute power, no matter where they were, lived in constant fear that they could be killed and their position taken by someone else. There were many reasons for them losing the throne. These included revolutions which came from the bottom-up, when those governed felt that the monarch failed to live up to certain standards, such as the provision of justice – and peace – to the people. Failure to achieve these goals could result in the loss of their throne. However, only a limited number of rebellions came from the grass-roots. This was most apparent with those who had absolutely no power – slaves – relatively obedient throughout this period of history. Although every regime attempted to limit the overtly inhumane treatment of slaves, none attempted to abolish the practice of slavery. This was despite the fact that the major regimes, Greeks, Romans and Islam, all had to deal with wars by slaves seeking to establish their own freedom. However, none of these wars was about trying to abolish the institution of slavery.

More commonly, civil war would break out when either a contender from outside the ruler's family, someone from within their family, or, most likely of all, someone in the military would try to take the throne. This became a clear pattern from China to Rome from the time that Caesar took absolute power. This pattern held under both pre- and post- Christian influences. In all instances, the pattern was the same – the holding of absolute power attracted others who wanted it. This incessant desire meant that dynasties were often short-lived, lasting no more than a few generations. In best-case scenarios, transitions could be carried out with minimal bloodshed beyond the mess of a palace coup. A large number of transitions in Egypt and Byzantium matched this pattern, although in both cases civil wars still occurred. In worst-case scenarios, entire empires could split apart. Assyria, the western side of the Roman Empire, and its successor, the realm of Charlemagne, were all examples of this. This was particularly likely to occur if the disputes about who held absolute power were mixed with external pressures. The history of China is a classic example of this problem. In all cases, the root cause was the quest by one person to take the absolute power of another.

The exceptions to the overwhelming dominance of one person governing the state were the options of government by an aristocracy or a democracy. The democratic tradition was one which existed only in pockets of ancient Greece. Democracy, in the sense of the equality of (a limited) citizenship, was born as a reaction against all of the power being held by one man as a tyrant or a monarch, or the power being held by a few, as in an aristocracy. It survived a tide of wars in which both Greek communities and later Rome fought for the autonomy of Greek cities to decide their own political choices. By the time that Rome became involved, although such areas could retain their own democratic institutions, they did not have the ability to commit to an independent foreign policy. Democracy in Greece was eventually extinguished by Rome, after a series of failed uprisings in which the people had been attracted to complete autonomy. It was extinguished by Rome, which was, in essence, acting under an aristocracy through their senate. The aristocracy of Rome was no more peaceful than democracy. There were continual struggles between those beneath the aristocracy and those who sought to get above it. When Caesar and his successor gained power over the aristocracy, the pattern reverted to one of absolute control being in the hands of one man.

The final theme that this work identified as having a large impact upon warfare was religion. Religion created common ritual and cult ceremonies through which intensive social cooperation became more habitual and the social as well as political goals more legitimised. This was achieved through the consolidation and legitimisation of power – especially that held by one person. Kings from all epochs claimed their power from gods. In all instances, it was claimed that the gods fought on their side and assured victory. A mutually reinforcing bond between those in power and the religious legitimiser is the pattern of the periods examined in this book. The ancient Near East provides numerous stories in this area, from Sumer to Israel. Christianity later picked up and used this idea from the macro level of the empire, through to the micro level of individual kings carving out countries in the west during the Dark Ages. The overlap between the papacy and kings, as both used each other to advance their positions, is hard to ignore. India, too, followed this pattern, as did China, although in China's case the question was one of a given mandate, rather than the gods actually picking up weapons. In India, the Hindu faith was particularly notable for introducing the idea that dying in war could result in religious reward. Both Christianity and Islam would later take up the same theory. Other religions from India, such as Buddhism and Jainism, also came to accept the possibility of just wars and when emperors of these faiths were in power, although remorse was recorded, armies were not disbanded and warfare was not repudiated.

In a number of instances, the importance of the domination of religion over enemies can be found. Tolerance of conquered faiths only emerges with the Persians. Buddhists were largely tolerant, although their tolerance was not always reciprocated. Persecution of Buddhism by competing Confuciasts, Daoists, Hindu and Islam forces is well recorded. Tolerance was also a feature of both the Greek and Roman epochs, during which religion and the state were largely separated. This changed with the rise of the super-rulers Alexander and Caesar (and their successors), who believed that they were gods on earth. Even then, tolerance of others was largely accepted if the opposing faiths did not challenge the ruling class or the glue that held society together.

Whilst Rome managed to navigate through its wars with the Jewish people on such questions, it could not manage the same success with Christians. Rome could not turn a blind eye when the early Christians refused to perform traditional Roman rituals. The oppression that followed created a movement that thrived on martyrdom and the creation of a radical new world view which quickly eclipsed the theological distance and staleness that had become characteristic of Rome. Although Rome came to tolerate Christians, when the Christians were in power, they did not reciprocate. Within the Christian empire, paganism was the first belief system to be suppressed. Anti-Semitism was also rife, and clearly rose in tempo from the sixth century onwards.

The tolerance of Christian Rome towards those having different religious faiths outside the empire – particularly Persia, and then Islam – was more difficult. In the case of Persia, both sides recognised the importance of tolerance of each other's faith within contested territories such as Armenia or at least, letting the locals choose their own paths. During three centuries of warfare, both sides returned to this conclusion, in which there was a general respect for the other. This was not the case from the end of the fifth century onwards, when the warfare on both sides became more comprehensive. Persia emerged from a civil war over questions of religious orthodoxy with a new fervour, which gave their forces unprecedented military success against Byzantium. Byzantium, responded with an unprecedented degree of religious rhetoric, as a core theme in its justifications for conflict.

The extreme nature of the final clash between Persia and Byzantium provided a perfect precedent for the emerging faith of Islam. Whilst exhibiting a relative tolerance of most of the different religious communities that it conquered provided that they paid a poll tax, Islam was rarely at peace with those outside its borders. Aside from the questions of the concept of a just war within Islam, the practice during 350 years up to 1000 CE was one of continual expansion. The Islamic conquests of India, the clash with China, and the advances against both Byzantium and western Europe were remarkable. The catalyst for advance was often the unwillingness of opponents to accept the rule of Islam. Aside from the instance of China, peace with external powers was never permanent, and warfare was only slowed when the forces were brought to a standstill, or a truce was bought. Usually, the truces – or retaking of former lands – occurred when Islamic forces turned on themselves.

Toleration of questions within their own faith, in which orthodoxy was challenged, was not a feature of Islam, Christianity, or Persian society. In all three cases, there was a grave risk of civil war when the orthodoxy was challenged. In the case of Christianity, the threat of military conflict over different interpretations of Scripture, could be either subtle, as with the Arians, or overt, as with the Paulicians. In the case of Islam, the faith split itself into two branches, Sunni and Shiia, over issues related to interpretation and practice on the question of leadership of the Muslim community within a very short period of time. Although this subject would cause untold bloodshed within Islam, it would be the saving of many other countries.

Index

www.ingramcontent.com/pod-product-compliance
Lightning Source LLC
Chambersburg PA
CBHW081415220926
51613CB00010B/201
9781849465007